Reporting to duty at the Supreme Court, 1939

THE WHITE HOUSE
WASHINGTON

April 15, 1939.

Dear Bill:

I have received your official resignation as
Commissioner of the Securities and Exchange Commission
and it is hereby accepted prior to your elevation to
the Supreme Court.

May I express my gratitude and that of the
Government to you for the very constructive service
you have given on the Securities and Exchange Commission
and especially because of the fact that you have been
so thoroughly cognizant of the human equations which
enter into the national task of protecting the Nation's
investors and, at the same time, by maintaining the
efficiency of the Nation's business on a high moral
plane.

To you as Associate Justice of the Supreme
Court go all of my good wishes for the years to come.

Faithfully yours,

Franklin D Roosevelt

Honorable William O. Douglas,
Chairman, Securities and Exchange Commission,
Washington, D. C.

HARRIS & EWING

Justice Louis D. Brandeis

Chief Justice Charles Evans Hughes

The Court visit to President Roosevelt in 1942:
Justices Jackson, Murphy, Douglas, Frankfurter,
Reed, Black, Roberts and Chief Justice Stone

With Edith Allen and David Ginsburg, secretary and law clerk during WOD's first term on the Court

HARRIS & EWING

Justices Frank Murphy and Felix Frankfurter

Justice Hugo Black

Dear Bill:

I certainly hope that your Endo case will go down. It is a good job and the problems are handled to my complete satisfaction. I do think, as I understood you did, that it would be better practice in situations like this for one Justice to write both cases. At least, this has ordinarily been the way such intimately related cases are handled. I should personally regret it very much if the CJ should reassign Endo, and I shall tell him that if he says anything to me about it. There is no feeling of any kind on my part about your writing, but as stated I think assignments of related opinions should be to one writer save in exceptional circumstances. The only feeling I have as to you personally in connection with it is one of admiration for the fine way in which you have done it.

Sincerely
H.B.

Letter from Hugo Black on the Endo *and* Korematsu *cases, 1944*

Reception honoring the Judiciary, October 1961

With President Lyndon B. Johnson

GO EAST, YOUNG MAN
The Early Years

William O. Dou...

...n O.   Kata

William O. Douglas

WEST OF THE INDUS

POINTS OF REBELLIO...
William O. Do...
Associate Justice of the Su...

William O. Douglas
FAREWELL TO TEXAS
A Vanishing Wilderne...

William O. Douglas
THE THREE HUNDRED YEAR WAR
A Chronicle

BEYOND THE HIGH Himalayas

A Wilderness Bill of Rights

Six Steps toward World Peace
INTERNATIONAL DISSENT
William O. Douglas
Associate Justice of the Supreme Court

WILLIAM O. DOUGLAS
THE ANATOMY OF LIBERTY

EXPLORING THE HIMALAYA

THE CREDO SERIES
RUTH NANDA AN...

By WILLIAM O. DOUGLAS

*Justices Clark, White,
Black, Brennan, Chief Justice
Warren, Justices Stewart,
Douglas, Goldberg and
Harlan, 1963*

"WE'RE THE INVESTIGATING COMMITTEE."

JUSTICE DOUGLAS

GOP HOUSE LEADER FORD

With Eric Sevareid in Goose Prairie, 1972

With Earl Warren and Abe Fortas at a party celebrating the publication of
Go East, Young Man

With Cathleen Douglas on the annual walk along the C & O Canal

In the Court Rotunda, where Earl Warren lay in state

*Justices Harlan, Marshall, Black, Stewart, Chief Justice Burger, Justices White,
Douglas, Blackmun and Brennan, 1970*

*With Dean Michael
Sovern, Sidney Davis and
Simon Rifkind, on the
fiftieth anniversary of WOD's
graduation from the Law
School of Columbia
University, May 29, 1975*

DOUGLAS

12/5/75

The
Court Years

The
Court Years
1939-1975

The Autobiography of
William O.
Douglas

Vintage Books
A Division of Random House
New York

First Vintage Books Edition, October 1981
Copyright © 1980 by the Estate of William O. Douglas
All rights reserved under International and Pan-American
Copyright Conventions. Published in the United States by
Random House, Inc., New York, and simultaneously in Canada
by Random House of Canada Limited, Toronto. Originally
published by Random House, Inc., New York, in October 1980.

Library of Congress Cataloging in Publication Data
Douglas, William O. (William Orville), 1898-
The court years, 1939-1975.
Originally published: New York: Random House, 1980.
Includes index.
1. Douglas, William O. (William Orville), 1898-.
2. Judges—United States—Biography.
I. Title.
KF8745.D6A28   1981   347.73'2634 [B]   81-40191
ISBN 0-394-74902-2   347.3073534 [B]   AACR2

Manufactured in the United States of America

The world is as it were a city: For which other commonweal is it, that all men can be said to be members of? From this common city it is that understanding, reasoning, and law is derived unto us, for from whence else? . . . shalt not thou say of the world, Thou lovely city of God?

—Marcus Aurelius, *Meditations*

If a man does not keep pace with his companions, perhaps it is because he hears a different drummer. Let him step to the music which he hears, however measured or far away.

—Henry David Thoreau, *Walden* (1854)

Only when you have worked alone—when you have felt around you a black gulf of solitude more isolating than that which surrounds the dying man, and in hope and in despair have trusted to your own unshaken will—then only will you have achieved. Thus only can you gain the secret isolated joy of the thinker, who knows that, a hundred years after he is dead and forgotten, men who never heard of him will be moving to the measure of his thought—the subtle rapture of a postponed power, which the world knows not because it has no external trappings, but which to his prophetic vision is more real than that which commands an army.

—Oliver Wendell Holmes
February 17, 1886

Publisher's Note

In 1974, to mark the anniversary of Justice William O. Douglas' thirty-fifth year on the Supreme Court, Sidney M. Davis, a distinguished New York lawyer and Princeton University professor who was Mr. Justice Douglas' long-time friend, wrote:

> Mr. Justice Douglas has grown older but he is not old. He continues, as he has always been, to be the most active member of the Court, producing his characteristically unorthodox, sharp and terse opinions at phenomenal speed. He is a most extraordinary man for these most unusual times. As long as Mr. Justice Douglas sits on the Court, and writes books, and lectures to those who come to hear him, the voice of freedom will still be heard and the cry for Justice will not be stilled.

William O. Douglas suffered a stroke late in 1974 and retired from the Court on November 12, 1975. He died on January 19, 1980. But his voice, "the voice of freedom," is not stilled. With the publication of this book, the second volume of his memoirs, his remarkable mind, his legal scholarship, his unique character and personality, his passionate belief that the function of the Constitution and of the Supreme Court of the United States is to "keep the government off the backs of the people" continue to resound.

The greater part of this book had been written by 1973 at the time its publication was contracted for. Over the next several years, most often during the summers in his home in Goose Prairie, Washington, Justice Douglas worked intensively on the manuscript. He would, for example, when significant events occurred, bring up to date the status of the legal issues and national events in which he was interested. He also worked to clarify complex legal matters for the lay reader and, most important, he enriched the book with personal recollections of his friends and associates in and out of government, including the six Presidents and the Supreme Court Justices with whom he served.

His relationship with the other Justices is perhaps best summed up in a letter that Mr. Justice Douglas wrote to his colleagues on the Court at the time of his retirement in 1975:

My Dear Brethren:

Your message, written on my retirement from the Court, filled my heart with overflowing emotion. You were kind and generous and made every hour, including the last one on our arduous journey, happy and relaxed.

I am reminded of many canoe trips I have taken in my lifetime. Those who start down a water course may be strangers at the beginning but almost invariably are close friends at the end. There were strong headwinds to overcome and there were rainy as well as sun-drenched days to travel. The portages were long and many and some were very strenuous. But there were always a pleasant camp in a stand of white bark birch and water concerts held at night to the music of the loons; and inevitably there came the last campfire, the last breakfast cooked over last night's fire, and the parting was always sad.

And yet, in fact, there was no parting because each happy memory of the choice parts of the journey—and of the whole journey—was of a harmonious united effort filled with fulfilling and beautiful hours as well as dull and dreary ones. The greatest such journey I've made has been with you, my brethren, who were strangers at the start but warm and fast friends at the end.

The value of our achievements will be for others to appraise. Other like journeys will be made by those who follow us, and we trust that they will leave these wilderness water courses as pure and unpolluted as we left those which we traversed.

As to the place of these memoirs in his life, Mr. Justice Douglas talked about this book, worked on it and gave it serious thought almost to the time of his death. He obviously considered it an important part of his life's work.

The Editors
Random House

April, 1980

Contents

Contents

The
Court Years

Chapter I

Early Years
on the Court

It seemed to me that I had barely reached the Court when people were trying to get me off. Most of them saw a political role for me starting, perhaps, in the executive branch; some were promoting me for the presidency. Negative decisions in these matters were not difficult for me, as I never wanted to run for office—not even for superintendent of schools in Yakima. Running for a state office or for Congress never occurred to me. The fangs and claws of politics and campaigning had no appeal to me ever. As to any other job in the executive branch, I was not interested. I saw none that caught my fancy and I was sure none could measure up to the challenge, interest and excitement of my old job with the Securities and Exchange Commission.

I was content to stay put for a while. The SEC job had paid $10,000 a year, which people in Yakima thought was a handsome income. And so it was in the thirties, but Washington, D.C., was an expensive place. I had a wife and two children, and while at the SEC, I ran into debt at the rate of $5,000 a year just supporting the family. This was all money borrowed from banks and insurance companies and that debt hovered ominously over me. More public life meant more debts, but my salary on the Court was $20,000, so although at the start I did not particularly enjoy the work of the Court, I settled into it for the long haul with no thought of resigning.

The Court's routine was a new one for me, and it took time to become adjusted. Ever since I was a boy I had been accustomed to living on the run. The SEC days had accentuated that pace: the hours were busy, the appointments many, the days long. But at the Court, there was no need to see anyone; appointments dropped off; the routine of reading and research set in. It took me two years or more to get used to that new workday, but in time I came to love the routine as well as the institution itself.

In the first years I did a lot of night work. As Justice Harlan F. Stone said, it takes some years "to get around the track," meaning that since there are so many new fields of law that come into focus through our cases, it takes time for the newcomer to get on speaking terms with them. And so it does.

Yet the myth grows that the Court is overworked. That was not the fact in my time. Indeed, it was not long before I realized that the job of an Associate Justice took four days a week. The problem was what to do with the other days, a problem that could be resolved in terms of one's interests and one's energy.

Within a few years I came to appreciate the privacy and quiet of the job and its demand for research and reflection. I enjoyed the leisure that it offered and the freedom from high-pressure work I had known in Wall Street and at the SEC. And I prized the long vacations when, in the mountains of Oregon or Washington, I could go over mailbags of petitions for certiorari (petitions for consideration of cases by the Court), many of them from prisoners or from indigent people.

When I took my seat in 1939, the Court had been in its new building for only two years. Cass Gilbert, Cass Gilbert, Jr., and John R. Rockart were the architects who designed it after the Parthenon on the Acropolis in Athens. My first arrival in Athens, years later, was at sunrise on a summer day, and as the plane approached the airport, there was the Supreme Court building below us in all its glory.

For nearly one hundred years before the present building was erected, the Court had sat in the old courtroom under the dome of the Capitol. It was small and intimate, and its acoustics were perfect. It lacked facilities, however, for the Clerk's Office and for the Library, and the Justices had to have their offices at home. Back in the twenties, Justice Louis D. Brandeis thought that a wing should be added to the Capitol for those purposes. But William Howard Taft, who had opposed Brandeis for the Court, also opposed him on this; and as Chief Justice, Taft had the Grecian temple built.

Nineteen thirty-seven, the year the Court moved into the new quarters, was also the year of President Roosevelt's Court-packing plan. "The transfer of the Court to the new building," Brandeis told me, "was symbolic of the clash between the Court and the other branches of government."

By the time I took my seat, four of the members of the old Court—Charles Evans Hughes, James Clark McReynolds, Pierce Butler and Owen J. Roberts—had moved their offices into the new building; only Harlan Stone continued the old habit with both his home and offices at Wyoming Avenue and Twenty-fourth Street, N.W. The Justices were located on three sides of the Courtroom. Brandeis, who preferred to work at home, never moved into the new building. He would, as a senior (he was appointed in 1916), have had the choice of a better suite (each comprised three rooms), but he took what was left over, number 108; and when I went to the Court on April 17, 1939, taking Brandeis' place, I moved into 108, kept the office for twenty-three years and later, in 1972, repossessed it. The reason I was able to do this was that Chief Justice Burger got the funds from Congress to remodel the interior of the building, enlarging each suite so as to accommodate the burgeoning number of law clerks. I found safety from any expansion in my old office as there was a stairway at each end, making it impossible to enlarge the three rooms in suite 108.

When I came to the Court there were many traditional habits and ways of doing things that were in time to be changed. In those days we sat from twelve noon until two o'clock, adjourning for thirty minutes for lunch. Then we returned to the Bench, sitting from two-thirty to four-thirty. (Our Conference—the weekly Convocation of the Court—was on Saturday at noon.) Historically, Congress had convened on weekdays at noon, and the Court, housed for so long in the Capitol Building, followed suit. These hours were ideal for me, as I discovered they were with Hughes. We were both early risers; and prior to noon one could get a day's work done.

We had difficulty with the acoustics in the new Courtroom, and though the ceiling was lowered and softer material used, that did not seem to help. Heavy red velvet curtains were placed behind and on the two sides of the bench in an effort to stop the echo and re-echo of voices. This helped some, but it did not greatly improve the situation. It was still difficult for a Justice who sat on one side of the bench to hear a question asked by a Justice on the opposite end; and members of the audience had great difficulty in hearing what either the lawyers or the Justices were saying. The condition was eventually corrected by the introduction of a loudspeaker system with a switch at each seat on the bench. In time, a recording machine was installed that took down on tape every oral argument.

In the forties, when Fred M. Vinson was Chief Justice, he tried to get a crescent-shaped bench substituted for the old one, but he had difficulties with the budget. At long last Warren Burger got the item approved and in 1972 a crescent-shaped bench, costing about $35,000 appeared. It was as useless and unnecessary as a man's sixth Cadillac, for the loudspeaker system was adequate for the old table. But it was symbolic of a change, which was important to President Nixon. Money was hard to come by at that time for salary raises for the underpaid court employees, but it was easy for items that publicized changes in the institution.

In the early days Justice McReynolds, who had been on the Court since 1914, insisted that the Conference direct the Marshal to string a white muslin fringe across the ugly red velvet curtains behind the bench. That fringe remained there until the day McReynolds retired.

McReynolds had another prejudice or phobia. He would not sit for any photographer except Harris & Ewing. This gave Harris & Ewing a monopoly on all Court pictures. What was behind it I do not know, but he was steadfast in his stand, so no one except that firm could photograph the nine of us until McReynolds retired. When he did, we sent notice to all photographers and photographic news services that we would be available for a few hours when we sat as a body, letting everyone take the Court picture—an event that was always arranged when there was a change in the Court membership.

On October 1, 1946, the Government Printing Office established a branch in the basement of the Court and entrusted it with the duty of printing our opinions. When I took my seat the printing was done by Clarence E. Bright, head of the Pearson Printing Office, whose shop was at 519 Eleventh Street, N.W. We paid Mr. Bright $25,000 a year to print our opinions. He was a grand person, and there never was a "leak" from his shop, which was amazing because there it was on Eleventh Street, open to the public, for whom he printed such things as placards, posters and stationery. There were three linotype machines. He worked one himself and he had two employees on the other machines. Some Court opinions would be worth millions in the market, but their secrets were always kept. When I asked Mr. Bright how it happened, he told me that he never gave one linotypist the whole opinion. He would break it into two or three parts, reserving for himself the last few pages, where the fatal words "Reverse" or "Affirmed" would appear.

Once, in the twenties, Justice Willis Van Devanter had an opinion to write that was in the sensitive stock-exchange area. He took it down to Chief Justice Taft to ask his advice. "It's so delicate," Van Devanter said, "that perhaps I should not even have it typed, but should circulate it among the Brethren in this handwritten form."

Though it was ten o'clock at night, Taft called Mr. Bright, who came down at once. After hearing the problem, Mr. Bright walked over to Taft, took the opinion from him and said, "Mr. Chief Justice, now the problem is mine." He set the opinion in type himself, and as usual, there was no leak.

I was with Mr. Bright shortly before he died. He had been quite ill and I went to his home to see him. He had been an inveterate cigarette smoker all his life, but his heart condition was such that his doctors demanded that he quit. To help him get the coal tar and nicotine out of his system, they wrapped him naked in hot steaming sheets. The nurse was removing a sheet as I walked in, and he made her hold it up so I could see the marks on it.

"That's the body of Clarence E. Bright wrought out of nicotine," he shouted, and then added, "Douglas, let that be a lesson to you."

When I joined the Court, it comprised (besides the "old-timers" James McReynolds, Pierce Butler, Charles Evans Hughes and Harlan Stone) Hugo L. Black, Owen Roberts, Stanley F. Reed and Felix Frank-furter. Charles Evans Hughes, who was Chief Justice when I took my seat, was then seventy-seven years old. I was forty; and that differential served not to separate us but to bring us together. Perhaps he liked me. Perhaps he sensed that I would long shape up the stream of Court history from which he was about to depart and that he therefore should make me his confidant and emissary. Whatever the reason, he took me at once into his confidence. He would call me into his office, and with utmost propriety, express his concerns. He was particularly worried about the image Felix Frankfurter reflected. Behind the Chief's back, Frankfurter called Hughes "Bushy"; and the day I finally chose a different path from Frankfurter was when he said to me, "If we can keep Bushy on our side, there is no amount of rewriting of the Constitution we cannot do." He referred, of course, to the tremendous prestige of Hughes, who in the contest with FDR over the Court-packing plan had not come out second best.

Hughes naturally never knew that Frankfurter said that.

Hughes also had early worries about Black, but he came to respect Black for the all-out adversary that he was: true-blue, honest and never double-dealing. He tolerated Stone and Reed and had little truck with McReynolds and Butler. He spoke affectionately of Oliver Wendell Holmes and Benjamin Cardozo and Louis Brandeis, my predecessor.

Once in Conference the vote was close on a case and Reed could not make up his mind. "I am inclined to reverse Chief Justice," Reed said deferentially. Hughes replied with his customary twinkle, "Brother Reed, I will enter you in the docket as voting to reverse. For my experience is that if a Justice inclines a certain way, he has the facility and resourcefulness to marshal the reason to back his inclination."

It was shortly after that episode that Hughes made a statement to me which at the time was shattering but which over the years turned out to be true: "Justice Douglas, you must remember one thing. At the constitutional level where we work, ninety percent of any decision is emotional. The rational part of us supplies the reasons for supporting our predilections."

I had thought of the law in the terms of Moses—principles chiseled in granite. I knew judges had predilections. I knew that their moods as well as their minds were ingredients of their decisions. But I had never been willing to admit to myself that the "gut" reaction of a judge at the level of constitutional adjudications, dealing with the vagaries of due process, freedom of speech, and the like, was the main ingredient of his decision. The admission of it destroyed in my mind some of the reverence for the immutable principles. But they were supplied by Constitutions written by people in conventions, not by judges. Judges are, after all, not creative figures; they represent ideological schools of thought that are highly competitive. No judge at the level I speak of was neutral. The Constitution is not neutral. It was designed to take the government off the backs of people, and no wiser man than Hughes ever sat on our Court. I say that although his predilections, drawn from a different age, were not always mine. I never, for example, could envision Hughes in a boxcar filled with Wobblies (IWWs) roaring across the dusty plains of Washington State at night, but it was not difficult to picture Hugo Black, Wiley Rutledge, Felix Frankfurter and Frank Murphy there. I could, however, imagine Hughes as an advocate pleading our cause or as a judge putting into imperishable words the tolerance which government must show even the most lowly of us.

Holmes once called Justice Benjamin Cardozo "a great and beautiful spirit." Cardozo was a classicist. He loved to take old concepts from Greek and Italian jurisprudence and pour them into Anglo-Saxon ideology. Once I followed a train of thought he developed in a lecture and found myself reading a Florentine treatise entitled "On the Nobility of Law and Medicine," published in 1399. There I read a lively debate in which one side maintained that law was handed down directly from God amidst thunder on Mount Sinai, while science had been put into immutable form by Aristotle.

Cardozo was a man who was interested in man's relation with the cosmos whether he was doctor, lawyer, astronomer, navigator or architect. And he followed, with patience which few of us had, proponents of many schools of thought through their long, tedious and bombastic debates.

He sat on the New York Court of Appeals for eighteen years, and on the U.S. Supreme Court six years (in 1932 President Hoover appointed him to succeed Oliver Wendell Holmes). As a New York judge he spent a great deal of his life fashioning rules of the common law. Of his various creations, I suppose that *MacPherson* v. *Buick Motor Co.* (217 N.Y. 382), decided in 1916, was the most famous. That case held a manufacturer liable to the ultimate consumer for a latent defect in the manufactured commodity that could have been discovered by reasonable inspection. Another landmark decision, *Meinhard* v. *Salmon* (249 N.Y. 458), decided in 1928, and written by Cardozo, held co-adventurers in business transactions to high fiduciary standards. The accountability was not for profits accruing under the joint adventure but for those arising under a new and different venture after the first had ended.

Some have thought that the glory of Western law was in the creative ability of common-law judges. In their eyes, Cardozo was the shining example. Others believe that rules of law should not be judge-made but legislative in origin. It is in the latter tradition that the Jacksonian philosophy has flourished.

Curiously, it was the construction of legislation by judges that Cardozo discussed with me in our one and only extended conversation. He had become fascinated with writings of men such as James M. Landis of Harvard, who, with great skill, showed the problem of translating confused legislative jargon into a consistent mosaic. Legislators do not write with precision: vague phrases are used to mark compromises; a hiatus may be left in a statute as a matter of necessity occasioned by a deadlock of opposed forces, equally strong. Cardozo, as a member of the Supreme Court, met this problem more frequently than when he sat on the Court of Appeals in New York—and he had great facility in resolving it. He coined many golden phrases, but perhaps one of his most enduring was the remark describing freedom of speech as "the cornerstone of the free society."

An intellectual—always a recluse—he had a wonderfully illuminated face, an engaging wit and a penetrating mind. One of his long-term friends, the late Judge Jonah J. Goldstein of New York, told me that he only knew Cardozo to crack a joke once. While on the Court, Cardozo traveled to Albany to attend the inauguration of Herbert Lehman as governor. Judge Goldstein also attended, and hearing that Cardozo was in town, looked him up. He located him in the library of the Court of Appeals, walking slowly while he read a book. As Judge Goldstein approached, Cardozo removed his pince-nez and asked, "What can I do for you?"

Goldstein replied, "Nothing at all."

"What brings you here?"

"The inauguration. Hearing you were here, I dropped by to pay my respects. You see, Mr. Justice, we Jews look at you as the Catholics look at the Pope."

Cardozo's eyes twinkled as he said, "The difference, Goldstein, is important. You don't have to kiss my toe."

When I went on the Court I knew former Justices Willis Van Devanter and George Sutherland casually, and I had had very few contacts with James McReynolds and Pierce Butler. My chief encounter with these Four Horsemen had been at the Chevy Chase Country Club. (I never joined the club because it had blackballed Frank Murphy on the theory that he chased "wild women"—which was false.) But I had numerous friends who were members, and I was often invited to play golf. It was indeed an unlucky day when we teed off behind the old Four Horsemen. They were as slow as molasses, taking many shots and consuming what seemed like hours in putting. To make matters worse, they would not let any faster group through. So apart from their rulings in substantive due process, I had a poor impression of these four Justices when I reached the Court.

When I think of those four old gentlemen I remember the story often told by a hero of mine, Senator Sam J. Erwin, Jr., of North Carolina: "A gentleman who was rather prominent in his community attained his ninety-fifth birthday anniversary. On that day the newspaper reporters came around to interview him. And one of them asked how old he was. He said, 'This is my ninety-fifth birthday anniversary.'

"And the reporter said, 'Well, you have lived a long, long time and have seen many changes in your life.'

"And he said, 'Yes, and I was against every one of them.' "

Van Devanter, on the Court from 1910 to 1937, wrote few opinions. In his twenty-six years on the Court he wrote the majority view in only 346 cases. A conservative on most issues, his highest credentials were, as Brandeis said, that he was an honest, able, forthright and dependable man who always kept his word.

At the end of an argument he could summarize it, state the pros and cons and what the Court should decide. If his words had been recorded, they would have made a perfect opinion. Yet Justice Van Devanter's mind froze the moment he picked up a pencil or pen, and therefore he had the lowest record of any member of the Court in the number of opinions written.

I knew Justice Van Devanter partly because of mutual friends and partly because we had been members of the same college fraternity, Beta Theta Pi—though of course at different colleges. We were at opposite poles on many phases of constitutional law, but what drew me to him was our shared love of the outdoors. Van Devanter had been a hunter, fisherman and camper in his early years in Wyoming and I spent many hours listening to his tales. I found him a genuine human being.

The year 1939 was the centennial of Beta Theta Pi, and a big dinner was scheduled in New York City. I was invited to speak, and Van Devanter urged me to accept. So I went up, having prepared a sentimental talk on the eight Betas who had sat on the Court.

Wendell Willkie was also a Beta and he arranged with the dinner committee to speak last. When his turn came he cut me to ribbons. He used me as an example of Roosevelt's ruination of the Court. It was a campaign speech, as Willkie was then running for President, and I happened to be the vehicle he used to launch an attack on FDR. He ended by saying that perhaps in twenty years I would have learned enough to be a good Justice.

Willkie's theme that experienced judges should be named as Justices to the Supreme Court has been a recurrent one. If selecting Justices for their experience had been the practice throughout our history, we would have had Holmes, Cardozo and Rutledge on the Court but not Marshall, Hughes, Stone, Black, Murphy or Warren. As already noted, Stone saw that it took some years "to get around the track" but no lawyer in practice, no matter how varied his work, ever covers the many different facets with which the Court is concerned. Lower federal court judges cover some of them; state court judges only a few; and neither federal judges nor state judges are faced with the perplexing problems of federalism which come to the Court. Willkie, in his brash way, was right—but for a different reason than the one he gave.

When I was at the SEC, we in the executive branch deemed Justice Sutherland, on the Court from 1922 to 1938, to be an archdemon. We were, at first, relieved when he did not sit in *Jones* v. *Securities & Exchange Commission* (298 U.S. 1), testing the stop-order power of the commission. Then we were shocked when Sutherland, the absent Justice, wrote the opinion for the Court which put a serious crimp in the operation of the SEC laws. We, the outsiders, were unaware of the significance of Chief Justice Hughes's statement at the beginning of oral argument when there was an absent Justice: "Counsel will of course vouch Justice —— into the case"—meaning that the absent member would sit in the case, as though he were present.

Sutherland was, on most issues, a conservative and he often opposed government regulation of big business. Whatever our judicial differences, however, I realized that the Justice was a tempered and reasonable man who also, as his decisions indicate, was zealous in upholding the rights of individuals before the law.

I had heard about Sutherland's aversion to being photographed. At one point there were two men watching his house constantly to find out when he came and went. One day, with the knowledge that he was inside, they rang his doorbell and said, "Mr. Justice, we would like to take your picture." Sutherland was enraged. He told the photographers to clear out and slammed the door.

One of the men pretended to leave, but hid in the bushes. The other rang the bell a second time, and just as Sutherland came out, brandishing a cane, the camera snapped. That photograph appeared on the front page of every newspaper in the United States showing this dignified Justice menacing the world, face aflame, cane raised.

Justice James Clark McReynolds, the tall, gruff, conservative Tennessean whom Wilson had appointed in 1914, was, when I came to the Court, senior in length of service. He was usually very severe in his relations with members of the Court. There were no jokes, no laughter, no pleasantness in his demeanor while he was on the Bench or in Conference. He had taken a particular dislike to Brandeis, whom he thought a "dangerous" man. I had, however, a special relationship to McReynolds born of the fact that we had a mutual friend, George Bates, a resident of Massachusetts whom I had come to know when I was teaching at Harvard Business School. Bates wrote McReynolds when I was named to the Court, saying he hoped McReynolds would get to know me. So Old Mac went out of his way to be nice to me. He greeted me every day with less than his usual gruffness. Morning after morning he would get me over in the corner of the Conference Room, after we were robed, and ask me questions about FDR.

The questions ran as follows: "The man is really insane, isn't he?" "Do you think he will ever regain his sanity?" "You say you were associated with FDR for five years. It is beyond my understanding how anyone could work for a crazy man that long. Can you please explain it?"

I told Old Mac that I was sure he would like FDR if he could get to know him. Whenever I said that, he would snort and get up and walk away.

Mac had the practice of announcing to any Justice who attempted to smoke in Conference, "Tobacco smoke is personally objectionable to me." Few ever undertook it and when they did they were stopped at the threshold. Mac had, however, a kind streak. He was extremely charitable to the pages who worked at the Court, and very tender in his relationship toward children. He lived in an apartment at 2400 Sixteenth Street, and though he was a bachelor, he entertained frequently. In view of our special relationship, he often invited me. I think the highlight of the social events I attended at his home was when he passed the cigarettes to his guests. I smoked at that time and took special pleasure in pretending that I had no match and in getting him to light the cigarette for me.

One of his favorite methods of entertaining was pancake breakfasts on Sunday morning at eleven—what later became known as "brunch." On these informal occasions in his own home he was the essence of hospitality and a very delightful companion.

The first opinion I wrote on the Court was *United States* v. *Powers* (307 U.S. 214), which was decided on May 15, 1939. It was in connection with this case that McReynolds lit into me—the one and only time during the months we served together. I reported at Conference that everybody had agreed with the opinion but that I had not heard from McReynolds. Hughes asked McReynolds if he was ready, and Mac went off on a tangent and made quite a speech. He said he hated to see the past being destroyed so quickly and that this opinion of mine helped to tear down some of the pillars. I was mystified. When I asked him why he felt the way he did, he replied that it was because I referred to something that Chief Justice John Marshall had said as "dictum." He added, "That, in my opinion, is just another way of insulting a great Virginian." I asked him if he would be satisfied if I changed "dictum" to "statement" and he said he would. And that is the way the opinion reads.

When *Schneider* v. *Town of Irvington* (308 U.S. 147) was being argued, McReynolds had a fit of temper. Counsel for Jehovah's Witnesses was Joseph F. Rutherford. (The Jehovah's Witnesses were successors to the Russellites of the seventeenth century, a militant, well-organized, closely knit religious group.) Rutherford had a long mane of hair; he wore a tan cutaway with a huge gold watch chain across his chest, and he had a wing collar with a flowing tie. After he had been under way awhile, McReynolds leaned over and said in a calm voice, "Counsel, why did this lady that was circulating religious literature for Jehovah's Witnesses not get a license? If she had only got a license, then she would not have this problem." Rutherford pushed himself back from the lectern, raised his right hand, and with his index finger pointing to the heavens, shouted, "You want to know why she did not get a license? I will tell you. She did not get a license because Jehovah God told her not to!" Hearing that utterance, McReynolds slammed down the book he had in his hand and left the Bench, not to return until the next day.

That weekend I told President Roosevelt, "Well, Old Mac was finally driven from the Bench." When I told FDR the complete story, he roared with laughter.

One day McReynolds went to the barbershop in the Court. Gates, the black barber, put the sheet around his neck and over his lap, and as he was pinning it behind him McReynolds said, "Gates, tell me, where is this nigger university in Washington, D.C.?" Gates removed the white cloth from McReynolds, walked around and faced him, and said in a very calm and dignified manner, "Mr. Justice, I am shocked that any Justice would call a Negro a nigger. There is a Negro college in Washington, D.C. Its name is Howard University and we are very proud of it." McReynolds muttered some kind of an apology and Gates resumed his work in silence.

McReynolds was rated as a conservative, yet on some issues he was quite liberal. For example, in 1925 he wrote the opinion for the Court in *Pierce* v. *Society of Sisters* (268 U.S. 510). He held it unconstitutional for a state to require all students to go to public schools, that it was part of the "liberty" of parents to send their offspring to parochial schools. In 1923 he ruled in *Meyer* v. *Nebraska* (262 U.S. 390) that a teacher could not be punished by a state for teaching the German language, even though the state had decreed that only the English language should be taught. The teacher's right to teach German and the parents' right to engage him for that purpose were within the concept of liberty in the Fourteenth Amendment. Justices Holmes and Sutherland dissented.

In *District of Columbia* v. *Clawans* (300 U.S. 617), the Court, speaking through Justice Stone, held that a jury was not required in a criminal prosecution for an offense carrying a fine of not more than $300 or imprisonment for not more than ninety days—a so-called petty offense. McReynolds dissented, saying that the Sixth Amendment meant what it said, that an accused in "all criminal prosecutions" was entitled to a trial by jury—the position taken by Justice Black and myself years later in *Baldwin* v. *New York* (399 U.S. 66, 74–76).

Everyone is apt to rush too quickly to the conclusion that a Justice is conservative or liberal, as the case may be, on only partial and often unfair evidence. Pierce Butler, on the Court from 1922 to 1939, was a bright, sharp antagonist, and one had to be well prepared to cross swords with him. While he was extremely conservative, I had great admiration for his intellect. And there were times, of course, when he was on the side of the more liberal members of the Court. He was one of the four who dissented in the famous wiretapping case, *Olmstead* v. *United States* (277 U.S. 438).

Butler lived at 1229 Nineteenth Street, N.W. (in a house which years later Abe Fortas purchased for use as a law office). Shortly after he came on the Court, I went to the Butler residence for a tea; he took me aside and gave me a personal tour of the house. As we were about to come down the stairs he stopped and referred to the Olmstead case. He spoke of the pernicious practice of detectives and government agents tapping wires, and the great revulsion he felt toward that practice. Then he mentioned that he had once been a prosecuting attorney in Minnesota and described some of the problems he had had there, particularly kidnapping—a crime that seemed especially offensive to him. He went on to say, "Wiretapping is unconstitutional. But if I were prosecutor and had a kidnapping case, by God, I would tap the wires!"

Pierce Butler—gruff, large-boned, broad-shouldered and tall—had practiced law in St. Paul for some years before Harding named him to the Court. He was associated in practice with a man of slight build by the name of Tighe. One day when the two were walking with their briefcases to the courthouse in St. Paul, Tighe said, "Mr. Butler, I cannot figure out whether you like me or not." Butler did not reply. Tighe repeated the question. Butler remained silent. A third time Tighe spoke up: "Please tell me if you like me or don't like me." There was a pause and then Butler said, "I never even thought about it."

Butler was able—very able. When the Court seat of Arthur R. Day of Ohio became vacant, two Catholic archbishops were contesting for two different candidates to be nominated. One was Butler; the other was Martin T. Manton, who had been named to the Second Circuit Court of Appeals by Wilson in 1918. (In time Manton was charged with obstructing justice and defrauding the United States government by accepting money for his decisions—one of the worst scandals touching the federal judiciary. He was convicted, and his conviction was affirmed by a specially constituted Court of Appeals consisting of Judge Charles E. Clark of that court and Justices Stone and Sutherland of the Supreme Court.) What influenced Harding toward Butler rather than Manton is not known, but the choice protected the Supreme Court against what would have left an awful scar.

Justice Owen J. Roberts, from Pennsylvania (on the Court from 1930 to 1945), was, on the whole, an extraordinarily fine human being. He was named by Hoover when John J. Parker of North Carolina failed in confirmation. Parker, then on the Court of Appeals, Fourth Circuit, was rejected by the Senate 41 to 39. The major complaints against him were, first, that he had enforced "yellow dog" contracts, whereby employees agreed not to join unions, and second, his belief in segregation of whites and blacks. Hoover thereupon sent up the name of Owen J. Roberts, who was unanimously reported by the Judiciary Committee and confirmed by the Senate without a dissenting vote.

I knew Parker and served with Roberts and concluded that, important as Senate confirmation is as a regulatory device, the wisdom of the Senate is not always apparent. The differences between Parker and Roberts in the broad sweep of the law were not marked. While Parker was abler, each sat way to the right of center and neither had the imaginative mind of Hughes or Stone, Brandeis or Holmes, Black or Frankfurter. Each was honest, honorable and decent, but neither was capable of dealing with the great forces that were beginning to shake the nation.

Roberts began to be known as the "swing" man—sometimes with the conservative majority, sometimes with the liberal minority—as I have described in *Go East, Young Man.*

Justice Harlan F. Stone had been my first professor of law at Columbia. He was Dean when I entered in the fall of 1922, and I took the course in Personal Property from him. He also taught Trusts and Mortgages, but he left at the end of my first year to become a partner in the firm of Sullivan and Cromwell. During the Teapot Dome scandal, President Coolidge brought Stone to Washington to replace Harry Micajah Daugherty as Attorney General, and the next year (1925) named him to the Court.

I had so many personal financial problems in my first year at the law school that I was a frequent visitor at the Dean's office, seeking Stone's advice. He remembered me from those days. He had also been very active in the Columbia Law Alumni Association, where I frequently saw him. When I came to Washington in 1934, I used to call on him at his home on Wyoming Avenue. He had built this home especially to accommodate his Supreme Court staff, which comprised his secretary, his law clerk and a messenger. They were housed in one commodious wing of the house. I used to go there at night to visit with him in his library and I was there shortly after *Colgate* v. *Harvey* (296 U.S. 404) was decided in December 1935. In this case the Court, in an opinion by Sutherland, gave rather expansive meaning to the Privileges and Immunities

Clause of the Fourteenth Amendment. Stone dissented from the opinion, and Brandeis and Cardozo joined him. I was to be on the Court with
Stone when that case was overruled in *Madden* v. *Kentucky* (309 U.S.
83). But the night in the winter of 1935 when I called on Stone, *Colgate*
v. *Harvey* was almost an obsession with him.

There have been, while I have been on the Court, three active prose-
lytizers: Stone, Black and Frankfurter. Most judges content themselves
with making up their own minds, but these three were evangelists, each
in his own right, each sincere, eloquent and unrelenting. Stone, the
evangelist, followed me out in this cold, bitter night onto the stoop
outside his library to denounce *Colgate* v. *Harvey,* and to state that the
Court in 1935 was getting back to about where the Court was in 1900
when it made the Due Process Clause of the Fourteenth Amendment
an engine of destruction. He ventured that the Privileges and Immunities Clause seemed destined to serve in the same role.

In the summer of 1937, after the great heat of the Court-packing
battle had passed, Van Devanter retired. FDR had promised the first
vacancy on the Court to Senator Joseph T. Robinson of Arkansas, one
of the most reactionary men I have known. His appointment would
have brought a mediocre conservative influence to the work of the
Court. Robinson was a loyal Democratic wheel horse, and in spite of the
fact that his law firm, from which he took fees while he was in the
Senate, represented utility companies, he had voted for the Public
Utility Holding Company Act of 1935. This act became law on August
26, 1935, having passed the Senate one hot night by only one vote. Yet
this one deed of his was hardly a credential for handling the great issues
which confront the Court.

In terms of the constitutionality of economic and social legislation, Joe
Robinson might have passed muster, and it was by that standard that
FDR was making his selections. Yet the standard was irrelevant to the
demands of the coming years. Substantive due process was on the
decline and the emerging problems dealt with civil rights. On those
issues Robinson would have been on a par with any of the old wheel
horses of the South.

When Robinson died suddenly on July 14, however, FDR reached for
a symbol of his opposition to the Court that the Senate might dislike but
would have to accept as a matter of traditional courtesy to one of their
own. He considered two senators: Hugo L. Black of Alabama and Sher-

man Minton of Indiana. FDR did not approach either of them directly. Rather, he had Attorney General Homer Cummings take the message to Minton and ask Minton to discuss it with Black, who was FDR's first choice.

FDR did not know Black well, but he was attracted to him by three factors: first, Hugo's use of the investigative role of the Senate to shape the American mind on the need for reforms; second, the message he had sent to FDR as he arrived in Washington for the first inauguration ("Do not appoint anyone to the Cabinet who has been involved in the shipping subsidies or the airline subsidies"); and third, Hugo's voting record.

Minton talked to Black in the Senate cloakroom late one afternoon, saying that although he, Minton, would like the job, he thought Black would make the greater judge. Black wanted to think it over and discuss it with his wife, Josephine. They talked that night and decided he should accept. Hugo told me that the central reason was that they had just learned that one of their sons, Sterling, might become permanently deaf. If he stayed in the Senate, Black would be able to spend little time with his children. If he was on the Court, he would have more time; and because of his son's deafness, that reason became decisive. And so FDR sent Black's name to the Senate on August 12, 1937.

Black, being a member of the Senate, was quickly confirmed. In a few days, however, a storm broke, for it was discovered that while Black was practicing law in Alabama, he had joined the Ku Klux Klan. A hue and cry went up for his removal. I recall one cartoon in the Portland *Oregonian* showing Black poised perilously on the gunwales of a vessel, the title being "Jump, Jump." I have written some of these details in a previous volume, but it seems appropriate to review here this aspect of Black's life.

Hugo Black was not attacked because of his technical and brief membership in the KKK. That was only the façade. The opposition came from those who had fought against his causes when he was a senator: minimum wages, the Fair Labor Standards Act, the Public Utility Holding Company Act, and so on. Yet even conservatives who were stalwarts rallied to his support on the newly engineered effort to remove him from the Court. Among them was Sylvester C. Smith, Jr., of New Jersey, later president of the American Bar Association who, believing fervently in an independent judiciary, defended Black in ABA circles.

The public outcry mounted. Black's house was picketed en masse, an experience that I think colored his decisions in all subsequent cases involving picketing, mass demonstrations, protest marches. Harassed, bombarded by telephone calls, denounced by radio broadcasts, Black, in order to clear up the matter, finally made a talk to the nation on coast-to-coast radio to explain his Klan membership.

I think the explanation lies in the fact that it is apparently the practice of politicians to join all sorts of vote-getting groups or societies. They are our original joiners. Not being a joiner, I do not appreciate the philosophy behind it, for if ever I joined an organization, I would feel committed, as I was with the American Legion and the American Bar Association until I learned their true character. At that point I resigned. But I am sure that Black never for a moment embraced the creed of the Ku Klux Klan.

He was, however, seared by the experience, just as Brandeis had been seared by his long inquisition before the Senate and the great delay in his confirmation. Neither one made many public appearances after going on the Bench, nor did they make speeches.

Black was "the tiger that Roosevelt tossed into the Court," according to Frank Maloney, who was in the Senate at the time. And there is truth in the statement. But Black had greatness also, as the years revealed. He was ridiculed by the press of the Establishment as having no "legal experience." He had, however, been a plaintiff's lawyer, a jury lawyer, in Alabama for years. He had also been a prosecutor. He actually brought to the Bench more courtroom experience than any Justice appointed in this century. He was also my closest friend on the Court, and my companion in many hard judicial battles.

Stanley F. Reed was FDR's second appointment to the Court. Reed, a Kentucky lawyer, had come to Washington under Hoover and served as counsel to various agencies, including the Reconstruction Finance Corporation. Then he became Solicitor General and argued many cases before the Court. He was working so hard that in 1935, while he was arguing the keystone case in FDR's agricultural program, *United States* v. *Butler* (297 U.S. 1), he fainted. Hughes called a short recess while Reed recovered. He bore the brunt of advocacy for most of FDR's program prior to his appointment to the Court in 1938.

Reed was a liberal in the frame of reference of the social and business problems that had become FDR's cause. Those problems, however, were soon to disappear and new ones would take their place. As civil rights cases emerged, Reed was usually on the side of government, which in one way made him consistent. The difficulty with his approach was that civil rights are often specifically protected against governmental action, while "property" interests have few particularized guarantees against regulation. For example, though the First Amendment provides that "Congress shall make no law abridging freedom of speech," there is nothing in the Constitution that says Congress shall make no law regulating hours of work, wages, labor-management relations, prices, and so on. Reed, as it developed, was one of the most reactionary judges to occupy the Bench in my time.

But he was also the most gentle, the friendliest, the most warmhearted individual one could meet. He never raised his voice; he never reflected anger or animus; he never said one unkind thing against another person. It was always a joy to be with him, though often he and I were poles apart. He recently joked to a friend of mine that he had broken me in on the Court—but that there had been times when he regretted it.

Both Cardozo and Brandeis were men who did not seem to enjoy life in the raw. They were happy, but their happiness was in the quiet determination that dominated their lives or in exquisite moments like those when the violin of an Isaac Stern took possession of an audience. Felix Frankfurter was more robust. He loved laughter and gaiety and the riposte. He was probably the best conversationalist that my generation knew. He would hold court in the drawing rooms of Washington, D.C., and show with splendor his scintillating mind.

But Frankfurter did not know wrong in the same sense as Brandeis and Cardozo. Rather, he was the eclectic whose inventive genius led to much improvising. He was primarily a teacher, and the habits he had acquired in that role carried over into all subsequent ones. Whenever a new Justice appeared at the Supreme Court, Frankfurter seemed to spend extra time and energy converting him to a particular school of thought that Frankfurter preferred. He was indeed a proselytizer extraordinary.

Early in his career he was identified with leftist causes, notably the Sacco-Vanzetti case. But Frankfurter was not leftist; he was always identified with the Establishment, though insistent that the Establishment proceed with meticulous care when it moved against a miscreant, whether he be left or right.

Most of Frankfurter's decisions at the constitutional level were eroded within a few years after he retired, in 1962, only to be refurbished when the Nixon appointees arrived. The Frankfurter decisions to which I refer dealt mostly with the extent to which Congress and/or the states can regulate speech, press, the right of assembly, and the other rights in the congeries of the First Amendment. Those decisions also included the restrictive way in which he applied the Bill of Rights to the states, as well as those in which he narrowly defined cases subject to judicial cognizance and broadly defined those that were "political" and therefore left to other departments for settlement. But the differences between Frankfurter and those of us whose views briefly prevailed until the Burger Court took over, in 1969, were, as my Brother Hugo Black once stated, "far less about the ultimate aims of our Constitution than they were about the most appropriate way for our Court to aid in achieving those aims" (78 *Harvard Law Review* 1521).

Frankfurter's greatest emphasis was probably on procedural due process, and although he would not extend the Bill of Rights to the states, he was quick to protest when municipal or state police tactics shocked his conscience.

The press was continually rife with untrue stories that Frankfurter and I were always at loggerheads. There was one press report to the effect that someone had hired a lip reader to attend our sessions to "read" what I was saying to one of the Justices next to me. The news was that I commented after one of Frankfurter's frequent questions, "Why doesn't the son of a bitch keep his mouth shut?" But that was wholly apocryphal.

We differed greatly, Frankfurter and I; and he was not one to let a difference lie. He was, as I have said, a proselytizer, and every waking hour vigorously promoted the ideas he espoused. Up and down the halls he went, pleading, needling, nudging, probing. He never stopped trying to change the votes on a case until the decision came down.

Frankfurter also indulged in histriónics in Conference. He often came in with piles of books, and on his turn to talk, would pound the table, read from the books, throw them around and create a great disturbance. His purpose was never aimless. His act was designed to get a particular Justice's vote or at least create doubts in the mind of a Justice who was thinking the other way. At times, when another was talking, he would break in, make a derisive comment and shout down the speaker.

We always had the most junior Justice in time of service act as keeper of the door to the Conference, but when anyone had a message to send out of the Conference, he took it himself, opened the door, waited for a page to appear and handed the message to the page, who took it to the part of the building indicated. Felix had one interesting innovation to this routine. Never would he hand his note to a page. Always he dropped it on the floor at the page's feet, even though the page held out his hand to receive the message.

I don't know why he did this. It was of course a form of compelled obeisance. But what psychological twist would induce a person year after year to make a servant stoop to pick up a paper from the floor? What barrier prevented the superior from handing the servant the piece of paper?

Frankfurter had a basic weakness. I think he had deep inside him a feeling of inadequacy. He was a man of short stature. Perhaps that was part of it. He longed to be accepted. He was an artist at teasing and taunting the Establishment and its advocates. He loved to see the Dean Achesons of the world squirm. But he also needed to be accepted by them and honored and admired by them. While he wanted the Establishment to be decent and civilized, his basic positions were ultimately aligned with it.

Frankfurter aroused people; they either loved him or hated him. He was not unique in that respect. Hugo Black, and I also, had that quality. It has always been a mystery to me why some men or women have that chemistry while others lack it. Arthur Houghton, a close friend of Joe Kennedy's, never met Felix but for some strange reason he hated him with ardor. Arthur was not a lawyer; he had been in the theatrical business and later had served on a voluntary censorship board established by the movie industry. Every time I saw Arthur he would let go at Felix. My defense of Felix only made Arthur more violent.

One Christmas I purchased an excellent photo of Felix and asked him to autograph it for Arthur Houghton. Felix hesitated, saying he did not remember him. I assured him that he was well remembered by Arthur. So Felix with some doubts signed the photo. I tipped off Joe Kennedy, and when I went to hand over the Christmas gift to Arthur, Joe was there. I made a sentimental presentation speech. Arthur, unwrapping the gift, became apoplectic, stormed up and down, denounced Felix, me, the Court and all who were friends of the aforesaid. With that he tossed the $25 photograph into the roaring fireplace. Thus a valued collector's item was lost in a burst of anger.

It was truly a joy to be with Frankfurter when he was tossing bits of conversation about. He had a keen sense of humor and the feminine quality of laying bare the essentials.

He loved stories that were a bit off-color. This one amused him: A prostitute (known as a woman of joy) was too poor to have a place of business. She garnered customers on the street, and if the man was a Protestant, took him to a secluded place in a Catholic cemetery. If he was a Catholic, she took him to a Protestant cemetery. Her price was standard and uniform: two bits. One day she got herself a traveling salesman who in settling the account offered her fifty cents. She looked up at him in shame and said, "You know very well I don't have change."

One night Felix and I spun out some chestnuts—not original with us, I believe. The two I remember are: Laws are like cobwebs which catch the small flies but are broken by the big ones; and God joined law and equity together but man put them asunder.

Felix and I constantly exchanged notes on the Bench. One lawyer— I forget the case—worked into his argument the old poem, "May there be no moaning of the bar when I put out to sea." In a flash a note came from Felix: "There will be when I do."

An argument in a Frazier-Lemke Bankruptcy Act case brought in the power of Congress over migratory birds. Felix wrote: "To interfere with McReynold's leisure there must be 'a public interest at least of the magnitude of ducks' "—a reference to a McReynolds comment intimating that foreclosure of farm mortgages were not of that stature. My reply to Felix almost cracked him up:

> When it comes to a duck
> or a really good * * * *
> public interest will carry the day.
> But banks do no harm
> to a poor debtor's farm.
> There is no public interest in hay.

Felix was not the only note-writer on the Bench. A night-club performer who was a friend of Frank Murphy's sent him a card saying she was opening in Washington on December 8, 1947. Frank sent me the card with a note: "I would be obliged if you would represent me at the lady's gala opening. If you can't make it, ask Wiley [Rutledge] to do so in an academic way." One would have to know Justice Wiley Rutledge to appreciate the humor. He was a quiet, dignified man with the presence of a parish priest. I say that not mockingly but with pride.

Frank Murphy came on the Court in 1940 and while he liked the Court work, he longed, I think, for an executive job, probably as Secretary of War. Frank never had a drink of alcohol in his life, and though he was always portrayed with a beautiful lady, his bachelor status was permanent. The legend persisted that he was a great playboy, which, as I have said, was not true.

I had great fun with Frank Murphy over the Court's decision in *Mortensen* v. *United States* (322 U.S. 369). It was a prosecution under the Mann Act against a couple, the Mortensens, who lived in Grand Island, Nebraska, and ran a house of prostitution there under the name of Nifty Rooms. The Mortensens had given their "employees" an out-of-state vacation; the criminal charge against them was that the return of the prostitutes to Grand Island constituted transportation across state lines "for the purpose of prostitution" under the Mann Act. The Court was divided five to four, Murphy writing for the majority, which held that the Mortensens had committed no federal crime.

The next summer I was driving East with my friend Sidney M. Davis, a New York lawyer. We stopped at Grand Island and looked for the Mortensens and for their place of business. The Mortensens had disappeared and the house known as Nifty Rooms was no longer in existence. What had happened, where the people had gone, no one knew. My plan had been to go to Nifty Rooms, obtain, if possible, some of its stationery, and write Justice Murphy a note of thanks. I did the next best thing. I went to the Chamber of Commerce, procured a sheet of its stationery and hired a secretary to type Murphy a letter thanking him warmly for protecting the "local industry" of Grand Island, Nebraska.

When I returned to the capital that fall, Frank showed me the letter and said something about "the good people" of Grand Island, Nebraska. Then he looked at me and asked, "You didn't write that letter, did you?"

Murphy was a special target of Frankfurter, who made fun of him behind his back. Murphy had a disease that caused poor blood circulation in his extremities. So he spent the hours in Conference rubbing his hands, massaging his fingers, and the like. Frankfurter pilloried Murphy for the habit, whispering that Murphy was so distraught that he was trying to solve legal problems by wringing his hands. Murphy did not have the technical competence of either Frankfurter or Reed or Stone —the three who probably disliked him the most. But he had common sense, a keen orientation to the Constitution and the Bill of Rights, and a sense of the relevancy of facts. He was a humanist in the best sense of the word. And though he and I did not always agree, I thought that he was a great Justice. In retrospect I realize I made more mistakes in not following him than in not following Frankfurter.

Frank Murphy was a very devout Catholic. One Sunday in New York City he attended mass at St. Patrick's with Joseph Kennedy. As Frank told the story to me, the two of them had climbed the steps together and were just about to enter the cathedral when Joe turned to Frank and asked, "By the way, Frank, are you still sleeping with that Miss Kelly?"

"Can you imagine it?" Frank asked me. "Here we are almost inside the holy place when Joe starts talking about fornication."

Frank was easy to spoof. One day he and I passed the Marshal's Office at Court and saw that it was packed with people.

"What are they doing here?" Frank asked.

"Waiting to see Felix," I lied.

Frank, ready to believe almost anything about Felix the fixer, asked, "You mean they are trying to see Felix to get jobs?"

"Jobs and contracts," I replied.

"What do you know!"

"The visitors are growing in such numbers," I added, "that Felix had to institute a new system."

"What's that?"

"Everyone now gets a ticket with a number."

"Just like a barber shop?"

"Exactly. And do you realize that yesterday the last ticket issued carried the number sixty-four?"

"What do you know about that!"

James F. Byrnes, who served for a year or so beginning in 1941, was a misfit on the Court and was himself the first to admit it. He disliked the Court work, perferring the helter-skelter life on the Hill, where he had served for years, or in the executive branch. His contribution to the Court was gaiety. Jimmy and his lovely wife, Maude, entertained frequently in their spacious apartment at the Sheraton Park. The food was delicious and the drinks abundant. Jimmy had a strong tenor voice, and after dinner he led the Justices and their wives in singing popular songs. The result was usually horrible, but Jimmy was undaunted.

Jimmy Byrnes wrote but one outstanding opinion, and that was in *Edwards* v. *California.* The case concerned an out-of-stater who had been barred from entering California because he was poor; like many others he had gone to California to get the sun on his back and reduce the cost of living. The case came before the Court in 1941 and the decision was reported in 314 U.S. 160. Jimmy reasoned that since livestock could pass state lines unless they were diseased, the same would hold for people, and it was that analogy that caused me to write a separate opinion. I wrote that the right to travel was a Privilege and Immunity guaranteed by citizenship and could not be challenged by a state.

When *Brown* v. *Board of Education* came before the Court, Jimmy was no longer a Justice and he was a disturbed man when that decision came down. He undoubtedly agreed with John W. Davis, a former congressman and Solicitor General, who made an impassioned plea in which he promised that South Carolina would get rid of the problem of segregation of the races by providing schools for blacks that were of equal quality to the whites.

Some time later I saw Jimmy when the American Bar Association held a convention in Portland, Oregon, and I was staying at the Benson Hotel. It was a lovely day and I was outside basking in the sun when the parade came by. Jimmy was in an open limousine, waving his hand, bowing to the ladies. There was a break in the parade, so I ran down to the car, put out my hand and said, "How are you, Jimmy?" He brushed my hand aside as if I were a peddler of cocaine or heroin or some other dangerous drug. That really hurt me, as we had been good friends for so long.

Years later, at another meeting I was attending in Portland, I was stopped by a gentleman who was a friend of Jimmy's from South Carolina. He said Jimmy was on his deathbed and the only thing that he could talk about was me and how he wanted to see me. Since Oregon is a long way from South Carolina, I thought that my coming would violate his views on interstate travel. In view of *Brown* v. *Board of Education,* it might set him back, so I reluctantly decided not to go to South Carolina. I have regretted that many times.

Wiley Rutledge took Byrnes's place early in 1943. Rutledge, who had tuberculosis in his youth, had gone west to Colorado, where he taught law. From there he went to Washington University, St. Louis, and then to Iowa. Irving Brant, a journalist and good friend of FDR's, knew him in St. Louis and admired him, and it was Brant who was largely responsible for Rutledge's judicial career. Ed Eicher, congressman from Iowa, who later served with me at the SEC, promoted Rutledge for the Court of Appeals in the District of Columbia, and Brant carried the idea through at the White House. I first met Rutledge in the waiting room of the Senate Judiciary Committee. He had been called there for confirmation to the Court of Appeals, I for the Supreme Court.

Rutledge had two habits that led to his early demise. He was an incessant cigarette smoker, a habit dating back to when he was eleven years old, and he was a prodigious worker. His gristmill ground very fine. He polished opinions with meticulous care. He worked more than any of us, staying at his desk night after night until the wee hours. He was a man I greatly liked; and he, Murphy, Black and I became somewhat of a foursome.

FDR had promised Robert H. Jackson, his gallant front-fighter on the Court-packing plan, that he would make him the next Chief Justice after Hughes. But by the time Hughes retired in 1941, FDR had named seven Justices to the Court, all from the Democratic Party ranks. So he decided it would be better to name Harlan Stone, a Republican, as Chief Justice. He broke the news to Bob, promising to make him Chief the next time around. At the time he settled on Stone as Hughes's successor, he sent Bob's name up to take Stone's place on the Court as an Associate Justice.

When Stone died in 1946, Bob Jackson was on leave of absence from the Court as U.S. prosecutor at the Nuremberg trials. He was planning to run for governor of New York and perhaps for President, so from a political viewpoint it was desirable for him to be our Nuremberg prosecutor, since the Jewish vote is important in many parts of our country. He was gone a whole year, and in his absence we sat as an eight-man Court. I thought at the time he accepted the job that it was a gross violation of separation of powers to put a Justice in charge of an executive function. I thought, and I think Stone and Black agreed, that if Bob did that, he should resign. Moreover, some of us—particularly Stone, Black, Murphy and I—thought that the Nuremberg trials were unconstitutional *by American standards.* I had talked with FDR about the matter several times. He had indeed sent Harry Hopkins to me to canvass the matter, as well as John Boettiger, husband of Anna Roosevelt and former editor of the Arizona *Times*. I told them what I still believe: that Hitler and members of his entourage should have been tried for murder. Instead, they were tried for waging "an aggressive war."

The difficulty with those trials was twofold: (1) By American standards, ex post facto laws are banned, and there was at the time no clear-cut crime of waging "an aggressive war." True, sharp lawyers could spell it out from treaties and conventions. But criminal law *by our standards* must be clear, precise and definite so as to warn all potential transgressors. No international ban on aggressive war had that precision and clarity. (2) The ban against "aggressive war" levied a penalty against the loser. As Stone said, "To be a winner, a nation under threats may have to move first or else be destroyed." His prophecy was borne out by Israel's victory over three Arab nations in 1967. In other words, the concept of "aggressive war" needs to be defined with precision to be a manageable affair under American criminal-law standards.

In any case, the Nuremberg trials were held and Bob Jackson did lawyerlike service there. But they turned out to be his undoing. His long absence and associations caused a deep family rift. Moreover, he was still abroad when Stone died and the question of who would be the new Chief Justice arose. Truman passed him over and appointed Fred Vinson. Rumors reached Germany that Black and I, particularly Black, had gone to Truman urging him not to appoint Jackson. That is not true. Truman never broached this matter to either of us, and neither of us sent any message to Truman. But Bob, advised to the contrary, let go a blast in a long letter to the chairman of the Senate and House Judiciary committees. He referred to "feuds" on the Court; and he had indeed had a "feud" with Black over the Jewell Ridge case (325 U.S. 161), in which Murphy wrote the majority opinion, with which Black agreed. The vote was five to four, Jackson writing the dissent.

In his letter to the committee that was considering Fred Vinson's nomination as Chief Justice, Bob said:

> The President has nominated an upright, fearless, and well qualified man for Chief Justice of the United States.
> Mr. Vinson's task is most difficult and long personal friendship with him as well as concern for the Court make me desire that he will succeed in his task. It is important that the magni-

tude and nature of the task which faces him shall not be minimized.

Many have assumed, and the impression has been cultivated, that he faces a mere personal vendetta among Justices which can be soothed by a tactful presiding officer. This is utterly false. The controversy threatens the reputation of the Court for non-partisan and unbiased decision.

Further suppression of facts will not help Mr. Vinson and will afford continuing basis for irresponsible rumor and innuendo.

This feud has been so much and so long publicized that Congress has a right to know the facts and issues involved. This is the appropriate opportunity so far as they involve myself and my participation in Court decisions. I also have personal reasons for wanting this situation made clear.

Such news as reaches me here indicates that in my absence, one of my colleagues made publicized threats to the President and that they have been exploited through certain inspired commentators and columnists to imply that offensive behavior on my part is responsible for the feud on the Court.

I could not defend myself even to the President while the appointment of a Chief Justice was pending without being in the position of pleading for the post. That I would not do. Now that the appointment is made I am free to answer and choose to do so not by inspired innuendos but over my signature.

In the balance of the letter Bob charged impropriety re Black's sitting in the Jewel Ridge coal case, since Black's ex-partner was the advocate for the winning party, the United Mine Workers. Bob ended his statement as follows:

It is high time that these stories of feuds cease to be mysteriously and irresponsibly fed out and that Congress have the facts.

If war is declared on me I propose to wage it with the weapons of the open warrior, not those of the stealthy assassin.

I want it understood that nothing in this statement is to be construed as the slightest reflection upon Fred Vinson. My knowledge of him leads me to the conviction that attempts to deal with him in the manner I have recited would be no more successful than they were with me. It is desirable to get the controversy all back of us now so that he can take up his task without the cloud hanging over the Court. Further, I do not want it inferred that I charge that Justice Black's sitting in the Jewell Ridge case involved lack of "honor."

It is rather a question of judgment as to sound judicial policy. There may be those who think it quite harmless to encourage the employment of Justices' ex-law partners to argue close cases by smothering the objections which the bar makes to this practice. But in my view such an attitude would soon bring the Court into disrepute. We do not sit like local judges, where lawyers and litigants know our relationships and characters. Our lawyers and litigants are usually, except when appearing for the Government, strangers who know us only by publicity, by our work and by appearances.

However innocent the coincidence of these two victories at successive terms by Justice Black's former law partner, I wanted that practice stopped. If it is ever repeated while I am on the bench, I will make my Jewell Ridge opinion look like a letter of recommendation by comparison. I have considered that the attacks upon me during my absence cannot in fairness to further work on the Court be left unanswered and that the responsible committees of Congress are entitled to the facts.

Whether a Justice should disqualify himself from a case is a matter of his own conscience. One's recent partner may be so much like a brother that the ties are too close for impartial judgment. One's distant partner may be pretty much a stranger. There is no fixed rule about it. Black, like Bob and the rest of us, was always quick to withdraw from a case when he felt there was a conflict. The weapon Bob used against Black was forged in passion and intemperance.

In retrospect, Bob's presence in Germany caused him to miss out on perhaps the one most enveloping ambition he ever had. Truman did not dislike Bob. As a matter of fact, he had thought so well of Bob as to consider him for his running mate in 1948. But he apparently never thought of Bob seriously as a Chief Justice and apparently never knew of FDR's promise to Bob. There was no one on this side close to Truman who could plead his cause. Frankfurter tried, but was ineffective. Bob's disappointment was bitter almost every day of his remaining life. As Fred Vinson, who succeeded Stone, told me, "I really think Bob Jackson will make a personal target out of everyone who sits here as Chief Justice."

Jackson was a country lawyer of great versatility. He had worked hard to be governor of New York but could not pass muster among the pros. He had a sharp pen and an incisive mind. He was a lone wolf on the Court, having no close friend except Frankfurter. He loved to write essays and publish them as opinions, not necessarily to illuminate a problem, but to embarrass or harass a colleague. In that sense he was petty, but some of his opinions are enduring and contain ringing declarations of the democratic ideal. But his ambition to be Chief Justice truly poisoned his judicial career.

Justice and Mrs. Owen Roberts were very gracious hosts and entertained at their home in Georgetown and also on their farm in Pennsylvania. Owen and Hugo Black became close friends, and Black used to spend weekends, especially in the spring of the year, at the Robertses' farm. While he and Roberts were not close ideologically speaking, they were extremely fond of each other. (To a certain degree Roberts felt the same toward me.) But Hugo's very happy relationship with Roberts soured. There were columns in the press then, as there always have been off and on, that predicted the way the Court would probably decide cases. When I was in the executive branch, that was our favorite indoor sport—lining up the judges and making our own private prediction—perhaps betting a dime or a quarter one way or the other. Sometimes we were right and sometimes we were wrong. The practice spread to the columnists. After I had been on the Supreme Court a few years, Drew Pearson predicted one Sunday with total exactness how a case was going to be decided the very next day. The case was *Bridges* v. *Wixon* (326 U.S. 135), holding that Harry Bridges was being illegally deported. I wrote the Court's opinion. Stone wrote a dissent, in which Roberts and Frankfurter joined. Jackson took no part in the decision. The case was scheduled to come down the following Monday.

Chief Justice Stone called a special Conference Monday morning and we decided to put the case off a week or two—not that anyone was going to change his mind, but Frankfurter rebelled at rendering Drew Pearson's story reliable. At this Conference Frankfurter charged me, Black and Murphy with "leaks" to Pearson. I denied it, Murphy denied it, Black denied it. And it was false, at least as far as I was concerned, and I am sure as far as the other two were concerned also. Drew told me years later who his source was; Felix had been far from the mark. Frankfurter, however, would not let the matter die and he built it up in Roberts' mind to such an extent that Roberts refused to shake hands or speak to Black, Murphy and me, and that condition continued until he resigned from the Court.

It is customary for the Justices to come to the Robing Room, shake hands with one another, line up in the Conference Room and then walk into Court. Roberts refused to go to the Robing Room. He would have the messenger come out in the hall and robe him, then he would stand in the hall waiting for the line to come by, and then step into his proper place so as to avoid shaking hands. The poison that Frankfurter dropped in the well ruined the later years of the life of a very fine human being.

Roberts outstayed FDR, resigning in 1945 and being replaced by Harold H. Burton, Truman's Republican appointee.

With the exception of Roberts, the men FDR named to the Court, plus Stone, constituted the so-called team to take over after the old Court passed on. They were, of course, not a "team." There were as many divisions within that group as there likely would have been had nine Presidents named the nine Justices.

Hughes told me in the early years, "You will find that the Justices will agree in about two thirds of the decisions they make. But as respects the other third, it will be impossible to get unanimity, no matter who makes the appointment."

Hughes was correct in his prediction. The issues in about one third of the cases are so controversial as to preclude unanimity. The reason, of course, is that the Constitution and the Bill of Rights are written in such broad language that a specific application can give rise to a contrariety of views. Freedom of speech and of the press is guaranteed. But does the guarantee extend to what is obscene, sacrilegious or seditious? Or rather, to what a majority thinks runs afoul of these categories? That is the kind of stuff out of which great constitutional debates arise. The Roosevelt Court was no more unanimous than any preceding it. And that will be true of the Court that sits in the next century.

In time I came to realize that Hughes was right when he said that a Justice's decisions were based 90 percent on emotion. The emotion that Frankfurter displayed in denouncing that Hughes dictum was a telltale sign that Hughes was right. Frankfurter was indeed the most obvious example in my time of the truth of the Hughes observation. Black was a close second. Each went at a problem with great feeling and charged with powerful emotions. Black was more frank about the process; he never took the Frankfurter stance that he was following "the law" and putting aside his own feelings and desires in reaching a decision. Frankfurter's skein of life was woven with a design that was duplicitous, for no one poured his emotions more completely into decisions, while professing just the opposite.

The Court Conference is not a public meeting. Only the Justices attend. Prior to 1910, there was a bar in the Conference Room with an attendant who served both soft drinks and hard liquor. It was, however, discontinued because alcoholic beverages did not mix well with the deliberative functions of the Conference.

The Chief Justice always presides, stating his views on every case on the Conference List—whether to deny certiorari (request for a hearing) or to grant the petition and hear argument; whether to dismiss an appeal or affirm or, on the other hand, to note probable jurisdiction and hear it on the merits; whether, as respects cases already argued, the judgment should be affirmed, reversed, vacated, modified, and so on. After the Chief Justice has spoken, the discussion proceeds around the table by seniority. When each has had his say, a vote is taken, each Justice recording the vote in a docket book in which every case is given a page.

The Conference discussion sometimes changes one's view of a case, but usually not. The chief function of the Conference is to discover the consensus. That is important when it comes to the assignment of opinions to write. British courts hand down seriatim opinions—that is, opinions by each of the members of the court. That was in Jefferson's eyes the better system. But Chief Justice John Marshall disagreed and established the practice of having, if possible, one opinion for the Court. To write for five or more men means, at times, trimming and qualifying to conceal sharp differences on the ultimate reach of a particular doctrine or its application. Yet knowledge of the consensus of the Conference is essential to the assignment of opinions and to a reduction in the number of opinions.

The Chief Justice assigns the opinion if he is in the majority. If he is in the minority, the senior Justice in the majority makes the assignment.

Every Chief Justice, when assigning opinions, has an eye to public relations and to history—and naturally so. A so-called liberal Justice will be certain to get the opinion holding a so-called liberal law unconstitutional. Brandeis was assigned the opinion holding the first Frazier-Lemke Bankruptcy Act unconstitutional (*Louisville Bank* v. *Radford*,

295 U.S. 555). Black, a long-time promoter of trade unionism, was assigned the opinion holding that states could enjoin unions from picketing to prevent enforcement of valid state antitrust laws (*Giboney* v. *Empire Storage & Ice Co.* 336 U.S. 490).

Harlan was assigned *NAACP* v. *Alabama* (357 U.S. 449), holding that disclosure of the NAACP's membership lists in Alabama in the 1950s would likely hinder the NAACP and its members from the collective efforts in lawfully promoting the interest of the black minority it represented.

For some reason unknown to me, Chief Justice Stone assigned *Korematsu* to Hugo Black and *Ex parte Endo,* argued and decided the same day, to me. In a much criticized opinion (*Korematsu* v. *United States,* 323 U.S. 214) *Korematsu* decided that in time of war the West Coast appeared to be defenseless until a Japanese army (which everyone assumed would land on the West Coast) reached the Rocky Mountains. Hence the approval of the evacuation program covering those of Japanese ancestry. The other opinion (*Ex parte Endo,* 323 U.S. 283), which I wrote for the Court, held that while the Army could evacuate the Japanese, it had no authority even in time of war to detain them in camps, as it was doing, absent evidence that those detained were not loyal to the United States. Why Stone assigned one to Hugo and one to me is a mystery. Hugo properly voiced his discontent after the opinions were circulated:

(no date)

DEAR BILL:

I certainly hope that your Endo case will go down. It is a good job and the problems are handled to my complete satisfaction. I do think, as I understood you did, that it would be better practice in situations like this for one Justice to write both cases. At least, this has ordinarily been the way such intimately related cases are handled. I should personally regret it very much if the CJ should reassign Endo, and I shall tell him that if he says anything to me about it. There is no feeling of any kind on my part about your writing, but as stated I think assignments of related opinions should be to one writer save in exceptional circumstances. The only feeling I have as to you personally in connection with it is one of admiration for the fine way in which you have done it.

Sincerely,
HLB

The examples are almost legion in which a Justice of one disposition is assigned to write an opinion expressing the opposed view that is generally contrary to his philosophy.

Earl Warren naturally kept to himself the landmark decisions: (1) segregation in public schools, *Brown* v. *Board of Education of Topeka, Kansas* (347 U.S. 483); (2) legislative apportionment, *Reynolds* v. *Sims* (377 U.S. 533); (3) the use of in-custody interrogation by the police to obtain confessions, *Miranda* v. *Arizona* (384 U.S. 436).

The idea of the Chief keeping these assignments did not reflect vanity. The prestige of the office of Chief Justice behind a controversial decision gives it strength and weight. I suppose that is why Hughes kept for himself the famous Gold Clause cases (*Norman* v. *Baltimore Ohio Railroad Co.*, 294 U.S. 240; *United States* v. *Bankers Trust Co.*, 294 U.S. 240; *Nortz* v. *United States,* 294 U.S. 317; *Perry* v. *United States,* 294 U.S. 330), which arose when Congress changed the monetary standard of U.S. currency. The owners and holders of gold coin, bullion and certificates were called on to deliver them over to the Federal Reserve Bank in exchange for paper money. This action was contested as unlawful and as a violation of the right of contract. A majority of the Court eventually decided to rely on the constitutionally stated authority of Congress to coin money and regulate its value (U.S. Constitution, Art. I, Sect. 8, par. 5).

The appointment of a new Chief commonly gives rise to talk that now the differences between Justices will lessen and greater harmony prevail. When former President William Howard Taft was named, in 1921, the New York *Tribune* said editorially:

> Mr. Taft has such tact and good humor, and has so unconquerable a spirit of fair play, that he is greatly beloved of his fellow citizens. These gifts and this character may not be the first ones sought for in a chief justice, but even the most eminent judges are none the worse for having them. With Justice Taft as a moderator it is probable that not a few asperities that mar the harmony of the celestial chamber, the consulting room, not a few of those asperities will be softened and that not quite so often in the future will the court divide five and four.

That was of course nonsense. Men sitting on the Court are never swayed by a smile or a slap on the back. Congenial relations in the corridors and at the luncheon table have no relationship with unanimity or dissent on the issues before the Court. Those issues cut too deep and mark such fundamental differences in legal philosophy ever to be erased or even conditioned by a smile or by acts of friendship from a protagonist.

The Court in my time always had amicable personal relations. The problem was to keep that feeling of compatibility active and alive, for the work of the Court involves fierce ideological conflicts of a very fundamental sort.

The outside criticism of the Court has been pretty much the same over the ages. Robert Jackson, long before his appointment, criticized the old Court because it sat "almost as a continuous constitutional convention which, without submitting its proposals to any ratification or rejection, could amend the basic law."

He was talking about the use of the Due Process Clause of the Fourteenth Amendment to strike down state laws touching social, economic and business problems, measures deemed by the majority to be unwise or unreasonable. In 1876 the Court, speaking through Chief Justice Morrison Remick Waite in *Munn* v. *Illinois* (94 U.S. 113), had sustained a state law fixing the maximum charges for the storage of grain. It refused to give the Due Process Clause a substantive meaning, saying: "For protection against abuses by legislatures the people must resort to the polls, not to the courts" (*Id.* 134). The Court, under the hammering of Justices like Stephen Johnson Field, who soon made up a majority, traveled the road of substantive due process and set back for decades experimental legislative programs in the states.

What Jackson said about the old Court, Senators Everett Dirksen and Strom Thurmond, speaking for the Republicans, and James Eastland, J. William Fulbright, Lister Hill and others, speaking for the Democrats, said about the Court of the 1950s and 1960s. Dirksen thought our reapportionment decisions should have been reached, if at all, only by constitutional amendment. The Southerners thought that segregation of the races, held constitutional in 1896 by *Plessy* v. *Ferguson,* was the only constitutional way of life, absent an amendment. I remember a biting comment made to me about our 1954 school desegregation decision by Lister Hill to the effect that the Court had rewritten the Constitution to suit its sociological views.

This was Jackson's criticism; and it will in the future be the criticism of any segment of American life that disagrees with the Court's consti-

tutional interpretations. These large swings in constitutional constructions are not due to political pressures on the Justices, though it is not
unusual to find those who think otherwise.

Mr. Dooley said, "No matter whether th' constitution follows th' flag
or not, th' supreme coort follows th' iliction returns." That witticism has
a grain of truth in it. The Court does move with political trends, as the
philosophy of newly appointed Justices commonly reflects a trend. And
community attitudes are not without their effect. The Court is not
isolated from life. Its members are very much a part of the community
and know the fears, anxieties, cravings and wishes of their neighbors.
That does not mean that community attitudes are necessarily translated
by mysterious osmosis into new judicial doctrine. It does mean that the
state of public opinion will often make the Court cautious when it
should be bold. That is usually reflected in what the Court does not do,
rather than in what it creates. That is to say, when the Court has
discretion to act or refuse to act, the state of public opinion may lead
it to find many reasons for not taking up a controversial issue at the
time. In the privacy of the Conference, that is often called "judicial
statesmanship." At times a Justice has illustrated the point by saying
that if the Court had been wise in the 1850s, it would never have taken
on the burden of trying to decide the explosive issues of the Dred Scott
case.* I would generally agree when it is clear that the decision to be
made would violate the conscience of mankind.

Some think that the famous Milligan case (71 U.S. 2)—generally limiting the power of military courts to try civilians—would never have been
written in the heat of the Civil War but mustered a majority of votes
only because it was decided late in 1866. That was the view of Robert
P. Patterson, federal judge and Undersecretary of War in World War
II, who once on a plane ride with me held forth at length on that thesis.
Others have felt the same way.

It may be that the military orders evacuating Americans of Japanese
ancestry from the West Coast in World War II would never have been
sustained except in the climate of war. My judgment is not the best

---

*In a six-to-three decision, the Court ruled in 1857 that a Negro slave did not
become free when taken into a free state, that Congress could not bar slavery
from a territory, and that Negroes could not be citizens (*Scott* v. *Sandford*, 60
U.S. 393).

because, as I have often said, my vote to affirm was one of my mistakes (see page 280). I was too close to the highly explosive atmosphere of the Rosenberg case (346 U.S. 273) to have an objective view. But if the *Korematsu* decision was the product of fear, *Rosenberg* was the product of the Cold War, not of reasoned law.

Black and I thought that the votes of all Justices should be recorded on all cases not taken for argument. The request was pertinent particularly to petitions for certiorari, which are taken only on a vote of four out of nine Justices. Often there were none voting to grant; sometimes one, two or three. It was our idea that because we were a public institution, we should make full disclosure of all our votes. The idea was never accepted, not because of the clerical burden it would impose but for Frankfurter's reasons: the cloak of apparent unanimity creates more public confidence than would follow if there was disclosure of the wide divisions within the Court. Since our idea was rejected, some of us, notably Black and myself, gradually adopted the course of noting in the Journal that we would grant certiorari, at least when the case seemed very important.

While Justice Frankfurter was adamant on his position that in general, dissents from denials of certiorari not be made public (see *Rosenberg* v. *United States,* 345 U.S. 1003-1004), he took an intermediate position, occasionally writing at some length to expose the merits on which he often felt strongly (see *Chemical Bank and Trust Co.* v. *Group of Institutional Investors,* 343 U.S. 982); and at other times he wrote explaining why denial of certiorari meant nothing (*Maryland* v. *Baltimore Radio Show,* 338 U.S. 912, 917-920), which most members of the bar still do not believe.

Opinions were announced on Mondays; and when I first took my seat it was customary to read the opinions in some detail. One week we read opinions all of Monday and all of Tuesday and part of Wednesday before we finished. It seemed to some of us that this was a needless expenditure of time and that reading opinions should be abandoned. Black and I proposed that the Chief Justice simply announce the result in each case —who wrote for the Court, who concurred, who dissented, and so on —and of course at that time all opinions would be released to the press and to interested members of the bar. That aroused Frankfurter's vehement opposition. He maintained that the oral announcements put the public on a wavelength with the Justices and gave them a better idea as to what kind of persons the Justices were. The arguments on this were long and passionate, and a majority took Frankfurter's view.

But the factor of time weighed heavily on us; besides, the oral announcements often had little relevancy to the written opinion. For example, one day McReynolds, who had written a rather prosaic dissent, announced it with heat and vigor. Hitting the bench with his fist, he shouted, "The Constitution is gone!" and proceeded to explain why he felt so. But none of that was in the written dissent. All of us, I suppose, deviated at times from the text. Once Frankfurter, speaking for the Court, ad-libbed at length, giving reasons for the decision that had no resemblance to the opinion. As we walked out, Stone said, "By God, Felix, if you had put all that stuff in the opinion, never in my life would I have agreed to it."

These excesses had a long-range effect. As the years passed, the announcements became more and more summary. In time I was sure that the suggestion we had urged years before would be adopted.

The announcement of opinions being the first item of business, the admission of lawyers who might argue before the Court was number two. Many of those who moved admissions were senators and congressmen, very busy people who often sat for hours waiting to move the admission of a constituent, and as I mentioned, once had to sit through all of Monday and Tuesday while opinions were announced. These men from the Hill missed many a roll call; they missed committee hearings; they lost hours of valuable time. Many of the congressmen would corner me and other Justices at social events, pleading for a change. "Why not make admissions of lawyers the first item of business?"

We discussed the problem at Conference after Conference but never could muster a majority vote to change the practice. Frankfurter was the leader of the opposition. He actually thought the pillars of the Court would tremble if we made such a change. The ritual of the institution was important, he said, and he cited British customs to bolster his point. (He might also have cited Catholic and Episcopalian precedents.) If we changed the order of business, we would be tinkering with precedent, and the results would be disastrous. He always concluded with the thought that with the lawyers and their sponsors waiting, we had an audience who could benefit from the announcements. I once replied that it was a "captive audience," repellent to the democratic ideal. But that idea only infuriated him. In any event, we never had a majority to change the practice under Hughes or under Stone.

But to the eternal credit of Fred Vinson, he took the bull by the horns without direction or approval by the Conference. One Monday we walked into the Court as usual and sat down. Vinson leaned over and called for the admission of lawyers. Frankfurter was fit to be tied, but there was no acrimonious aftermath. The press did not even notice the change. The pillars of the Court never even trembled. The matter was never mentioned in Conference. While the Court was often severely criticized, we were never criticized for admitting lawyers on Mondays before announcing opinions.

Another criticism of those of us on the Court is relevant to a letter Oliver Wendell Holmes wrote to Sir Frederick Pollock on March 17, 1898, when Holmes was on the Supreme Judicial Court of Massachusetts:

> As we don't shut up bores, one has to listen to discourses dragging slowly along after one has seen the point and made up one's mind. That is what is happening now and I take the chance to write as I sit with my brethren. I hope I shall be supposed to be taking notes.*

I too did a lot of writing on the Bench for the same reason Holmes described. I wrote few letters, most of my scribbling being dissenting opinions either in the case under argument or in some case recently argued. When I was not writing, I was doing research in the case under argument, sending to the Library for books, law-review articles, related court decisions, legislative history of acts of Congress, etc. The end of a four-hour day hearing argument was for me an exhausting time, as my output of energy during those hours was tremendous. Some unfriendly critics charged that I was writing books on the Bench. That was not true. The work I was doing was related to the week's work, and I had a knack of following the argument with my ears as I wrote with a pen or pencil on my long yellow sheets.

Once I was asked who, in my opinion, were the most outstanding Justices with whom I served. I modified the answer by compiling a list

The Holmes-Pollock Letters: Correspondence, 1874–1932. Mark DeWolfe Howe, ed. Vol. I (Harvard University Press, 1941), pp. 81–82.

of the outstanding men. The All-American team in my estimation (listed alphabetically) were:

> Hugo Black
> William Brennan
> Felix Frankfurter
> John Harlan
> Charles Evans Hughes
> Earl Warren
> Byron White

This list reflects not an ideological line, but basic ability and judicial attitude. These Justices would have adorned any Court in our history. They had differing philosophies and points of view, but only monotony springs from conformity.

By the 1950s and 1960s it had become customary for the President to write bar associations around the country for recommendations before selecting nominees for the federal bar. This was a practice that Hugo abhorred. The bar is usually the focal point of reaction. It reflects the status quo. It is part of the Establishment. The people deserve more than mouthpieces—mouthpieces of the dominant corporate interests. Much rides on the construction and interpretation of the generalities in the Constitution and the Bill of Rights.

Country lawyers very often are closer to the hearts and dreams of America than the prominent big-name lawyers who become judges. There was great merit in FDR's predilection for offbeat law professors and lawyers. It produced unique and outstanding federal judges: Charles E. Clark; Jerome Frank of the Second Circuit Court of Appeals; Henry Edgetron of the Court of Appeals of the District of Columbia; and Felix Frankfurter, to name only a few. These men were not bar-association prototypes and might not have passed muster there. If organized groups are to be consulted, farmers, teachers, labor and church groups should be included.

The courts are indeed the "great rock" over which all storms break leaving that "great rock" undisturbed. That may be a romantic view of the judicial function. But since Hughes and Warren functioned in that tradition, I always placed them with Marshall at the head of our distinguished list of Chief Justices.

Chapter II

Contending Schools
of Thought

The Constitution is written in general terms and uses terms like "due process" without definition. Moreover, the policy issues underlying one question or another are often controversial, leading individual Justices to plead for a special construction. During my time the press failed to educate the public as to the nature of the conflicts inside the Court. It usually tried to reduce these disagreements into terms of personal vendetta. But though feelings often ran high, there was never a personal vendetta on the Court in my time.

As I have explained, though the story was current that Felix Frankfurter and I were enemies, that was not the case. Although we differed greatly on the merits of many cases, we were not enemies. Learned Hand once said that Felix was a divisive force in any group of which he was a member. To my mind Felix did indeed stir dissension, but dissension and divisiveness are not synonymous.

I really think that out of the great differences on legal and policy issues coming before the Court there evolved a stronger Court, though, occasionally, the persuasive powers of individual Justices may have had undue influence.

Every Justice I have known feels in retrospect that he made mistakes in his early years. The problems sometimes come so fast that the uninitiated is drawn into channels from which he later wants to retreat. That happened to me in the Japanese detention-camp case (see page 279), and to Hugo Black, Frank Murphy and me when the first flag-salute case (*Minersville School District* v. *Gobitis,* 310 U.S. 586) was argued on April 25, 1940. In those days, Felix Frankfurter was our hero. He was indeed learned in constitutional law and we were inclined to take him at face value. We voted with him in the opinion holding that the state could subject the children of Jehovah's Witnesses to compulsory flag salute in public schools.

The Fourteenth Amendment provides that "No state shall . . . deprive any person life, liberty, or property without due process of law." Justice Hughes, writing for a seven-to-two Court in 1931, held that the guarantees of the First Amendment were included in the term "due process" as it was used in the Fourteenth Amendment (*Stromberg* v. *California,* 283 U.S. 359). The First Amendment guarantees the free exercise of religion as well as free speech and free press absolutely, without reference to due process. Frankfurter, we were later to discover, thought that freedom of speech and of press and the free exercise of religion, as guaranteed against state abridgment by reason of the Fourteenth Amendment, were watered-down versions of those rights as guaranteed by the First Amendment. Why watered-down versions? Because, he maintained, due process as applied to First Amendment freedom meant "due process" free speech, "due process" freedom of the press, "due process" free exercise of religion. Those freedoms could, in other words, be modified or controlled by the states so long as they did not violate due process. What, in his mind, was "due process"? It was a concept of "ordered liberty," a regime of reasonable regulation. Thus, for example, freedom of the press could be abridged, as long as due process was observed.

What does "due process" mean? It is not defined in the Constitution. But the guarantees of the first Eight Amendments—originally applicable only to the federal government—are pretty sturdy standards for "due process." Why not apply them to the states through the Fourteenth Amendment? It was far better we do that than leave "due process" to be defined according to the predilections of individual Justices. That was Black's position and mine. That was the position that the Burger court was later to steadfastly reject.

At the time of the first flag-salute case, we had not fully divined

Frankfurter's view. We were probably naïve in not catching the nuances of his position from the opinion he had been circulating for some time. No one knew for sure where Stone stood. Finally, on May 31, 1940, the day before the Conference at which Frankfurter's opinion was cleared for Monday release, Stone sent around his dissent. It did not, however, reveal the basic issue, and though Stone vaguely adumbrated his position, he did not, for once, campaign for it. In any case, by this time the vote for Frankfurter's opinion had solidified. It is always difficult, and especially so for a newcomer, to withdraw his agreement to one opinion at the last minute and cast his vote for the opposed view. A mature Justice may do just that; a junior usually is too unsure to make a last-minute major shift. But as the months passed and new cases were filed involving the same or a related problem, Black and I began to realize that we had erred.

Jehovah's Witnesses, the religious sect which had been the defendant in this case, took Exodus 20:4-5 literally. Saluting the flag was to them bowing down to a "graven image." When the issue was again presented in 1942 (*Jones* v. *Opelika,* 316 U.S. 584), and in 1943 (*West Virginia Board of Education* v. *Barnette,* 319 U.S. 624), Black, Murphy and I changed our minds, deserted Frankfurter and, in time, helped constitute a new majority, leaving Frankfurter and his 1940 views in dissent along with Roberts and Reed (*Id.* 624, 642, 646). The Frankfurter philosophy was finally exposed in that dissent: he held that although free exercise of religion was guaranteed by the First and Fourteenth Amendments, the legislature could nonetheless regulate it by invoking the concept of due process, provided they stayed within reasonable limits.

Stone, who came off a New Hampshire farm and always pronounced Iowa as I-oh-way, never knew how the other half lived, nor had he any speaking acquaintance with the offbeat nonconformists of his time. But during World War I he had an experience that was to influence him throughout his life. He was made a member of the three-man board of inquiry named by the Secretary of War on June 1, 1918, to review the claims of those who had refused military service on the ground of conscientious objection. This board traveled to the various containments, and the contacts, interviews and cross-examinations of the objectors deeply affected Stone. He talked to me a lot about this experience

45

and wrote an account of it. "It may well be questioned," he said in part, "whether the state which preserves its life by a settled policy of violation of the conscience of the individual will not in fact ultimately lose it by the process."*

I think it was this experience which made Stone peculiarly sensitive to the claims of Jehovah's Witnesses in the flag-salute case.

The old Court had used the Due Process Clause of the Fourteenth Amendment to strike down social and industrial legislation where there was no explicit guarantee in the Constitution that protected the matter on which the legislation acted.

In 1905 it struck down a maximum ten-hour day in bakeries as an interference with that "liberty" guaranteed by the Fourteenth Amendment (*Lochner* v. *New York,* 198 U.S. 45). In 1915 it held that a state law could not bar an employer from requiring employees not to become or remain a member of any labor organization (*Coppage* v. *State of Kansas,* 236 U.S. 1). In 1917 a state law was struck down providing that employment agents were not allowed to receive fees from workers for whom they found jobs, as it interfered with the agents' "liberty" protected by the Fourteenth Amendment (*Adams* v. *Tanner,* 244 U.S. 590). A minimum-wage law for women in the District of Columbia was likewise invalidated for that reason in 1923 (*Adkins* v. *Children's Hospital,* 261 U.S. 525). In 1927 a state law forbidding resale of theater tickets at a price in excess of fifty cents above the printed price was held to be an invasion of "liberty" within the meaning of the Fourteenth Amendment (*Tyson and Brother* v. *Banton,* 273 U.S. 418). In 1928 a state law fixing the fees chargeable by an employment agent met the same fate (*Ribnik* v. *McBride,* 277 U.S. 350).

This is not a complete catalogue, only illustrative. In one of these earlier cases Justice Holmes wrote in dissent:

> Some of these laws embody convictions or prejudices which judges are likely to share. Some may not. But a constitution is not intended to embody a particular economic theory, whether of paternalism and the organic relation of the citizen to the State or of *laissez faire.* It is made for people of fundamentally differing views, and the accident of our finding certain opinions natural and familiar or novel and even shocking

Columbia University Quarterly, Vol. XXI, No. 4 (October 1919), p. 269.

ought not to conclude our judgment upon the question
whether statutes embodying them conflict with the Constitution of the United States.

(198 U.S. 75–76)

There is nothing in the Constitution that says no state shall abridge
"the fixing of prices" or "employment agency fees" or "the right to fix
hours of work or wages." The Court coined the phrase "liberty of
contract." But as Holmes observed:

Contract is not specially mentioned in the text that we have
to construe. It is merely an example of doing what you want
to do, embodied in the word liberty. But pretty much all law
consists in forbidding men to do some things that they want to
do, and contract is no more exempt from law than other acts.

(261 U.S. 568)

The Constitution and the Bill of Rights, however, do ban legislation
on some things: bills of attainder, religious test oaths, freedom of
speech, freedom of press, free exercise of religion, and so on. Are those
bans complete or may the legislatures act in those fields if they do not
act "unreasonably"? The Frankfurter school of thought answered in the
affirmative: either the state—or Congress—has freedom to regulate, the
constitutional mandate being construed as only a constitutional admonition for moderation.

While Black, Murphy and I disagreed with the old Court when it sat
as a superlegislature reviewing the wisdom of legislation in the social,
industrial and financial field, we thought that when the Constitution
said in the First Amendment that there should be "no law" abridging
a specific right, it did not mean "some law, provided it is reasonable."

The right of free speech, all are agreed, does have its limitations.
Statutes which proscribe the use of epithets such as profanity, libel and
"fighting" words have generally been excluded from constitutional protection. Such was the case in *Chaplinsky* v. *New Hampshire,* in which
Mr. Chaplinsky addressed the town marshal as being a "damned Fascist" and a "damned racketeer" (315 U.S. 568 at 574). As Justice Murphy
wrote for the Court: "It has been well observed that such utterances are
no essential part of any exposition of ideas" (*Id.* 572). They normally do

not foster the promotion or discussion of public issues. Their use would in general promote the use of dueling and other forms of violence.

The usual way of stating the difference was that one school of thought was for "balancing" the need for, say, free speech against the need for law and order. The Frankfurter school was for "balancing." Black and I thought that all of the "balancing" had been done by those who wrote the Constitution and the Bill of Rights. They had set aside certain domains where all government regulation was banned. When it came to certain activities, the Constitution had taken government off the backs of men.

That was the great divide between us and the Frankfurter school, which grew wider and wider with the passing years as more and more civil rights clamored for protection.

The broad expansive construction of the Due Process Clause of the Fourteenth Amendment given by the old Court with regard to social and economic legislation was only one of the bones of contention that FDR had with that regime. Another quarrel was over the construction of the Commerce Clause. All that the clause says is: "The Congress shall have power . . . to regulate commerce with foreign nations, and among the several states, and with the Indian tribes" (Article I, Sect. 8).

Prior to our Constitution, the states had raised protective tariffs and duties against one another and had taken many forms of retaliatory economic actions against one another. They had treated one another as foreign nations rather than members of a great polity. States lacking seaports were particularly beset. As President Madison said: "New Jersey, placed between Philadelphia and New York, was likened to a cask tapped at both ends; and North Carolina, between Virginia and South Carolina, to a patient bleeding in both arms." This was because duties were assessed on goods coming from abroad and kept by the receiving state. Duties were also collected on merchandise brought in from other states. The problems at that time among the thirteen states were comparable to problems with which many foreign nations these days are wrestling in an effort to provide a common market. It was to this problem that the Commerce Clause was addressed, and the Marshall Court's liberal construction of it laid the foundation for the creation in this country of the greatest common market in the world. That Court in the first place construed "commerce" as broad and all-inclusive. In the second place, it construed the power of Congress to regulate as extensive. Third, it established the principle that a state law regulating commerce in conflict with a federal law was unconstitutional by reason of the Supremacy Clause. In the fourth place, it held that the states may not act in certain fields affecting commerce, even though Congress has failed to pass any statutes governing the same subject matter. That is to say, there are some areas that can be regulated only by Congress.

The states have of course police powers which they may exercise for the health, safety and welfare of their inhabitants, even though those measures may have an incidental effect on commerce. What has to be considered is the magnitude of the effect on commerce, whether the matter is primarily of local concern, allowing for diversity and experimentation, or of national concern requiring uniformity.

These principles were not firmly established by the Marshall Court. They merely appear as the broad outlines of the constitutional contours. But it was along these lines, projected by the Marshall Court, that the law was to develop: an open economy, a great common market characterized by free trade among the states, but in which the states have the requisite autonomy to deal with peculiar local conditions.

In 1895, however, the power of Congress to regulate commerce was given a narrow construction by an opinion which held that manufacturing, even by units of an interstate complex, was not commerce (*United States* v. *E. C. Knight Co.,* 156 U.S. 1). That decision had wide ramifications, and in later cases it came to mean that Congress did not have authority even to ban an interstate shipment of goods which were the products of child labor (*Hammer* v. *Dagenhart,* 247 U.S. 251 [1918]).

These decisions stood as a great dike against federal control over many of the pressing economic problems of the 1920s and 1930s. Holmes, in his dissent in the child-labor case, stated the Rooseveltian idea in the following words:

> The act does not meddle with anything belonging to the States. They may regulate their internal affairs and their domestic commerce as they like. But when they seek to send their products across the state line they are no longer within their rights. If there were no Constitution and no Congress their power to cross the line would depend upon their neighbors. Under the Constitution such commerce belongs not to the States but to Congress to regulate. It may carry out its views of public policy whatever indirect effect they may have

upon the activities of the States. Instead of being encountered by a prohibitive tariff at her boundaries, the State encounters the public policy of the United States which it is for Congress to express. The public policy of the United States is shaped with a view to the benefit of the nation as a whole.

(247 U.S. 281)

The philosophy of Holmes gradually won out; the narrow construction of the commerce power of Congress announced in 1895 was slowly eroded, many exceptions being created. But the old decision that manufacturing was not commerce (156 U.S. 1) was not overruled until 1948 (*Mandeville Farms* v. *Sugar Co.,* 334 U.S. 219, 229).

The National Labor Relations Act was sustained in 1937 both as respects practices or transactions in the "flow" of commerce and those "affecting" commerce (*NLRB* v. *Jones & Laughlin Steel Corp.,* 301 U.S. 1). The marketing program for agricultural products was upheld in 1939 (*Mulford* v. *Smith,* 307 U.S. 38) after a prior defeat of an agricultural program which tried to decrease the quantities of articles produced by increasing the prices (*United States* v. *Butler,* 297 U.S. 1).

In 1941 the Court, in a unanimous opinion written by Stone (*United States* v. *Darby,* 312 U.S. 100), overruled the old child-labor case (247 U.S. 251) and held constitutional an act of Congress which prohibited the shipment in interstate commerce of articles manufactured by employees whose wages were below a stated minimum and whose hours of work were above a prescribed maximum and which prohibited the employment of workers in the production of goods "for interstate commerce" at other than prescribed wages and hours. In upholding the new act, the Court returned to the philosophy of the Marshall Court. Thus Congress once more had the power to stand astride the stream of commerce and impose terms and conditions on those who were producing goods which after manufacture would enter that stream.

The newly restored power under the Commerce Clause reached its outward limits in 1942 when a unanimous Court, under an agricultural marketing act, upheld a sanction against a farmer who raised wheat not for the stream of interstate commerce, but only for consumption on his farm (*Wickard* v. *Filburn,* 317 U.S. 111). The Court said:

One of the primary purposes of the Act in question was to increase the market price of wheat, and to that end to limit the volume thereof that could affect the market. It can hardly be denied that a factor of such volume and variability as home-consumed wheat would have a substantial influence on price and market conditions. This may arise because being in marketable condition such wheat overhangs the market and, if induced by rising prices, tends to flow into the market and check price increases. But if we assume that it is never marketed, it supplies a need of the man who grew it which would otherwise be reflected by purchases in the open market. Home-grown wheat in this sense competes with wheat in commerce. The stimulation of commerce is a use of the regulatory function quite as definitely as prohibitions or restrictions thereon. This record leaves us in no doubt that Congress may properly have considered that wheat consumed on the farm where grown, if wholly outside the scheme of regulation, would have a substantial effect in defeating and obstructing its purpose to stimulate trade therein at increased prices.

(317 U.S. 128–129)

This was a decision that another unanimous Court followed in 1959 when Charles Whittaker was a member (*United States* v. *Haley,* 358 U.S. 644), though he later roundly denounced the Court for going to such extremes.

Commerce Clause cases continued to divide the Court, but the reach of the Commerce power was no longer much in dispute. The controversies involved construction of commerce legislation and its ambiguities. They also raised questions of whether a state law could coexist with a federal law or whether the federal law had pre-empted the field. These were often important questions, but they never reached the dimensions of the problems with which the Marshall Court or the Hughes Court dealt.

The old Court's limitations on the government's power to regulate social, industrial and business problems and conditions by reason of the Justices' conception of "liberty" as used in the Due Process Clause of the Fourteenth Amendment were also slowly eroded. Exceptions began to appear at least by 1908 (*Muller* v. *State of Oregon,* 208 U.S. 412). Finally, in 1937, a state law fixing minimum wages was sustained (*West Coast Hotel* v. *Parrish,* 300 U.S. 379), the prior contrary decision (*Adkins* v. *Children's Hospital,* 261 U.S. 525) being overruled. That attitude became a pattern, the new Court concluding that the wisdom, need or appropriateness of the legislation was none of its business (*Olsen* v. *Nebraska,* 313 U.S. 236), and declaring that no law would be struck down under the Due Process Clause if there was any rational basis on which it might rest. Most laws survived that test, an exception being an act of Congress which provided that if a person had been convicted of a crime of violence and possessed a firearm, it was presumed that the weapon was received in interstate commerce after the effective date of the act (*Tot* v. *United States,* 319 U.S. 463). The Court held that the presumptions concerning the receipt of the firearms were "violent, and inconsistent with any argument drawn from experience" (*Id.* 468).

Some laws, however, involved specific guarantees of the Constitution, such as free exercise of religion or freedom of speech and of the press, the privilege against self-incrimination, and the like. The question in those cases was whether those rights could be qualified by legislation—watered down, so to speak. If it was "reasonable" that free speech be suppressed or free exercise of religion be qualified, was a law that reached that result constitutional? If that was the test, then the Justices would determine what was "reasonable." In that event they would in a sense sit as a superlegislature. Certainly their views on reasonableness would vary quite widely. We would then have a regime of constitutional law that turned on the subjective attitudes of the Justices rather than on the Constitution. That regime would give the Court vastly more power than it would have if the Constitution were taken more literally.

That was the type of problem posed in the flag-salute cases. It was to appear over and again as civil rights cases mounted. After World War II these cases began to multiply. The work of the Court always mirrors the worries and concerns of the people of a particular age. Since World War II, individual rights have been more and more in balance—as a result of racial tensions, the demands of religious minorities, the trend to conformity and the accompanying revolt, the search for ideological strays in the loyalty and security hearings, the Cold War and the mounting lists of its victims, and many other factors related to the growing power of government and the growing importance of the individual.

The contest within the Court in my early years was between the Frankfurter school, which thought that even specific constitutional guarantees could be watered down by "reasonable" regulations, and those of us, especially Black and myself, who read those specific guarantees more literally as part of the plan of the Framers to take government off the backs of the people when it came to specified civil rights.

With the passage of time the Frankfurter school of thought came to be sponsored by Burger and Blackmun—though they were quite inappropriately called "strict constructionists—" and it will probably endure. Black's death gave this view great momentum. Underlying the differences in the Court on this issue was the more basic conflict that concerned the question of the extent to which the state powers had been restricted by the Fourteenth Amendment. While it established that no state can deny any person life, liberty or property without due process of law, the Amendment does not define due process.

One group on the Court led by Black and me thought that due process in the Fourteenth Amendment meant the prerogatives and procedures set forth in the Bill of Rights. This was the so-called incorporation theory, coming first to a shattering head in 1947, in *Adamson* v. *California* (332 U.S. 46), in which Frankfurter wrote that the Fourteenth Amendment did not incorporate the Bill of Rights.

Black and I took the opposite view, and in those days we spent many long hours going through the dusty volumes of Civil War history and law trying to ascertain the meanings of the drafters of the Fourteenth Amendment.

The Fourteenth Amendment speaks of the privileges and immunities of citizens, and Black and I could never think of a greater privilege or immunity than the right to speak one's mind or to follow one's own conscience in choosing one's religion. Black wrote a powerful dissent in *Adamson,* in which he laid bare the critical features of the Fourteenth Amendment, supporting the view that Congress, in the recommendation of the Fourteenth Amendment, had in mind making applicable to the states *all* of the provisions in the Bill of Rights which had previously been applicable only to the federal government.

To Frankfurter that was heresy—a wrongful construction of history. Charles Fairman, a Frankfurter disciple who wrote one of the volumes on the Supreme Court in the Holmes series, takes the view that Black was dead wrong and that Frankfurter was dead right. This is an old argument that goes way back into the 1890s. At that time a state condemned the property of a corporation but did not pay just compensation. The question came to the Court, and it ruled that the Just Compensation Clause of the Fifth Amendment was applicable to the states by reason of the Fourteenth Amendment.

If the Due Process Clause in the Fourteenth Amendment makes applicable to property rights the principles and procedures of the Bill of Rights, it is difficult to see why there should be a difference when it comes to individual rights, such as the right to be secure against the police coming in at night to search the house without a search warrant; and why it isn't applicable to the Self-Incrimination Clause contained in the Fifth Amendment.

The great work of the Warren Court was in making the standards of the Bill of Rights applicable to state action. The Fourth Amendment was held to be covered in *Mapp* v. *Ohio* (367 U.S. 643); the privilege against self-incrimination was also held applicable to the states in *Malloy* v. *Hogan* (378 U.S. 1).

The ban against cruel and unusual punishment in the Eighth Amendment; the Double-Jeopardy Clause of the Fifth Amendment was treated the same way as was the right to a trial by jury and the right of an accused to be represented by counsel and advised of his rights, as spelled out in the Sixth Amendment and in *Gideon* v. *Wainwright* (372 U.S. 335).

Indeed, all of the important protective safeguards afforded to the accused by the Bill of Rights have been made applicable to the states. As this was happening a great howl went up in some quarters that states' rights were being abridged and the lives of criminals made easier.

Making the Bill of Rights applicable to the states raised the level of law enforcement practices that states may permissibly use. In *Miranda* v. *Arizona* (384 U.S. 436) we stated that once a person is held by the police in custody and is under examination, that examination as a practical matter is the start of his trial, and that he therefore is entitled to be represented by a lawyer and advised of his constitutional rights. It is indeed difficult to see how a civilized society could demand less. The *Miranda* decision, written by Earl Warren, came in for a lot of abuse and was said to be responsible for increased crime rates. But those knowlegeable in the field know that crime springs from poverty, insufferable living conditions and from involvement in drugs. The presumption of innocence is proclaimed not only for the rich and prestigious members of the community but also for the lowliest members.

Murphy and Rutledge, joining Black's opinion in the Adamson case, filed a separate opinion that said that they thought that the guarantees of due process were not necessarily limited to the provisions of the Bill of Rights but include other privileges and immunities—a decision with which I, in the years to come, was inclined to agree.

The other great cleavage of the Frankfurter school concerned the so-called hands-off policy, by which many Court-made rules promote the policy of judicial abstinence. This tradition meant that the Supreme Court would have symbolic value but little beyond that. That Court would sedulously avoid meeting contentious issues and would sit in resplendent dignity aloof from the issues of the day. That was later to be the Burger philosophy.

Those who take the other view of the role of the Court are called the "activists"; and this was the label that the Harvard cabal used against Brennan, Black, Warren and myself. My view always has been that anyone whose life, liberty or property was threatened or impaired by any branch of government—whether the President or one of his agencies, or Congress, or the courts (or any counterpart in a state regime)—had a justiciable controversy and could properly repair to a judicial tribunal for vindication of his rights.

Men protested that they were being sent to Vietnam to fight when no "war" had been declared by Congress. By the Constitution, only Congress can declare a "war"; the idea of a "presidential war" is foreign to our charter. If "property" is taken in violation of the Constitution, the owner has a justiciable claim. In 1952 the Court so held when Truman seized the steel mills during the Korean "war" (*Youngstown Sheet & Tube Co.* v. *Sawyer*, 343 U.S. 579). Life and liberty are ranked as high as property in the Due Process Clauses. They are indeed the trinity that appears both in the Fifth and in the Fourteenth Amendments. A man whose life may be taken or whose legs may be shot off in Vietnam has as high a right to judicial protection as did the steel mills in the Korean "war."

I wrote numerous opinions stating why we should take these cases and decide them. Once or twice Potter Stewart and Bill Brennan joined me. But there was never a fourth vote. I thought then—and still think—that treating the question as a "political" one was an abdication of duty and a self-inflicted wound on the Court.

If the judiciary bows to expediency and puts questions in the "political" rather than in the justiciable category merely because they are troublesome or embarrassing or pregnant with great emotion, the judiciary has become a political instrument itself. Courts sit to determine questions on stormy as well as on calm days. The Constitution is the measure of their duty. And it is the Constitution, not the judges' individual preferences, that marks the line between what is justiciable on the one hand and, on the other, what is political and therefore beyond the reach or competence of courts. A question is "political" only if the Constitution has assigned it to one of the other two departments for solution. (For further discussion of this subject, see Chapter 6, "Separation of Powers.")

Chapter III

Loyalty-Security Program

Harry Truman launched the loyalty-security program in 1947, which laid the ground for the most intensive search for ideological strays that we have ever known. I doubt that any spy or saboteur was ever caught by that program. The unpopular person, the offbeat, the nonconformist was the victim. Twenty million people were screened, and thousands were cast into the outer darkness.

The House Un-American Activities Committee (HUAC) had been waving the flag and "burning the witches"; and Truman doubtless thought that his executive order directing government department heads and the FBI to investigate the loyalty of federal employees would put the investigations into more responsible hands. Truman made a bow to that House committee by designating its files "as a source of information on suspect employees" and the committee at once took credit for Truman's move and continued as the official flag waver of the nation.

That committee became the most un-American agency in our history, for it made a specialty out of probing people's beliefs, conscience and thoughts—matters put beyond the reach of government by reason of the First Amendment.

Perhaps some such program was politically necessary, as the nation was frightened of Russia and the Cold War was reaching a white heat. I always thought, however, that no such program was necessary. Certainly the British got along without one. Of course they had spies and defectors in their midst, but so did we. The saving feature of the British system was that a department head had vast discretion to move a person out of "security" positions, as he chose, without branding him or her as a "poor security risk" or as a "disloyal" person. No aspect of the witch hunt appeared in England.

The vice of HUAC was not that it pursued "leftists"; its impropriety would exist if it only went after Minutemen, the Klan or the fascist Silver Shirts. As Congressman Don Edwards put it, HUAC had no business investigating any group, for that role made it "a usurper of the judiciary's exclusive jurisdiction over trial and punishment, as a violator of the First Amendment, and as an instigator of bills of attainder."

Our loyalty-security program had pronounced un-American characteristics: an employee was never finally "cleared." He was open to successive investigations and accusations and hearings on the same identical evidence. The strategy was to keep trying to get a "tougher" panel which would bear down hard and get rid of an unpopular person. That was done over and again.

The charges were vague and lacked specificity. A person was often charged with being pro-Communist without definition and notice of what the charge meant.

The tribunals that sat in judgment were not impartial; they were subject to political pressures; no member could be challenged for cause.

One defect of constitutional proportions was the absence of the right of confrontation. This right, reflected in our criminal law, is based upon the sound policy that the truth of a person's accusations can best be tested by putting him face to face with the person he is accusing. Under cross-examination the accuser may change his recollection of facts or his interpretation of them.

Kenneth A. MacDonald, a Seattle lawyer who handled many loyalty-security cases for employees, came across only one instance in which a living witness testified. That witness took the position that he had seen the employee at Communist Party meetings. The hearing board gave MacDonald permission to ask the witness to describe the employee in the employee's absence. The witness testified so poorly that MacDonald got permission of the board to ask six people plus the employee to come into the room for a line-up. The witness, who supposedly had seen the employee at Communist Party meetings, picked out two men, neither of whom was the employee. This case of mistaken identity led to the reinstatement of the employee.

The right of the accused to confront and cross-examine his accuser is at least as old as the persecution of the Christians by the Romans. Thus Festus, in Acts 25:16, tells us: "It is not the manner of the Romans to deliver any man to die, before that he which is accused have the accusers face to face, and have license to answer for himself concerning the crime laid against him." And the Roman Emperor Trajan instructed the governor of Bithynia that "anonymous accusations must not be admitted in evidence as against anyone, as it is introducing a dangerous precedent, and out of accord with the spirit of our times."

In the loyalty-security hearings, the federal agencies did not have the subpoena power to compel informers to attend. Thus, employees were discharged on the basis of information supplied by faceless people who whispered evil tidings in any available ear. Many of these informers were ex-Communists who displayed, in their period of reform, the same emotionalism that had drawn them into the party in the first place. Their conception of the truth was likely to be warped. They attempted to proclaim their new loyalty by denouncing everyone in sight. I learned from the records coming before the Court that many were paid informants and professional witnesses and that several of them turned out to be perjurors. In other words, they had a definite interest in demonstrating their worth to their employers, and there was no surer way to do this than by accusing someone previously beyond reproach.

Although the question of confrontation was often presented to the courts and although the Supreme Court had several opportunities to rule on it, it always avoided the issue. Once when it was squarely presented there were only eight judges sitting (Black, Reed, Frankfurter, Douglas, Jackson, Burton, Minton and Vinson). The lower-court judgment, holding that there was no right of confrontation, was affirmed by an equally divided Court (*Bailey* v. *Richardson*, 341 U.S. 918). Those employees under the barrage of the hearing boards continued to have no opportunity to cross-examine the accuser to show whether the charge made came from the mouth of a venal person or from a psychopath or from some other unreliable individual.

Another major defect of these hearings was that the charges against employees were worded in the broadest possible terms. The usual pattern was to charge the employee with "sympathetic association" with named individuals or named organizations. There was no statement of why the employee was deemed to have been in "sympathetic association" with those persons or organizations. The agency revealed as little as possible. It seemed that the more serious the charge, the less was revealed. The reason given for this procedure was that the boards did not want to disclose the confidential sources of information. The theory was that the truth was better obtained by vague accusations because the employee would not have an opportunity to cover up and manufacture a story concerning a specific charge. Thus the basic philosophy of an employee was searched to see if he was in some way nonconformist. The Constitution provides free speech for everyone, but in these hearings anyone who thought that even an alleged Communist should enjoy free speech was certainly doomed.

One of the other problems of the loyalty-security program was the lack of written decisions setting forth the findings and grounds for decision. Without such a record, it was almost impossible to determine what factors were persuasive with the agency board. The charges and hearings often ranged over the employee's entire life; information was elicited about every aspect of his career. Without an available written decision there was no way of knowing what evidence had been accepted as true and what rejected as false; there was no way to determine what evidence had been considered as relevant, or what weight was given to specific evidence.

The absence of reasons for governmental action has a long history of abuse. The King of England used to withhold from the courts the reasons for detaining prisoners who sought release by habeas corpus. In *Darnels Case* (3 St. Tr. 2, 59), decided in 1627, the absence of a reason for detention was held to justify the detention. "Mr. Attorney hath told you that the King hath done it, and we trust him in great matters, and he is bound by law, and he bids us proceed by law, as we are sworn to do, and so is the King; and we make no doubt but the King, if you seek to him, he knowing the cause why you are imprisoned, he will have mercy."

In the same way, the accused employee had the burden of proving that he was innocent. Yet how could anyone possibly prove that he was not disloyal? In these and in other like ways, we lived under a totalitarian regime that tried men and women for beliefs, thoughts and social philosophy.

One man was discharged for his "behavior, activities, or association." But the evidence did not relate to them: this employee saw no reason why the people could not amend the Constitution to provide for a socialist regime if they so desired. He thought that Franco in Spain was an undesirable influence, that we had helped West Germany come back too fast, that the Peking regime should be admitted to the United Nations, and that it was a mistake to give the foreign aid we had been giving to Formosa.

In answer to the question of what he thought of Communism today, he answered:

A. Well, a person doesn't know what to think, really. They can't produce the way we do—the farming situation is as bad as can be, so that isn't much of a recommendation for them.

. . .

Q. Do you read a lot of Supreme Court decisions?

Q. Have you read any book containing Justice Douglas's opinions on the Communist Party case?

Q. You rather like Justice Douglas?

. . .

Q. You do not want to preclude yourself from voting for the Communist Party if they came up with a candidate you liked? For instance, Justice Douglas, if he decided to run for President on the Communist Party?

A. Well, here is the deal. If it is a legal party but as long as it is under a shadow the way it is now, not only the Communist Party but some other minority party, if they would invite some popular man to run and if there was a chance for him to be elected, there would be people following him.

Q. What about you? Would you be one of the followers?

A. It all depends on his principles. If there were principles he stood for, I can see myself standing up and being counted.

The questions covered not "behavior, activities, or association" but this man's views across a broad spectrum of philosophy, sociology and politics; his views on automation, a shorter work week, federal control of the distribution of manufactured goods, relief for people unemployed, socialization of the forestry and lumber industry, etc.

Tastes in music and theater were treated as indicia of disloyalty. At one point the possession of Paul Robeson records was damning. One employee's preference for the works of Prokofiev and Khatchaturian was suspect. Another had reproductions of paintings by great masters —Renoir, Matisse, Picasso. He was questioned as to whether there was any connection between the paintings and the Communist Party, the reason being that these artists were suspect.

The doctrine of "guilt by association" was not limited to membership in or sympathetic association with subversive organizations. It extended to sympathetic association with suspect individuals—sympathetic association with a person who was in sympathetic association with a subversive organization. Thus the employee was placed in the anomalous position of not only having to defend himself, but also having to defend his friends or the musicians or artists he enjoyed. The former task was difficult enough; the latter was all but impossible, for the boards took the position that the friends were not on trial, thus cavalierly dismissing an employee's attempt to prove that his friends were not disloyal. Sympathetic association was often nothing but contact with a person suspected of disloyalty. And the contacts might be slight, or in the distant past. A working relationship, attendance at a party, an innocuous conversation have all been bases for a charge of sympathetic association.

Questions regarding an employee's voting were not infrequent:

"How many times did you vote for Henry Wallace? How about Norman Thomas?"

". . . you indicated . . . that you at times voted for and sponsored the principles of Franklin Delano Roosevelt, Norman Thomas, and Henry Wallace."

Advocating the advancement of peace through international cooperation was also suspect:

"At one time you were a strong advocate of the United Nations. Are you still?"

"The file indicated that you were quite hepped up over the one-world idea at one time, is that right?"

Integration of the races in schools was a telltale sign of disloyalty:

"Would you mix blood plasma of Negroes with blood plasma of whites?" An affirmative answer was fatal.

"Should a Communist enjoy the right to free speech?" An affirmative answer was fatal.

"Should the Communist Party be suppressed or allowed on the ticket?" One who chose the latter was doomed.

One who thought that the French should get out of Vietnam was obviously a Communist, as was anyone who read *Das Kapital* or subscribed to Russian magazines.

One who thought we should recognize the Peking regime was an outcast.

Truman cast a blight across the nation with this inquisition into people's beliefs. His program stifled individuality; it narrowed the spectrum of permissible ideas. Only a person with "safe" ideas could be employed by the federal government.

Senator Joseph McCarthy came to the Senate in January of 1947, and remained there until his death in May of 1957. During that ten-year period he became a symbol of the intolerance which swept America during the 1950s. On February 9, 1950, McCarthy made a speech saying that there were 205 Communists in the State Department, that of these only 80 had been discharged, that the others remained, and that they were "bad security risks because of their Communistic connections."

A couple of days later he said in Reno that he had in his hand "fifty-seven cases of individuals who would appear to be either card-carrying members or certainly loyal to the Communist party, but who nevertheless are still helping to shape our foreign policy."

Another time he stated that he had records of 81 Communists in the State Department, but that he hesitated to disclose their names to the Senate. He referred to a group as "the Big Three, No. 1 and No. 2 and No. 81" that made up an "espionage ring in the State Department."

From time to time he mentioned other cases by numbers, giving credence to his representations that the government was honeycombed with Communists. For each case number he had a factual summary—vague, inconclusive but nonetheless very damning; and the total picture was one of an unsuspecting people about to be undermined by a host of subversive characters operating in government.

Actually, none of these charges proved to be true. In 1954 McCarthy was censured by the Senate. But the harm he and his ilk had done to the country was incalculable.

I knew McCarthy, meeting him through the Kennedys, who, sad to say, had helped finance his Wisconsin campaign. He was a lawyer but not one of distinction. He always greeted me in a friendly way, but his face always showed tension and anxiety. I never knew the reason for this, though I soon learned that he was an alcoholic. And in time I came to realize that he was a sick man with a very troubled psyche. He was not, of course, the first sick man to plague the world.

He often had lunch at the Carroll Arms, a restaurant near the Senate Office Building, and it was there that I would come across him. His conversation was never about the "witch hunt" but about some genuine concern he felt on foreign or economic matters. When I saw him during the days of ordeal leading to censure, he had the appearance of a hunted man, fleeing from something horrible and finding a sanctuary in liquor.

While President Truman stood up against McCarthy, he did not have the shrewdness to see that his loyalty-security program and McCarthy's techniques were cut from the same cloth. The result was a hideous perversion of the American ideal, and these two men together set loose in this country a regime of terror. People actually became frightened to espouse anything that was not wholly and utterly orthodox.

Truman did more than oppose McCarthy. To his credit, he in time protested the effort to put the government "in the thought-control business" when he vetoed the Subversive Activities Control Act of 1950, which Patrick McCarran in the Senate and Richard Nixon in the House had eagerly promoted. The act stated that an organization would be a "communist-front organization" within the meaning of the act if "the positions taken or advanced by it from time to time on matters of policy do not deviate from those of the communist movement. Such an organization would have to register and its members would be barred from obtaining passports." Truman in his veto put the objection in enduring words.

I was not proud of the Court's record on these loyalty cases. As I have said, it approved four to four a decision denying an employee the constitutional right to have his accuser face him and make the charge. When that issue was again presented, the Court evaded it, resting its decision on narrow technical grounds (*Peters* v. *Hobby,* 349 U.S. 331). And while the Court in other cases construed the regulations strictly in favor of the employee (e.g., *Vitarelli* v. *Seaton,* 359 U.S. 535), it never made the resounding declaration of human rights that was sorely needed. In the neighboring field of congressional investigations it often set aside convictions of contempt on procedural grounds (e.g., *Yellin* v. *United States,* 374 U.S. 109; *Russell* v. *United States,* 369 U.S. 749; *Flaxer* v. *United States,* 358 U.S. 147), and once it declared that what a person believes is protected from congressional investigation by the First Amendment: "Abuse of the investigative process may imperceptibly lead to abridgment of protected freedoms. The mere summoning of a witness and compelling him to testify, against his will, about his beliefs, expressions or associations is a measure of governmental interference. And when those forced revelations concern matters that are unorthodox, unpopular, or even hateful to the general public, the reaction in the life of the witness may be disastrous" (*Watkins* v. *United States*, 354 U.S. 178, 197).

But there was no carry-through that made continuing and clear the constitutional mandate that Big Brother can be concerned only with men's actions, not with their ideas.

I became alarmed about these invasions of privacy and in 1951 expressed my fears in an address called "The Black Silence of Fear," which I delivered at Brandeis University.

I said that to understand what was happening, a person would have to leave the country, go into the back regions of the world, lose himself there and become absorbed in the problems of the peoples of different civilizations. When he returned to America after a few months, he would probably be shocked. He would be shocked not at the intentions or purposes or ideals of the American people, but at the arrogance and intolerance of great segments of the American press, at the arrogance and intolerance of many leaders in public office, at the arrogance and intolerance reflected in many of our attitudes toward Asia. He would find that thought was being standardized, that the permissible area for calm discussion was being narrowed, that the range of ideas was being limited, that many minds were closed to the reception of any ideas from Asia.

We carried over to days of peace the military approach to world affairs. Diplomacy took a back seat. The military approach conditioned our thinking and our planning.

We thought of Asia in terms of military bases, not in terms of peoples and their aspirations. We wanted the starving people of Asia to choose sides, to make up their minds whether they were for us or against us, to cast their lot with us and against Russia.

We did not realize that to millions of these people the difference between Soviet dictatorship and the dictatorship under which they lived was not very great. We did not realize that in some regions of Asia it was the Communist Party that had identified itself with the so-called reform programs, the other parties being mere instruments for keeping a ruling class in power. We did not realize that the choice between democracy and Communism was not, in the eyes of millions of illiterates, the critical choice it was for us.

We forgot that democracy in many lands was an empty word; that its appeal was hollow when made to illiterate people living at the subsistence level. We asked them to furnish staging grounds for military operations whose outcome, in their eyes, had no perceptible relation to their own welfare. Those who rejected our overtures must be Communists, Truman said. Those who did not fall in with our military plans must be secretly aligning with Russia, he thought.

After World War II the military effort involved more and more of our sons, more and more of our budget, more and more of our thinking. The military policy so completely absorbed our thoughts that we mostly forgot that our greatest strength, our enduring power was not in guns, but in ideas. In Asia we were identified not with ideas of freedom, but with guns. At home we were thinking less and less in terms of defeating Communism with ideas, more and more in terms of defeating Communism with military might and suppression of ideas.

Mrs. Helen Rogers Reid, wife of Ogden Reid, owned the New York *Herald Tribune* and was a bright, friendly person with liberal tendencies, judged by American standards. She was very civic-minded, and from the thirties into the fifties she sponsored the Herald Tribune Forum, in New York City, where speakers presented various points of view on current topics of public interest. Mrs. Reid often approached me to participate in the forum and once in a while I accepted. She also sought out Thurman Arnold, a distinguished attorney. One night in 1947 at a forum at which he spoke, Thurman sat next to Mrs. Reid and told her what he and his associates were doing about the loyalty-security program, the dozens of cases they had, the hopelessness of the plight of any employee charged, and of a recent dismissal of ten State Department employees for reasons not disclosed.

Mrs. Reid got steamed up about what Arnold told her and assigned her top reporter, Bert Andrews, to the job of finding out what was going on. She gave him the front page of the *Tribune* for ten days. Beginning on November 2, 1947, Bert turned out some amazing articles, and as a result he was awarded the Pulitzer Prize in journalism in 1948. Mrs. Reid was responsible for the major investigative reporting on the miserable un-American procedure under which a person charged with being disloyal could never know even the name of his accuser, let alone face him and cross-examine him.

In 1948 Bert Andrews published a book summarizing his investigation called *Washington Witch Hunt*. He wrote that at his first interview with State Department officials, one of them said that anyone could be made "the victim of a complete frame-up, if he had enough enemies in the Department who were out to get him." Bert was shocked that a person could say that "without being shocked himself," and from that point on dug deep.

In World War I, Andrews pointed out, the search for "Reds" had started with the Executive; this time it had started in Congress. The Department of State was the first suspect. Chiang Kai-shek was losing ground in Asia; charges were being made that our overseas people were too friendly with Mao. So in 1946 Congress gave the Secretary of State power to discharge any department employee "in his absolute discretion . . . whenever he shall deem such termination necessary or desirable in the interests of the United States." The Atomic Energy Commission got the same power (42 U.S.C. 2011). Congressional pressure "for scalps," as Andrews put it, mounted. Ten State Department employees were fired. There was a tug of war between Congress and the Executive to see who would get the glory and the credit. Truman won with his executive order of March 22, 1947.

Three of the ten were allowed to resign "without prejudice." Abe Fortas, Thurman Arnold and Paul A. Porter—all partners in the law firm of Arnold & Porter—were retained by the seven other employees. These distinguished attorneys served without a fee and had several battles royal with the State Department. A "Mr. Blank" had been discharged as "a potential security risk" without ever being informed of the nature of the charges against him and without being confronted by his accusers. He was given a "hearing" before a four-man committee of the State Department. The discharge was final, the committee said; the only purpose of the "hearing" was to tell Mr. Blank that and to let him make any statement he wished for the record. The FBI had tailed Mr. Blank and given the department a report that it believed Mr. Blank was a Communist. He denied ever having joined any group. He was discharged not for being disloyal, but for being a security risk. But why, he could not be told. No shred of evidence which the accusers relied on was disclosed.

The press and radio denounced the procedure. Arnold & Porter insisted either on a full hearing or on letting Mr. Blank resign. Finally, after two weeks, during which heat on the department mounted, it announced the seven accused men could resign. Even so, it took Mr. Blank, a highly rated economist, about a year until he finally found a job.

The next year an interesting debate took place between Paul Porter and Richard Nixon. It was at the New York Herald Tribune Forum, in

October 1948, and Bert Andrews presided. In his comments Porter proclaimed as "fundamental American precepts" the following: "That guilt is personal, that the accused is entitled to be confronted by witnesses against him, that there is a presumption of innocence until guilt is proved, that our cherished freedoms of speech and assembly are sacrosanct and that the opinions of any American citizen are his private possession, not to be abridged, coerced, classified or otherwise tampered with."

Nixon followed Porter on the platform and in reply stated what an awful menace the Communists were and why the security program had to go forward. He did, however, propose some changes: "Any individual who is charged with loyalty risk should have an opportunity to present his side of the case in the same forum in which he was accused. He should have the right to counsel at all times and should have the right to present witnesses in his own behalf and to make statements which are pertinent to the issue involved. No report reflecting upon an individual's loyalty should be made by a committee until hearings have been held and until the individual involved has had an opportunity to appear."

Nixon proposed reforms, but the reforms never touched the two basic defects in the procedure: under the Nixon regime, the accused need never know who his accuser was; and under the Nixon regime, a person could be condemned not for his actions, but merely for his thoughts or beliefs.

In the debate Porter said, "I wish the next President would designate General Eisenhower to head a committee to study the present uncontrolled drift toward suppression of all freedoms, including the freedoms of inquiry of the campus, of the graphic arts, of radio, of the screen: Yes, and even of the town hall and the cracker barrel."

It is ironic that Eisenhower was the next President and Nixon the Vice President and the two of them "reformed" the loyalty-security program, not in the way Nixon had proposed in October 1948, but by making practically irrefutable the presumption of guilt.

When Eisenhower moved into the White House, the loyalty-security program was stepped up. Eisenhower's executive order of April 27, 1953, changed the program in two important respects: (1) a person against whom a charge was made was instantly removed from the payroll, placing on him the burden of proving that he was loyal and not a security risk; (2) a person who disproved the charges and was cleared would still not be restored to the payroll unless the agency head decided that it was "clearly consistent with the interests of national security that he be reemployed." This was a burden of proof that even Eisenhower would have had difficulty meeting!

Yet Eisenhower's instincts, at times, seemed to be against such procedures. I was at the head table at the Mayflower Hotel on November 23, 1953, when he spoke of Kansas, his home, and the tradition of "Wild Bill" Hickok, the nineteenth-century stagecoach driver, Union Army scout and U.S. marshal. During his career he killed many thieves and outlaws but, as Eisenhower said, Wild Bill never shot a man in the back; he always faced the culprit. That was the American way, said Ike. "In this country, if someone dislikes you, or accuses you, he must come up in front. He cannot hide behind the shadow." His speech got huge applause, but his aides and Nixon were terribly upset. And Ike, finally, like Truman, perpetuated a program that did just the opposite of the views he expressed that night.

I should add as a postscript an interesting historic episode involving Nixon and Truman. The FBI had made a report on Dr. Edward U. Condon, Director of the National Bureau of Standards and a noted nuclear scientist. The hound dogs in the House, headed by Parnell Thomas and Richard Nixon, started demanding that the report be made public. On March 13, 1948, Truman issued a directive that no FBI report on any individual be made public. The House debated the matter on April 22 and passed a resolution (302 to 29) demanding the report on Condon. Speaking on the motion, Nixon said:

> I am now going to address myself to a second issue which is very important. The point has been made that the President of the United States has issued an order that none of this information can be released to the Congress and that therefore the Congress has no right to question the judgment of the President in making that decision.
>
> I say that the proposition cannot stand from a constitutional standpoint or on the basis of the merits for this very good reason: That would mean that the President could have arbitrarily issued an Executive order in the Meyers case, the Teapot Dome case, or any other case denying the Congress of the United States information it needed to conduct an investigation of the executive department and the Congress would have no right to question his decision.

Any such order of the President can be questioned by the Congress as to whether or not that order is justified on the merits.

Truman stood steadfast: the FBI Report on Condon was not disclosed, and in the 1970s Nixon was reversing himself, and as President, going even further than Truman in asserting executive privilege over papers under his control.

What his pursuers had against Condon was that he attended sessions of the American-Soviet Society, the kind of association that ended ultimately in the Pugwash Conference, where concerned scientists from both sides could face the cold realities of the risks of atomic war and try to build a détente into the relationship. The other thing against Condon was that in writing J. Robert Oppenheimer, another fine man cruelly treated by our fanatics, Condon had expressed his concern about the "close security policy" governing his work:

> I do not feel qualified to question the wisdom of this since I am totally unaware of the extent of enemy espionage and sabotage activities. I only want to say that in my case I found that the extreme concern with security was morbidly depressing—especially the discussion about censoring mail and telephone calls, the possible militarization and complete isolation of the personnel from the outside world. I know that before long all such concerns would make me be so depressed as to be of little if any value. I think a great many of the other people are apt to be this way otherwise I wouldn't mention it.

(94 *Cong. Record* 4785)

Another brilliant reporting job on our loyalty-security program was made by Joseph and Stewart Alsop in the September 1954 *Harper's* magazine. The case concerned Dr. Oppenheimer, renowned physicist retained by the Atomic Energy Commission and head of the Los Alamos Project that produced the atomic bomb which we dropped on Hiroshima. Oppenheimer had been cleared for security and loyalty, time and again, but in 1953 his security clearance was suspended by the AEC. There was nothing new that had not been examined over and again. He had never been a member of the Communist Party, but in the thirties he had favored some committees that were later branded as "Communist First" organizations, and he had made contributions to them and to the Spanish War Relief. He knew some Communists, but who did not in that multi-ideological world? There was no iota of evidence that he had ever disclosed any "secret" to anyone unauthorized to receive it, nor to any Communist or Communist-affiliated person.

The AEC named Gordon Gray, Thomas A. Morgan and Ward V. Evans (hereafter called the Gray Board) to pass on Oppenheimer's loyalty-security. Hearings were held, Oppenheimer being represented by counsel including Lloyd K. Garrison and John W. Davis. The board was represented by Roger Robb, an attorney later to be named by Nixon to the Court of Appeals of the District of Columbia.

The Gray Board, after reviewing the menace of Communism, said: "This proceeding presents the almost unrelinquishable opportunity for a demonstration against communism, almost regardless of the facts developed about the conduct and sympathies of Dr. Oppenheimer." In other words, it was admittedly the witch hunt, the search for a culprit. It turned out to be a "trial," not an inquiry.

The board reviewed all the evidence of Oppenheimer's association with Communist groups and individuals a decade earlier when he had been cleared at a loyalty-security investigation. It proved him loyal. Then why did the Gray Board not acquit him? Because he was a poor security risk. Why was he a poor security risk? Because he was opposed to the development of the hydrogen bomb. But so were most of the scientists at that time. Truman decided to go ahead with the H-bomb in 1950, and Oppenheimer diligently followed. Yet his reluctance to promote the H-bomb made him a poor security risk!

The distinguished scientist Dr. Vannevar Bush told the Gray Board that calling Oppenheimer a security risk because he was opposed to the hydrogen bomb was "like placing a man on trial because he held opinions and had the tenacity to express them." And he added, "If this country ever gets that near to the Russian system, we are certainly not in any condition to attempt to lead the free world . . . We have been slipping backwards in our maintenance of the Bill of Rights . . . I think . . . no board should ever sit on a question in this country of whether a man [served] his country or not because he expressed strong opinions. If you want to try that case, you can try me."

So, Oppenheimer's suspension was urged because he opposed development of the H-bomb. That was the finding of the Gray Board in a ten-to-one decision, with Ward V. Evans vigorously dissenting.

But what did the AEC do? Or rather, what did Lewis L. Strauss, former Kuhn Loeb partner and now an Eisenhower-Nixon hatchet man, do? He did not rely on Oppenheimer's reluctance to promote the H-bomb. Strauss went back over the old, old stuff about Oppenheimer and Communist acquaintances and Communist First organizations. All of that had long been known and rejected: and as Henry D. Smyth, the only member of the AEC with guts enough to dissent, said, "The communists that Oppenheimer knew were his brother and sister-in-law, his wife (who left the party before their marriage) and a former frau."

Ward V. Evans in his dissent from the Gray Board decision said that its failure "to clear Dr. Oppenheimer will be a black mark in the escutcheon of our country."

The Alsops reporting showed that the pique of pious and sensitive Lewis Strauss was acquired in a conflict with Oppenheimer over the export of radioactive isotopes to our allies. In June 1949 the Joint Committee on Atomic Energy had held hearings on the wisdom (security) of sending radioactive isotopes to Norway. Strauss bitterly opposed it. Oppenheimer (then head of the Institute for Advanced Study at Princeton), made mincemeat out of Strauss.

The Alsops concluded that the AEC was guilty "of a shocking miscarriage of justice" in the Oppenheimer case. They accused Strauss "of venting the bitterness of old disputes through the security system of this country." They accused "the security system itself, as being subject to this kind of ugliness and as inherently repugnant in its present standard and procedures to every high tradition of the American past."

One who reads the record, studies the tactics of Roger Robb and Lewis Strauss, and puts a microscope on the reports will see how manipulation of power to serve selfish and popular ends, as used in the Oppenheimer case, was the forerunner of the professional disgrace of the lawyers in Watergate. In the 1970s there was much discussion of the moral decline in the lawyers around Nixon. Most of what was said was true. But the moral decline started slowly under Truman and then picked up tremendous momentum when Nixon was Vice President.

Lawyers dominated the loyalty-security hearings. The respected Seth W. Richardson headed the panel of the Civil Service Commission called the Loyalty Review Board. He knew about the First Amendment and the sanctity of one's beliefs. He knew about the American tradition of being allowed to meet one's accuser face to face, but he presided over the loyalty-security program beginning in 1947, and sanctioned and enforced the program that was part of the great witch hunt in America.

Roger Robb was a lawyer practicing in the District of Columbia, described by the Alsops in their article as "a man best known as the lawyer for Senator Joseph R. McCarthy's chief journalistic incense-swinger, Fulton Lewis, Jr." Robb committed the unforgivable sin of turning a search for "facts" into a "trial," using documents as a basis for examining the accused which the accused either had never seen or had not seen for years. Robb used "highly classified" documents from the Air Force in which "the zealots spewed out their suspicions of Oppenheimer." They were not shown to Oppenheimer, who was forced to answer accusations never specified nor openly made, yet these documents were later publicly released to start a counter-fire against the man. Roger Robb belittled the legal profession by using anonymous poison-pen letters to destroy a citizen in the sacred name of national security. He took a leaf out of the Communist book. Moreover, though the Gray Board had promised that its record would be forever confidential, all 992 pages of it were released eighteen hours before the date of the Strauss decision. Robb fed the report first to his star client Fulton Lewis, Jr., who with advance help sorted out the juicy bits and released it on his sensational "I Caught a Communist" radio program. Lewis headlined the charges of disloyalty that the Gray Board had disbelieved. The rest of the press, hurrying to catch up, had no time to absorb the 992-page report and generally parroted Lewis. Thus, by legal tactics in the best Nixon tradition was an honest, solid, prestigious American smeared.

Gordon Gray was a lawyer and had served with distinction in the federal service. He knew the Bill of Rights and the constitutional guarantees of freedom in our society. Yet, as we have seen, he announced that the hearings "present the almost unrelinquishable opportunity for a demonstration against communism"! Why not a unique opportunity to examine dispassionately, while the mob cried for victims, the sober truth of these politicized accusations against Oppenheimer?

The monstrous nature of the final AEC decision that Oppenheimer was not a good security risk was shown by its false statement that it relied on the record made by the Gray Board. But it also relied on "reports of Military Intelligence" which were never available to Oppenheimer or his counsel. Since Strauss and the others were condemning Oppenheimer's "character," it is shocking that they relied on secret information. Dr. Smyth, in dissent, stated that "any implication . . . that further substantial evidence exists in the investigative files to support these charges is unfounded."

Are we to trust the AEC commissioners more than Oppenheimer? There was a long line of witnesses on Oppenheimer's behalf, men who knew him and had worked with him: James B. Conant, former president of Harvard; Vannevar Bush, who had long been active in atomic research; General Leslie R. Groves of the Pentagon, who worked with Oppenheimer at Los Alamos; John Von Neumann, a colleague of Oppenheimer at Princeton; David E. Lilienthal, who had been Chairman of the AEC and who swore Oppenheimer was no security risk; Sumner T. Pike, former member of the AEC; Hartley Rowe of United Fruit Company and a former member of the General Advisory Committee to the AEC; John J. McCloy, former High Commissioner in Germany and later chairman of the board of Chase National Bank and president of the Ford Foundation; George F. Kennan of our foreign service and former ambassador to the Soviet Union; General James McCormack, Jr., of the Air Force; Dr. Isidor Rabi, eminent physicist; Mervin J. Kelly of Bell Telephone; Karl T. Compton, once head of MIT; Frederick Osborn, formerly on the AEC; Hans Bethe, Cornell scientist; James B. Fisk of Bell Telephone; Norris E. Bradbury, who succeeded Oppenheimer at Los Alamos; Lee A. DuBridge of Cal Tech; Harry A. Winne of General Electric; Charles C. Lauritsen, Cal Tech physicist; Jerold R. Zacharias, MIT physicist; Oliver E. Buckley, Bell Telephone; Robert F. Bocher, Cal Tech physicist. Could Strauss have marshaled such a talented group that would swear as to his "good character"? I doubt it.

Moreover, who is a "security risk"? McCloy said, "I know that I am a security risk and I think every individual is a security risk. You can always talk in your sleep. You can always drop a paper that you should not drop, or you can speak to your wife about something, and to that extent no human being is an absolutely secure person."

As to security risks, it was demonstrable that Eugene Zuckert, Chairman of the AEC from 1952 to 1954—as well as Strauss—was a greater security risk than Oppenheimer. On Friday, June 11, 1954, Zuckert left on a train for Stamford, Connecticut, to see his father. He took with him a digest of all the secret investigative files on Oppenheimer and read the digest on the train, falling asleep in the process. He awoke as the conductor bellowed "Stamford," collected his personal belongings and disembarked. Only after the train pulled out did he realize that the FBI data and the Pentagon data on Oppenheimer were still on the train.

He called Strauss to report the loss. The next day Strauss called a meeting of the commission and announced first that the file had probably been stolen "by the Communists," and in a day or so Strauss ordered that the massive Gray Board record—which every witness was assured would remain forever confidential—be printed. Someone objected, saying that that would break the promise of secrecy. So Strauss hired a staff to call all witnesses and get a waiver from each. He put the heat on the Government Printing Office and got it to complete the printing job on Wednesday, June 16. Meanwhile, one commissioner—Murray, I believe —suggested that the Lost and Found department of the New Haven Railroad in Boston be called. Sure enough, the crew that cleaned the cars found the secret digest and turned it in. Thus Strauss's vision of a Communist plot evaporated.

But my point is that Zuckert, who left a confidential file on a Pullman car, was more of a security risk than Oppenheimer, who never, never, never leaked or caused to be leaked any secret in his fifteen years of government work.

Between 1943 and 1947 Oppenheimer headed up the Los Alamos Project, which produced the atomic bomb, and never leaked a bit of evidence concerning that secret. After the war he became chairman of the General Advisory Committee to the AEC. That was in 1947, and everyone who sat on the case conceded he was not "disloyal." In the same year he was made director of the Institute for Advanced Study at Princeton, with which Albert Einstein was then associated. Strauss, who wrote the AEC opinion against Oppenheimer, was president of the institute. Oppenheimer left the General Advisory Committee in 1952 and was appointed consultant of the AEC, but he was consulted very infrequently. His contract as consultant was up on June 30, 1954. The Gray Board hearings were from April 12 to May 6, 1954. The Gray Board filed its adverse report with the AEC on May 27. K. D. Nichols, AEC manager, agreed with the Gray Board, though he had cleared Oppenheimer for Los Alamos in 1943, knowing all the facts. Nichols' report to the AEC was on June 12, 1954. The AEC members had to work fast if they were to smear Oppenheimer before his contract with the AEC ran out. On June 16 the AEC published an edited version of the record made before the Gray Board—edited in the sense that classified material is indicated by asteriks. Finally, on June 28—two days before Oppenheimer's contract would run out—the AEC voted not to give him security clearance. On June 29 the AEC decision was made public, just in the nick of time. There was no law, rule or custom that would have made it necessary to renew the contract.

Why did the AEC rush to condemn an eminent scientist who was more responsible than any other for the atomic bomb? He had indeed a record of complete loyalty to this nation.

In his book *The Oppenheimer Case,* the distinguished lawyer Charles P. Curtis of Boston exposes the picayune, pee-wee little points that Strauss, Zuckert, Murray and Campbell of the AEC made. I know Strauss; therefore, his conduct was predictable. Senator Joe McCarthy was on the scene and ready to force Oppenheimer through his meat chopper. And if he went through the chopper, Strauss would go through too—for Strauss, knowing all the facts he now relied on to condemn the man, had cleared Oppenheimer for security with the AEC in 1947. Strauss had also named him to the Institute for Advanced Study at Princeton. If McCarthy went after Oppenheimer, he would catch Strauss, too; hence the haste to condemn Oppenheimer before June 30. After that the AEC would have no jurisdiction, for Oppenheimer would not be an employee.

It was an easy maneuver for Strauss because once an employee's "security" was questioned, it was up to the accused—in this case Oppenheimer—to prove the negative. So Strauss merely warmed over the old accusations; he was no longer seeking the truth; he was allowed to generate a doubt and rest on that and become a great national hero. Knowing Strauss, I venture to say he would have done the same to his grandmother. In my mind, Strauss was the real "security" risk, since he would toss a man of talent to the dogs to ensure that he himself remained "safe." Strauss had lots of company in the 1950s.

John Paton Davies was discharged from the State Department in 1954 because of his views on China. Those who fired him were the real "security" risks, as they were tools of Chiang Kai-shek and quite ignorant of the tremendous revolution in China. John Paton Davies went down the drain along with others because he saw Mao Tse-tung as the wave of the future.

The timid, frightened, cautious men were the real "security" risks. They cast into oblivion the men of talent. That is the price we pay when we forsake the formula of an open society. Everything is of some risk: being alive is the riskiest of all. But to refuse to trust men whose performance is immaculate is to go the totalitarian way. Then, to survive, man must be homogenized and not stand above the crowd. If he does, if he is unusual, then a Lewis Strauss or an Edward Teller always appears, and jealous whispers of doubt and distrust destroy a great Oppenheimer. Yes, the Tellers along with the Strausses were our great security risks. The physicist Teller was the real antagonist, spurring Strauss on. His testimony shows him very jealous and therefore very antagonistic to Oppenheimer.

Teller had nothing critical to say of Oppenheimer's loyalty, but he did testify:

> In a great number of cases I have seen Dr. Oppenheimer act . . . in a way which for me was exceedingly hard to understand. I thoroughly disagreed with him in numerous issues and his actions frankly appeared to me confused and complicated. To this extent I feel that I would like to see the vital interests of this country in hands which I understand better, and therefore trust more. In this very limited sense I would like to express a feeling that I would feel personally more secure if public matters would rest in other hands.

Gray then asked Teller this question, "Do you feel that it would endanger the common defense and security to grant clearance to Dr. Oppenheimer?" Teller replied that to the extent that the question was "directed toward intent, I would say I do not see any reason to deny clearance." Teller went on to say, "If it is a question of wisdom and judgment, as demonstrated by actions since 1945, then I would say one would be wiser not to grant clearance."

What were Oppenheimer's "actions since 1945" to which Teller objected? They amounted to his opposition to the H-bomb project in 1949. In that year no one knew how to make such a weapon. In fact, even if it had been produced in 1949, it was clear that it would have had to be "delivered by oxcart." Oppenheimer was therefore opposed; so were most of the other scientists involved. In 1951 Teller came up with new discoveries in this area; Oppenheimer gave him credit for the H-bomb; and the scientists, including Oppenheimer, then went to work producing it. But Oppenheimer's original opposition or lukewarm attitude to the H-bomb was the sole reason the Gray Board recommended he be denied clearance. Strauss did not even mention it. Yet behind the scene was Teller, brilliant, competitive and petulant, using the barrage of a "doubt" about Oppenheimer to destroy the man.

The abuse of power by men like Teller, Strauss and Gray was like the tactics employed by Nixon and the other lawyers who climbed the political ladder to greater positions of power by flouting constitutional guarantees, by tossing due process to the winds, and by using any shortcut to reach a desired end. Case after case before the Un-American Activities Committee, case after case before the Loyalty Security Board, dealt only with the beliefs of men and women. Thousands were cast into the outer darkness because they deemed those questions to be unconstitutional invasions of privacy—which they were—or because their ideas were unpopular. The Nixons of those days lived outside the law and climbed to power on the corpses of those they destroyed. It is no wonder that the people reaching the top continued to operate outside the law. Nor is it a wonder that young eager men working for Nixon and his likes assumed that positions of power enabled them to operate with impunity outside the law.

These zealous men cast aside constitutional restrictions and fashioned procedures to serve their own selfish ends. They operated outside the law hoping to be cheered on by the mob or rewarded, as most of them were, by the choice plums in government, business and finance which were at the disposal of the Nixons, the Strausses, and the other small men with power of our time.

Robert Oppenheimer was the most prestigious citizen whom they delivered to the mob for the awful sacrifices being produced in the fifties, sixties and seventies.

I did not know Oppenheimer at the time of these events. I met him only later at the Institute for Advanced Study. He had written to me to drop by and see him when I was next at Princeton University. We visited perhaps a half-hour. This total stranger asked me if I would honor him by writing his biography. I thanked him but declined, saying I was too involved in Court work and in outside activities to take on additional commitments. Shortly after that, he died; and I felt that I had been honored by the chance to meet one who was perhaps not learned in American ways, as he had largely been educated in Europe, but who had lived much more greatly than those who did him in.

Joseph McCarthy flourished for about a year after Eisenhower became President. It was during that time that the Rosenberg case arose. Julius Rosenberg and his wife, Ethel, were prosecuted for espionage on the charge that they had procured atomic secrets for Soviet Russia.

They were convicted in a New York federal court and sentenced to death. Their convictions were sustained by the Court of Appeals, and the Supreme Court denied certiorari, Mr. Justice Black (344 U.S. 889) and I (345 U.S. 965–966) voting to grant.

In June 1953, as the Court was about to adjourn for the summer, new lawyers entered the case and applied to the Court for a stay of execution. Emanuel H. Bloch, counsel for the Rosenbergs, had never raised the question as to the impropriety of the death sentence because the conditions specified in the intervening Atomic Energy Act of 1946 had not been satisfied (see page 80). He apparently had refused to raise the point when it was urged upon him (346 U.S. 282). When it came to us in June 1953, it was a brand-new issue never once raised previously in the protracted litigation.

There is in the law the "next friend" doctrine, especially applicable to habeas corpus proceedings. This procedure serves to allow friends of prisoners who may not be able to reach a court to bring an action on account of the prisoners. One Edelman was the "next friend" who, through Fyke Farmer of Nashville, Tennessee, filed a writ of habeas corpus in the Rosenberg case, accompanied with a motion for a stay. I did not grant the writ, only the motion; and it was my motion that the entire Court considered when it met in Special Term on June 18 (*Id.* 273).

Bloch filed a brief against vacating my stay, though he did not even then rest on the key point made by Fyke Farmer. My own impression was that Bloch never raised the point because the Communist consensus of that day was that it was best for the cause that the Rosenbergs pay the extreme price. That is a harsh thought; but it must be remembered that Stalin was still in power.

I call the ambiguity in the act the "key" point as far as the death penalty was concerned because of what Judge Jerome Frank later told me. It was he who wrote for the Court of Appeals sustaining the convictions in 1952 (195 F 2d 583). He said that the "key" point had never been raised prior to the "next friend" application to me and that if my stay had not been vacated and my ruling had reached the Court of Appeals, as it would have, there was no doubt that the Court of Appeals would have held that the imposition of the death sentence was improper.

The practice in processing an application for a stay is to refer it to the Circuit Justice, who in this case was Jackson. But the lawyers, hearing that I was leaving the city for the Far West the next morning, presented the application to me, as this was Tuesday and the Rosenbergs were to die on Thursday. This was, in other words, the last chance to present the application to me. I, however, referred it to Jackson, who instantly responded by saying that I should consider it in light of the lateness of time and my imminent departure for the Far West.

I accordingly set down the application for a hearing in my chambers. That was Tuesday, June 16, 1953. After hearing the oral argument, I was deeply troubled. The point presented had never been considered by any court that reviewed the case. It was briefly the following: the Rosenbergs were charged with a conspiracy that ran from 1944 to 1950. At the time the conspiracy started, the relevant statute, the Espionage Act of 1917, provided for the death penalty. In 1946, while the alleged conspiracy was still under way, Congress, to ameliorate the punishment, amended the law in the Atomic Energy Act so as to make the death penalty applicable *only in case the jury recommended it.* In the Rosenberg case the jury had made no such recommendation; and the trial court had proceeded on the ground that only the original act was applicable. So the question was analogous to the case in which, while a burglar was entering a house, the penalty for burglary was lightened. Which penalty should be applied, the heavier or the lesser one?

The Rosenberg case was an aggravated application of that principle, as human lives were at issue. (It is elemental law, in Continental Europe as well as in the Anglo-American world, that any ambiguity in a law should be resolved in favor of life, not against it.) The problem was, theoretically speaking, interesting, but what made it loom large was the fact that the incriminating evidence against the Rosenbergs, as revealed in the record, were events happening *after* the 1946 amendment that ameliorated the punishment.

Washington was a powder keg. Pro-Rosenberg pickets were picketing the White House; and anti-Rosenberg pickets were picketing the pickets. A crowd was milling around the Supreme Court building. Our police told me that two hundred newsmen and photographers were inside waiting for me. At one o'clock in the morning I went out a back door and drove my car to Fred Vinson's apartment. After I told him I had almost decided to issue the stay, we talked for an hour. He tried to dissuade me, and I finally decided to sleep on the matter and come to a decision in the morning.

I took a hotel room and slept late. Before noon the next day (Wednesday, June 17) I issued the stay and left town by car for the Far West.

Before I had left Washington, while I was still considering the stay application, I had received a telegram from my hometown of Yakima which stated the mood of the country: "If you grant the Rosenbergs a stay, there will be a lynching party waiting for you here." I had wired back: "If there is to be a Yakima lynching party you'll have to furnish your own whiskey."

My first stop was to be Collinsville, Illinois, where my friend Irving Dilliard lives. I had left the Chief Justice a memo telling him the route I was following and my destination. I was on that route when dusk overtook me not far south of Pittsburgh. I saw a motel, stopped and registered, and while I was moving my bags inside I had the car radio on, listening to a symphony. Suddenly the music stopped and a voice announced that the Chief Justice had called a Special Term of Court for noon the next day to review my stay of execution.

I called my secretary, Mrs. Edith Allen, at once to see if the news was correct. She told me it was, and on inquiry advised me that Vinson had never tried to reach me, as he easily could have by alerting the state police of Pennsylvania. An eight-man Court would sit the following day to review my action! I told Mrs. Allen to inform the Chief that I'd be there.

Chief Justice Vinson of course had no authority to convene a Special Term of Court. That could be done only by a vote of five out of nine Justices. Black raised the point and vigorously objected, but I decided to waive the point, as a majority of the Court was clearly of a mind to ratify the action of the Chief. So the Conference considered the first question on the merits: Should my stay be upheld? Upholding it would mean only that the District Court would consider the question and rule on it, before fall the Court of Appeals could pass on it, and it would then be ripe for decision by us in October. Black, Frankfurter, Burton and I urged that course. No harm would be done; the Rosenbergs were behind bars; they could be executed in October as well as in June. But we could not muster the fifth vote from Vinson, Reed, Clark, Jackson or Sherman Minton. So we put on our robes and went into the courtroom to hear oral argument on the merits of the stay.

The arguments lasted several hours before an audience more tense than any I have ever seen. We adjourned to a Conference in which the vote was six to three to vacate the stay, the dissenters being Black, Frankfurter and myself. Opinions were feverishly written that afternoon and evening and circulated in the morning. At noon on Friday,

June 19, we convened Court and announced the decision and the dissents (346 U.S. 273). The Rosenbergs were executed that night.

And when that happened the people of this country experienced a thrill. Mrs. Rosenberg was the first woman to be executed. She, like her husband, was electrocuted and her death received the greatest publicity. What does a woman who has received a lethal electric shock look like? The photographers were accommodating. The front pages the next day showed Mrs. Rosenberg's face as the electric charge hit her body. Her face at once became bloated. There were visible liquid excretions through the skin. It was as if one were an eyewitness to the suffering and torture that a sinner receives in hell. Many people in the nation felt a glow of sadistic satisfaction in viewing this picture.

What I lived through in the Rosenberg case reminded me of the saga of Raymond Swing, our greatest radio commentator in the thirties and forties. Fred Friendly, formerly with CBS, said Swing was "the closest thing broadcasting ever had to a Walter Lippmann." Ray put the sweep of the news into political essays for the listeners. He spoke to nearly forty million people for less than fifteen minutes Monday, Tuesday, Wednesday and Thursday nights. He not only related what had happened; he also placed in national or global perspective the growth and development of seemingly unrelated news items. I remember men and women saying, as a week of bad news filled the papers, "I can't wait to hear what gleam of hope Ray Swing may find in this mess."

On November 6, 1945, HUAC zeroed in on seven radio commentators, the most prominent of whom was Raymond Swing. They asked for copies of all broadcasts and said that they were making the request because of public complaints about the "communist views" expressed by Swing and others. A spokesman for HUAC said, "The time has come to determine how far you can go with free speech."

That summons was the start of the decline of Ray Swing. His sponsors got nervous and asked, "Who in the world would want to be known as the seller of communist cigars?" Down, down, down went Ray Swing. His "sin" was praising the Soviet army's fighting, labeling Chiang Kai-shek as a fascist, and calling Douglas MacArthur a reactionary. HUAC never held a hearing, but it issued a report (H.R. 2233, 79th Cong., 2d Sess.) in which it pilloried the commentators for promoting socialism and Communism. So sensitive was American business to having its products associated with anything "subversive" that Ray Swing went from pillar to post looking for jobs that finally petered out. In 1953, after I issued the stay in the Rosenberg case, he saw me and said, "Bill, they will get you. For you have touched the most sensitive, the most emotional issue that has swept the nation in our time."

In 1913 Justice Holmes said, "When twenty years ago a vague terror went over the earth and the word socialism began to be heard, I thought and still think that fear was translated into doctrines that had no proper place in the Constitution or the common law. Judges are apt to be naïve, simple-minded men, and they need something of Mephistopheles."

In my time the fear of Communism worked the same wrong on the law. Perhaps the Justices did not feel any immediate threat of Communism, but they certainly were aware of the hysteria that beset our people, and that hysteria touched off the Justices also. I have no other way of explaining why they ran pell-mell with the mob in the Rosenberg case and felt it was important that this couple die that very week —before the point of law on the legality of their sentence could be calmly considered and decided by the lower courts.

The Rosenberg affair had much in common with what I had seen years earlier in Afghanistan when a murderer would be put in a wire cage and hung from a tree at or near the site of the crime. He was of course given no food or drink. He would in time die of pneumonia. Meanwhile passers-by could throw rocks at him, shake their fists at him, denounce him. This form of capital punishment, I decided, best served the cause, as it gave the sadistic public the fullest possible participation in the execution. The only other method anywhere equal to it was the Middle Eastern custom of letting a whole community take up the hue and cry against a man accused of rape. Those who got there first could kill the accused in their chosen way. Another Middle Eastern custom gave the father or brother of a female member of the family who was raped or killed the pleasure of shooting the defendant after he had been convicted—a system that broke down when a man killed his wife, the execution falling to the eldest son. The mullahs balked at that and preserved the system by substituting an uncle for the eldest son.

What I had seen in the Rosenberg case brought home to me vividly that capital punishment is barbaric, that its only value is in the orgasm of delight that it produces in the public, that if we were truly civilized, we would find other ways to satisfy the animal urges of people. We know that capital punishment is no deterrent. We know it when we compare the felony statistics in Minnesota and Michigan—two states that abolished capital punishment years ago—with the felony statistics in California and New York that led the way in executions. There was no major difference in the incidence of felony crimes in the two former states as compared with the latter two. Rehabilitation of criminals has seldom been attempted. Killing them or locking them up is the tried-and-true ancient method. Why not turn our faces toward rehabilitation? New techniques are evolving and some show promise. This was the train of thought that the aftermath of the Rosenberg case quickened in my mind.

After that case, as before, I allowed many people to be executed, as my role was not to fix the punishment but to make sure the trial had been free of constitutional errors. But in the dozens of executions that took place in my circuit after the Rosenberg case, I shared the agony of the family of the victim.

I know of no more serious danger to our legal system than occurs when *ideological* trials take place behind the façade of *legal* trials. Perhaps the most eloquent statement on this subject comes from Bartolomeo Vanzetti when he was asked if he had "anything to say why sentence of death should not be passed":

> This is what I say: I would not wish to a dog or to a snake, to the most low and misfortunate creature of the earth—I would not wish to any of them what I have had to suffer for things that I am not guilty of. But my conviction is that I have suffered for things that I am not guilty of. I am suffering because I am a radical and indeed I am a radical; I have suffered because I was an Italian, and indeed I am an Italian; I have suffered more for my family and for my beloved than for myself; but I am so convinced to be right that if you could execute me two times, and if I could be reborn two other times, I would live again to do what I have done already.

My brother Arthur told me an interesting aftermath to the Rosenberg case. In August 1953 he was at the Boston Statler on business. The American Bar Association was meeting there, and among its guests was Fred Vinson. Fred called Art and asked if he would come up to his suite. The two sat and talked over glasses of "bourbon and branch water," as Fred always described his favorite drink. Finally Fred told Art that he was sorry about the Rosenberg case and the Court's treatment of me and the stay, that I had been right and he had been wrong and that he wanted a Douglas to know what the Chief Justice actually felt. Whether Fred had a premonition of his death I do not know. Within a month, however, he was dead of a heart attack, fulfilling Dr. George Draper's prediction. Fred had large bags under his eyes, he smoked cigarettes incessantly, he was paunchy and never took a bit of exercise. "The ideal candidate for a coronary" were Draper's words.

As a result of my action in the Rosenberg case I became temporarily a leper whom people avoided, just as later old friends avoided Judge J. Skelly Wright in Louisiana because of his court orders desegregating the public schools. I was dropped from social lists, which did not bother me, as I much preferred to spend winter days in the Potomac Valley looking for wild persimmon trees and their sweet fruit, or conversing with an old barred owl on a cold crisp morning, or walking the old C&O Canal towpath at night in a thickening fog when the Virginia deer were on the move.

One special dividend of my social isolation was in the form of the time I had for backpacking along the Appalachian Trail. Eventually I backpacked or hiked along the trail in all the states from Maine and Vermont to Georgia and participated in efforts to preserve it against "civilization," as when a power company planned to convert lovely Sunfish Pond on Kintaniny Ridge in New Jersey into a vast reservoir system. In 1953 and 1954 I hiked from October to June in the Virginia and Maryland sectors of the trail. One weekend I went by car, alone as usual, to Paris, Virginia, and picked up the trail at the point where the highway going west bisects it. I turned north to a shelter below which lies a moss-lined spring of cold water. It had been raining in the valley and even there it was cold, though there was no ice on the roads. On the ridge the drizzling rain had frozen on every twig and every branch of every tree. It was the most beautiful silver freeze I have ever seen in the woods—a condition of beauty that turned into danger the next day when the temperature rose and avalanches of ice dropped to the ground.

So much for the dividends of being ostracized. There was sadness too. It hurts when old friends cut one down. Lyndon Johnson, a dear friend whom I loved then, as I did until he died, was one of those who did just that. He was in politics and fearful that the aura of any left-wing person would touch him. One day I was on the train going up to New York City. I spotted him in the same car. As he walked by I shouted, "Hi, Lyndon, my friend!" He did not stop, but looking through me and beyond me, went by in stony silence. That hurt.

It also hurt when Congressman W. M. Wheeler of Georgia introduced a resolution in the House (H.R. 290, June 14, 1953) to impeach me. When I had issued the stay, the press interviewed senators and congressmen, and with few exceptions everyone interviewed denounced me. I remember particularly the cutting remarks of George A. Smathers of Florida, who knew nothing of the legal point of the case, but who made political capital with the "crackers" of Florida by being anti-Communist. Congressman Wheeler took those sentiments literally by introducing his resolution.

In the long history of the Court an impeachment was brought only against one Justice, Samuel Chase. That was in 1802, and it was as politically inspired as was the resolution aimed at me. Chase was actually tried before the Senate and acquitted. His acquittal put an end, until my time, to political reprisals against federal judges. His counsel, Joseph Hopkinson, said to the Senate:

> All governments require, in order to give them firmness, stability and character, some permanent principle, some settled establishment. The want of this is the great deficiency in republican institutions. Nothing can be relied upon—no faith can be given either at home or abroad to a people whose systems and operations and policy are constantly changing with popular opinion. If, however, the judiciary is stable and independent, if the rule of justice between men rests upon known and permanent principles, it gives a security and character to a country which is absolutely necessary in its intercourse with the world and in its own internal concerns. This independence is further requisite as a security from oppression. All history demonstrates from page to page, that tyranny and oppression have not been confined to despotisms, but have been freely exercised in republics both ancient and modern—With this difference: that in the latter the oppression has sprung from the impulse of some sudden gust of passion or prejudice, while in the former it is systematically planned and pursued as an ingredient and principle of the government. The people destroy not deliberately and will return to reflection and justice, if passion is not kept alive and excited by artful intrigue, but

while the fit is on, their devastation and cruelty is more terrible and unbounded than the most monstrous tyrant. It is for their own benefit and to protect them from the violence of their own passions that it is essential to have some firm, unshaken, independent branch of government, able and willing to resist their frenzy. If we have read of the death of a Seneca under the ferocity of a Nero, we have read too of the murder of a Socrates under the delusion of a republic. An independent and firm judiciary protected and protecting by the laws would have snatched the one from the fury of a despot and preserved the other from the madness of a people.

(14 Annals of Congress, 8th Cong., 2d Sess., 1802, p. 363)

In the case of the post-Rosenberg resolution to impeach me, Congressman Wheeler demanded a hearing, and a five-man subcommittee of the House Judiciary Committee, headed by Louis E. Graham, held one on June 30, 1953. Wheeler testified that, through issuing the stay, I had committed treason by giving aid and comfort to the Communists. The committee never reported out the bill; the commotion over the episode died by the fall of 1953; and Congressman Wheeler was defeated for re-election in 1954.

The Washington *Post* said editorially on July 2, 1953:

Whether Mr. Justice Douglas was right or wrong in granting a stay of execution to the Rosenbergs after the Supreme Court had recessed, he had indubitable authority to do so. The act, whether wise or mistaken, was based upon a conscientious conviction on his part that a substantial question of law had been raised. Given the atmosphere of excitement in which it was projected, it was an act of courage and of moral stature. If judges were to be subject to impeachment every time some know-nothing Congressman disliked one of their decisions, the independence of the judiciary would become a fiction. The House subcommittee acted wisely to protect the integrity of our courts.

The same day Congressman Abraham J. Multer of New York spoke of the matter in the House:

Liberty cannot survive without justice. Justice must perish if not sustained by our courts. Our courts will be destroyed if they are not kept free from legislative influence, cajolery and threats. To the extent we lose or impair liberty, justice or the courts which protect and dispense liberty and justice, we lose or impair our democracy.

(99 Cong. Record A4148)

Another such incident had arisen out of an issue having nothing to do with any suggestion of Communism. In June 1950, in a contest between the federal government and Texas over the tidelands, the Court held that paramount interest in all lands lying seaward of the low watermark in the Gulf were in the United States (*United States* v. *Texas,* 339 U.S. 707). The opinion followed the earlier precedent in the case of California and Louisiana. Only seven Justices sat, Jackson and Clark having dealt with the matter while they were in the Department of Justice. The seven decided four to three, the four being Vinson, Black, Burton and myself. Vinson assigned the opinion to me.

Then, on January 16, 1951, S. J. Isaacks introduced a resolution in the Texas House of Representatives calling for my impeachment:

> That we request the United States Senators and Members of the House of Representatives from Texas to institute and prosecute impeachment proceedings against Justice William O. Douglas, the member of the Supreme Court of the United States . . . for the first time in the Court's history to ignore a solemn contract entered into between the United States and another nation.

(Texas House Journal, 52nd Legislature, Vol. 1)

The resolution passed the Texas House, eleven voting in the negative. One of the eleven was Maury Maverick, Jr., son of one of my close New Deal friends.

I was both flattered and amused at the news that I had caused Vinson, Black and Burton, otherwise honorable men, to agree with me. For in my long service, I had never tried to persuade any Justice that I was right and he was wrong. I was probably the one Justice in the long history of the Court never to proselytize.

Nothing was done in Washington about the proposed impeachment. In time Texas obtained more complete satisfaction than any impeachment could have brought. In 1953 Congress passed the Submerged Lands Act ceding the submerged lands to the states. When the constitutionality of that cession came to the Court, only three who had sat in the 1950 Texas case survived. The new Chief Justice, Earl Warren, took no part, as he had been active as governor in the California case. The eight divided six to two, upholding the cession (*Alabama* v. *Texas,* 347 U.S. 272), Black and I being the sole dissenters. In 1960 the Court held that Texas could claim dominion not over a three-mile belt like the other States but over a three-league belt (*United States* v. *Louisiana,* 363 U.S. 1, 36–64). This time I was the sole dissenter.

So Texas, represented by powerful interests in the nation's capital, won back all she had lost by our 1950 decision, though she lost out on an impeachment.

Three other episodes out of Texas burned in my memory the importance of academic freedom and its perversion under political manipulation. In 1951 I was in Yugoslavia and saw how Communist orthodoxy was being modified by the infiltration of ideas from other ideologies. Among other things, a team of professors from the University of Texas were there, teaching at the university in Belgrade under an AID project. They were well thought of and their ideas were raising the sights of the students and broadening their perspectives.

No sooner had I returned home when I read that a regent of the University of Texas had learned that this group of distinguished Texas teachers was on assignment in a Communist country. He denounced the project and demanded that the regents order the withdrawal of these teachers—which they immediately did. This episode, minor in the global scene, seared me, for I knew that communicating with Communist lands was the only sure way of developing a cooperative world regime.

Another Texas episode proved how benighted the University of Texas had become. I had been drawn to Frank Dobie, distinguished author and teacher, by his book *The Voice of the Coyote.* Dobie loved that canine as did I; and out of his love grew an expertise in the importance of coyotes to our environment and the uplift that their calls give the spirit of man. So I sought him out and came to know him casually. Dobie was a free spirit like Walt Whitman in many ways; he was steeped in Texas folklore; he was teacher extraordinary. He also spoke out on controversial issues and made clear his stand. He said, for example,

"When I get ready to explain homemade fascism in America, I can take my example from the State Capitol of Texas."

Dobie criticized universities that suppress plays, as well as newspapers that suppress news or distort it. In writing about rattlesnakes, he left the impression that he was writing about the governor—Lee (Pappy) O'Daniel and later about Coke Stevenson, who appointed regents to purge the university faculties of nonconformists. Dobie was unperturbed. When the legislators proposed to close the university to students from other states on the ground that they occupied housing needed for Texans, Dobie spoke up. The danger of outside students, Dobie said, was that "they bring new ideas," and he added, "There are few people who need ideas more than Texans do."

As a result of this kind of statement, Dobie was a ready target for Texas orthodoxy. The powers that be denounced him as a troublemaker (which he was, in the same sense that Socrates was), and manipulated their rules and squeezed Dobie out of the faculty. He was a true Jeffersonian and his life was a dramatic illustration of First Amendment values. He would say, "Positive zest for life and positive opposition of the strangling of life go together." He once wrote in the student paper, the *Texas Ranger:* "I do not see how anybody who cherishes liberty for others as well as for himself can be intolerant of ideas. I do not see how a vast country, the life of which is bound up in vast complexities, can be governed wisely except by intellectual ability."

I was always indebted to the coyote for bringing Frank Dobie and me together. We communicated not through letters but through that wondrous canine and through the golden eagle, which was being cruelly slaughtered by ignorant and lawless Texans, and through the gnarled mesquite trees and live oaks which distinguish the Southwest. "I have never smelled incense in a church as refreshing to the spirit as the spring laden with aroma from a field of those wild lupines called bluebonnets," Frank once said.

His love for that environment was a part of his love of life. Another part was his love for the emancipators of the human mind—including Jefferson, Paine, Emerson and Thoreau. Freedom of the mind was beauty to Frank Dobie, a beauty he considered essential to all men who desire to stay fully alive.

On March 5, 1974, years after the firing of Frank Dobie, I landed in Austin on invitation from the student body. I was to give a lecture on

"Points of Rebellion" expanding the theme of a book I had written earlier which touched off the Nixon-Agnew-Ford project to impeach me. As I walked into the airport I was served with an order entered that day by a state court judge in Texas on petition of a TV station owned in part by former Governor Alan Shivers. The order enjoined my speech unless I agreed to have it recorded on tape. The reason may have been that taping the lecture would enable someone to search it diligently later on to see if I had uttered any "subversive" thoughts. Or perhaps the purpose was to get a tape that, with editing, could be made to sound "subversive." Tapes can be—and often are—edited. A "no" can be cut out and moved forward or backward to take the place of a "yes." Or a proposition the speaker seems to endorse can be manufactured from the other segments of the tape. The voice remains the same; the only thing changed is the meaning.

As a result, when I spoke in Texas, it was *without a manuscript.* I also specifically asked that my talk not be taped. When I went to the platform to address the three thousand students in the auditorium, I explained the situation and said that out of obedience to the state court, but not of respect for it, I would not give my lecture. I would, however, stand to questions. I stayed for an hour and a half trying to answer the questions that were put to me. TV cameras, radio microphones, and the newspaper press were all crowded up front to record the meeting, but in about fifteen minutes most of the crowd of three thousand rose to their feet and hissed the press out of the room. I did not give my "Points of Rebellion" lecture; but I said many so-called extreme things that would make the Alan Shiverses of the state have fits.

Chapter IV

Judicial Treatment
of Nonconformists

The radical has never fared well in American life, whether he was dubbed anarchist, socialist, Bolshevik or Communist. Public passions have always run high against him; and that feeling has radiated from judges as well as from newspapers and the people on Main Street. The result was manifest not only in cases like *In re Debs* (158 U.S. 564)* but whenever the Bench felt the "tremor of socialism" Holmes had referred to.

The seeds of Communist thought which were spread throughout the world following 1917 fell, therefore, on inhospitable soil. America has long been and remains a very conservative nation. In the 1950s, when the Cold War flourished, the resulting climate of opinion made the dispensation of justice very unlikely when one was merely charged with being a Communist, let alone a person who was, in fact, a hard-core member. Juries were almost bound to reflect the dark suspicions which most Americans harbored about dispensers of a foreign ideology. Judges were not much more independent; it often seemed that they were being whipsawed by public passions and transformed into agents of intolerance. State judges, elected to office, were often mere mouthpieces of the most intolerant members of the community. Michael A. Musmanno of the Pennsylvania Supreme Court was a notorious example of this kind of official, but even federal judges, named for life, were

*For a description of the case, see Chapter 7 (pages 159–160).

affected, as is illustrated by the long series of sad episodes which resulted in federal prosecutions.

The break with tradition in my time came with *Dennis* v. *United States* (341 U.S. 494), decided in 1951. The indictment charged a "conspiracy" under the Smith Act (18 U.S.C. 371) to teach Marxist thought and Marxist doctrine. (Using this rationale, any faculty of a school or college which undertook to offer such courses could also be categorized as taking part in a "conspiracy.") The only difference in *Dennis* was that the defendants were in fact Communists. Instruction in Communist ideology by Communists must therefore, it was said, be "advocacy"; and advocacy was taken to mean the hope that the doctrine would become acceptable and put into operation.

In my dissent in *Dennis*, I said:

> Communism in . . . the world scene is no bogeyman; but Communism as a political faction or party in this country plainly is. Communism has been so thoroughly exposed in this country that it has been crippled as a political force. Free speech has destroyed it as an effective political party. . . . In days of trouble and confusion, when bread lines were long, when the unemployed walked the streets, when people were starving, the advocates of a short-cut by revolution might have a chance to gain adherents. But today there are no such conditions. The country is not in despair; the people know Soviet Communism; the doctrine of Soviet revolution is exposed in all of its ugliness and the American people want none of it.
>
> (341 U.S. 588)

Certainly freedom of expression as used in the First Amendment includes more than teaching in the abstract; it means all shades of advocacy from lukewarm endorsement to partisan promotion, as the Court held in *Terminiello* v. *Chicago* (337 U.S. 1). To be sure, that idea had been qualified during World War I by the "clear and present danger" test first adumbrated by Holmes in *Schenck* v. *United States* (249 U.S. 47, 52). Advocacy at some point can come so close to the line where action commences that the two become brigaded. Since the legislature can ban the action, it can ban the advocacy that is closely blended with the action.

But that idea was perverted in *Dennis*. The "clear and present danger" test was restated to mean that it was the intent of the defendants in teaching the Marxist creed to overthrow the government "as speedily as circumstances would permit" (341 U.S. 509–510).

Thus, those who believed in Communism and hoped it would take hold here and taught the creed became criminals, while those who were more detached—that is, did not believe in Communism—could teach it with impunity. Yet from the academic viewpoint, the deeper a person was immersed in a subject and the more passionately he felt about it, the better teacher he usually was—whether the course be one on Wordsworth, Henry George or Karl Marx.

At the time of *Dennis* the danger of Communist advocacy was magnified by two related considerations: first, the Communist world seemed even more monolithic than the Catholic Church, all units working for one central cause; second, control of the American Communist Party seemed to be in the hands of Moscow and the other capitals of Eastern Europe. These factors made American Communism look like a powerful and destructive foreign force. Yet if that was the reason for reformulation of the "clear and present danger" test by the Court in *Dennis,* does the new, relaxed, easygoing test apply only in Communist cases or to any minority of dissidents whether they are advocating Black Power or are Jehovah's Witnesses or sharecroppers?

In the October 1943 Term, there had been a similar case from the Eighth Circuit Court of Appeals, *Dunne* v. *United States* (138 F 2d 137), in which we denied certiorari. The case involved two conspiracies—advocacy of the overthrow of the government by violence, and advocacy of disloyalty and insubordination in the armed services. No overt acts were charged apart from advocacy. Yet the case, emotionally speaking, was less appealing than *Dennis* because *Dennis* was in the classic framework of teaching.

Murphy and Rutledge, joined by Black, voted to grant the petition. If I had done likewise, there would have been four to grant and the Court would have heard the case. It was clear that the majority of five —Stone, Roberts, Reed, Frankfurter and Jackson—would have voted to affirm; and it seemed to me at that particular point in history unwise to put the Court's seal of approval on that doctrine. Better let the issue be presented at a more auspicious time! That is why I did not vote to grant the petition.

Such a judgment is often made at Conference, and everyone who has been on the Court has succumbed to that influence. But the study of

Dunne reveals how unwise such deferrals may be. In 1943 and 1944, *Dunne* would have been a five-to-four decision. By the time *Dennis* arrived, Rutledge and Murphy had passed on, and there were fewer votes on the libertarian side than there would have been a decade earlier. The moral is to take important cases whenever four votes are available and not to speculate as to what time in the future will be more auspicious. In 1943 Black, Douglas, Murphy and Rutledge looked like a long-term, enduring bloc of votes. But death was to play a conspicuous role.

We will discuss later the 1947 Attorney General's list of subversive organizations. What is interesting to note here is not that the executive branch issued such a list but that the lower courts sustained the action. When the question of the list reached our Court in *Joint Anti-Fascist Committee* v. *McGrath* (341 U.S. 123), decided on April 30, 1951, we reversed, only Reed, Vinson and Minton dissenting.

But while the Court ruled that the organization called "subversive" had a right to a hearing before being so branded, an individual employee charged with being disloyal or a poor security risk had no right to confront his accuser and have a full-fledged hearing in the Western sense of the term (*Bailey* v. *Richardson,* 341 U.S. 918).

Such vagaries of decision could be explained by the changing personnel of the Court. The same Justices who decided the Anti-Fascist Committee case decided the Bailey case. The former decision was in defense of liberty, while the latter restricted it. That seeming inconsistency can be explained only on the ground that the majority of five in the Anti-Fascist Committee case included Burton, who went off on a construction of an executive order as not authorizing what the Attorney General had done. Had he reached the constitutional question, he would have been with the dissenters. The alignment in the Bailey case reflects that fact.

In 1950 the Court held that Congress could require officers of unions employing the services of the National Labor Relations Board to sign affidavits that they were not Communists. This interference with First Amendment rights was justified as protecting commerce against political strikes (*American Communications Association* v. *Douds,* 339 U.S. 382). Clark, Minton and I took no part—I was on a long convalescence in Arizona. Vinson wrote for the Court. Only Black dissented, saying that the First Amendment forbade penalizing a person for the political views he held. How that view could be refuted I never knew. The majority said, of course, that Congress could legislate against "political" strikes. But that is only another way of saying that Congress may make some laws abridging freedom of expression.

The states, like the federal government, made lists of "subversive" organizations; and some, like New York, disqualified members of such an organization from public employment—for example, from working as a teacher. A teacher held ineligible was entitled to a hearing; but he or she could not challenge the finding that the organization he or she was accused of joining was "subversive." Moreover, the mere fact of membership raised a prima facie case of his or her own guilt. The chance of proving innocence in the face of membership was nil when the witch hunt was on. Yet it is common knowledge that people join even the Republican Party with private disavowals of some of its aims.

The system of spying and surveillance which follows in the wake of such laws is obvious; in particular, its effect on academic freedom is shattering. Yet in 1952 the Court sustained the law (*Adler* v. *Board of Education,* 342 U.S. 485). In 1954 the Court in *Barsky* v. *Board of Regents* (347 U.S. 442) authorized suspension of a physician from practice because he had been convicted of failing to produce before the House Un-American Activities Committee documents which it subpoenaed from an organization on the Attorney General's subversive list engaged in opposing Franco in Spain. This suspension order against Barsky was sustained, even though there was not a shred of evidence that he was not a competent doctor, nor that he used improper conduct toward his patients. It was obvious that he lost his right to be a doctor merely because of his political beliefs and his mistaken notion that his constitutional rights entitled him to defy the House committee.

Dennis, Adler, Bailey and *Barsky* show the Court running with the hounds and joining the hue and cry against unpopular people.

In other cases decided during the mid-fifties—*Peters* v. *Hobby* (349 U.S. 331), *Cole* v. *Young* (351 U.S. 536), *Vitarelli* v. *Seaton* (359 U.S. 535), *Service* v. *Dulles* (354 U.S. 363), and in *Greene* v. *McElroy* (360 U.S. 474), decided in 1959—the Court swerved its course and acted to protect the rights of those same people by limiting the thrust of the anti-subversive program.

The arrival of Earl Warren made part of the difference. Moreover, I think the notorious and high-handed way in which the loyalty security program was administered was making itself felt on the judicial conscience. In any event, the Court construed executive orders and regulations concerning the discharge of "subversives" from government employment quite strictly, to give the accused employees a full measure of procedural due process of law.

The individual states also got involved in the "roundup" of suspected radicals. The Court decided *Pennsylvania* v. *Nelson* (350 U.S. 497), involving a prosecution under a state sedition law. There is no question that a state may proscribe sedition against its own government. The prosecution in *Nelson,* however, was for sedition against the *federal* government, a matter which Congress had dealt with in the Smith Act (54 Stat. 670). The Cold War was at its peak and every local prosecutor was trying to get into the act. Think what a political plum it would be for a prosecutor to catch a Communist! But the FBI also was hot on the trail of all known Communists for prosecution under the Smith Act, and J. Edgar Hoover, in his talks with state agencies, emphasized how much damage an eager state prosecutor could do by flushing a suspect before the FBI had cast its net and rounded everyone up. It was, in other words, in the national interest to entrust protection of the nation to federal officers.

The Court held that state prosecution for sedition against the nation had been pre-empted by the Smith Act and that enforcement of a state prosecution of this kind presented a serious danger of conflict with the administration of the federal program. It accordingly upheld the Pennsylvania Supreme Court, which had ruled to the same effect.

The resulting uproar was loud and incessant. About seventy bills were introduced to change the result in the Nelson case; all but four died in committee. The others were debated on the floor of the Senate and the House and failed of passage. The gist of these bills was that nothing but an express provision in a federal law should prevent a state from prosecuting acts of subversion or sedition against the federal government. The FBI must have been greatly relieved that none of these measures was enacted.

Then, in 1956, came *Slochower* v. *Board of Education* (350 U.S. 551), in which the state of New York discharged a teacher for invoking the Self-Incrimination Clause of the Fifth Amendment. The teacher testified before a committee of the Congress that he was not then a member of the Communist Party but refused to testify about his alleged membership in 1940 and 1941 on the ground that his answers might incriminate him. Thereupon he was discharged from his job. Invoking the privilege, we held, was a means of protecting "the innocent who otherwise might be ensnared by ambiguous circumstances" and may not properly be taken as a confession of guilt. The *Slochower* decision raised another howl concerning states' rights.

During the next Term two other so-called states' rights cases were decided. One Schware was denied admission to the New Mexico Bar for lack of "good moral character." The main evidence against him was that for seven or eight years he had been a member of the Communist Party, resigning from it in 1940 after disillusionment. He had never engaged in illegal activity, nor had he done anything that was morally reprehensible as a member of that party. During the time he was a member, the party was a lawful political party on the ballot in most states. The Court refused on that record to infer that all members shared the "evil purposes" and the "illegal conduct" of some members. The Court concluded that there is "no evidence in the record which rationally justifies a finding that Schware was morally unfit to practice law" (*Schware* v. *Board of Bar Examiners,* 353 U.S. 232 at 247).

On the same day the Court decided *Konigsberg* v. *State Bar of California* (353 U.S. 252). Konigsberg had been denied admission to the California Bar for lack of "good moral character." There was testimony that he had attended Communist Party meetings in 1941, at a time when the party was lawful in California. There was no evidence linking him to any illegal or disloyal activities, though he had criticized the United States' role in the Korean "war," our *Dennis* decision and racial discrimination. But, as the Court held, such expressions of political views are no evidence of bad moral character. Konigsberg had refused to answer questions concerning his political opinions and associations, including his membership in the Communist Party, on the ground that the question invaded his First Amendment rights. This was held to be no basis for concluding that he had a bad moral character. And the Court further held that there was no evidence that he advocated overthrow of the government by force.

These cases were followed by *Sweezy* v. *New Hampshire* (354 U.S. 234). A state legislature had defined a subversive person very broadly and entrusted the Attorney General to find out if there were any in the state. Sweezy, a teacher and lecturer was examined, and he answered most of the questions by saying that he had never been a Communist, never taught violent overthrow of the government, never knowingly associated with Communists, but that he was a socialist who believed in peaceful change and had belonged to some organizations on the Attorney General's list. He refused, however, to answer questions concerning (1) a lecture he had given at a university; (2) his and his friends' activities in the Progressive Party; and (3) his opinion and beliefs. For these refusals he was held in contempt and our Court reversed.

Among the questions at which he balked were the following:

What was the subject of your lecture?

Didn't you tell the class at the University of New Hampshire on Monday, March 22, 1954, that Socialism was inevitable in this country?

Did you advocate Marxism at that time?

Did you in this last lecture on March 22 or in any of the former lectures espouse the theory of dialectical materialism?

I have in the file here a statement from a person who attended your class, and I will read it in part because I don't want you to think I am just fishing. "His talk this time was on the inevitability of the Socialist program. It was a glossed-over interpretation of the materialist dialectic." Now, again I ask you the original question.

The Court emphasized that the questions at which Sweezy balked were in the First Amendment area: academic freedom, including the right to pursue ideas to the horizon; and "the right to engage in political expression and association."

Watkins v. *United States* (354 U.S. 178) likewise created a tempest. Watkins was convicted of contempt of Congress. He had been a member of the Communist Party and testified fully regarding all of his activities. He also was willing to testify about anyone who still was a member of the party, but he refused to testify about those who once had been members but long since ceased to be such. It was for such refusal that he was convicted.

In reversing, the Court said that the power to investigate is part of the lawmaking power. Since Congress, by the First Amendment, is barred from making a law abridging freedom of speech, press or assembly, the First Amendment is a barrier to certain questions. Thus, "there is no congressional power to expose for the sake of exposure."

But the promise contained in the *Watkins* opinion was not kept.

Barenblatt v. *United States* (360 U.S. 109), decided on June 8, 1959, and *Wilkinson* v. *United States* (365 U.S. 399) and *Braden* v. *United States* (365 U.S. 431), both decided on February 27, 1961, gave the House Un-American Activities Committee broad powers to probe a person's ideas and beliefs. In effect, they allowed the committee to subpoena anyone who had criticized the committee, and to examine all facets of his life, holding him up as a subversive or a traitor and, if he was man enough to defy the committee, to see that he went off to jail for his contempt. Moreover, the authorization of the committee in these three cases was the same as it had been in *Watkins*—to make investigations of "the extent, character and objects of un-American propaganda activities in the United States." Criticizing the committee was brought under that heading. What had been six to one for *Watkins* became five to four against *Barenblatt, Wilkinson* and *Braden*.

In the first Konigsberg case, the Court did not consider whether Konigsberg's refusal to answer questions concerning his past or present membership in the Communist Party was a proper ground for barring him from law practice. So when the case went back to California, it was referred back to the bar committee, which asked him questions concerning that membership, questions he refused to answer. His refusal to answer was the basis for denying his admission to the bar, and the case came to us again (366 U.S. 36).

By 1961, when the Konigsberg case returned to the Court, Stewart and Whittaker had been appointed and confirmed, and they, together with Frankfurter, Clark and Harlan, formed a new majority of five that finally kept Konigsberg from the California Bar on the ground that his refusal to answer prevented a full investigation of his qualifications.

On the same day that we decided *Watkins* in support of the First Amendment, we also decided *Yates* v. *United States* (354 U.S. 298), making four decisions all told on a day which some critics called Red Monday. The crime alleged was a conspiracy to "organize" the Communist Party in this country in alleged violation of the Smith Act (18 U.S.C. 371, 2385). The party had been organized in 1945 and the indictment returned in 1951. We held that the prosecution was therefore barred by the three-year statute of limitations. Since the Smith Act did not define "organize," we followed the old rule that criminal statutes are to be strictly construed and therefore gave the word its narrow meaning.

The Smith Act also made criminal advocacy of the desirability or propriety of overthrowing the government by force and violence. The Court held that advocacy of mere abstract doctrine of forcible overthrow was not punishable. The advocacy, to be criminal, must be reasonably and ordinarily calculable to incite people to action. The voices on the Hill protested the narrow construction of the word "organize." But they did not criticize the Court's construction of the word "advocacy," which followed the construction in the Dennis case and ended in a great dilution of First Amendment rights.

Then came *Scales* v. *United States* (367 U.S. 203), decided on June 5, 1961. Scales was convicted under the Smith Act of being an active member of the Communist Party with knowledge of the party's illegal purpose and with a specific intent to accomplish the overthrow of the government "as speedily as circumstances would permit." No illegal actions were charged. His "crime" was belief, advocacy of action, and teaching Marxism in practical operation. Sedition or treason in the area of politics, and heresy in the field of religion had, in times past, made *beliefs* criminal acts. We came to this country to get away from such punishment for what was in our minds.

In *Scales*, the right of advocacy for the purpose of incitement, as well as for education, was lost by a five-to-four decision. But free speech traditionally had included both. The First Amendment says Congress may make "no law" abridging freedom of speech. After *Dennis* and *Scales*, Congress may make *some* laws abridging freedom of speech.

The American philosophy was that anyone, no matter how unpopular or disliked, was entitled to the due process guaranteed by the Constitution. Yet some of the press dubbed a Justice "Communist" whenever he ruled in favor of anyone charged with being a member of that party. Thus it was that some of us were put into tables and charts showing we were 90 percent or more "Communist," while other Justices were only 35 percent "Communist."

The Court was severely criticized for the modest stands it took to protect the civil rights of this despised minority. In a mature society it would have been roundly criticized for the shameful performance in *Dennis* and in *Scales*.

Dennis and *Scales* mark the greatest decline in free speech in the history of the nation. The constitutional theory, expounded by Jefferson and Madison, was to let the people believe what they choose and to talk as they like, putting reliance on public debate to expose the fallacy of ideas and to correct errors. Government has no rightful concern with interfering except and unless beliefs and ideas break out into violent acts. Under that view, Communists would not be driven underground. They would have the hustings, the printing press, advocacy, propaganda and all the tools which other publicists enjoy.

That course is the constitutional standard; and it does presuppose a mature people. It turned out that we as a nation were as intolerant of this opposed ideology as Russia is to advocacy of free enterprise. We keep a wider part of the spectrum open for discussion than does Russia, but where the clash of ideas is clear and vivid, we follow the Soviet pattern. The majority in *Scales* reflected the public attitude on that issue, and they firmly believed that the safety of the republic did not permit the other choice.

Yet the only evidence of addiction to force and violence in these Communist cases was the classical writings of Marx, Engels, Lenin and Stalin. These writings, however, did not indicate that Communists in the United States were geared for a coup. Lacking such evidence, it is impossible to square the Smith Act prosecutions with our own Declaration of Independence, not to mention the First Amendment.

Once in a while the judiciary gets a scunner against a group, and disregarding high principles and standards of justice and equality, allows government or individuals to get after a person or a class of people. In my time it happened three times: first, the case of John L. Lewis, illustrated by *United States* v. *United Mine Workers* (330 U.S. 258). The 1947 case was supercharged with feelings about John L. Lewis and led, I think, to extreme strictures on his union. Second, the case of Hughes Tool Co.—a Howard Hughes company—involving a money judgment close to $200 million which the Court set aside on January 10, 1973 (*Hughes Tool Co.* v. *Trans World Airlines, Inc.*, 409 U.S. 363). Hughes, who had refused to answer a subpoena to testify, drew the wrath of the entire Second Circuit, which showed no mercy in piling damages on top of damages in a case that had no business being in court at all. Third, the long series of Communist prosecutions under the Smith Act in which there was not a shred of evidence that any defendant had ever raised his hand against the government or even threatened to do so. And, as I indicated above, their theory of violence closely coincided with the one we expressed in the Declaration of Independence.

These were all unusual situations, illustrating that no matter how high-minded the judges may be, an emotional factor may send a court off on a false trail. It is fortunate that it does not happen often.

In the winter of 1951–52, after *Dennis* was decided, there was a Columbia University dinner in New York City (Dwight Eisenhower was then Columbia's president). This night Tom Dewey was the toastmaster. (Tom was a short man, and when speaking, he usually stood on a big fat dictionary so as to look tall. There was a story about him to the effect that he should start each speech by saying, "My friends, I'm not standing in a hole.") I, as an alumnus of the law school, sat at the head table. During the preliminaries and before the main course was served, Dewey was performing. There were announcements to make and a few jokes to tell; and then, for some reason, he got going on the Supreme Court. His main theme was that the Court was too leftist for the country. He may have been thinking that had he defeated Truman he would have made some Supreme Court appointments and they would—Allah save us—have been more conservative than Vinson, Burton, Clark and Minton. Whatever the reason, Tom Dewey gave the Court quite a flailing.

At the end he talked about the Dennis case, and changing his voice to indicate surprise, said, "Never, never did I dream that the Court would have the guts to send those Communists off to prison."

That remark got a thunderous applause—and I left the head table and the dinner, never to return. For to me it was sad that educated lawyers would think that sending the miserable defendants in *Dennis* off to prison had saved the country. The Communist Party—as dull and oppressive as any party I have ever read about—was at its lowest ebb in America and could not have elected a dogcatcher to office.

Tom Dewey downgraded the First Amendment that night as much as any member of the House Un-American Activities Committee ever did.

It was sometimes said that Hugo Black and I initially went along with the "clear and present danger" test but later repudiated it. What we did was meet the arguments of the majority as in *Dennis* that the "clear and present danger" test had been satisfied. We rejected that as a legitimate test at any time.

After *Dennis* the words "clear and present danger" were sometimes used, but only trivially. The test thereafter used, as illustrated by *Yates,*

Scales and *Noto* v. *United States* (367 U.S. 290), looked to the speaker's *intent* and the *content* of his advocacy, not to the probability or danger or the imminence of its success. A person teaching Marxism was not held a criminal unless he was a fervent believer and his advocacy was intense. At the same time, intentional incitement to concrete lawless action, no matter how distant or unlikely, was not protected speech.

Whitney v. *California* (274 U.S. 357) was decided in 1927. Yet when in 1969 *Whitney* was overruled by *Brandenburg* v. *Ohio* (395 U.S. 444), the Court, speaking per curiam* (in an opinion drafted by Justice Stewart), ruled that a state may not "forbid or proscribe advocacy of the use of force or of law violation except where such advocacy is directed to inciting or producing imminent lawless action and is likely to incite or produce such action" (*Id.* 447). Some scholar commented at the time that this test would certainly surprise the defendants in *Dennis,* who went to jail only for teaching Marxism (in which they believed), when there was no proof that their teaching (advocacy) was directed "to inciting or producing imminent lawless action."

It is a long and weary trail from *Schenck,* in 1919, and *Gitlow* v. *New York* (268 U.S. 652), in 1925, to *Brandenburg.* The First Amendment says that "Congress shall make no law . . . abridging the freedom of speech, or of the press." And by reason of *Stromberg* v. *California* (283 U.S. 359), the Fourteenth Amendment makes that mandate applicable to the states.

Most of the cases involved acts of legislatures directed against specified speech. Any law aimed at speech would obviously seem to violate the First Amendment; whether there was also "conduct" which constitutionally could have been punished would be irrelevant to the sanctity of the "speech" guarantee. The absence of power of federal or state legislatures to punish (abridge) speech seems obvious in the face of the First Amendment. As to conduct, different considerations apply. *Schenck* involved an act written in "nonspeech" terms, such as acts "to obstruct the recruiting and enlistment service" in World War I (249 U.S. 49). The act was plainly constitutional, as it had no conflict with the First Amendment and was within the reach of the traditional police power of the state. Whether "speech" or "advocacy" could constitutionally be proof of violation of the act was the question. That is when and how the "clear and present danger" test came into being, the test which, after

*An unsigned decision by the majority of the Court.

long neglect, was substantially readopted in *Brandenburg*.

Speech is "abridged" whenever it is punished; and I have never been able to conclude that it could be punished no matter what the degree of the "danger" was unless it was as closely synchronized with "conduct" as was falsely "shouting fire in a crowded theatre," to use Holmes's expression (*Schenck* v. *United States,* 249 U.S. 47, 52).

Making laws "abridging" speech is beyond legislative power. It is not beyond legislative power to treat only conduct. The test of "incitement" is beyond the mark, since many ideas do incite and the fact that some do not has never meant that only inoffensive utterances are protected. Obscenity, which has plagued the Court more than subversion, is offensive speech or utterances—at least the literature and pictures and movies coming to us in civil and criminal cases were obnoxious to me personally. But many other things are also: i.e., the Court's decision in *Dennis,* or the Court's holding in *San Antonio Independent School District* v. *Rodriguez* (411 U.S. 1) that there was no violation of the Equal Protection Clause for a state to let a poor district finance its schools, and rich ones their schools. Watergate was obscene to me, and very offensive. So were the passionate denunciations of Hugo Black and Earl Warren from the right. The twisting and distortion of the news by the Communist press and by some of our mass media were shocking to me. So were some laws pushed through Congress by powerful lobbies to line their own pockets. But one judge's standard of offensiveness is not a constitutional standard.

The First Amendment tolerates a wide range of utterances. Whether in the field of obscenity or subversion, an utterance which incites to unlawful acts is irrelevant to the protection afforded by the First Amendment. Of course a legislature can deal with sexual conduct; unfortunately, the easy way is to strike at the speaker and suppress him. Our constitutional philosophy is that mature people will pick and choose among speakers, writers and publishers, turning their backs on those ideas that are repulsive but suppressing none. But in politics there are the untouchables, just as in religion there are heretics. Until Americans grow up and become sophisticated, they will continue to produce legislators and judges who will find applause somewhere in the mob.

One of my most vivid memories of China came from a prison in which one third of the inmates were there because of "counterrevolutionary" activities. On close analysis it turned out their crime was that they espoused the cause of capitalism; similarly, all that the defendants in our Dennis case did was to espouse causes of socialism. We profess great enlightenment; yet we have a degree of intolerance that puts us on a par with most other people—in spite of our boasting about the First Amendment.

The cases we have discussed so far arose
1. Under Truman's and Eisenhower's executive orders
2. Under the Smith Act, making advocacy of the Communist cause or organizing that party criminal
3. Under state programs to control "subversives"
But the most pervasive law passed "concerning the Communist menace" was the Subversive Activities Control Act (50 U.S.C. Sec. 781 *et seq.*), enacted in 1950.

The record of the Court under this act was by my lights much better. The arrival of Earl Warren, Abe Fortas and Arthur Goldberg made some of the difference.

The act established a Subversive Activities Control Board (SACB) with broad powers to investigate and to require organizations it found to be "Communist" to register. The act made it a crime for a member of an organization required to be registered to apply for a passport. That provision was struck down in 1964 in *Aptheker* v. *Secretary of State* (378 U.S. 500) because, *inter alia,* it interfered with a person's constitutional right to travel and his right of freedom of association.

The next year the Court considered *Albertson* v. *SACB* (382 U.S. 70). The board had directed the Communist Party to register with the Attorney General, and when the Party failed to do so, the Attorney General obtained from the board an order requiring that the members register. The Court held that such registration ran afoul of the Fifth Amendment because an admission of membership in the Communist Party might be used to prosecute a registrant under the Smith Act. Congress thereupon amended the act to abolish registration and to give the board power to determine if a group is a "Communist" organization or if a person is a member of it. The procedure under that section was held unconstitutional in 1969 in *Boorda* v. *SACB* (421 F 2d 1142), since no distinction was made between those members who shared the illegal aims of the party from those whose only aims were constitutionally protected.

In 1967 we held in *United States* v. *Robel* (389 U.S. 258) that Congress could not indiscriminately make it a crime for a member of the Communist Party to work in a defense facility, in this case a shipyard. The statute made irrelevant the fact that the worker was a passive or inactive member, that he was unaware of the party's unlawful aims, that he disagreed with those unlawful aims, or that he occupied a nonsensitive position in the defense facility. Those innocent associations were held to be protected by the First Amendment. While Congress can legislate against espionage, the laws it enacts must be "narrowly drawn" to hit the precise evil so that guilt is not determined by association.

There were minor aspects of this act which survived. Its essential features, however, ran afoul of the Constitution and the Bill of Rights. There was a detention-camp provision in the act under which "subversives" could be locked up. In 1971 this detention-camp provision was repealed because popular sentiment was strongly adverse to it. The vote in the House was 356 to 49 (117 *Cong. Record,* sec. 31781). The repeal added a new provision that no one could be imprisoned or detained for "subversion" except pursuant to an act of Congress. Thus Congress evinced an intent that no President should be allowed to repeat what was done in World War II when Americans of Japanese ancestry were put into camps (*Id.* sec. 31753 *et seq.;* H. R. 92–116, 92d Cong., 1st Sess.).

The Subversive Activities Control Board slowly became defunct. The appropriation for the board was $350,000 in 1973, but the next year it was not funded at all. Thus ended the Subversive Activities Control Act, one of the most repressive measures enacted by Congress since the Alien and Sedition Act of 1798.

When the act was passed by Congress, Truman vetoed. (His veto message had been falsely attributed to Felix Frankfurter.) The veto was overridden in the House by a vote of 286 to 48. Fred Vinson, shortly to become Chief Justice, voted with the majority, as did Richard Nixon and Jack Kennedy. Those voting in the House *not* to overrule included Henry (Scoop) Jackson, Helen Gahagan Douglas, Andy Biemiller and James Roosevelt (96 *Cong. Record* 15632). The vote in the Senate was 57 to overrule and 10 to sustain Truman. Hubert Humphrey, Paul Douglas and Estes Kefauver were among the ten (*Id.* 15726).

Truman's veto message said, as we have seen, that the act would put the government "in the thought-control business" and that it would give "government officials vast powers to harass all our citizens in the exercise of their right of free speech." Truman did not underrate the Communists, but he was convinced that requiring Communist organizations to divulge information about themselves is "about as practical as requiring thieves to register with the sheriff."

He pointed out that an organization would be a "Communist-front organization" within the meaning of the act if "the positions taken and advanced by it from time to time on matters of policy do not deviate from those" of the Communist Party. This was what became known as "parallelism." He who believes in Medicare is a Communist because Communists favor Medicare!!

This was a historic veto (*Id.* 1562 *et seq.;* 5726). It anticipated in an uncanny way the court decisions which over the years would invalidate the crucial provisions of the act because they ran against America's constitutional traditions and way of life.

The Court also did a shade better when it came to loyalty oaths. The vice of many loyalty oaths is that they look to the past, not to present fitness or future promises of behavior. They punish a person for acts which may not have been unlawful when committed. They have all the essential earmarks of bills of attainder historically used to inflict punishment on unpopular minorities. A person seeking a public post can of course be tested for present loyalty and for his disposition toward law and order. But disqualifying him because of past actions or thoughts that are not necessarily relevant to present fitness is punishment for acts which may have been innocent when done. Certainly a person put on the blacklist for public employment suffers punishment of an acute and measurable amount.

Loyalty oaths are an old familiar means of hounding unpopular people. In 1966, in *Elfbrandt* v. *Russell* (384 U.S. 11), the state of Arizona required an oath of a teacher under which she might be guilty of perjury if she attended the Pugwash Conference, which was allegedly predominantly Communist. Freedom of association is a First Amendment right; a person should be able to expose herself to any group, to any school of thought, without being tagged as a subversive. The very presence of an oath requiring one official to swear he is a true believer puts pressure on all to take the oath lest they too be persecuted as ideological strays.

The loyalty oath has a special and severe impact on teachers. It is wholly inconsistent with the ideal of the university, never better described than by my friend Robert M. Hutchins:

> Now, a university is a place that is established and will function for the benefit of society, provided it is a center of independent thought. It is a center of independent thought and criticism that is created in the interest of the progress of society, and the one reason that we know that every totalitarian government must fail is that no totalitarian government is prepared to face the consequences of creating free universities.
>
> It is important for this purpose to attract into the institution men of the greatest capacity, and to encourage them to exercise their independent judgment.
>
> Education is a kind of continuing dialogue, and a dialogue assumes, in the nature of the case, different points of view.
>
> The civilization which I work toward and which, I am sure, every American is working toward, could be called a civilization of the dialogue, where, instead of shooting one another when you differ, you reason things out together.
>
> In this dialogue, then, you cannot assume that you are going to have everybody thinking the same way or feeling the same way. It would be unprogressive if that happened. The hope of eventual development would be gone. More than that, of course it would be very boring.
>
> A university, then, is a kind of continuing Socratic conversation on the highest level for the very best people you can think of, you can bring together, about the most important questions, and the thing that you must do, to the uttermost possible limits, is to guarantee those men the freedom to think and to express themselves.
>
> Now, the limits on this freedom cannot be merely prejudice, because although our prejudices might be perfectly satisfactory, the prejudices of our successors, or of those who are in a position to bring pressure to bear on the institution, might be subversive in the real sense, subverting the American doctrine of free thought and free speech.

In my time that ideal of the university was greatly blurred. The university and college became corrupted by many influences. The "witch hunt" seriously seared many. Secret use of CIA funds corrupted others. The $16 billion a year spent by the Pentagon for "research and development" was largely distributed through universities; and the recipients, usually individual professors, became research adjuncts of the Pentagon, not scholars in pursuit of truth. Pentagon money allowed science to outweigh the humanities; it resulted in many unseemly faculty contests and stirred much student unrest. Beyond all these influences was the growing domination of university thought by financial backers. Faculties became more and more defenders of the status quo. A young lecturer who was bold enough to propose that Peking be admitted to the United Nations had little or no chance of ever becoming a full professor.

With the passage of the loyalty security programs, university environments did not relax; rather they hardened. The lessons of conformity and the rewards it brought became subtle influences in academic circles. Faculties walked more and more in goose step to the tunes of the Establishment. Universities were no longer places of ferment but became more and more institutions dispensing information on how to get ahead and sedatives that made students less and less responsive to the mighty forces of rebellion that were making the nation seethe.

I believed, with William M. Birenbaum, that "a campus without disruption is polluted, like a river without fish or a defoliated forest along the Ho Chi Minh Trail. . . . The campus is now like the compulsory ghetto."*

Something for Everybody Is Not Enough: An Educator's Search for His Education (New York: Random House, 1971).

Chapter V

Separate but Unequal

Plessy v. *Ferguson* (163 U.S. 537), decided on May 18, 1896, was an eight-to-one decision holding that segregation of blacks on railroad coaches was constitutional, that state laws requiring such segregation did not violate the Equal Protection Clause of the Fourteenth Amendment. It was a predominantly Northern Court that made the decision. Justice Henry B. Brown of Michigan wrote for the majority, and the first Justice John Marshall Harlan, a Kentuckian—and a former slave owner—was the lone dissenter stating the now famous dictum, "Our Constitution is color-blind" (*Id.* 559). This decision sanctioned the black codes that adopted segregation as a way of life not only in public facilities such as railroads but in schools. Thus dual school systems were adopted by many states, not all of them Southern.

This 1896 decision enabled the black codes to be tightly fastened on the South and encouraged the spread of their philosophy into the North. In 1927, while Holmes, Brandeis and Stone were on the Court, the Justices voted unanimously to extend that holding to Chinese. The state of Mississippi required that Chinese attend black schools, and did not admit them into white schools. The Court, basing its opinion on *Plessy* v. *Ferguson,* approved (*Gong Lum* v. *Rice,* 275 U.S. 78).

By the thirties, discontent was in the air. Missouri's dual school system provided a law school for whites but none for blacks. Missouri sought to remedy this by paying blacks reasonable tuition fees for attending a law school in "any adjacent state." In 1938 the Court, speaking through Chief Justice Hughes, held that such a program did not satisfy the federal right of a black to have the "equal opportunity for legal training" in Missouri, and the denial of the right meant he must be admitted to the white law school in Missouri (*Missouri* ex rel. *Gaines* v. *Canada,* 305 U.S. 337, 352). Only Mr. Justice McReynolds and Mr. Justice Butler dissented.

By the forties, cases of racial discrimination were mounting. We held in *Mitchell* v. *United States* (313 U.S. 80) that a black with a first-class ticket who demanded Pullman accommodations on an interstate train could not constitutionally be relegated to second-class accommodations. In *Sipuel* v. *Board of Regents* (332 U.S. 631) we ordered that a black be admitted to Oklahoma's white law school, there being no other legal education offered by the state.

Texas established a separate law school for blacks, but in 1950 we held in *Sweatt* v. *Painter* (339 U.S. 629) that it was not equal to the white law school and that the black who applied must, therefore, be admitted to the white institution. Vinson wrote feelingly in rejecting the claim of Texas that it would constitutionally take care of black law students in a new school recently opened: "Whether the University of Texas Law School is compared with the original or the new law school for Negroes, we cannot find substantial equality in the educational opportunities offered white and Negro law students by the State" (*Id.* 633).

In *McLaurin* v. *Oklahoma State Regents* (339 U.S. 637), a black seeking a doctorate in education was, under compulsion of our decisions, admitted to Oklahoma's white graduate school but was required "to sit apart at a designated desk in an anteroom adjoining the class room." He was not allowed to use the desks in the "regular reading room" of the library, and was to eat separately and at a different time from other students in the school cafeteria" (*Id.* 640). We held that the imposition of these conditions deprived the black of "his personal and present right to the equal protection of the laws" (*Id.* 642).

The presence of blacks in white schools began to appear in geographical areas that had been completely segregated. In the North and in the West a different pattern had developed and, at least legally, blacks enjoyed full equality in public educational facilities, in parks, on railroads, and the like.

And so the parade of separate but unequal cases mounted in the

Courts. After McReynolds and Butler were gone from the Court, it was quite unanimous in agreeing on what treatment of blacks was not "equal" by the test of *Plessy* v. *Ferguson.* There was some discussion as to whether the "separate but equal" doctrine should not be reconsidered and overruled. Some briefs were urging it but the Court did not move in that direction until 1952. At that time *Brown* v. *Board of Education* (344 U.S. 1) was set for argument with four other cases, each of which seemed, on the records before us, to present dual school systems where the facilities and curricula and teachers were "equal." Thus the continued validity of *Plessy* v. *Ferguson* was presented.

The cases were argued on December 9, 1952. On June 8, 1953, we set them down for reargument and suggested that five questions be argued (345 U.S. 972). When the cases had been argued in December of 1952, only four of us—Minton, Burton, Black and myself—felt that segregation was unconstitutional. Vinson was Chief Justice and he seemed to be firm that *Plessy* v. *Ferguson* should stand, and that the states should be allowed to deal with segregation in their own way and should be given time to make the black schools equal to those of the whites. Justice Reed held that segregation was on its way out and over the years would disappear, and that meanwhile the states should be allowed to handle it in their own way.

Frankfurter's view was that it was not unconstitutional to treat a Negro differently from a white but that the cases should be reargued. Jackson felt that nothing in the Fourteenth Amendment barred segregation and that it "would be bad for the Negroes" to be put in white schools, while Justice Clark said that since we had led the states to believe segregation was lawful, we should let them work out the problem by themselves.

It was clear that if a decision had been reached in the 1952 Term, we would have had five saying that separate but equal schools were constitutional, that separate but unequal schools were not constitutional, and that the remedy was to give the states time to make the two systems of schools equal.

The cases were ordered reargued, and Black and I were greatly relieved when that vote carried. By that time Vinson had died and Earl Warren had taken his place. The new Chief, sensing the deep division in the Court, did not press for a decision but made it clear he thought segregation was unconstitutional.

On December 12, 1953, at the first Conference after the second argument, Warren suggested that the cases be discussed informally and no vote be taken. He didn't want the Conference to split up into two opposed groups. Warren's approach to the problem and his discussions in Conference were conciliatory; not those of an advocate trying to convince recalcitrant judges. Frankfurter maintained the position that history supported the conclusions in *Plessy* that segregation was constitutional. Reed thought segregation was constitutional, and Jackson thought the issue was "political" and beyond judicial competence. Tom Clark was of the opinion that violence would follow if the Court ordered desegregation of the schools, but that while history sanctioned segregation, he would vote to abolish it if the matter was handled delicately.

It was suggested and decided that the new Chief Justice try his hand at this opinion. Opinions are usually typed by the Justice's office and sent to the printer in the basement, and then two or more printed copies are circulated to each of the other Justices' offices. This time we suggested that the Chief Justice's opinion not be circulated but that it be given to each individual Justice privately so that each could express his doubts and uncertainties before a formal opinion was circulated. When circulations are made formally there is always the possibility of a leak, and it was felt we should take the time needed to come up with an opinion that reflected the true opinion of the Court. With these thoughts in mind Chief Justice Warren personally handed to each of us one copy of his first draft of his opinion.

The four of us who had stood against *Plessy* v. *Ferguson* the first time these landmark cases were argued transmitted our approval of his opinion to him either orally or by a written note. With Warren we were in the majority, but a five-to-four decision was the last thing any of us wanted. It would not be a decisive decision historically. It would make the issue a political football and would make the filling of the next vacancy on the Court a Roman holiday.

As the days passed, Warren's position immensely impressed Frankfurter. The essence of Frankfurter's position seemed to be that if a practical politician like Warren, who had been governor of California for eleven years, thought we should overrule the 1896 opinion, why should a professor object? The fact that a worldly and wise man like Warren would stake his reputation on this issue not only impressed

Frankfurter but seemed to have a like influence on Reed and Clark. Clark followed shortly, Reed finally came around somewhat doubtfully, and only Jackson was left. Jackson had had a heart attack and was convalescing in the hospital, where Warren went to see him. I don't know what happened in the hospital room, but Warren returned to the Court triumphant. Jackson had said to count him in, which made the opinion unanimous. We could present a solid front to the country, and it was a brilliant diplomatic process which Warren had engineered.

The storm broke on May 17, 1954, the day the decision in *Brown* v. *Board of Education* was initially announced (347 U.S. 483).

The opinion, though unanimous, did not represent that solidity which unanimity implies. The first worries were expressed in the remedies to be decreed, the terms of the judgment to be entered. So we put down for reargument the question of relief (*Id.* 500). *Brown* was reargued April 11–14, 1955, and decided on May 31, 1955 (349 U.S. 294). We emphasized that the federal courts should require the local boards to "make a prompt and reasonable start toward full compliance with our May 17, 1954, ruling" (*Id.* 300). We recognized that additional time might be needed "arising from the physical condition of the school plant, the school transportation system, personnel, revision of school districts and attendance areas into compact units to achieve a system of determining admission to the public schools on a non-racial basis, and a revision of local laws and regulations which may be necessary in solving the foregoing problems" (*Id.* 300–301). We remanded the cases to the District Courts to move "with all deliberate speed" (*Id.* 301).

That phrase was put in because of Frankfurter's persuasion. He pointed out that it was an old equity expression, that Holmes as state judge had used it, that it expressed the tolerance and yet firmness which was required. (I later did research on the use of that phrase and I think Frankfurter overstated its history.) Some, including Black and me, were opposed, but everyone eventually acquiesced.

That phrase became a signal for delay. In Arkansas a District Court approved a desegregation program and then suspended the initiation of the program for two and a half years in order that new Arkansas laws, promoted by Governor Orville Faubus, could be challenged and tested in the courts. The Court of Appeals reversed the District Court, and in September of 1958 we affirmed the Court of Appeals (*Cooper* v. *Aaron*, 358 U.S. 1).

In 1957 some blacks were admitted to a high school in Little Rock, Arkansas. Local police removed them and Eisenhower sent federal troops to enforce the Court decree—and properly so. It is the duty of the President to "take care that the laws be faithfully executed" (Article II, Sect. 3 of the Constitution). Court decrees are of course part of "the laws." As a result of Eisenhower's order to move troops to Little Rock, eight black children attended the white high school for one school year (358 U.S. 12). But in 1958, on petition of the school board, the District Court—finding that "chaos, bedlam, and turmoil" had existed at this high school—changed the order approving the delay of the board's desegregation plan for two and a half years. It was that order the Court of Appeals reversed and we disapproved in *Cooper* v. *Aaron.* It was the governor and legislature of Arkansas that had created "violent resistance" to desegregation (*Id.* 15). "Thus law and order are not here to be preserved by depriving the Negro children of their Constitutional rights" (*Id.* 16).

Article VI of the Constitution makes the Constitution the "supreme law of the land" (*Id.* 18). Law and order are important. But it is not Faubus or Wallace or Nixon "law and order" but "constitutional law and order" that must be maintained.

Many areas in the North and East and West had segregated school systems, though not statutory dual systems. When it is shown that school authorities have installed a systematic program of segregation, the case is no different than a "dual system" so far as remedies are concerned. That appeared to be the case in Denver, which, we concluded in 1973, had used the "neighborhood school" concept as a manipulative device to encourage segregation (*Keyes* v. *School District No. 1, Denver, Colo.,* 413 U.S. 189). We remanded the case for full findings on these issues, and if the prima facie case shown by the black and Chicano minorities was made out, our direction was "all-out desegregation of the core city schools" (*Id.* 214).

All sorts of subterfuges were adopted. "Freedom of choice" was adopted in Virginia to block dismantling of a dual school system, and in 1968 we disapproved it (*Green* v. *County School Board,* 391 U.S. 430). Arkansas had a similar plan, which we also disapproved (*Raney* v. *Board of Education,* 391 U.S. 443). Mississippi used a plan giving a student the right freely to transfer to a school of his choice, zone residents having priority and no bus service being provided. After a year, all black elementary schools were all black, and only token transfers of blacks to white schools had been made. Fourteen years to come up with that plan was not using "all deliberate speed" (*Monroe* v. *Board of Commissioners*, 391 U.S. 450).

Not only did local authorities impede progress, but the decree, of course, bound only those states which were parties to the action. While most of them moved promptly, other states that had the same problem and that were advised that the segregated way of life was unconstitutional delayed and did nothing about the dismantling process.

The federal district judges faced with the problem of granting decrees which would result in the dismantling of dual school systems almost always resorted to busing as a remedy. Busing had been used prior to *Brown* as one means of preserving a dual school system. Thus many blacks were bused for miles to get them into a black school and to deprive them of attending the neighborhood school which was either all white or mixed.

Out West, where I come from, busing was not used to handle any racial problem; it was used extensively in small towns which otherwise would have been able to afford only a one-room school house in which students often would be crowded together from the first to the eighth grade. As the consolidated school movement gained momentum, local resources were pooled, and superior facilities were constructed and faculties assembled. Buses were used to bring the students to this better school. The youngsters who grew up in Goose Prairie, Washington, for example, would travel forty-eight miles in the morning to the school way down in the valley in Naches, and then back those forty-eight miles at night.

In the more recent cases involving *Brown,* busing was commonly used as the device best suited to putting an end to the dual school system. Many parents were upset that their children had to travel long distances. It was not an ideal solution, but in terms of coercion in the effort to dismantle the dual school system, it was effective.

But even with the busing, the dismantling process went very slowly. The problem kept coming back that usually the local school boards were predominantly white. Moreover, the school boards were resolved to keep the education of blacks at an inferior level. There were many competent black teachers, but the segregated way of life had so infected the nation that superior faculties which were 100 percent black were hard to find.

Ideally, a decree ordering that the inferior school buildings be razed and that new school buildings be erected in areas that would attract both whites and blacks would seem to have been a better remedy. But that would have been an expensive decree to supervise and administer, involving the raising of money locally for that purpose.

In 1972, eighteen years after our *Brown* decision, Virginia was still impeding the dismantling of its dual school system by establishing a new school (*Wright* v. *City of Emporia* (407 U.S. 451), and North Carolina was making a like effort (*United States* v. *Scotland Neck City*, 407 U.S. 484). While we struck down both schemes, they were both five-to-four decisions. Further division of the Court appeared in *Bradley* v. *State Board of Education of Virginia* (462 F 2d 1058), which we affirmed by an equally divided Court (412 U.S. 92), Mr. Justice Lewis F. Powell taking no part. The affirmance meant that the District Court was barred from uniting three school districts in a desegregation school plan in order to prevent the blacks in Richmond from being locked into a permanently black school, the end product of one dual school system.

A state ban on busing for and in school desegregation was held invalid in 1971 in *North Carolina State Board of Education* v. *Swann* (402 U.S. 43). Busing was a conventional means of implementing plans of desegregation which we approved the same year in *Swann* v. *Charlotte-Mecklenburg Board of Education* (402 U.S. 1, 30). Busing was not an issue on which the Court was in contention. The Court divided on the issue of the use of two or more school districts in metropolitan areas as the framework for a desegregation school plan. The practice first appeared in the Bradley case in 1973, in which we divided four to four. That fracture grew in 1974 in the Detroit school case, *Milliken* v. *Bradley* (418 U.S. 717), where the suburban area had the resources and the sophistication to command excellent schools, while the disadvantaged residents of the Detroit inner city did not.

Milliken, taken together with *San Antonio Independent School District* v. *Rodriguez* (411 U.S. 1) of 1973 is a great setback for school desegregation in metropolitan areas. *Rodriguez* involved a Texas scheme whereby each school district financed itself, the state sharing none of the costs—which meant that a school district with a ghetto had fewer funds for education than a plush white suburban area! *Rodriguez* was a five-to-four decision, holding that there was no violation of the Equal

Protection Clause of the Fourteenth Amendment when a state made poor school districts pay their own way. White, Douglas, Brennan and Marshall dissented.

That decision, coupled with *Milliken,* brought school desegregation to a halt in metropolitan areas where (as Richmond and Detroit illustrated) the ghetto core of the cities is black or some other racial minority, and the surrounding suburbs, in separate districts, white.

But even beyond the problems of *Swann* and *Rodriguez* was the controversy raised in another case, in 1974. It had become common practice for some graduate schools, law schools and bar associations to keep the entrance requirements high for whites but to admit blacks who might apply with lesser credentials. The question was extensively argued in *DeFunis* v. *Odegaard* (416 U.S. 312), which came out of the University of Washington Law School. The reasoning was that black people were at such a disadvantage in the educational system in American that they needed some concessions if we were to have black lawyers and judges, black dentists and doctors. Some argued that the Court should adopt a pro rata system: if a community was half black and half white, half of the entering class for a law school or medical school should be black also. This same argument was extended to bar associations. That seemed to me to be a wholly un-American practice, quite inconsistent with equal protection. It would promote aristocracy in this country —not an aristocracy of wealth or an aristocracy of race, but an aristocracy of talent, the best talents being recognized in all minority groups and each entitled to take his or her place at the top. I wrote out my views in *DeFunis,* but the Court did not rule on the case. Believing the case had become moot, it dismissed the issue. But, I felt the Court would have to revisit *DeFunis* in the future and decide which is the right path, for it is a constantly recurring question. The later Bakke and Weber cases, of course, were in the same area.

I feel that if blacks or any other minority are poorly prepared for the legal profession but are nevertheless admitted, the situation of the minorities will worsen. Many law schools admit blacks even though their credentials are not up to par, and this leads to the following tragedy: the black student graduates, enters the job market and is hired, perhaps as a law clerk. It is soon apparent, in these instances, that he cannot research a problem, or prepare a relevant memo, or draft a contract or a will. Years pass and he goes on from one law firm to another and finally ends up in the street—a wholly discredited professional person. This has a more deadly, killing impact than if he had been turned down at the entrance of the law school because he possessed inadequate credentials. Having reached the top and entered the market, he is told in no uncertain terms that the society that needs lawyers has no place for him.

The progress under *Brown* v. *Board of Education* was outrageously sluggish. "All deliberate speed" was used to drag feet, but even without that phrase the progress would have been slow, for the spirit of revolt against the Court's decision ran high. Legislators, governors and others running for public office thought up ingenious as well as ingenuous plans to forestall such programs.

They were encouraged to do so by President Eisenhower. This was one Court decision Eisenhower opposed and he so told a group of Southern governors, as related by Arthur Larson in *Eisenhower: The President Nobody Knew.* His words were: "I personally think the decision was wrong." It was common knowledge in Washington that such were Ike's views. He had played golf too long with the "wrong" people, those who preferred a caste system, to think otherwise. There was tragedy in that attitude, for if he had gone to the nation on television and radio telling the people to obey the law and fall into line, the cause of desegregation would have been accelerated. Ike was a hero and he was worshiped. Some of his political capital spent on the racial cause would have brought the nation closer to the constitutional standards. Ike's ominous silence on our 1954 decision gave courage to the racists who decided to resist the decision ward by ward, precinct by precinct, town by town, and county by county.

The *Brown* decision was, of course, violently opposed by Southern leaders. Debates, speeches and articles denounced the decision with vehemence. On March 12, 1956, nineteen senators and sixty-three congressmen, all from the South, signed a manifesto against the *Brown* decision. After reviewing the history of the "separate but equal" doctrine, this manifesto continued:

> This interpretation, restated time and again, became a part
> of the life of the people of many of the States and confirmed
> their habits, customs, traditions, and way of life. It is founded
> on elemental humanity and commonsense, for parents should

not be deprived by Government of the right to direct the lives and education of their own children.

Though there has been no constitutional amendment or act of Congress changing this established legal principle almost a century old, the Supreme Court of the United States, with no legal basis for such action, undertook to exercise their naked judicial power and substituted their personal political and social ideas for the established law of the land.

This unwarranted exercise of power by the Court, contrary to the Constitution, is creating chaos and confusion in the States principally affected. It is destroying the amicable relations between the white and Negro races that have been created through 90 years of patient effort by the good people of both races. It has planted hatred and suspicion where there has been heretofore friendship and understanding.

The statement concluded:

Even though we constitute a minority in the present Congress, we have full faith that a majority of the American people believe in the dual system of government which has enabled us to achieve our greatness and will in time demand that the reserved rights of the States and of the people be made secure against judicial usurpation.

We pledge ourselves to use all lawful means to bring about a reversal of this decision which is contrary to the Constitution and to prevent the use of force in its implementation.

It was common criticism to say that the Court was changing the Constitution to suit its tastes. Segregation was, of course, not ensconced in the Constitution. *Plessy* v. *Ferguson* had approved segregation of the races in public facilities. While that was a constitutional decision, the Court never had hesitated to overrule a constitutional adjudication. Throughout our history, dozens of such decisions had been overruled by subsequent Courts and at least one of those was over ninety years old (see *Erie R. Co.* v. *Tompkins,* 304 U.S. 64). The question was not whether the case was too old to overrule; the overriding consideration was whether the old interpretation suited modern needs, modern problems.

If a state had required Jews to ride separate trolleys, use separate toilets, attend separate schools, I suppose no one would have thought that system would provide "equal protection." Rather, it would seem to contain the seeds of rank discrimination—a setting apart of one group because it was thought to be inferior, obnoxious, harmful to society, or the like. Historically, unpopular people had been confined to certain quarters or regions of a city. Segregation is kin to that separateness of treatment.

All of this was, of course, known in 1896 when *Plessy* v. *Ferguson* was decided. Why was not the segregation of the blacks therefore obviously unequal protection of the laws? The reason, I think, was that the blacks never got rid of the shadow of slavery. Emancipation meant escape from slavery, not escape into full first-class citizenship. Under that theory, white people justified the lesser type of discrimination in the form of segregation.

Moreover, the limitation of federal courts to "cases" or "controversies" means that court decrees run to only a small group in one case. Johnny Jones may win his case against a school board, but that does not help Susie Smith against her school board. Those who opposed *Brown*, therefore, could fight pupil by pupil, school by school, district by district; and they did just that, dragging out the problem indefinitely.

Such progress as the Court made was due entirely to the lower courts. Of the lower courts, the most important were the district courts. Their findings of fact could, if slanted against *Brown*, give refuge to segregationists for years. District judges who stood firm gave solidity to what in Washington was a rather fragile structure. While *Brown* v. *Board of Education* was unanimous, there were differing views in our councils. Only the firmness of district judges gave stability to our decision. The district judges had the great tradition of living "under the law" and obeying it. I cannot name all of those who gave solid foundation to *Brown*, but I want to mention J. Skelly Wright in Louisiana and Frank M. Johnson in Alabama, who deserve a great deal of credit for what progress was made in this area.

Skelly Wright, a native of Louisiana, came from a poor family and worked his way through Loyola Law School. He was admitted to the Louisiana Bar and was Assistant U.S. Attorney in New Orleans from 1937 to 1946, and later United States Attorney from 1948 to 1949. He argued several cases before our Court. The one I best remember was *Francis* v. *Resweber* (329 U.S. 459), in which a man who was sentenced to death withstood the electrical charge and brought suit to enjoin the second attempt to execute him. Skelly Wright's claim was that his client had been denied due process by reason of the infliction of cruel and unusual punishment in violation of the Fourteenth and Eighth Amendments. Only Murphy, Rutledge and I shared that view, so Francis was successfully electrocuted.

Wright was appointed federal district judge by President Truman in 1949, and that was the beginning of a very distinguished judicial career. He was soon the center of many storms gathering around the rights of blacks in a state which at the time was dominantly racist, as least as far as its leaders were concerned.

In 1950 Wright wrote for a three-judge court, which included Judges Wayne G. Borah and Herbert W. Christenberry, that consistent with the Equal Protection Clause, Louisiana could not refuse admission of a black into its white law school if the state created law schools for blacks that did not afford "educational advantages equal or substantially equal to those that he would receive" at a white law school (*Wilson* v. *Board of Supervisors,* 92 F Supp. 986, 988).

In 1954 the legislature of Louisiana passed a series of acts to circumvent *Brown* v. *Board of Education.* It amended the state constitution to mandate separate schools for whites and blacks, and to give each superintendent of schools in each parish the right to determine what school each child should attend. The standard of these determinations was segregation and Judge Wright enjoined the operation of that law (*Bush* v. *Orleans Parish School Board,* 138 F Supp. 337).

When Judge Wright ordered the New Orleans School Board to file a desegregation plan, it replied that Louisiana laws barred it from doing so. The court of Judges Wright, Richard T. Rives and Christenberry filed its own plan of desegregation. Louisiana sued the school board to restrain it from desegregating the schools. The legislature then quickly passed a law giving itself, the legislature, the right to determine what schools should be desegregated. Wright and his colleagues held that no legislature had the right to decide whether a public school should be segregated or not (*Bush* v. *Orleans Parish School Board,* 187 F Supp. 42). That clearly was one teaching of the *Brown* case. Louisiana passed another law putting the schools in the hands of the governor until such time as the legislature should determine what schools should be desegregated. The Wright court held that law unconstitutional, as it permitted the governor to operate the schools on a segregated basis (*Id.* 44). Another act of the legislature gave the governor the right to close any school that was ordered integrated. That act was also held unconstitutional (*Id.* 45). Still another act withheld, under criminal sanctions, free school books, supplies, lunch and all state funds from integrated schools, and that act was also held to be unconstitutional (*Id.* 45).

In response to the first Bush case, the Louisiana legislature took further action. The Court's proposed integration plan was modest, involving initially only the first grade. The New Orleans School Board finally admitted five black girls into the first grade at two white schools. The legislature then undertook to vest control of the public schools in itself and to deny the school board any control of its own funds. Wright and his two associates held those acts invalid in a 1960 decision (*Bush* v. *Orleans Parish School Board,* 190 F Supp. 861, 866). It also declared the school board to be the rightful owner of its own bank accounts. The legislature also appointed the state Attorney General as counsel for the school board, replacing the board's counsel. While that normally would be a local question, the court struck down the action on the ground that it was part of the harassment of the legislature against the school board because the board had undertaken a first step toward integration (*Id.* 867).

In the third Bush case (194 F Supp. 182), the United States asked the Wright court to declare certain acts of the Louisiana legislature unconstitutional. One act punished a parent for accepting anything of value as an inducement to sending a child to a desegregated school. A companion act made it a crime to offer a child, parent, teacher or school employee anything which might influence that person to perform any act "in violation of any law of this state." The Wright court noted that these acts were "invidious weapons of a state administration dedicated to scuttling the modest program of desegregation which has been initiated in Orleans Parish" (*Id.* 185). The Court noted that although federal courts rarely enjoined state criminal prosecution, these acts were subterfuge measures to defeat the court's orders and forestall the regime of *Brown* v. *Board of Education.* It therefore enjoined their enforcement.

The last school decision by Judge Wright was another Bush case (204 F Supp. 568). It was decided in 1962, shortly before he was nominated to the Court of Appeals for the District of Columbia. The school board assigned all children to racially segregated schools in their residential areas. First graders—and first graders only—were subjected to tests.

After testing, only 4 black first graders out of 134 applicants were allowed to transfer to the white schools nearest their homes, and only 8 black children out of 66 passed the second year. As a result only 12 of the approximately 13,000 black children entering the first grade during those two years were allowed to attend predominantly white schools. Judge Wright ruled: "[A] pupil placement law may only be validly applied in an integrated school system and then only where no consideration is based on race. To assign children to a segregated school system and then require them to pass muster under a pupil placement law is discrimination in its rawest form" (*Id.* 570–571).

Judge Wright also held that black schools were more crowded than the white, that the pupil-teacher ratio was higher for blacks than for whites, that the black schools were quite unequal to the white schools in violation even of *Plessy* v. *Ferguson,* which had sanctified separate but equal treatment. Thereupon Judge Wright amended his prior order and allowed all children in grades one through six to attend white public schools nearest their homes or the formerly all-black public schools nearest their homes, at their option. He also authorized the transfer of children from one school to another as long as the transfers were not based on race. In addition, he prohibited the Louisiana Pupil Placement plan from being applied as long as the New Orleans School Board operated a dual school system based on racial segregation.

That case was decided on April 3, 1962. By May 23 Judge Frank Ellis (who retired after three years because of a disability) had taken Judge Wright's place, and while in the main he supported Wright's position, he revoked Wright's order to desegregate the first six grades and substituted a provision that one grade a year should be integrated, and the dual system as respects each grade abolished at the same time (205 F Supp. 893).

Earlier in 1962, Judge Wright had decided *Guillory* v. *Administration of Tulane University* (203 F Supp. 855). Tulane claimed to be a "private" institution, but a Louisiana statute required that Tulane admit only whites, and that act was permissible under the state constitution. Hence the state sanctioned racial discrimination, which it could not legally do under the *Brown* decision. Judge Wright held that the long relation between Tulane and the state made it a state agency and thus subject to *Brown.* His decision was based on the fact that the university held a special legislative franchise, it had a tax exemption from the state, it received revenues from state lands, and three public officials were on its board. In December of 1962 Judge Ellis granted a rehearing and held that Tulane was not a state agency but a private institution (306 F 2d 489).

The Court of Appeals of the Fifth Circuit said that the Bush case (308 F 2d 491) was "Exhibit A" for the slowness of "all deliberate speed." The action had started in 1951 when black parents asked that the New Orleans public schools be desegregated. Suit started in 1952, but it was suspended while *Brown* worked its way through the Court. After *Brown* was decided, the Bush case went to trial with Judge Wright ordering desegregation "with all deliberate speed," but in 1962 the litigation was still pending and the issue not fully resolved. If it were not for Judge Wright, any measurable "speed" would have been unlikely.

Judge Wright's decisions, which he unwaveringly made, made him and his family targets of hostile people. A cross was burned on his lawn one night, hate mail poured in to him, much of it threatening his life. His wife, Helen, at home alone with a small son, received a barrage of telephone calls hour after hour, day after day. These were threatening, insulting, vulgar calls from people promising retribution against her and the child for her husband's opinions.

The Wrights were cut to the quick by many episodes. Old acquaintances, seeing them coming down the sidewalk, would cross the street to avoid them. In private homes some guests were so hostile they would not shake hands with them. A long-standing friend of Helen's who had worked with her on a cancer problem said she was now embarrassed to be seen with her. Jim Wright, then thirteen years old, was badly hurt by the jibes of his contemporaries. Skelly Wright was called Smelly Wright. Attorney General Jack Paul Faustin Gremillion, who was later accused and convicted of other crimes, was cited for contempt for his disrespectful remarks about the Wright court. In an aside to the press table, while he was leaving the courtroom, Gremillion had said, "This is a kangaroo court."

In November 1960 the legislature was in constant session, passing twenty-nine bills designed to thwart desegregation. Wright and his colleagues struck down all of them. As a result the community was so hostile that six detectives were assigned to protect the Wrights around the clock, two at a time in eight-hour shifts.

William Rogers, Attorney General in Washington, let the U.S. Attorney General intervene in the cases before Judge Wright and sent marshals to escort black girls into schools. On November 14, 1960, Wright enjoined the legislature from interfering with school integration. That day, black buttons, called mourner's buttons and stamped with "11/14/60," appeared by the thousands, and petitions for impeachment of Skelly Wright were circulated.

Often Judge Wright sat alone on a case nursing it along until violence had ebbed a bit. He may have delayed decisions at times because of the mob attitude, but he never changed his opinion and did not shift even one degree to the left or to the right. He was committed to the Constitution and applied it as he understood it.

His two staunch judicial allies in the most tumultuous days were Circuit Judge Richard Rives and District Judge Herbert Christenberry, with whom he sat on many of the explosive issues. Skelly Wright, however, was always in command and the chances are that if an opinion was per curiam (not bearing the author's name), Skelly Wright wrote it. At least that is what the intrinsic evidence indicates.

The time came during Jack Kennedy's Administration when there was a vacancy on the Supreme Court, and he asked me if I had any suggestions. I said he should name Skelly Wright. Jack was undecided at first and then concluded that he could never get Judge Wright by Mississippi Senator James O. Eastland of the Senate Judiciary Committee.

"You can get him by, Mr. President," I replied, "although it may take six months."

"It would be a terrific battle."

"But that is the kind of battle to pick—and you would win," I said.

Sometime later Bobby Kennedy, who was then Attorney General, called me to say that it could not be Skelly Wright for our Court. There was, however, a vacancy on the Court of Appeals for the Fifth Circuit, which is in the South, and Bobby asked, "How about Skelly for that?" I said it was not as good as having him on the Supreme Court, but it was second best. More time passed and Bobby came back to me saying there would be a fight getting Skelly confirmed for the Court of Appeals. My reply was "Hogwash."

In the end, Bobby told me they were sending up the name of J. Skelly Wright to fill a vacancy on the Court of Appeals for the District of Columbia. It was a bitter pill for me to swallow because the South needed a Skelly Wright on one of its courts and the Supreme Court needed a Skelly Wright on it, for on racial problems our Court was much more fragile than the appearances indicated.

Unfortunately, politics shunted Wright to Washington on a lower court. Jack Kennedy, being in his first term, was playing for solidarity with the South—which meant solidarity with the racists.

Another champion of the Constitution, believer in the supremacy of the law and stalwart defender of civil liberties is Judge Frank M. Johnson, the district judge for Alabama's twenty-three southeastern counties. He was named to the bench in 1955 by President Eisenhower when he was only thirty-seven, which made him one of the youngest federal judges in the nation. It was Frank Johnson and his interpretation and enforcement of the U.S. Constitution that brought about social and political changes that affected all of Alabama, the South and the nation.

Frank Johnson grew up in northern Alabama's Winston County. Winston County, many have forgotten, seceded from Alabama in 1861 when the state seceded from the Union, saying the county was "not going to take up arms against the rebels, but at the same time it is not going to shoot at the flag of our fathers', Old Glory, the flag of Washington, Jefferson, and Jackson."

The people who settled in the hills of northern Alabama started homesteading in the 1820s and 1830s. The land was not suited to the plantation way of life. Only a few had slaves, with the bulk of the settlers having a rough time eking out a living. Perhaps the sectionalism that grew up between the northern hill country of Alabama and the rest of the state was due in part to slavery, but there were earlier differences, particularly as to the allotment of seats in the state legislature. (The conditions suffered by the people of "The Free State of Winston," between Confederates conscripting men and Yankees raiding the hill country, is told by Wesley S. Thompson in a book by that name which was published in 1968.) In 1867 the people of Winston County organized a Republican Party. Frank Johnson was from a family that played a leading role in Republican politics: his great-grandfather was the first Republican sheriff of Fayette County, and at one point his father was the only Republican in the Alabama legislature.

Frank Johnson took his law degree at the University of Alabama, and one of his classmates was George Wallace. As governor, Wallace defied desegregation, while Judge Johnson promoted it, delicately but firmly and unambiguously; and it is a wonder to many how the sensitive problem was managed without Governor Wallace being cited for contempt.

The fifties and early sixties were not easy years for Frank Johnson and his family. His mother had her home bombed in retaliation, and the recriminations against Judge Johnson, his wife and his son were bitter. Nevertheless, he went his own dogged way, never deviating from the straight path indicated by the Constitution. A wife, more dependent on social affairs, is apt to suffer more, and so is a son who faces the jeers of those of his own generation. Periodically Frank Johnson had bodyguards, but even during the most troubled times he was as unruffled as a professor presiding over a boisterous class. He, in Alabama, and Skelly Wright, in Louisiana, brought new dignity and meaning to "constitutional law and order."

Frank Johnson emphasized his belief in the supremacy of the law in a speech to newly naturalized citizens on May 1, 1967:

> It is necessary, now more than ever, that the responsible American citizen realize and discharge his obligation constantly to support and defend the proposition that our law is supreme and must be obeyed. This means that irresponsible criticism—by those who can hardly read the Constitution, much less study it and interpret it—must not be allowed to stand unchallenged.
>
> When those who frustrate the law, who undermine judicial decisions, run riot and provide uncurbed leadership for a return to nothing more than medieval savagery, for the responsible American citizen to remain silent is tantamount to cowardice; it is a grievous injustice to the proposition that in America the law is supreme.

Brown was decided in 1954, yet no black attended white primary or secondary schools in Alabama until 1963. Even when resistance declined, integration was at a token level. In 1963–64, eleven states in the South had only 1.17 percent of their black students in schools with whites. In 1964–65 it reached 2.25 percent, and in 1965–66 it reached 6.01 percent; but even then, Alabama had less than one percent of blacks attending schools with whites. By 1966, though most of the school districts were officially in compliance, the *actual* attendance of blacks in formerly all-white schools was still under 16 percent.

In 1953, prior to *Brown,* the Alabama legislature appointed a committee to prepare for maintenance of segregated schools. The Alabama constitution in Section 256 expressly prohibited the operation of desegregated schools. The committee proposed its repeal and the substitution of three measures.

1. It recommended a pupil assignment law which contained a clause requiring students to continue in their old schools unless their parents applied for a transfer.

2. It provided for a system of administrative review and appeal to the state courts which would make such parent applications moot by the time it could reach a federal court.

3. It permitted a parent to keep his child out of any school "in which the races are comingled" and gave state aid to children who withdrew from integrated schools.

By 1958 the Alabama legislature repealed the compulsory school-attendance laws and authorized school districts to close any of their schools if the local board determined that their operation would create "such tensions, friction or potential disorder or ill will" as substantially "to impair effective standards or objectives of education," or impair "peace, order and good will" in the community or school district. The local boards were authorized to turn the closed schools over to "private" schools created to avoid desegregation. The legislature also passed a law making a school board non-suable. Thus, when a personnel board refused to allow a black to take a competitive examination to become a policeman, the state courts held the board non-suable (267 Ala. 108).

The greatest weapon the state had was the threat to close the public schools rather than desegregate. That issue was decided by the Supreme Court in a Virginia case, *Griffin* v. *County School Board* (377 U.S. 218), in an opinion written by Hugo Black which was handed down in May of 1964. Mr. Justice Clark and Mr. Justice Harlan disagreed with the holding that the federal courts are empowered to order the reopening of the public schools in question, but they otherwise joined in the Court's opinion.

Meanwhile Judge Johnson had ordered Macon County to prepare a desegregation school plan by the fall of 1963. It undertook to do so, adopting a partial plan, but Governor Wallace sent out the troopers and closed one high school. When the school reopened a week later, whites were admitted but blacks were denied entrance. Johnson and his colleagues enjoined Wallace from such action. The whites thereupon transferred to all-white schools in other towns or to private segregated schools.

In 1963 Judge Johnson ordered twelve black students admitted to all-white Tuskegee High School. The State Board of Education, of which the governor was a member, closed Tuskegee High School and transferred the black students to an all-black school. Johnson ordered that the blacks be admitted to the schools in the nearby town to which the whites had been transferred. The mayor of that town then prevented blacks from entering, claiming that their attendance would create a fire hazard. Johnson enjoined the mayor (231 F Supp. 772), but the white students withdrew and the schools remained open with only blacks in attendance.

A few years later a three-judge court, with Judges Rives and Grooms also sitting, ordered state-wide desegregation of the schools (231 F Supp. 743). It overturned the tuition-grant statute; it ordered that, beginning in 1967, plans for desegregation be adopted within twenty days covering all grades. It also ordered desegregation of state trade schools and some colleges; and it required equalization of facilities in all public schools (267 F Supp. 458). That was on March 22, 1967. Satisfactory desegregation plans were adopted by 28 of the 99 school systems in the state.

The 1967 Alabama legislature gave public school students the right to choose the race of their teacher and authorized the governor to withhold public funds from any school district failing to require students to make that choice. Judge Johnson and his associates held both acts unconstitutional.

The freedom-of-choice plan resulted in a school board closing one black school because only two blacks were in attendance in an otherwise all-white school. A state court ordered the school reopened and Judge Johnson's court held that the state court had transgressed the federal decree.

Alabama had operated dual athletic programs. Judge Johnson's court ordered the two athletic associations to merge (283 F Supp. 194).

By reason of Johnson's court orders, 598 black teachers were assigned to formerly white schools, and 400 white teachers to formerly black schools. Piece by piece, the entire school system of Alabama became more and more desegregated. The supervision of Judge Johnson's court was painstaking in detail and thorough in its reform (317 F Supp. 103).

The Department of Health, Education and Welfare had issued guidelines for school desegregation. The legislature passed a law prohibiting the boards from following those guidelines. That, too, was held invalid (269 F Supp. 346).

Frank Johnson's racial decisions, like those of Skelly Wright, touched on numerous aspects of the problem: voting rights, criminal prosecutions for violating the civil rights of citizens, recreational facilities such as parks and other municipal areas. Each stood tall and firm in all of these racial issues.

Judge Johnson presided over *United States* v. *Eaton,* a criminal trial under 18 U.S.C. 241. Viola Luizzo was killed while participating in the Selma demonstrations in 1965. Three whites were charged with her murder in a state court and acquitted. Then a federal prosecution was brought under Sec. 241 charging a conspiracy to deprive citizens of their civil rights, which in the case included petitioning government for redress of grievances, a right protected by the First and Fourteenth Amendments. The federal jury convicted, and Johnson sentenced each defendant to ten years.

What Judge Johnson said in his charge to the jury contains the principle of the supremacy of the law which he and Judge Wright brilliantly represented in a troubled time:

> I cannot be, as Judge of this court, and you cannot be, as jurors serving in this court on this case, if we discharge our duty and responsibility in the manner that our oath requires, be concerned with the wisdom or the policy of the law. Because we are a government of laws, we are required in matters involving the law and the application of the law to, whether we like it or whether we don't like it, accept the law and make a proper and an unbiased application of it in any given instance.

Chapter VI

Separation of Powers

Perhaps the deepest division in the Court in my time, as we have discussed in the chapter on "Contending Schools of Thought," concerned the "political" question; an issue which has always plagued American law. In the federal system, Article III of the Constitution gives federal courts jurisdiction only over cases that are questions or controversies, but not every controversy presents a justiciable question. Should this country have an ambassador at the Vatican, and if so, who should be named? Which of two competing candidates should be seated by the Senate or the House? Should a law passed by Congress be approved or vetoed? Issues of that kind often present great controversies, but they are not suited for resolution from the judicial branch, since, according to the Constitution, they have been entrusted to the other two branches of government for deliberation and eventual solution.

The main test, as stated in *Baker* v. *Carr* (369 U.S. 186, 217), is whether there can be "found a textually demonstrable constitutional commitment of the issue to a coordinate political department." But whenever the Executive or Congress moves in on the individual, arrests him, fines him, imprisons him or causes him to suffer some disability, the theory is that a case or controversy fit for *judicial* determination has been presented.

Dean James Bradley Thayer of Harvard Law School had a great influence on many jurists including Holmes, Learned Hand and Frankfurter. Many of his works, particularly his biography of John Marshall and an article published in the *Harvard Law Review,* substantially cut down the kinds of questions that were justiciable and enlarged the number of cases which were "political."* These views were often quoted in our reports (e.g., *Board of Education* v. *Barnette,* 319 U.S. 667–670) by those who believed in the policy of judicial abstinence. Thayer's theory was that if a citizen could run to a court to resolve a question, the republican form of government would suffer because most citizen's complaints were better answered by the legislative branch of government, and going to the legislature would tend to promote a more active citizenry. This philosophy had, I think, a profound effect on Holmes, who was of the Harvard school, and it also had a profound effect on Frankfurter. I think he gave special credence to it because of Holmes.

Holmes did our society a grave injustice when, in 1903, writing for a majority of six, he held that Negroes could not bring an action in the federal courts to protect their constitutional right to vote by forcing state officers to register them (*Giles* v. *Harris,* 189 U.S. 475). Why? Because, he said, the issue was "political" not "justiciable." The remedy, in other words, was to be found in political procedures; there was not a judicial remedy.

Yet imagine! What "political" remedies did black people have in Alabama at the turn of the century? The votes were with the whites, and control was in the hands of the anti-black political machine. The voices of blacks were muted, for they had no audience. The whites put them in their "proper" place, and kept them there. They were citizens by reason of the Fourteenth Amendment, but their citizenship was second-class. There are, of course, as Holmes said, many "political" issues which are left either for the executive or the legislative exclusively, issues in which the judiciary has no hand. But the protection of the right to vote, expressly conferred by the Constitution, is grist for the judicial mill, as dozens upon dozens of cases illustrate. When Holmes rejected the Negroes' plea in 1903, he left them without an effective remedy for sixty years. Congress in time acted, but meanwhile two

**John Marshall (New York: Houghton Mifflin, 1901); and "The Origin and Scope of the American Doctrine of Constitutional Law," *Harvard Law Review,* Vol. 7, No. 3, pp. 129–156.

generations of black people were denied the franchise. Political equality, as envisaged by the Constitution, was long defeated, and conditions in the ghettoes festered.

If the ballot a man casts is not counted, a wrong is done and there are remedies. If a man casts his ballot and someone stuffs the ballot box with phony ballots, diluting his ballot, there are remedies in the federal courts. Why, then, should there not be a remedy in the courts for comparable wrongs, as for example when one person's vote is diluted by a state legislature in more sophisticated ways?

State legislatures frequently allowed what is known in England as rotten boroughs to be created—for example, giving a district that was sparsely populated as much representation as a heavily populated district, or giving a rural district as much voting power as an urban district with twenty times the population of the rural district. The obvious remedy was for the citizens of the states to get legislative action, but the legislatures were not easily moved and the problem continued to rankle. This was, indeed, the heart of the county unit system in Georgia which enabled the rural vote to control the state (*Gray* v. *Sanders,* 372 U.S. 368).

Some judges, notably Frankfurter, held that the apportionment of votes was not fit business for the federal courts (*Colegrove* v. *Green,* 328 U.S. 549, 556). The area was dubbed a "political thicket" which the federal courts should not enter. And the Frankfurter view was often cited by authors as being the view of the Court.

But the Court had never so held. While a majority had each time refused to entertain such a suit, the reasons varied. For example, it was common to say that the particular suit had "no equity" in the sense that the challenged election would be over before a federal court could adjudicate the merits. When *Baker* v. *Carr*—which challenged the failure of Tennessee to reapportion state legislators among the counties despite substantial population changes—triggered a careful analysis of the apportionment decisions, it became clear that the Court had never endorsed the Frankfurter view.

The Conference vote on whether the question of reapportionment was "political" rather than "justiciable" was five to four. Justice Stewart was one of the five, though his vote was tentative, dependent on whether thorough research and a close analysis of the cases would disclose that the question was not foreclosed by prior decisions. If it had been previously decided that the question was "political," he was inclined to follow precedent and not change course in such turbulent times and on such a controversial issue.

Chief Justice Warren assigned the opinion to Justice Brennan on the theory that if anyone could convince Stewart, Brennan was the one. Brennan worked long and hard on the opinion, its length being due to the exhaustive and detailed examination of precedents which he undertook. When he finished the first draft he showed it to Stewart, who approved; and there was a broad Irish grin on his face when he told me that the fifth vote was secure. He then circulated the opinion and quickly obtained the concurrence of the Chief, Black and myself. The dissents were circulated; and just before the Conference at which *Baker* v. *Carr* was to be cleared for Monday release, Tom Clark circulated a concurring opinion. Without talking to anyone, he had changed his mind and written a short concurrence, which, if it had happened earlier, would have made Brennan's long, scholarly but tedious opinion unnecessary.

Baker v. *Carr* came down six to two (Charles E. Whittaker did not participate in the decision of the case), holding that reapportionment was within the judicial competence. That case was followed in 1964 by *Reynolds* v. *Sims* (377 U.S. 533), holding that the constitutional principle of "one man, one vote" was the standard by which an apportionment was to be judged. Thus did the Court mark the beginning of the end of America's "rotten boroughs." Thus was the bugaboo of the "political" question put to rest.

Between 1962, when *Baker* v. *Carr* was decided, and 1970, thirty-six states had reapportioned either voluntarily or under pressure of judicial decrees, making a reality of the constitutional standard "one man, one vote," reversing a long tradition of making certain blocs of voters more powerful than others.

By its long neglect of these problems, the Supreme Court added greatly to the tension that produced the explosions in the 1960s. Holmes had shut the door of the federal courts for relief against denial of the right to vote. A segregated way of life, imposed by the Black Codes in the South after the Civil War, had received the constitutional blessing of the Court on an eight-to-one vote in 1896. As a result of these two Court decisions, the country wasted precious years while racial problems increased.

The issue was more emotional than rational. Racism sanctified, justified and rationalized segregation. As a result, the issue was seldom debated or discussed in terms of the mandate of the Fourteenth Amendment: that a state should accord all her citizens equal protection, irrespective of race, creed or color.

That is a very important value judgment. But it is a value written into our Constitution by the Fourteenth Amendment. Some critics have said that the Court should apply only "neutral" principles. But, on most issues, the Constitution is not "neutral." It vigorously champions freedom of expression, not censorship; it declares against self-incrimination, not for inquisition; it proclaims against the establishment of a religion by the state; and in numerous like ways, picks and chooses one set of values as against others. The Constitution is not neutral when it comes to race; and a Court, therefore, that undertook to pose as neutral would not be faithful to the constitutional scheme.

It was common in those days for Congress to take retaliatory steps once an unpopular decision was handed down by the Court. Usually a bill was introduced modifying the Court's appellate jurisdiction, which Congress has some power to do under Article III of the Constitution. For example, if a state decision was reversed, holding that the state could not bar a man from practicing law because he was a so-called subversive, a bill would be introduced depriving the Court of appellate jurisdiction over cases from state courts concerning admission to practice law. At other times a constitutional amendment was proposed. On July 5, 1957, largely in response to our *Brown* decision, a Joint Congressional Resolution was offered which provided the following amendment:

> The Senate of the United States shall comprise a court with final appellate jurisdiction to review decisions and judgments of the Supreme Court of the United States where questions of the powers reserved to the States, or the people, are either directly or indirectly involved and decided. The Senate's exercise of such final appellate jurisdiction shall be under such rules and regulations as may be provided by the Senate, including the time within which appeals shall be taken. A decision of the Senate affirming, modifying, or reversing a decision or judgment of the Supreme Court of the United States shall be final.

None of these legislative measures was adopted, but they were numerous, running into the dozens over a period of a decade.

• • •

The other side of the "political" question is that, of course, the Court must guard itself against the influence of "politics." Mr. Justice Holmes once wrote in a famous dissent:

> Great cases like hard cases make bad law. For great cases are called great, not by reason of their real importance in shaping the law of the future, but because of some accident of immediate overwhelming interest which appeals to the feelings and distorts the judgment. These immediate interests exercise a kind of hydraulic pressure which makes what previously was clear seem doubtful, and before which even well settled principles of law will bend. What we have to do in this case is to find the meaning of some not very difficult words. We must try, I have tried, to do it with the same freedom of natural and spontaneous interpretation that one would be sure of if the same question arose upon an indictment for a similar act which excited no public attention, and was of importance only to a prisoner before the court. Furthermore, while at times judges need for their work the training of economists or statesmen, and must act in view of their foresight of consequences, yet when their task is to interpret and apply the words of a statute, their function is merely academic to begin with—to read English intelligently—and a consideration of consequences comes into play, if at all, only when the meaning of the words used is open to reasonable doubt.*

We have on a few occasions taken cases from the Court of Appeals prior to judgment. *Ex parte Quirin* (317 U.S. 1) was one, and it was unfortunate the Court took the case. It involved German saboteurs who landed in the United States and were tried by a military commission. We heard the case on July 29–30, 1942, and on July 31 issued a per curiam setting forth our conclusion that the military trial was lawful and that there was no cause to discharge the prisoners by habeas corpus (*Id.* 19).

We filed a full-dress opinion written for the Court by Chief Justice Stone on October 29, 1942. While it was easy to agree on the original per curiam, we almost fell far apart when it came time to write out the

Northern Securities Co. v. *United States* (193 U.S. 197, 400–401).

views. The Attorney General, Francis Biddle, told the Court that the claims of the saboteurs were so frivolous, the Army was going to go ahead and execute the men whatever the Court did; that the Executive would simply not tolerate any delay. That was a blatant affront to the Court. Whether FDR had authorized it I don't know. Biddle, a man of facts and not given to impulsive action, was telling the Court that he had little respect for its intrusion. That view was at war with the idea that the Pentagon—our most powerful federal agency—like the humble person in the ghetto, lived under a regime of law which it could not manufacture to suit its mood.

In 1947 we took *United States* v. *United Mine Workers* (330 U.S. 258) from the Court of Appeals before judgment. A District Court had held John L. Lewis in contempt of court and fined him $10,000 and his union $3.5 million. The case came on in a blaze of anti-Lewis public sentiment. The Court was divided; Chief Justice Vinson was convinced that John L. Lewis was "too big for his britches." It was a bad day for law. The majority of our Court haggled over the fine the union should pay. All but Vinson thought $3.5 million was too much. It was finally set at $700,000. How our Court had the power to set a fine in a criminal case which it never heard at the trial level is strange indeed. For the first time I saw passion sweeping my Brethren and sending them pell-mell to a public stand against John L. Lewis. The man had his weak points, but he battled as no union leader had ever done for the rights of coal miners. He was arrogant and a master at creating pungent phrases, as when he called Jack Garner "an evil, whiskey-drinking, poker-playing old man." But the coal operators were also arrogant. We had no business taking sides. But Washington, D.C., seemed to heave a sigh of relief when Vinson lowered the boom on John L. Lewis.

In June 1974 we lifted the Nixon case out of the Court of Appeals for the District of Columbia before judgment and sat on July 8 to hear argument (*United States* v. *Nixon,* 418 U.S. 683). Burger and I had strongly opposed taking the cases. The Court of Appeals had resolved an earlier dispute between the District Court and the White House over tapes withheld from the grand jury (487 F [2d] 700). The new cases involved not the grand jury but the criminal trial of six defendants. The Court of Appeals, having decided the grand jury case, would promptly have decided the new Nixon cases. Brennan felt strongly that we should take the cases, and so did Marshall. If we declined to do so, Brennan said he would write in dissent. As the discussion passed around the table the opinion seemed to be shaping up in the minds of Stewart, Blackmun and Powell that the cases should be taken. There seemed to be a feeling that the Court had a "duty" to step in and clarify the Watergate mess. I felt we should refrain. I said the Court of Appeals would quickly affirm the District Court on the basis of its opinion in 487 F(2d) 700 and that we could quickly deny certiorari. We should deny it, I said, because the legal and constitutional claims were "frivolous" and insofar as they involved the "impeachment" process, they were "political," not justiciable.

When the briefs were filed and I studied them, it was plain that the Nixon lawyers were angling for us to muddy the waters so as to slow down the impeachment procedure.

There was a cleavage in the Court which reflected, in part, differences of opinion about the First Amendment as it concerns trial by jury. I refer to the area of law known as contempt by publication.

It had long been settled in England and in many states in this country that a newspaper commenting upon pending litigation in a court could be punished for contempt by a judge in a similar proceeding. The test was whether the news article or editorial had a reasonable tendency to obstruct the administration of justice or to cast doubt upon the fitness of a judge to sit. The traditional view was that this power of the courts was an implied authority to protect the judiciary against assaults and to vindicate its authority. Many great battles were raised over the years in this area, but the problems that emerged were phrased not so much in terms of the First Amendment as in terms of the right to a jury trial. The Sixth Amendment of the Constitution guarantees a jury trial in all criminal prosecutions. A contempt proceeding initiated by a judge was different in some respects from the one initiated by the prosecutor. There was no information charging offenses by the grand jury. The judge himself instituted the proceedings, and he tried the case without the benefit of a jury.

During the last century, Congress dealt with this problem and had greatly narrowed the power of a federal judge to hold a person in criminal contempt. The statute as rewritten by Congress defined crimes punishable as contempt as conduct in the presence of the court or so near the court as to obstruct the administration of justice. The statute came before the Court in 1917 in the case of *Toledo Newspaper Co.* v. *United States* (247 U.S. 402), in which the Court held that a newspaper editor could be tried in a summary proceeding for contempt for publishing news stories and editorials that pointed rather sharply to a rate case pending before the local court and indicating how the judge should rule.

The Court sustained the conviction, Mr. Justice Holmes writing a vigorous dissent. The opinion stated that newspaper comment on pending cases, having a reasonable tendency to interfere with or obstruct the normal operation of the judicial system, could be so punished.

The problem returned to the Court in *Nye* v. *United States* in 1941 (313 U.S. 33), in which the *Toledo* decision was overruled. *Nye* demonstrated an even more obnoxious form of interference with judicial administration than *Toledo,* but the decision rested on the statute conceding that though under other provisions of the criminal code those acts of obstruction of justice could be punished, they would follow the normal course of indictment and trial by jury, rather than summary contempt proceedings. Trial by jury in "all criminal cases" was an important ingredient in construing this act narrowly in the Nye case.

In the summary contempt cases the judge is the accusor as well as the judicial officer ruling on the case. In many instances the judges are personally involved—they have been personally attacked. So the importance of trial by jury looms rather large because a jury drawn from the community would be apt to be a counterweight to the judge and to prevent runaway convictions having no statutory limitations on the amount of the fine or the number of years of imprisonment that could be inflicted.

Of course parties acting outside the view of a judge may be obstructing justice and may be punished under the criminal code. But in the trial they would have the right to trial by jury, a guarantee designed at least in part to protect defendants against the wrath of judges who historically often turned out to be tyrants.

Our overruling of the *Toledo* decision and our narrow construction of the summary contempt statute left important problems unsolved. The climate of opinion in a community may be manipulated by the papers or by TV and radio so as to make it difficult for a named accused to get a fair trial. Apart from citing the news media for contempt there are two other remedies. One is reversal of convictions on appeal, another is a change of venue to another locale that is free of the unfriendly propaganda against the accused.

We have had numerous instances of each variety. Perhaps the most notorious was the case of Dr. Sam Sheppard of Cleveland, Ohio, in which the trial was held after the sheriff had put the accused on television and had him re-enact the crime. The event drew headlines all over the nation. A woman had been murdered and the accused was her husband, a prominent doctor. Suspicion settled on him and the local press started beating the drums for conviction.

I had written the Nye opinions, strongly supported by Black and joined by Frankfurter, though he was more dubious. The result was that in courthouse talk about such decisions I was often ridiculed for my views; and when a case like Sam Sheppard's broke in the news the Brethern would ask, "What do you propose to do about that?" I had no roving commission in that area, but since my opinion in *Nye* had changed the current of law in this country, I followed the cases of this kind coming up rather closely.

In the Sheppard case, the District Court issued a writ of habeas corpus and the Court of Appeals reversed. When a petition for certiorari was presented to our Court, seven voted to take the case and only Black voted to deny. He felt that Sheppard was guilty. After argument the majority of the Court voted to reverse the judgment of conviction because of the publicity. Warren, Black and White voted to affirm. We ordered the federal writ of habeas corpus to issue discharging Sheppard from custody unless he was retried within a reasonable time (*Sheppard v. Maxwell,* 384 U.S. 333).

Warren assigned the opinion to me and I worked long and hard on it, reading every word of the record. As a result of my research I could not write to reverse because I concluded that Sheppard was guilty and that the issuance of the writ would indeed be an abuse of the federal habeas corpus statute which was designed primarily to protect the *innocent* but also was broad enough to protect one who might be guilty but had been railroaded to the gallows.

Books have been written about Sam Sheppard's travail and suffering, and eloquent pleas made, but, in the end, I did not think that the press had persuaded the jury as much as the lawyers argued. For if the press is muzzled, the spotlight of publicity might never be cast on ugly goings-on in the courtroom. The press has a potential for evil in these situations, especially when the accused is of a minority race or despised for his social or political views, but it is better that the press be free than muzzled. The judicial world can reek with passion and prejudice which only full publicity can crush.

So at the next Conference I reported I could not write to reverse. After the Conference had been canvassed again, Warren assigned the opinion to Tom Clark, who did a commendable job. I ended up joining the opinion, believing it to be within permissible limits of the record. So the writ was issued and Sheppard got a reprieve. A later jury acquitted him.

An incident involving the extent to which a state may cut down on First Amendment rights was present in 1941 in *Bridges* v. *California* (314 U.S. 252). The case arose out of a territorial conflict between the then separate American Federation of Labor and Congress of Industrial Organizations. The A.F. of L. sponsored the International Longshoremen's Association (ILA) and the CIO sponsored the International Longshoremen-Warehousemen's Union (ILWU). The case unhappily had inflammatory aspects because the defendant president of the ILWU, Harry Bridges, was reported to be a Communist and was a very controversial labor leader on the West Coast.

The officers of the local ILA chapter decided to abandon it and merge with the ILWU. They directed the funds and other assets of the ILA local toward that end. An injunction was sought by members of the ILA to prevent the officers from continuing to use the chapters' assets in this fashion. The judge issued the injunction ordering the officers to reimburse the ILA local for the misspent funds and also appointed a receiver to conduct the affairs of the ILA in accordance with its articles of incorporation.

The defendant officers of the ILA then filed a notice of intention to seek a new trial and a notice of a motion to vacate the judgment. On that same day, Harry Bridges sent a stinging telegram to the Secretary of Labor calling the court's decision "outrageous." He was cited for contempt for obstructing justice because the newly filed motions were still pending before the court. The Los Angeles *Times* printed Bridges' statements that as a result of the court's decision a "coast-wide" strike of maritime workers would be called. The *Times* was also cited for contempt. The issue before us, then, was whether or not the contempt citations were valid under the "free speech" and "free press" guarantees of the First Amendment. In a sharply divided five-to-four decision,

Justice Black wrote for the majority that neither Bridges nor the *Times* could constitutionally be held in contempt because there was "no clear and present danger" of obstruction of justice as a result of their activities.

In 1896, as we have seen, long before Holmes was on the Court, it had held in *Plessy* v. *Ferguson* that segregation of the races in public facilities was constitutional (163 U.S. 537). To review the history: in 1927, while Holmes, Brandeis and Stone were on the Court, the Justices voted unanimously to extend that holding to Chinese, and in 1931, just before Holmes retired, the Court reaffirmed the 1896 decision allowing Negroes to be segregated in public schools (*School District No. 7, Muskogee Country* v. *Hunnicut,* 283 U.S. 810) and refused review in other cases (see *Salvatierra* v. *Independent School District,* 284 U.S. 580). So my hero, Holmes, by action as well as inaction, helped create for blacks a second-class citizenship.

Vinson wrote for the Court in 1948 holding that it was unconstitutional for a state to throw its weight behind restrictive covenants governing the sale of residential property by allowing its courts to enforce those covenants (*Shelley* v. *Kraemer,* 334 U.S. 1). Restrictive covenants on real estate deeds had been widely used in fencing blacks, Orientals and Jews out of choice residential areas. While Vinson stood firm in 1948, by 1953 he had weakened. In that year a suit over another restrictive covenant was before the Court. This time, enforcement was not asked; only damages for its breach. The Court held that a state could no more put its weight behind damage suits to enforce restrictive covenants than behind equity suits. Vinson was the lone dissenter (346 U.S. 249, 260 *et seq.*).

By the early fifties the demands were growing for riddance of segregation, and the pressure was becoming noticeable in the Conference of the Court. Vinson, who was from Kentucky, was adamant and spoke sternly against letting those fences of the law break down. His allies in this regard were Reed, also of Kentucky, and Clark of Texas. Vinson had two others on his side—Frankfurter and Jackson—which made five for Vinson's views. Frankfurter was not an ideological ally, nor was Jackson. But Frankfurter kept talking about not doing anything which would pull down "the pillars of the temple." In his opinion, a decision desegregating public facilities would doom the Court. He mouthed the Holmes idea that questions of such great public moment were truly "political questions" which the Court should avoid. Jackson had pretty much the same idea, but his motivation, I think, was to make rulings which would not upset the Establishment. And the elders of Washington, D.C., were Southerners.

The legal and constitutional phase of the civil rights movement was largely won when Congress passed the Civil Rights Act of April 10, 1968, and included housing in the series of laws protecting the "rights" of blacks. The Fair Housing Act certainly did no good to the low-income or no-income black struggling to make ends meet in the ghetto. Yet he was the chief victim of America's racial problem. The legal battles were only part of the struggle—and in some ways the minor part, at that. The real struggle was to admit blacks in full equality in our economic, business and social life.

Over the years our ghettos had housed Jews, Irish, Poles, Russians and others. While the first generation were largely prisoners locked into the ghettos, the second generation escaped and entered all areas of our life. But, for the black, the escape was not easy. When the great black migration to the North took place, in the 1940s, his unskilled labor was no longer greatly in demand. He was not admitted to many trade unions and was barred from some schools and most suburban areas. He had few entrepreneurial opportunities, including bank loans. Slavery and subsequent periods of long male unemployment made the black family matriarchal. The result was, in many instances, loose family ties for the husband and high rates of desertion. The "American dream" had meant escape from the ghetto for most whites. To the black it meant imprisonment. That imprisonment was due to a caste system with roots in slavery. My friend Harry Golden described it in testimony before a Senate Committee in 1966:

> But why did Tammany Hall and private philanthropy with less funds accomplish in the Jewish, Irish, Italian, and Polish ghettoes in 1905 what the present government has found so difficult to accomplish in 1966 with huge funds and noble administrators?
> The reason is that earlier the philanthropists and politicians did not contend with caste. Caste goes deep in the human consciousness, so deep that it makes a machinist in Cicero,

Illinois, where the average wage is $2.84 an hour, cheer a politician from a State where the average wage is $1.72 an hour. Caste makes one set of Americans determined not to grant equity to another set of Americans.

A huge percentage of the black population lives in a state of poverty. Median family income for blacks is considerably lower than for whites, and unemployment is higher among blacks, particularly among young men, than for whites.

The "caste" system we created for the black was more vicious than the "caste" system created in India for the untouchables. Once India obtained her independence, she abolished her caste system, writing into the laws many sanctions against discrimination. There were positive, as well as negative, aspects to those sanctions. Untouchables, long excluded from higher education, the professions and the foreign service, were given quotas in those various fields—quotas that could not be filled by others. The caste system of the untouchables was, of course, not abolished overnight; prejudice against that "caste" long persisted in the villages. But progress was made. Some of the outstanding Indian leaders have indeed come from that caste.

The black "caste" is, however, more difficult to break down. After all, the untouchables of India were of the same race and color as all other Indians. Color made the black's escape from the "caste" much, much more difficult in spite of all our laws.

In the spring of 1967 I went to New York City to attend a dinner and make a speech. The sponsoring group was made up mostly of Democrats—white and black; and my talk was partly on civil rights, mostly on economic opportunities and the prospects of mounting disemployment due to technological advances. The question I posed was: When the private sector is unable to supply full employment, what will the public sector offer?

We have already had three generations of people on relief. Part of the deep unrest in our society was the growing idea that those at the bottom were "being paid to be poor." In fact, what people wanted were jobs; work was a powerful therapy. If there was no work in the private sector, we must provide it in the public sector.

In talking with the blacks afterward, I found little interest in concrete ideas of this character. The mounting feeling, in that period, was that violence was the solution. Moreover, in that black group, at that time, there was a deep-seated anti-Semitic attitude. It poured from the lips of a millionaire singer, and from Stokely Carmichael, too. Those two had never suffered as their people had. Yet they were not promoting remedies; they were promoting hatred, retaliation and violence. They denounced Jewish moneylenders, Jewish merchants, Jewish brokers in Harlem, where most Harlem businessmen and financiers are in fact not Jewish at all.

They expressed violent attitudes against those blacks who were looking for practical solutions without violence—people like Thurgood Marshall and Whitney Young. They called them "house niggers"—i.e., spies for their white masters. They downgraded Martin Luther King, Jr.— one of the greatest men of this century—because he disavowed violent methods.

The year 1967 awakened me to the realization that great volcanoes were about to erupt, and when King was assassinated in the spring of 1968, those eruptions started. They evidenced a polarization between whites and blacks that was extremely dangerous to the whole country. Without the mucilage of good will, any community will be torn asunder.

My own mail became filled with anonymous postcards saying, in effect, "now your chickens have come home to roost," meaning that the civil rights decisions of the Court had turned the black people loose. What actually happened was that a century of neglect, aided and abetted by the Court, had caused the problem to fester until a really dangerous infection had reached the bloodstream of America.

The fault was not that of the "uppity Negro" but the "unreconstructed white"—and the latter did not live in the South alone.

Catherine May, congresswoman from my hometown, Yakima, voted against the Fair Housing Act of April 10, 1968. That single fact was appalling to me. My generation had made tremendous progress in some areas, but when it came to racial tolerance we were mostly bankrupt. The death of King forced the Fair Housing Act out of a reluctant Congress, but the smoldering attitude of the whites promised recurring trouble.

Racial discrimination is not easy to see in places like Yakima, Washington, or even San Diego, California. There are no signs to tear down. People deny there is a problem. They profess dedication to equality. Many of our Western towns and cities are communities without commitment. The racial problem—concerning Chicanos as well as blacks— is hidden under the surface because people optimistically think it will

147

go away if it is not stirred. Meanwhile, the deep frustrations of the black community festers. The dream of a multiracial society seems more distant today than when I was a boy.

The use of violence usually carries a penalty, but recourse to violence is deep in the American tradition. It started at least as early as the Boston Tea Party and continues to this day. It is a crude, irrational, extravagant mode of expression. The philosopher will say that violence has no place in a civilized society, since in a people's democracy, debate, argument, electioneering and the ballot box are the remedies; and these leave no place for violence. That may be theoretically true. But in reality, citizens are often caught in a pot of glue and are utterly helpless when it comes to obtaining relief from an injustice.

What do ghetto people do about rats or about the barriers erected against job opportunities because of racial intolerance?

What do people do to escape the terrible injustices of the welfare system and the paralysis caused by prejudiced or corrupt officials?

How do people face an all-powerful bureaucracy—a Bureau of Public Roads, Forest Service, Corps of Engineers—that knows no limits to its discretion and plows under the helpless individual?

What does the individual do to resist the corrupting influence of the CIA or to combat the all-powerful military-industrial complex that now commands our lives?

The helplessness of the individual against the modern array of governmental power frequently causes explosions. There is a point beyond which suffering will no longer be tolerated.

Farmers do seize trains and trucks and dump offending milk in the streets.

People do set fire to their own homes once their grievances are piled high enough.

Laws are violated and penalties inflicted for those shows of violence. But the violence, being symptomatic of a vast disorder in society, sounds a public alarm; and it may be effective in obtaining relief.

We know little about mob psychology and the deep springs of action behind public demonstrations. They may indeed be primeval methods of expression, having to do with the emotions, not the minds, of men. But the expression of emotions is philosophically within the ambit of the First Amendment. Indeed, people make decisions based on emotions more commonly than on reason.

How do we produce a multiracial, multireligious, multi-ideological nation that accommodates all minorities and their idiosyncrasies, dispenses equal justice under law, and provides equality of opportunity? The democratic ideal is an aristocracy of talent which draws from all the springs of genius and ability wherever they may be found. That is the theory, though we are far from living up to it. That is also the central problem of the world, for wherever one goes one finds that racial, religious and ideological differences generate suspicion, hate and conflict.

Racism has cast a shadow across this country that at times seemed to be ever lengthening. During argument of one case involving racial discrimination, a judge interrupted counsel to say, "What you are really arguing is that I must like this racial minority. Yet for the life of me, I do not see how by legislative command, executive direction, or judicial decree, I can constitutionally be required to like any person or any race."

That of course was not the argument; and few would be brash enough to make it. The argument has concerned the extent to which the individual can enlist the power of the state to enforce his prejudices on the racial issue. In the 1971 Term, *Johnson* v. *Committee on Examinations* (407 U.S. 915) came to the Court on a petition for certiorari to the Arizona Supreme Court. Petitioner was a white applicant for admission to the Arizona bar. The passing grade was 70 percent, and he on three occasions received 68.3 percent, 68.6 percent and 69.5 per cent. He showed that blacks who received similar failing grades were admitted, the failing grades being waived in their cases. Petitioner claimed he was the victim of reverse discrimination. I was the only one to vote to grant, saying to the Conference that racial discrimination against a white was as unconstitutional as racial discrimination against a black. The only one who replied was Thurgood Marshall, who said, "You guys have been practicing discrimination for years. Now it is our turn." I noted my dissent from the denial of certiorari.

If the White Citizens Council can summon the police on its side of the white-black conflict, the Black Muslims can do the same once they are in control. And so it has been and is across the world: the dominant group shapes the laws to reflect its racial prejudices.

That is why I long felt and finally stated, in *Keyes* v. *School District No. 1, Denver, Colo.* (413 U.S. 189), my view that white control of a school board was often the root of the whole problem. Though this situation has changed in recent years, it was apparently true in the North during those years, when white school boards often sat in judgment of school questions even where the blacks were in theoretical control because they outnumbered the white residents. With such large populations, their voice should be heard at the administrative level. Our school decrees should have contained directives for District Courts to approve only those school plans submitted by school boards on which both races were represented. Absent that, they could order that election be held with the seats fairly apportioned.

Hands went up that those were "political" questions, unfit for courts. If that is true, then *Plessy* v. *Ferguson,* as well as *Brown* v. *Board of Education,* were "political" question cases, unfit for the judicial process. But that would make the matter of race—which had constitutional guarantees—of lesser importance than matters of property, speech and privacy, which also had constitutional guarantees. If one was fit for judicial protection, then so were the others.

In *Sterling* v. *Constantin* (287 U.S. 378), owners of oil and gas interests sued in a federal court to enjoin the governor and other officials of Texas from enforcing oil pro-rating orders. The governor had declared martial law in the area and sent the National Guard in to enforce his mandate. The District Court issued a restraining order, and the state officers were cited for contempt. The Court, speaking through Chief Justice Hughes, said that while martial law may be declared by a governor, its constitutional limits render them "judicial questions" (*Id.* 401). The Court held that "there was no military necessity" that justified the governor's restriction of oil production (*Id.* 404) and that the District Court acted properly in 1932 in enjoining the military intervention.

In 1969 *Powell* v. *McCormack* (395 U.S. 486) involved a suit by a congressman who had met the constitutional standards for office and had been clearly elected by the voters of his district but yet for collateral reasons was not seated by the House. It was the office and its prerogatives which he claimed and to which our decree asserted he had a constitutional right. The Court held that under the Constitution (Article I, Sect. 51) there was a "textually demonstrable commitment" to Congress (the test under *Baker* v. *Carr*) to judge *whether* he met the qualifications set forth in the Constitution, not to add to them (*Powell,* 548). No confrontation with the House was involved. No injunction was issued against the House; the members of the House were dismissed from the suit, and final judgment was only against House employees

(*Id.* 550), in the form of a declaratory judgment declaring Adam Clayton Powell's rights; this was sufficient as a basis for recovery of his salary.

In 1936 the Senate had tried to bar my old friend William Langer, Senator-elect of North Dakota, from a seat, and at long last the Senate voted it had no power to exclude when the candidate had the proper credentials and possessed the constitutional qualifications (*Id.* 558–559).

Federal courts do not sit to fashion new remedies; the remedies come from Congress. Apart from rights rooted in the common law, in the federal regime they come from Congress or are specified in the Constitution or the Bill of Rights. By Article IV, Sect. 4, of the Constitution the states are guaranteed a republican form of government. In 1849 it was held in *Luther* v. *Borden* (48 U.S. 1) that that guarantee had only political sanctions and was not justiciable. It is, however, extremely doubtful if that view has survived *Sterling* v. *Constantin, Powell* v. *McCormack* and *Baker* v. *Carr.*

Courts do not—and should not—undertake to run the country, but where individual or group rights are created by the Constitution or laws of the United States, a Court is niggardly which does not enforce them, unless their enforcement has been entrusted by the Constitution to one of the other branches of government.

It should be noted here that the Court never considered the question of executive privilege in any specific way, though it was referred to peripherally from time to time. The Nixon case was the first time the issue came directly to us.

There were many challenges during the Vietnam years. At least nineteen cases were filed with the Court, in no one of which the Court granted certiorari. I noted my dissent in each case and in some wrote out my views (*Mitchell* v. *United States,* 386 U.S. 972; *Mora* v. *McNamara,* 389 U.S. 934; *Massachusetts* v. *Laird,* 400 U.S. 886). Article I, Sect. 8 of the Constitution says: "The Congress shall have power . . . to declare war." The "presidential war" which we experienced in Vietnam has no sanction in the Constitution. The main objection to taking a case raising the constitutional question was usually phrased in terms of the issue being "political" rather than "justiciable."

There had been no declaration of war on Korea in the steel seizure case, when Truman seized the mills during labor trouble to keep production under way. As we have seen, the Court in a six-to-three decision held the seizure unconstitutional, since Congress had not acted by declaring war or otherwise granting the Commander in Chief authority to seize property.

If it is "justiciable" when the Executive seizes property, why not when he seizes persons and forces them to go overseas to fight an undeclared "war"? Life and liberty are supposed to be as important as property under our constitutional system.

Each of these cases arose when a draftee objected to being forced into the Army for overseas combat. To make the claim "justiciable" would mean that only a small percentage who were opposed would not be required to serve. Those who opposed going to Vietnam faced the prospect of court orders against the President, the Pentagon and all officials giving impetus to the war effort. Whether some of those remedies would not be manageable as "justiciable" questions need not be reached in the simple habeas corpus case, by which a person seeks release from custody leading to overseas service.

However the cases might come out on the merits, I thought the Court did a great disservice to the nation in not resolving this, the most important issue of the sixties to reach the Court.

Chapter VII

The Court and Big Business

Even from the beginning of our country's history, moneyed corporations were often suspect. In 1816 Jefferson wrote that

> virtue and interest are inseparable. It ends, as might have been expected, in the ruin of its people, but this ruin will fall heaviest, as it ought to fall, on that hereditary aristocracy which has for generations been preparing for the catastrophe. I hope we shall take warning from the example and crush in its birth the aristocracy of our monied corporations which dare already to challenge our government to a trial of strength and bid defiance to the laws of our country.*

But the Court, in 1819, speaking through Chief Justice John Marshall, sealed their fate by ruling that corporations are legal persons, endowed with perpetual life:

> A corporation is an artificial being, invisible, intangible, and existing only in contemplation of law. Being the mere creature of law, it possesses only those properties which the charter of its creation confers upon it, either expressly, or as incidental to its very existence. These are such as are supposed best cal-

*Letter to George Logan, November 12, 1816.

culated to effect the object for which it was created. Among the most important are immortality, and, if the expression may be allowed, individuality; properties, by which a perpetual succession of many persons are considered as the same, and may act as a single individual.*

On January 31, 1938, the Court rendered a historic decision in *Connecticut General Life Ins. Co.* v. *Johnson* (303 U.S. 77). Justice Stone, writing for the majority, held that California's tax on the corporation violated the Due Process Clause of the Fourteenth Amendment. Only Black did not agree, the main thrust of his dissent being that a corporation is not a "person" within the meaning of the Fourteenth Amendment, which says that no state shall deprive "any person of life, liberty, or property without due process of law." The Court had previously held that "person," as so used, meant a "natural" person, a human being (*Western Turf Assn.* v. *Greenberg*, 204 U.S. 359, 363). The Fourteenth Amendment, said Circuit Judge William B. Woods (later Associate Justice) in 1871 (*Insurance Co.* v. *New Orleans*, 1 Woods 85, 88), does not include corporations in its coverage, adding that the Amendment's history (it was adopted in 1868) is "so fresh in all minds as to need no rehearsal."

The Fourteenth Amendment was passed to give blacks first-class citizenship. Section 2 apportions representatives among the states "according to their respective numbers, counting the whole number of persons in each state, excluding Indians not taxed." Certainly corporations would not be counted as voters. Section 3 says that "no person" shall be a senator or representative in Congress who has engaged in sedition. Certainly, in this instance also, "person" does not include corporations. Section 1 of the Amendment talks about citizens as being "born or naturalized" here. Certainly such language excludes corporations. Yet in 1886 the Court, in *Santa Clara County* v. *Southern Pac. RR. Co.* (118 U.S. 394, 396), held that a corporation is a "person" within the meaning of the Equal Protection Clause of the Fourteenth Amendment. The Court was so sure of its ground that it asked neither for briefs on the point nor for oral argument. Chief Justice Waite merely announced from the bench: "The court does not wish to hear argument on the question whether the provision in the Fourteenth Amendment

The Trustees of Dartmouth College v. *Woodware* (17 U.S. 518, 616).

to the Constitution, which forbids a State to deny to any person within its jurisdiction the equal protection of the laws, applies to these corporations. We are all of opinion that it does" (*Id.* 396). And soon the corporation came under the protective cover of the Due Process Clause as well.

I was at the SEC when Justice Black's dissent came down on January 31, 1938. Robert E. Healy, a commissioner, walked into my office that afternoon with a copy of the opinion and read it out loud to me. And then we sat and talked an hour or so about it.

"What a great difference in American history his dissent would have made," Healy observed, and I agreed. There are some people who have always claimed that the main thrust of the Constitution is to protect property. "And this decision will prove their point," Healy added.

The corporation already had the sword of financial power, the big American names, the big prestige behind them. Now they had the shield as well as the sword—the shield of the Constitution. And they used that shield from 1882 to 1937 to lay low most of the social legislation of the day which attempted to regulate hours of work, the minimum wage, utility rates—ad nauseam. "Liberty" in the setting of the Fourteenth Amendment meant the "liberty" of the corporation to exploit labor, to pay cheap wages and then to get most or all of them back in the company stores they owned and ran. Liberty also meant "liberty" for the seven-year-old lad to work for ten cents a day. This was Adam Smith in an extreme version.

At SEC, Healy and I touched on the grotesque line of cases that had ensued—in hours of work, the minimum wage, control of factory conditions and in the inequitable taxes laid on corporations. We discussed the populist movement, which arose earlier in the century in connection with these issues and gave rise to William J. Bryan, Robert La Follette, the Farmer's Alliance, as well as the populists of a later vintage, including Huey Long, who was just then in the forefront. We ended up, of course, talking about FDR's Court-packing plan, which had been inspired by the constitutional shields given the corporation by the Court. At the time of our discussion, the plan was already marked for rejection.

Years later, in 1949, in *Wheeling Steel Corp.* v. *Glander* (337 U.S. 562, 576) the question was again whether or not a corporation is a "person" within the meaning of the Equal Protection Clause of the Fourteenth Amendment. The Court decided it is, and I filed a dissent, noting my agreement with Justice Black in his 1938 dissent. I was joined, in this later case, only by Black.

• • •

In the nineteenth century, politicians as well as judges lined up pro and con on the issue of economic competition. One of the most eloquent pleas for a competitive society was made in 1890 by Senator John Sherman when he proposed the bill that became the Sherman Antitrust Act:

> If the concentered powers of this combination are entrusted to a single man, it is a kingly prerogative, inconsistent with our form of government, and should be subject to the strong resistance of the State and National authorities. If anything is wrong this is wrong. If we will not endure a king as a political power we should not endure a king over the production, transportation, and sale of any of the necessaries of life. If we would not submit to an emperor we should not submit to an autocrat of trade, with power to prevent competition and to fix the price of any commodity.
>
> (21 *Cong. Record* 2457)

In those days the nation had become frightened of the "trusts" (though they had less justification for their fears than they would have had by the 1970s). On a roll-call vote in the Senate on April 8, 1890, Rufus Blodgett of New Jersey was the only senator to vote against the Sherman Act (21 *Cong. Record* 3153).

The antitrust laws, as early construed by the Court, gave carte blanche to corporate monopoly in certain areas. Thus American Sugar Refining Co. purchased the stock of four other refineries and "acquired nearly complete control of the manufacture of refined sugar within the United States" (*United States* v. *E. C. Knight Co.*, 156 U.S. 1, 9). Creating a monopoly in violation of the Sherman Act? Certainly not. Why? Because the act as applied did not give Congress power to regulate commerce. Why? "The fact that an article is manufactured for export to another State does not of itself make it an article of interstate commerce" (*Id.* 13). Marketing of goods, transportation of goods between the states—that was "commerce" in the constitutional sense, said the Court, but not manufacturing. That decision was made in 1895, five years after the Sherman Act was passed. Only one Justice dissented—the first Justice Harlan. He claimed that commerce, as viewed in the Constitution, includes not only movement of goods interstate but "interstate trade in any of its stages" (*Id.* 24). And he added: "A citizen of Missouri has the right to go in person, or send orders, to Pennsylvania and New Jersey for the purpose of purchasing refined sugar. But of what value is that right if he is confronted in those States by a vast *combination* which absolutely controls the price of that article by reason of its having acquired all the sugar refineries in the United States in order that they may fix prices in their own interest exclusively?" (*Id.* 37).

Northern Pacific and Great Northern were competing railroads, operating separate systems from the Midwest to the Pacific. Together, they purchased the stock of Chicago, Burlington & Quincy, a railroad serving the Midwest and extending to Cheyenne and Billings, where it connected with Northern Pacific. A holding company, Northern Securities Co., was thereupon formed, which acquired either the capital stock or a controlling interest in the capital stock of these rail systems. The two magistrates behind this were James J. Hill of Northern Pacific and John Pierpont Morgan of Great Northern. Teddy Roosevelt was President. The opinion of the Court on the merger was written by Justice Harlan (*Northern Securities Co.* v. *United States,* 193 U.S. 197). It was a five-to-four decision, holding that the combination violated the Sherman Act.

As previously mentioned, Holmes was one of the four dissenters, expressing at the start of his opinion an idea soon to become foreign to him: "I think it useless and undesirable, as a rule, to express dissent" (*Id.* 400). Suppression of competition was not the aim of the act, he maintained. So to hold, he said, "would make eternal the *bellum omnium contra omnes* and disintegrate society so far as it could into individual atoms. If that were its intent I should regard calling such a law a regulation of commerce as a mere pretense. It would be an attempt to reconstruct society" (*Id.* 411).

As indeed it was. For Holmes lived long enough to join his Brethren in supporting Congress in its broad attempts to "reconstruct society" through the Commerce Clause.

Holmes, nominated by Teddy Roosevelt, lost favor at the White House as a result of this dissent and was not invited back for some time. The example is one of many I use in telling people who bemoan new appointments to the Court, "Cheer up. Presidents are notorious for making mistakes."

Justice Brandeis had a different view of restraints of trade, monopoly and competition. He tried to educate Holmes, but I really do not believe he made much progress. The philosophy of Holmes, adumbrated in *Northern Securities,* was that the end product of competition was that some of the competitors would be destroyed.

He best expressed his view in 1896, when he was still on the Supreme Judicial Court of Massachusetts:

> [I]t is plain from the slightest consideration of practical affairs, or the most superficial reading of industrial history, that free competition means combination, and that the organization of the world, now going on so fast, means an ever increasing might and scope of combination. It seems to me futile to set our faces against this tendency. Whether beneficial on the whole, as I think it, or detrimental, it is inevitable, unless the fundamental axioms of society, and even the fundamental conditions of life, are to be changed.
>
> One of the eternal conflicts out of which life is made up is that between the effort of every man to get the most he can for his services, and that of society, disguised under the name of capital, to get his services for the least possible return. Combination on the one side is patent and powerful. Combination on the other is the necessary and desirable counterpart, if the battle is to be carried on in a fair and equal way.
>
> (*Vegelahn* v. *Guntner,* 167 Mass. 92, 108)

This Holmes philosophy has become the heart of the apologia tendered by economists like John Kenneth Galbraith for the domestic and international planning by American corporations as of the 1970s.

In 1911 the Court decided *Standard Oil Co.* v. *United States* (221 U.S. 1), a civil suit under the Sherman Act to break up the Standard Oil trust. That act makes illegal every "contract, combination . . . or conspiracy in restraint of trade or commerce." The Court construed that language to mean "an undue restraint" (*Id.* 60), and by modifying the decree to which the oil company objected, the Court allowed subsidiary corporations of the great cartel to create new combinations—as long as they did not re-create the existing one (*Id.* 80–81).

Justice Harlan dissented, saying that the majority "legislated" when it restricted the act to "undue" or "unreasonable" restraints of trade (*Id.* 103). In fact, the Court fashioned its own restraint of trade in this case. *United States* v. *American Tobacco Co.* (221 U.S. 106), decided shortly thereafter, held that the Tobacco Trust violated the act. Justice Harlan again dissented. While the majority had condemned the conspiracy as a "monster combination" (*Id.* 190), it remanded the case to see if the parties could not succeed in "re-creating out of the elements now composing it, a new condition which shall be honestly in harmony with and not repugnant to the law" (*Id.* 187). Justice Harlan could see no justification for giving clear-cut law violators a second chance to get some benefits from "the vicious methods" they had used (*Id.* 190).

Thus, from the very start, the giants of corporations engaged in free-wheeling destructive tactics and received soft, easy treatment at the hands of the Court. The Court unwittingly laid the groundwork for the enormous power of the corporations by the time of Nixon's second term.

While corporate business fared quite well under the Sherman Act, labor soon felt the full sting of the new law. In 1913 Samuel Gompers, founder of the American Federation of Labor, testified in support of the Clayton bill (which bĕcame the Clayton Antitrust Act in 1914 supplementing the Sherman Act). According to Gompers, the courts readily held labor unions to be illegal combinations in restraint of trade, going so far as to dissolve a union.* The most spectacular episodes grew out of the Pullman strike in 1894. Pullman had established a "company town" in Illinois for its employees, the company performing all municipal functions. (Many years later in another setting the Court, speaking through Justice Black, held in *Marsh* v. *Alabama* [326 U.S. 501] that people living in company towns were free citizens, that by virtue of the First and Fourteenth Amendments, they could not be prosecuted by the state for distributing religious literature on the streets against the regulations of the company.)

Pullman's "company town" was all glitter and glow on the outside but boiling with discontent on the inside. For example, the residents believed that the charges the company made for rent, heat, gas and water were excessive. The wages of the employees were miserable, from thirty-six cents to $1.51 a day.

In 1894 Eugene Debs had led a strike against the Pullman Company

*Hearings before Judiciary Committee on Trust Legislation 4965, Vol. 1, p. 62 at pp. 16–17 (Dec. 16, 1913).

for better wages, and in response the Department of Justice moved in and got an omnibus injunction against the strike. While never advocating violence or lawlessness, Debs stood firm on the strike. Yet he was cited for criminal contempt, found guilty and sentenced to prison (64 Fed. 724). Thereupon he sought habeas corpus in the Court, which denied relief. The Court sustained the injunction not under the Sherman Act but under other federal acts extending national control over railroads. Debs had asked for a trial by jury. The Court held that no jury trial was necessary (*In re Debs*, 158 U.S. 564, 595). That was the view for many years.

The Sixth Amendment provides for trial by jury in "all criminal prosecutions." In 1937 the Court, speaking through Justice Stone, held that "all criminal prosecutions" did not extend to "petty" offenses and that a crime carrying a penalty of imprisonment for ninety days was a "petty" offense. Justice McReynolds and Justice Butler—often referred to as reactionary—dissented, saying that "all" meant "all" (*District of Columbia* v. *Clawans,* 300 U.S. 617, 633).

That was the view that Black, Warren and I expressed in 1958 in *Green* v. *United States* (356 U.S. 165, 193). In 1966 Black and I adhered to that opinion in all its permutations in *Cheff* v. *Schnackenberg* (384 U.S. 373). Finally, in 1968, the Court accepted the view which had been rejected in *Debs* and held that in "serious criminal contempt cases, a trial by jury was required, save for summary punishment for contempts committed in the presence of the Court" (*Bloom* v. *Illinois* 391 U.S. 194, 208). Thus the principle for which Clarence Darrow and other lawyers for Debs contended before the Court in 1895 were approved seventy-three years later.

Debs was decided on May 27, 1895. On May 29 the Court held the federal income tax unconstitutional (*Pollock* v. *Farmers Loan & Trust Co.,* 158 U.S. 601), a decision which resulted in the Sixteenth Amendment in 1913.

Debs and *Pollock* brought good tidings to the moneyed interests, and the indications were that they savored the *Debs* decision even more than *Pollock.* In prison Eugene Debs turned to socialism and emerged to proclaim that "industrial slavery" would be abolished. The entire episode caused many to conclude that the Court was nothing but a servant of the moneyed interests. The decisions rendered in *Knight, Debs* and *Pollock* were the trilogy that made clear to many on which side the Court was aligned.

That view was fortified in 1908 when the Court held unanimously, in the famous Danbury Hatters' case, that the American Federation of Labor violated the Sherman Act when it used its pressures and persuasion to get 70 percent of the eighty-two manufacturers of the country to accept the working conditions demanded. This was a "combination to restrain and destroy interstate trade and commerce," in the view of the Court (*Loewe* v. *Lawlor,* 208 U.S. 274).

One of the several purposes of the Clayton Act was to remove labor unions from the category of unlawful combinations, but Court injunctions against strikes continued, over the protests of Brandeis, who kept dissenting in such cases. (See *Duplex Co.* v. *Deering,* 254 U.S. 443, decided in 1921.) Finally, in 1932, the Norris–La Guardia Act was passed, greatly restraining the use of injunctions in labor controversies to very select special situations (47 Stat 70).

The Senate report on the bill said: "A man must work in order to live. If he can express no control over his conditions of employment, he is subjected to involuntary servitude" (S.R. 163, 72d Cong., 1st Sess., p. 9).

In 1941 the Court at long last gave the Norris–La Guardia and Clayton acts full recognition as a congressional policy to leave labor largely alone in its peaceful pursuits of better wages and living conditions (*United States* v. *Hutcheson,* 312 U.S. 219).

The Clayton Act also barred the setting up of holding companies, a common device to create a monopoly by stock acquisition. But the Clayton Act did not bar mergers as a result of one company acquiring the assets of another, and big business exploited that loophole.

In the famous Aluminum case in 1945 it had been held that 90 percent control of the industry by one company was a monopoly (*United States* v. *Aluminum Co.,* 148 F 2d 416, 429), but the *Aluminum* decision would probably affect fewer than six companies. And the Court went on to say that it was doubtful that 64 percent would be enough to constitute a monopoly and that 33 percent certainly was not sufficient (*Id.* 424).

In 1948 the Court held that the acquisition of the largest steel fabricator on the West Coast by the largest steel producer on the West Coast, which in turn was the subsidiary of the largest steel producer in the nation, did not violate the Sherman Act (*United States* v. *Columbia Steel Co.,* 334 U.S. 495). I wrote a dissent in which Black, Murphy and Rutledge joined.

It was decisions like these that in 1950 led to the Celler-Kefauver Act, which amended the Clayton Act, giving the Federal Trade Commission authority to bar the acquisitions of either stock or assets of one corporation by another corporation "where in any line of commerce in any section of the country the effect of such acquisition may be substantially to lessen competition or to tend to create a monopoly" (64 Stat. 1125, 1126). The Court has in general been an "activist" in that it applied the antitrust laws grudgingly and niggardly in failing to constrain these corporate mergers. The Court in 1974, as evidenced by its five-to-four decision in *United States* v. *General Dynamics Corp.* (415 U.S. 486), was still very anti-antitrust.

I was always denounced as an activist; so were Black, Warren, Tom Clark, Brennan and others. And we were "activists"—not in reading our individual notions of the public good into the Constitution and/or the laws, but in trying to construe them in the spirit as well as the letter in which they were enacted. We doubtless made many errors. But we never followed the funeral march that buried the antitrust laws or deprived them of vitality by making them mere husks of what they were intended to be.

In my time, Tom Clark probably contributed more insight into antitrust problems than any other Justice. His experiences in various roles at the Department of Justice were illuminating. Abe Fortas would have added greatly in this area had he remained on the Court, for he had had a lively law practice in antitrust cases.

Teddy Roosevelt was of course a great proponent of antitrust laws. But in his big "crusade," the entire Antitrust Division of the Department of Justice consisted of only five lawyers and four stenographers. Taft, who followed Roosevelt, likewise was of that view. When he campaigned in 1911 he said, "We must get back to competition. If it is impossible, then let us go to socialism, for there is no way between." Taft, on leaving office, wrote a book entitled *The Anti-Trust Act and the Supreme Court* (1914) which gave a rosier picture of "progress" against monopoly than was justified. It was not until the late thirties, when Thurman Arnold headed the Antitrust Division (from 1938 to 1943), that any measurable progress was made.

Business first sought monopolies through "pools," which were agreements to fix prices, restrict production, divide markets. But "pools" gave way to more effective "trusts." Each company forming trusts turned in its stock to trustees, who issued trust certificates in exchange. The trustees had the voting power of all the combined companies. The

Standard Oil trust of 1879 gave the trust complete control of the oil industry without investing a dollar in it. Those trusts were what Brandeis inveighed against. There was no federal control at that time. States moved against trusts, but they were seldom effective. New Jersey amended its corporation law to permit one corporation to own the stock of another. So extensive pyramids of companies were created, pyramids the states could not attack, as they were legal in the state of incorporation. That is why at long last a conservative Republican Congress passed the Sherman Act.

Holmes, who voted against applying the Sherman Act in the Northern Securities case, wrote Sir Frederick Pollock in 1910: "I don't disguise my belief that the Sherman Act is a humbug based on economic ignorance and incompetence." Thurman Arnold believed that Holmes "had faith in the benevolence and efficiency of the rich." Felix Frankfurter had traces of that philosophy. So did Butler, McReynolds and Roberts. Years later Lewis Powell was quite outspoken in the same vein, as were most Nixon appointees. Not all Eisenhower nominees felt that way, Brennan being very much of the opposed view. So was Fortas, a Johnson nominee, and Goldberg, named by Kennedy. Hugo Black held the populist view; so did Tom Clark and Earl Warren and these, with Brennan, were the most articulate in my time in antitrust matters. And so the curve marking progress and decline under the Sherman Act went up and down depending on the economic and political philosophies of the Justices, who often read the statutory words "unreasonable restraints" of trade to reflect their own concept of the public good.

There is much that the Court has done to keep some stability in the antitrust laws.* But the aim to check abuses of economic power by law has fallen far short of the goal. The value of antitrust is that it looms over the shoulders of malefactors who are thereby somewhat restrained. The most potent weapon in both the Sherman Act and the Clayton Act has been the provision for the private suit for treble damages. Many cases with this penalty have ensued.

For example, the use of a patent may not be tied up by means of an agreement to use, with the patent, an unpatented article owned by the

*The best overall account is by a Britisher, A. D. Neale, *The Anti-Trust Laws of the U.S.A.,* 2nd ed. (Cambridge U. Press, 1970).

patentee (*International Salt Co.* v. *United States,* 332 U.S. 392, and *Mercoid Corp.* v. *Mid-Continent Investment Co.,* 320 U.S. 661).

"Tying" arrangements are illegal. A railroad that sold or leased adjacent land subject to a covenant that the buyer would give that road a preference in shipping commodities was in violation of the Sherman Act (*Northern Pacific Ry. Co.* v. *United States,* 356 U.S. 1). And the Clayton Act as well as the Sherman Act is violated when a distributor of films, commanding a "substantial market" will sell its top films only if the franchise also will take older and less attractive films (*United States* v. *Loews, Inc.,* 371 U.S. 38).

Joint actions by two or more businesses to keep others out of a particular market is a *per se* violation of the Sherman Act (*United States* v. *General Motors Corp.,* 384 U.S. 127), as is price fixing (*United States* v. *Socony-Vacuum Oil Co.,* 310 U.S. 150). Many other examples could be given.

After the turn of the century, the Court began to broaden the scope of the Commerce Clause, which had previously reached only interstate commerce and foreign trade. But when Hughes, then Associate Justice, wrote for the Court in the famous Shreveport Rates case in 1914, he held that the Interstate Commerce Commission, which had power to fix interstate rail rates, could also fix *intrastate* rates, if the low intrastate rates attracted trade, so as to "affect" interstate commerce (*Houston & Texas Ry.* v. *United States,* 234 U.S. 342, 354–355).

The development was not in a straight line; there were many deviations. Congress had power under the Commerce Clause to ban the movement of articles, goods or even persons deemed contrary to national policy. Thus the Pure Food and Drug Act was sustained, in 1911 (*Hipolite Egg Co.* v. *United States,* 220 U.S. 45), as was the law prohibiting the interstate transportation of women for immoral purposes, in 1913 (*Hoke* v. *United States,* 227 U.S. 308), to mention only two acts of a long list of such legislation. But when Congress undertook to ban the products of child labor from interstate commerce, the Court in 1918 held the act unconstitutional, saying production was in the domain of the states (*Hammer* v. *Dagenhart,* 247 U.S. 251). The decision was five to four, Holmes writing the dissent. Thus little pockets of corporate exploitation flourished, in spite of separate attempts of Congress to wipe them out. It was not until 1941 that the Holmes dissent was vindicated, in *United States* v. *Darby* (312 U.S. 100, 116), which held that

Congress had power to legislate concerning wages, hours of work, and factory conditions in plants that were "producing goods for consumers."

On the other hand, the constitutionally imperiled Holding Company Act of 1935 was saved by the Hughes Court. When he was practicing law, John Foster Dulles, among others, had made many forecasts, giving legal opinions that the act was plainly unconstitutional because a holding company that merely held controlling stock interests in scattered public untilities was not engaged in commerce. In 1938 the Court, speaking through Chief Justice Hughes, held that this regulatory power *was* encompassed by the Commerce Clause, since even a holding company uses the mails and instrumentalities of interstate commerce extensively (*Electric Bond & Share Co.* v. *SEC,* 303 U.S. 419); and in 1946 Justice Murphy, writing for the Court, sustained the law in the application of standards which simplified holding-company structures and required honest capital structures (*North American Co.* v. *SEC,* 327 U.S. 686).

Thus the Court, in time, removed the chief barriers to the control which the Roosevelt Administration sought to assert—the full reach of the Commerce Clause. The other row FDR had had with this old regime was its use of "substantive due process" to strike down social legislation. Typical of this use had been *Ribnik* v. *McBride* (277 U.S. 350), which held that a state was constitutionally barred from setting the fees which an employment agency might charge. That was overruled in 1941 by *Olsen* v. *Nebraska* (313 U.S. 236). Dozens of other relics from the early Court days when the corporate and financial philosophy dominated our jurisprudence were likewise overruled. FDR lost the Court-packing war, but he won several decisive battles.

Only occasionally did we hand down corporate decisions that had the flavor of the philosophy of the robber barons. In *Salyer Land Co.* v. *Tulare Water District* (410 U.S. 719), the weighting of votes in a water district concerned with conservation was at issue. Four corporations owned 85 percent of the land, one corporation having such large holdings that its vote elected a majority of the board of directors. The other 185 landowners in the district were therefore subdued and controlled. The corporation used its control to protect its holdings in the district to the ruination of some of the landowners and to the damage of all the others. "One man, one vote," which we exalted in *Reynolds* v. *Sims* (377 U.S. 533), was extended to include one corporation, one vote. The result was the creation of "a corporate political kingdom" which was performing a governmental function. This was not a decision in the dim past of the 1880s and 1890s when the vicious powers of the corporate world may not have been fully appreciated; it was a decision handed down in a year of enlightenment—1973. Three of the five remaining Warren Court Justices dissented.

Big unions grew in the shadow of big business. The National Labor Relations Act of 1935, as amended by the Taft-Hartley Act of 1947, makes it an unfair labor practice for a union to engage in a secondary boycott (29 U.S.C. 158(b)(4)). The aim of the law, in the mind of Congress, was to make the ban on secondary boycotts the national law, enforceable only by the National Labor Relations Board. That led to situations in which, when states tried to act, their action was pre-empted by federal law. Even though the NLRB refused to act because it lacked, for example, funds or personnel, the pre-emption was upheld, leaving a "no-man's-land" (*Guss* v. *Utah Labor Board,* 353 U.S. 1, 11). This "no-man's-land" had been created by an act of Congress. We had no choice but to hold that if an activity of a union is "arguably" subject to the secondary-boycott provision of the amended National Labor Relations Act, the state as well as the federal courts must defer the matter to the sole discretion of the NLRB (*San Diego Building Trades Council* v. *Garmon,* 359 U.S. 236, 245).

The result allowed the Teamsters Union to create great mischief. Secondary boycotts were used by the Teamsters to destroy businesses that really had no problem with them. It was a situation that cried out for relief by Congress. I hesitated to join some of the opinions being handed down on the subject, but judges are not supposed to rewrite statutes, though these practices of the Teamsters Union were very provocative.

To be sure, the corporation did not owe its rate of growth and its size to the fact that it was a "person" for Fourteenth Amendment purposes. That only gave it defensive power against state regulation. And so it waxed in power and strength—reducing its tax burdens under the cover of "equal protection"; escaping a host of state factory and industrial controls because it was a constitutional "person"; wielding enormous financial power that led to the money trust, entering politics with its moneybags not in Nixon's 1972 election alone but by increasing use of its wealth to control elections even prior to 1900.

By the 1960s and 1970s the corporation dominated American life. Its lobbies ran Washington, D.C., the power behind almost all of the federal agencies. Federal agencies had been entrusted by Congress with carrying policies into practice that were consistent with the "public interest." In practical effect, "public interest" became impregnated with "corporate interest"; the agencies, not viciously and corruptly, but nonetheless effectively, became vehicles whereby the corporate lobbies dictated or influenced agency policies.

In 1970, for example, Congress defeated a law which would have increased the cutting of timber on public lands. Under that bill the old forests would be cut at an increasingly fast pace; multiple use would be abandoned; all national lands with timber would be marked for cutting unless they were already reserved for another purpose—for example, national parks (H.R. 12025, 91st Cong., 1st Sess.). This bill would have directed the Secretary of Agriculture immediately to establish programs that would develop national-forest and commercial-forest land into optimum productivity as soon as possible. This bill was the fulfillment of the lumber company's dream—the rape of public forested lands (*Id.* 91–655).

Though the bill was defeated, Richard Nixon reached practically the same result by executive action through the Forest Service by providing that the allotment of cuttings on public lands meet the standards in the defeated law. By 1973 we were cutting 11.8 billion board feet in national forests; and the pressure continued for more and more cutting. Our exports of timber rose to 3 billion board feet, 85 percent of which went to Japan, thereby putting many American workers out of jobs. But the timber companies gloried in Nixon's regime because the White House recognized the master's voice. In 1974 someone protesting a plan to cut virgin timber on Forest Service or Bureau of Land Management land could get no relief from the agency. If he called the White House, the operator would give him or her a telephone number to call; and that number was not the Forest Service or BLM, but the offices of the lumber lobby.

There was, however, in my time, no overreaching, no semblance of any improper action by any company with cases before the Court—with one exception. That exception is the El Paso Natural Gas Company, which pulled out all the political stops to get the Court to reverse its decision requiring El Paso to divest itself of an illegally acquired competitor (see page 233). But El Paso did not win. No other corporate interest ever even tried to tamper with the Court. And I can say the same of any labor union, any senator, any congressman.

We are not a perfect society, but the tradition of a truly independent judiciary has been one of our greatest assets.

Chapter VIII

Law Clerks

When I arrived at the Court, the Chief Justice had two law clerks, and the Associate Justices one each. The practice of appointing law clerks started in 1886, when Congress authorized stenographer-clerks (24 Stat. 254), some of whom were lawyers. These people not only rendered stenographic services but served as law clerks as well. In 1919 law clerks, as such, were authorized by Congress for the first time (41 Stat. 209), the appropriation for that purpose being made in fiscal 1920 (41 Stat. 686–87).

Each law clerk usually served for only a year. Roberts, who had a law clerk from 1930 to 1931, then brought in Albert J. Schneider, a lawyer from his Philadelphia law office who stayed with him from 1931 until Roberts resigned. McReynolds, during his long term from 1914 to 1941, had a total of nineteen law clerks. The story around the Court was that Old Mac's law clerks served "as long as they could stand it."

Hughes had a law clerk, of course, but he paid out of his own pocket a stenographer to the law clerk who also was a law school graduate. He was Albert W. Shupienis, who served from 1934 to 1939.

In 1946 two clerks were authorized for each Justice, and in the same year three were authorized for the Chief Justice. My first law clerk was David Ginsburg, who came with me from the Securities and Exchange Commission. Dave was so close to me he was practically a son. He now has a busy law office in Washington, has been very active in civic affairs, and was a key man on several commissions dealing with civil rights. He also managed Hubert Humphrey's campaign for the Democratic nomination in 1968.

For many years most law clerks were graduates of the Harvard, Yale or Columbia law schools. Columbia was anxious for me to take one of its graduates, since I was an alumnus of that school, but because Stone already took a Columbia graduate every year, I decided I would take my law clerks from the graduates of the law schools located in the Ninth Circuit, to which Chief Justice Hughes had assigned me as Circuit Justice. The circuit included Washington, Oregon, California, Idaho, Montana, Nevada and Arizona. Most of these states had law schools, but none of their graduates were ever chosen as law clerks.

How should I select a clerk? It was too expensive for applicants to make the long trip to the capital for an interview. At first I interviewed the applicants when I reached the West each June, but I soon discontinued that practice, as many good candidates had accepted other jobs by June, and I could not get West in the winter.

For several years I let the Dean and faculty of the law school at the University of Washington select a clerk, but again, that restricted the choice. So I compromised, telling the Dean of the University of Washington Law School that I would pick one of his graduates but would not be able to interview any of them until June. I tried that system for a couple of years and ended up with two extraordinary men, Stanley Soderland and Vern Countryman. Stanley went on to practice law in Seattle and in time ran for the Superior Court judgeship, and for the trial court in that state. He was elected, and by the 1960s was recognized by the bar as the outstanding trial lawyer in that state.

Vern Countryman became Dean of the University of New Mexico Law School at Albuquerque, and later full professor at Harvard Law School. I once asked him how he could stand being in that oppressive environment. He replied with a wry smile, "It appeals to my sadistic instinct."

Vern served a unique role in the failure of G. Harrold Carswell, a Nixon appointee to the Court, to pass muster in the Senate. Vern was, in a sense, the key to undoing what seemed almost certain Senate approval. Hugo Black knew Carswell and thought he would be a good Justice. I did not know him then and did not meet him until much later.

Vern compiled all of Carswell's opinions both as District Court judge and as judge of the Court of Appeals. He then sent dozens, perhaps hundreds, of letters across the country asking if the recipient would like to have the list. The demand was enormous; and those who received the list apparently read the opinions. The avalanche of telephone calls and letters pouring in on the senators turned the tide against Carswell.

Eventually I turned to Max Radin, who at the time was on the Berkeley Law faculty, for the actual selection of clerks. Max—Latin scholar, Roman law expert, distinguished historian, humanist—undertook the task of finding a law clerk for me. On Max's death Stanley Sparrowe, a former law clerk practicing in Oakland, California, took over. In the late sixties he asked to be relieved, and another former clerk, Thomas Klitgaard of San Francisco, carried on. And in 1970 a committee of three —Charles E. Ares of Tucson, Bill Cohen of Stanford, and Jerry Falk of San Francisco—took on the task. For each of these men it was a labor of love that exacted days of work—all without compensation. And they supplied me with wonderful men and women.

My clerks chosen from the Ninth Circuit law schools held their own with the best from the better-known schools and served me well. While each of the other Justices had his own circuit, no one else followed my practice of giving the patronage of their prized law clerkships to graduates of schools in their respective circuits. Hugo Black usually chose a southerner, but there were no restrictions on the law school from which he came. Earl Warren, while taking one clerk from the University of California Law School at Berkeley, took the rest from wherever he could find them. Felix always had Harvard graduates. Harlan did the same, but his clerks always first served for a term with a judge in the Second Circuit.

I was the first Justice to have a female law clerk. Back in the 1940s the very able and very conscientious Lucille Lomen of the University of Washington Law School served with me. She later worked at a distinguished career with General Electric. Many of my former clerks settled down in the Far West for practice or teaching.

I did not know how the other Justices used their clerks. Holmes, before me, took a clerk largely as a companion. Brandeis used a clerk as researcher for the voluminous footnotes often found in his opinions. Stone would dictate his opinions, and when he stated a principle of law he would say in parentheses "Cite cases." The draft would go to the clerk, who would then look for the cases supporting Stone's position. Woe unto him if he overlooked an opinion or even a dissent that Stone himself had authored. Franfurter and I labeled Stone's passion for citing his own opinions as "Stone's disease."

Justice Murphy kept Eugene Gressman for six years, a most able man who later practiced law in Washington, D.C. Murphy relied heavily on Gressman in preparing the first draft of his opinions for the Court. The philosophy was Murphy's and the final draft was Murphy's.

There is intrinsic evidence that in later years some other Justices followed the Murphy precedent. If you know a Justice, you become accustomed to his style and pace. Reading the circulated opinions, you sense when someone other than the Justice is the author. In fact, the presence in one opinion of varied styles often meant that several law clerks were assigned respective chunks to write out for the Justice, though he, of course, had the final responsibility. This was never true of Black or myself, but it was true of most of the others. This situation was fairly well known and led to the proposal on the Hill that all law clerks, as well as Justices, be confirmed by the Senate.

I used my law clerks primarily to certify the accuracy of my opinions as to facts and precedents. They did not need to agree with the opinions, and I always welcomed criticism of what I wrote. The law clerk would write a memorandum on each petition for certiorari and on each jurisdictional statement, but I went over each case independently of him. At times I sent a law clerk to the library to collect material for footnotes or appendices. And at times I asked him to draft a concurring or dissenting opinion for me, which I in turn would revise or rewrite. But Court assignments—opinions I had been chosen to write on behalf of the majority—were always my own creation.

Under Earl Warren the demand for more law clerks continued. There were to be four, instead of three, for the Chief, and three, instead of two, for the Justices. One day when the matter was discussed at Conference I made a countermotion to abolish all law clerks. "For one year," I pleaded, "why don't we experiment with doing our own work? You all might like it for a change." My proposal was met by a few smiles but mostly by stony silence.

Brandeis used to point to one mark of distinction that the Court enjoyed. All other agencies of government had vast hierarchies where the man or men at the top were serviced by subordinates. In commissions the usual practice was for department heads or bureau chiefs or their staffs to draft the opinions, which would be passed on to the commissioners and usually adopted *in toto,* except for dissents. If the headman was a Cabinet officer, his opinions were seldom, if ever, prepared by him—even his mail was drafted by staff members—and it was customary for him to sign letters without even reading them. Brandeis knew these things and realized how irresponsible officials had become. Their essential thinking was done for them by others. "On the Court, it is different," he would say. "Here all the work of making decisions and writing opinions is done by the individual Justices." But with the multiplication of law clerks, that ceased to be the case.

When Warren, Reed and Clark retired, they too had law clerks, but since they seldom used them, the new Chief arranged to use them when they were otherwise not engaged.

As the years passed, it became more and more evident that the law clerks were drafting opinions. Brandeis, I think, was correct in believing that the totality of one decision should rest wholly on the Justice. That simply could not happen unless he was the architect, carpenter, mason, plumber, plasterer and roofer who put the whole structure together.

Frankfurter used his law clerks as flying squadrons against the law clerks of other Justices and even against the Justices themselves. Frankfurter, a proselytizer, never missed a chance to line up a vote. His prize target was Charles Whittaker, named to the Court by Eisenhower in 1957.

Whittaker would make up his mind on argument, only to be changed by Frankfurter the next day. In Conference, Whittaker would take one position when the Chief or Black spoke, change his mind when Frankfurter spoke, and change back again when some other Justice spoke. This eventually led to his "nervous breakdown" and his retirement for being permanently disabled in 1962. No one can change his mind so often and not have a breakdown.

Whittaker was duck soup for Frankfurter and his flying squadrons of law clerks. In one case when the vote was five to four, Whittaker was assigned the opinion for the majority. I had already written the dissent and went to his office to discuss a wholly different matter. When I entered he was pacing his office, walking around his desk with pursed lips as if possessed. I asked him what was wrong. He said, referring to the five-to-four decision, that he had been trying to write the majority opinion but simply could not do it.

"That's because you are on the wrong side," I said.

"Not at all. Not at all. I am right but I can't get started."

"Would you like me to send you a draft of the majority opinion?"

"Would you, please?"

Within an hour the draft was in his office, and when the opinion came down (*Meyer* v. *United States,* 364 U.S. 410) it was one of the few in which the majority and minority opinions were written by the same man.

Near the turn of the century, legend has it, one law clerk (or perhaps it was a stenographer-clerk) leaked a forthcoming opinion of the Court to stock-market operators and was later disbarred. Whether that is true, I do not know. But in the long years I served, there was never any suspicion that a clerk violated a confidence of the Court.

For years I had only one law clerk, choosing instead to have two secretaries. But in the summer of 1970, after Court adjourned, Chief Justice Burger decided that the *in forma pauperis* cases (involving people who cannot afford to pay legal costs) would be reviewed not by the clerks in his office, who since the days of Hughes had been preparing "flimsies," or memos, in these cases for every office and then circulating the petitions and records in the capital cases, but by the Justices themselves, which was a good idea. So he bough Xerox machines and had the petitions duplicated, each Justice getting a copy. He wrote me that to handle the *in formas* he had hired three extra law clerks and had assigned one to my office.

I replied that if I was to have an extra law clerk, I would pick him and asked the Burger clerk to leave. Burger replied that there was no money for another clerk and that he refused to fire the one just hired. So I answered that I could get along with only one. In September, Burger wrote that he had scraped together enough money to hire another law clerk for me. So I had Tom Klitgaard in San Francisco pick me a second one, Dennis Brown, and send him on to Washington, D.C. He and Lucas "Scot" Powe were with me in that Term.

When in 1971 Congress authorized four law clerks for the Chief and three for the other Justices, I finally acquiesced, but I decided I would try to take the third from some other discipline. I turned to Richard Neustadt of the Kennedy School of Government and he sent me William A. Alsup, who was specializing in sociology. Since Alsup was a welcome addition, I decided to try clerks from other fields as well—government, psychiatry and economics—to see if fresh air blowing from other disciplines would ventilate the law.

In 1972 there was a staff problem in my office and David Ginsburg found a young man for me who had just finished clerking for Irving

Kaufman of the Second Circuit Court of Appeals. He was Peter Kreindler who led his class at Harvard Law School. He was indeed a rare "find" and had a reputation for excellence that appealed to Archibald Cox, special prosecutor for Watergate. At Archie's request I released Peter a few weeks early so that he could be in on the ground floor of the Watergate prosecution.

During that Term I often said to Peter, "Imagine me ending up with a Harvard clerk when I made all those speeches over the years saying that Harvard's only ability was to teach law at a distance of a thousand feet."

The reference, of course, was to the large box-office classes at Harvard as contrasted to the small clusters of seminars we ran at Yale.

By the start of the 1973 Term, Chief Justice Burger had acquired a permanent law clerk and other Justices were thinking in the same direction. It was to me a sad development. Under that system the law clerks would acquire more and more power, with no fresh minds coming in annually to ventilate the old stuffy chambers; under such a system the ideas of the "boss," usually stuffy and stereotyped, would never be challenged. That movement would mean the end of the seasoning of the pudding—it would eliminate the spice that fresh young minds brought to the job. Luckily, the plan hasn't worked out too well and there are now only one or two such "permanent" clerks.

Under the Burger Court many law clerks did much of the work for the Justices, and that was not right. A Justice is confirmed for what he appears to be; it is his personal decision that is constitutionally required. Delegation of work merely increases the length of the week—unless the Justice is to be a mere rubber stamp for the clerks. I felt that Congress should demand that no more than one law clerk be authorized for each Justice.

In 1972 Burger suggested the pooling of law clerks to pass on all petitions for certiorari and on appeals. He proposed picking four law clerks, who would be replaced in a few weeks or months by another group of four. The purpose was to prepare memos on all incoming cases and to circulate those memos among the Justices. I opposed the idea, repeating that we were already overstaffed and underworked and that each Justice had a job that "does not add up to more than about four days a week." I emphasized the value of having the Justice go over the cases, as "different eyes see different things." I concluded my memo by saying that law clerks "have never been confirmed by the Senate and the job here is so highly personal, depending upon the judgment, discretion, and experience and point of view of each of the nine of us that in my view the fewer obstacles put in our way, the better." I meant no criticism of anyone. Burger, however, was upset, replying: "I contemplate giving each case individual study and consideration as I have been doing for nearly 17 years as a judge and for 20 years as a practitioner."

The mounting pressure for law clerks was in a sense our undoing in still another way. Each Justice had three rooms—one for himself, one for his secretary, one for his law clerks and messenger. Three law clerks and a messenger meant enormous crowding, for their room was small. That meant moving the messenger into the secretary's office. Yet that was not always satisfactory. As the demand for law clerks grew, Burger came up with the idea of remodeling the interior of the building. One office was to be added to each suite by knocking out an interior wall.

As I have mentioned, I solved my problem by moving back to my original office—number 108—which could not be enlarged because there was a stairwell at each end. That meant I could never have more than two law clerks, which was a way of killing two birds with one stone.

Chapter IX

The Advocates

John W. Davis said that a lecture on how to argue an appeal should come from a judge, not a lawyer. "Who," he asked, "would listen to a fisherman's weary discourse on fly casting if the fish himself could be induced to give his views on the most effective method of approach?" Justice Robert Jackson often spoke to the point, emphasizing two things: first, it is the lawyer's argument, not his eminence, that is important, and second, the purpose of a hearing is that the Court may learn what it does not know, and what it knows least are the facts. To be a successful advocate, he admonished, one preparing for oral argument should hear nothing but his case, see nothing but his case, talk nothing but his case.

Bob Jackson, advocate extraordinary, once told of a lawyer arguing a case before a country judge. "He had barely stated his contention when the judge said, 'There is nothing to your proposition—just nothing to it.' The lawyer drew himself up and said, 'Your Honor, I have worked on this case for six weeks and you have not heard of it twenty minutes. Now, Judge, you are a lot smarter man than I am, but there is not that much difference between us.'" I have always been on the lawyer's side of that kind of argument.

William T. Gossett, former law clerk of Chief Justice Hughes and later his son-in-law, found the following in Hughes's notes concerning advocacy:

The advocate learns to be courteous, but never obsequious, always the gentleman. He learns how important it is to keep one's temper, never to appear nervous or to lose poise; never to be petty, wordy, repetitious; to know when to keep still; to express himself candidly, concisely, always going directly to the power; to use a rapier rather than a club; to have one's papers so arranged that whatever may be needed will be immediately at hand so that he does not have to fumble; to be so well prepared that he is ready for any emergency; not to be tied down by brief or memoranda and always to show spontaneity as well as alertness.*

The all-time record holder of cases argued before the Court by one counsel was set by Walter Jones of the Virginia Bar; between 1801 and 1850 he argued 317 cases. Daniel Webster of the Massachusetts Bar is second with nearly 200. John W. Davis of the New York Bar is third with 140 cases argued between 1913 and 1954. A close runner-up to Davis is Erwin N. Griswold of the Ohio Bar and the Massachusetts Bar, who by 1974 had argued 114 cases.

During my time on the Court we heard both great arguments and miserably poor arguments. When some incompetent soul was wasting our time trying to present a case, I often sent a note to Felix Frankfurter. Sometimes it read: "I understand this chap led your class at Harvard Law School." Sometimes it read: "Rumor has it that this lawyer got the highest grade at Harvard Law School you ever awarded a student." Almost always Felix would be ignited, just like a match.

There are few creative forces in the law because it is, by its nature, rooted in the past. A lawyer's advice is his prediction, based on that past, as to what a court will do tomorrow. Judges come and go, so there is a constant recasting of the constituency of the bench. Yet the judges, no matter who appoints them, or whether they are elected, are not revolutionary characters. They are not protagonists of change; their oaths quite properly commit them to maintain the existing order. Since law must change under pressure of new conditions and newly discovered facts, the result is that apart from convulsions created by constitutional conventions, the change in law is like a glacial movement, slow but relentless.

In 1949 I gave the Cardozo Lecture at the Bar of the City of New

*New York County Lawyers Association lecture, March 15, 1973.

York. After nearly a decade on the Court, I felt the need for constitutional law to be rid of the restrictive constructions adopted by the majorities who preceded me to serve the financial interests of the corporate world, not the public. To dramatize my point, I said that I would rather create a precedent than find one. In 1972, Erwin Griswold, former Dean of Harvard Law School and then Solicitor General under Johnson and Nixon, delivered the Cardozo Lecture on the same platform and took me to task for such a light-hearted, irresponsible philosophy. Stability, he said, was what we needed in the law, not new precedents. Yet technology was changing, and with it, critical problems arose. Electronic surveillance was in its heyday. Should not the law keep up? I speak of the Fourth Amendment designed by James Otis to keep government agents from ransacking a man's home or his files. But now the ransacking can be done electronically with no physical intrusion. Must the law stand still while politicians, hungry for more power, seek to level all the necessary barricades to liquidate or destroy their opposition?

The Griswold point of view was the Nixon philosophy. As his Solicitor General, Griswold was obeying his master. And that is the way it has been since the beginning—the clash of ideas of opposed philosophies. The run of lawyers in the 1960s and 1970s were in the Griswold-Nixon tradition. Those who sat in Philadelphia in 1787 had a broader vision of the public welfare.

The lawyer building a record is supposed to be the architect who, familiar with the grand design, tries to shape the facts through the lips of witnesses and through exhibits so as to meet the requirements of precedents and to show telling differences that will mark a new and different development. He who argues a case on appeal underscores the facts that he hopes will send the case down the mainstream or divert it into a different channel.

The man who tries the case is ideally the man to argue it on appeal, provided of course he knows the grand design of the law pertaining to the particular problem. Some country lawyers, indeed most of them, are timid when it comes to the last appeal and send the case on to a sophisticated advocate with a reputation for appellate work. This lawyer—who by the law of averages is likely to be mediocre—usually makes a worse argument than his correspondent would have, for he is apt to treat a cold record less intelligently than would the man who tried the case.

The less successful appellate lawyer spends his time telling the Justices what their opinions mean, often reading excerpts from them. The pre-eminent appellate advocate makes a distillation of the facts to show why the case fits neatly between two opposed precedents and why this particular case should follow one rather than the other. It is the education of the Justices on the facts of the case that is the essential function of the appellate lawyer.

The country lawyer who bellows at the Justices as if they were jurors usually makes a great mistake. For then the Bench gets more wind than light. The color and cunning of the country lawyer may, however, make a lively and interesting case out of a dull problem. Judges do perk up at such tactics and often get a new and wholly different impression of a case because of a colorful presentation of the facts. But, to repeat, the facts of a case are the essentials. Once they are divined, it is easy indeed to fit the case into accepted categories of the law.

Even the sophisticated advocate to whom the country lawyer is tempted to send his case is often greatly overrated. One such was Dean Acheson, too pontifical, too much the Episcopalian bishop to be a good advocate. Dean would speak *ex cathedra,* pretty much like Erwin Griswold. These men spoke from the premise of the status quo in the law, of the past and its precedents; they considered any deviation an error. Each knew the art of obfuscation and used his time not to enlighten, but to smother a case with his own personal philosophy, even though it was way out of line with the trend of decisions. They were unsuccessful, unenlightened advocates who missed great opportunities to mold the law because they lectured the Justices on their alleged shortcomings.

In my time on the Court the questioning from the bench was often relentless. The story is that when Justice Brandeis sat at one end and Justice Clark at the other, they often went at an attorney hammer and tongs. One lawyer was so beset by them that he hardly had time to argue his case. When his time was up, Chief Justice White brought a halt to the argument.

"But, Chief Justice, your two end men have used up all my time!"

To which White replied, "It is not the concern of the Court how an attorney spends the time allotted him."

I shared that attorney's concern, feeling that the time set aside for a lawyer was his time, not mine. So over the years I asked very few questions. The other Justices were not as reticent. Black and Frankfurter probably led the list in intensity of questioning. Whoever the questioner, I soon learned that the idea was not to throw light on dark spots but to expose one's own view, with the hope of convincing one or more of the Brethren that the questioner was right. Questioning from the bench was, in other words, a form of lobbying for votes.

Some of us would often squirm at Frankfurter's seemingly endless questions that took the advocate round and round and round. One day Felix kept shouting at the lawyer, "Give me one case that stands for that proposition!" Over and again the same question came to the bewildered advocate. Finally I leaned over and said, "Don't bother to send Justice Frankfurter the list he wants; I'll be happy to do it myself." For once Felix stayed quiet.

At times some interesting and unexpected events occurred in the courtroom. In one case, involving a judgment obtained by fraud and the remedies for correcting it (*Hazel-Atlas Co.* v. *Hartford-Empire Co.,* 322 U.S. 238), the questioning from the bench was very searching. The critical document was, as I recall, an affidavit; and I asked an attorney, "Who prepared this affidavit?" He instantly fainted, falling to the floor and hitting his head against a table as he went down. Chief Justice Stone recessed the Court while attendants and a doctor administered to the stricken lawyer. In due course the Court reconvened, and the lawyer, now recovered, though a bit shaky, turned to me and said, "In answer to your question, I drafted the affidavit." I admired him for his frankness and for his guts.

As I have described elsewhere, when Stanley Reed was Solicitor General he fainted while arguing a case before the Court, but shortly revived. In 1973 James A. Chanoux of San Diego passed out when arguing a Fourth Amendment case. He was removed to a hospital and the case was reargued the next week, by a colleague who came on from San Diego. (See *Almeida-Sanchez* v. *United States,* 413 U.S. 266.)

Prew Savoy argued *Soriano* v. *United States* (352 U.S. 270) on December 5, 1956, and died within thirty-six hours. At the time of argument he was in the last stages of lung cancer and had to fortify himself for the oral argument with blood transfusions, but he had lived with his case a long time and felt so keenly about it that he wanted to argue it even on his last day on this earth.

Prew was an expert fisherman and loved to drop a dry fly on a shaded pool where a trout usually lies in wait. There are not many such streams along the mid-Atlantic coast. One runs near Thurmont, Maryland, not far from Camp David, the presidential retreat. The river is a series of pools covered by low-hanging branches. Brown trout up to eight pounds have been caught there.

Prew helped form the Order of the Jungle Cock, which held an annual meeting at a lodge on the side of this creek. Every member was to bring to the annual meeting a young man fifteen years of age and teach him fly casting. I was a member and joined Prew there on several occasions. In those days he was a wiry, agile person who could work his way easily up a treacherous riverbed. When he argued the Soriano case he was a gaunt wisp of a man whose voice was barely audible and who had to cling to the lectern as he talked.

I often saw Justices snoozing on the bench, a performance that seemed to me an insult to the bar. I swore I would never sleep there; and I kept my promise, though once I had a close call.

My doctor, Hill Carter, and I had arisen one April morning at four o'clock to go trout fishing in Virginia on the opening day. We were fishing an hour later and back at his hut having a sandwich and a drink by ten. In those days the Court opened its session at noon, and I was there on time. But by a quarter after twelve the voice of the lawyer came and went, at times almost entirely fading away. By twelve-thirty he seemed almost to dissolve before my eyes. At that point I left the bench, repaired to my office and slept an hour, to awaken refreshed.

There were nervous, worrisome lawyers who were very much on edge during oral argument. William C. Wines, who represented Illinois in many cases, was such a person. He was conscientious to a fault, and while arguing, he would wring his hands as if he were in great internal turmoil.

No one ever argued with greater intensity, precision and force than Robert H. Jackson when he was Solicitor General. He wore a pince-nez and looked very much like a professor (which he was not) as he lifted his eyes from his notes and gave the Court a piercing look over his spectacles.

Those who represented a particular agency of government usually were long-term employees. As a result, members of the Bench came to know them intimately. They came to know who was brilliant and who was pedestrian. They came to know, by the person who stepped to the lectern to argue the case, what the agency thought of the merits. When one of several lawyers (whose names I do not reveal) appeared to argue, the word went up and down the bench: "The Department of Justice is about to confess error." Actually there was no formal confession of error in such a case, but the low caliber of the lawyer was a telltale sign that the department did not rate its side of the case very highly.

Few truly good advocates have appeared before the Court. In my time 40 percent were incompetent. Only a very few were excellent.

The best Solicitor General as far as advocacy was concerned was Charles Fahy, who served from 1941 until shortly after FDR's death in 1945. His virtue was not only clarity and precision, reflecting a sharp-edged mind, but his complete honesty. He never overstated his case; he never stretched a finding of fact to serve his end; he was always frank in stating what the shortcomings of the record were. That is to say, he was meticulous in pointing out the factual weaknesses in the record so far as the merits of his case were concerned.

During his regime the briefs filed by the United States were completely reliable, their accuracy and scholarship outstanding. Under Truman their quality deteriorated. Under Eisenhower two great Solicitors General, Simon Sobeloff and J. Lee Rankin, brought great integrity to their work; and their tradition was continued by Archibald Cox under Kennedy. But under Johnson there was again a great deterioration, no one ever daring to trust any statement of fact or law in a United States brief.

Over the years the Solicitor General's office sent us many able advocates. Oscar Davis, Philip Elman, Daniel M. Friedman, Arnold Rauh and Beatrice Rosenberg were among them. Ramsey Clark, formerly Attorney General, would have rated with the very best of them if he had had opportunities to appear frequently and develop his great talents.

Bruce Bromley and John W. Davis, representing the Establishment, were by all odds its best advocates at the appellate level. I had carried Bromley's briefcase when I was a young lawyer in the Cravath firm on Wall Street. I thought then that he had few peers as a trial lawyer. Of the many cases he argued, perhaps the outstanding one was *Hannegan* v. *Esquire, Inc.* (327 U.S. 146) in which Truman's Postmaster General sought to use his control over second-class mail to prevent the use of the mails for the dissemination not only of "obscene" literature but also of publications which in his judgment did not "contribute to the public good and the public welfare" (*Id.* 150), a requirement that obviously "smacks of an ideology foreign to our system" (*Id.* 158).

What made Bromley so effective at the appellate level of our Court was, first, an easy relaxed manner of presentation; second, the knack of reducing a complicated case to one or two starkly simple issues; third, illuminating those issues with homely illustrations; and fourth, never using the full time allotted to him.

John W. Davis, debonair and eloquent, also had pretty much the same virtues, though he was inclined to be more long-winded. He was counsel to both South Carolina and Virginia, in the school-segregation cases under *Brown* v. *Board of Education* (347 U.S. 483) Such was the last case he argued before this Court; and I felt sad that his professional swan song was in support of a principle of racism that promised to tear the country to pieces. His last words to us were, "May it please the Court. I ask you to remember that the good is sometimes better than the best."

Along with John W. Davis of the old school and Bruce Bromley of a later vintage but in the same tradition was George Wharton Pepper of Pennsylvania. He was in his early seventies when I took my seat and he lived until he was ninety-four. He was a dignified man and most meticulous in his choice of words. He spoke slowly, his eyes moving across the bench. He never consulted any notes. Whether his argument was memorized I do not know, but it was well laid out in his mind, as he never faltered. Questions did not bother him. After an interruption he would resume his argument at the precise point he had reached when the question was put to him.

Pepper, Davis and Bromley—these were advocates of the early years who knew no equal.

Helen R. Carloss, a gray-haired lady from Mississippi, represented the Tax Division of the Department of Justice from 1928 to 1947 in many cases. If seen by a stranger, she would doubtless be identified as a housewife. But she was an advocate *par excellence*—brief, lucid, relevant and powerful. Typical of the complex and important questions which she presented is *Kirby Petroleum Co.* v. *Commissioner* (326 U.S. 599) concerning the right of the lessor of oil and gas land to the depletion allowance where the lease is for a cash bonus, a royalty and a share of the net profits.

Bessie Margolin of the Department of Labor argued many Fair Labor Standards Act cases, and never for years lost one. She was crisp in her speech and penetrating in her analyses, reducing complex factual situations to simple, orderly problems. Typical perhaps of the worrisome but important issues which she argued was *Phillips Co.* v. *Walling* (324 U.S. 490), holding that an exemption from the Fair Labor Standards Act of employees "engaged in any retail . . . establishment" does not include warehouse and central office employees of an interstate retail-chain-store system. As Earl Warren said at a dinner honoring her retirement, she helped put flesh on the bare bones of the Fair Labor Standards Act and made it a viable statutory scheme.

In the sixties and seventies, more and more women appeared as advocates. Their average ability and skill were the same as the male advocates and their presence was no cure for the mediocrity of most arguments before us. I remember four women in one case who droned on and on in whining voices that said, "Pay special attention to our arguments, for this is the day of women's liberation." Several of us did express the view that any law which drew a line between men and women was inherently suspect. That view had not prevailed over the majority saying a discrimination classification in sex would be sustained if "reasonable."

During this argument by the four wondrous Amazons, I sent a note along the bench saying I was about to change my mind on sex classifications and sustain them if they were "reasonable."

Charles H. Houston, noted black lawyer, pleaded civil rights cases before us. One of his best was *Steele* v. *Louisville & Nashville R. Co.* (323 U.S. 192), in which the Court held that a union representing a craft had the duty to represent both the black and the white employees equally. One of his last was the leading case involving the constitutionality of restrictive covenants, decided in 1948 (see *Hurd* v. *Hodge,* 334 U.S. 24). He was a veritable dynamo of energy guided by a mind that had as sharp a cutting edge as any I have known.

Constance Motley, later a federal District Court judge in New York City, was equal to Houston in advocacy of cases. She argued only a few before us; but the quality of those arguments would place her in the top ten of any group of advocates at the appellate level in this country.

As I have said, the unknown country lawyer who has tried the case, lived with it and knows the record inside and out often stands head and shoulders above the sophisticated appellate advocate. In 1942 we had a case raising the question whether the minimum wage provided by the Fair Labor Standards Act was payable to redcaps working in rail terminals, in addition to any tips they might receive. The Court (Black,

Murphy and I dissenting) held that in computing the minimum wage that was payable, the tips must first be deducted (*Williams* v. *Jacksonville Terminal Co.,* 315 U.S. 386). Charles H. Hay of St. Louis, who argued for one group of redcaps, made a powerful and moving argument based on the facts of that labor problem and its economic aspects. Booming voices often conceal cloudy thinking. But Mr. Hay's resonance was matched by penetrating analysis and incisive thinking. He ended his argument by paraphrasing the position of the employers: "The voice is the voice of the Negro but the hand is the hand of the railroad."

Three Harvard Law notables deserve honorable mention, though none was a great advocate. Charles Wyzanski, who was to make a distinguished record as federal District Court judge, was bright and flashy, given to nourishing his reputation by remembering leading cases not only by their names but also by the volume and page of the reports where each was published. Paul Freund, who went on to Harvard as a so-called expert on constitutional law, also had a gimmick—the ostensible profundity of a scholar. Actually he was the dispenser of warmed-over theories of law that seemingly were objective but actually were tools to keep the "proper" people in control of society.

Frederick B. Weiner, a grandnephew of Sigmund Freud, was pompous and learned and an "expert" on military law, but much too conceited to be taken seriously.

These three Harvard notables had reputations promoted by sycophants. But lesser lights and lawyers not well known brought greater distinction to advocacy at the appellate level: Oscar Davis (later to serve on the Court of Claims), Daniel Friedman and Beatrice Rosenberg (all of the Department of Justice) made more enduring contributions to the art of advocacy before us than most of the "big-name" lawyers.

Edward Bennett Williams, best known perhaps as a criminal lawyer, would certainly be in any list of the top appellate advocates who appeared in my time. He argued both civil and criminal cases and had the rare capacity of being able to reduce a complicated record to a few simple capsules that marked the heart of the case.

Perhaps his leading civil case was *Costello* v. *Immigration Service* (376 U.S. 120), in which an immigrant who had become a citizen was convicted of two offenses involving moral turpitude. Later he was denaturalized and after that happened was ordered deported. The Court held, on the basis of the federal statutes, that crimes committed by a citizen did not make him deportable after he had become an alien by virtue of denaturalization proceedings.

In my time probably the best single legal argument was made by Abe Fortas in 1963 in *Gideon* v. *Wainwright* (372 U.S. 335). The Court had appointed him to represent Gideon, an indigent who had been tried and convicted in a Florida state court for a felony, without counsel to represent him, although he had requested the trial judge to assign him a lawyer. In 1942 the Court (Black, Murphy and I dissenting) had held that save for capital offenses, a state could require an indigent to stand trial for a felony without counsel to represent him (*Betts* v. *Brady,* 316 U.S. 455). A unanimous Court reversed that decision in 1963, not so much because it had changed its mind on constitutional theory, but because the failure of defendants to have counsel at their criminal trials resulted in a host of habeas corpus petitions which years later raised constitutional questions that would have been brought up at the trial had the accused been allowed a lawyer.

Abe Fortas made a powerful argument. His advocacy was a skillful combination of the evolution of state laws, the practical impact of the old rule on criminal administration, and the service of the Due Process Clause of the Fourteenth Amendment in conditioning the procedure of law enforcement at the state level.

Clark M. Clifford was a trial lawyer of note when he practiced in St. Louis, Missouri. Though his Washington, D.C., practice was largely corporate, he kept fresh his art of advocacy, in part by accepting assignments to represent indigents in appellate courts. His arguments before us, though not numerous, were good. Perhaps his best argument was in *Ashe* v. *Swenson* (397 U.S. 436), a state case involving double jeopardy which we had assigned to Clifford for argument.

He had been on the White House staff during Truman's years; when Kennedy took over, he was brought in as an occasional adviser. The same happened when Johnson was President; in fact, each President who asked Clark for advice came to lean on him more and more. They found in him a high type of advocacy.

Lawyers who are "house counsel" tend to become obsequious, giving the advice their "boss" wants to hear. Outside counsel in the Clark Clifford tradition are coldly objective and brutally frank in their advice. At the start, Clark was convinced that LBJ's policy in Vietnam was the correct one, so he gave advice within that framework. He hewed strictly to a professional line, not deviating in order to effect a compromise with opposing advisers.

This trait pleased LBJ in the early days of the war, for he found Clark furthering the hard core of his thinking. He found Fortas equally convincing. Thus LBJ told me of a meeting when the Joint Chiefs of Staff, along with Robert McNamara and Dean Rusk, presented various views as to what to do in a given situation. "I turned to Clark and asked him what he thought," LBJ said. "I asked Abe what he thought," he added, "and he agreed with Clark." According to Johnson, Clark and Abe spoke with clarity and emphasis ("They hit the nail right on the head"), LBJ meaning that they tapped his innermost desire.

"After the meeting McNamara came up to me and asked, 'Mr. President, I can't understand why you bother consulting your experts. For in a pinch you pick two guys off the street, bring them in, ask their views, which are opposed to the views of the rest of us, and follow their advice.'"

When LBJ found his advisers hopelessly split, he hated to make a decision. He would wait patiently for one strong voice that confirmed his own opinion of what he should do. When consulting with Clark and Dean Acheson (who grew far apart as Clark's position on Vietnam gradually changed), he began to get contrary views; and these he disliked. So he'd say, "The two of you go out and thrash it over and come back with your recommendation."

Out they went and talked and talked, neither changing one whit. So when they returned, LBJ was faced with the dilemma of having to announce his own deep-seated prejudice, not being able to pin it on some adviser.

By the time Clark was made Secretary of Defense, in February 1968, he began to have doubts about LBJ's "presidential war" in Vietnam. But his views had not yet changed significantly.

He had not been at the Pentagon long when the doubt began to evolve into an opinion, and by March, less than a month later, that opinion had evolved into a conviction. I relate in a later chapter how that conviction was converted into action, causing LBJ to promise "peace talks" that at last ended in Paris, and convinced him not to run for re-election.

The most outstanding advocate of all was Simon H. Rifkind, my classmate at Columbia and my lawyer in the impeachment proceedings against me. He was a powerful and animated advocate, putting into a capsule the essential facts of the case and relating them to the existing or emerging pattern of the law. He had a bright conscience, an astute mind and a sense of relevance of facts. His leading argument before us was probably *First National Bank* v. *Cities Service* (391 U.S. 253), in which the Court was divided, I being disqualified. Si Rifkind's training as a federal District Court judge had been stern and demanding, and he utilized that experience and training in perfecting his extraordinary advocacy. We had also named him as Special Master* in *Arizona* v. *California* (373 U.S. 546), in which he rendered an outstanding report on a complicated matter involving the amount of water various states might use from the Colorado River and its tributaries. The Court, speaking through Black, agreed with him, while I dissented.

One of the worst advocates before us in my time was a classmate of mine at Columbia whom I had tutored in vain as a student. He presented a notable array of cases before the Court—and lost every single one. He took his losses with anger, for, as he once told me, Stone, also a Columbia Law man, was on the Bench and was the cruelest of all in his questions. But no courtroom encounter should be expected to be a tête-à-tête.

After Earl Warren became Chief Justice we instituted the practice of recording on a tape machine, visible to everyone, the entire oral arguments of each case. Later in the sixties we arranged with the National Archives to keep those tapes in perpetuity. I was on the committee of the Court that finalized the arrangements with the Archives. I learned that the tapes were quite popular and very much in demand. I had assumed that members of the bar, professors of law, graduate students in law and government would be those who used the tapes most. Not so. Those who sent for copies or came to the Archives to hear the tapes played were teachers and students of public speaking. Lawyers may imagine that the substance of their polished phrases were the enduring contributions; but it is not their ideas that live on so much as the manner of their speech.

*A Special Master may be appointed by the Court to serve as "a referee, an auditor, an examiner, a commissioner, and an assessor." See *Moore's Federal Practice,* Vol. 5A, Ch. 53 (1976), pp. 2901 *et seq.*

Chapter X

Judicial
Conferences

In the early years Justices of the Supreme Court "rode circuit." Beginning in 1789 there were federal District Courts and federal Circuit Courts, which covered a larger geographical area than the District Courts. The Circuit Courts were composed of three judges: one district judge and two Justices of the Supreme Court. The Circuit Courts heard civil cases involving $500 or more in which the United States was a party, or an alien was a party, or citizens of different states were involved. They also heard certain defined criminal cases (1 Stat. 73).

A storm arose over the power of Congress to require Supreme Court Justices to sit as circuit judges. The legislation, the Circuit Court Act of 1802, was a Republican measure and the Justices were all Federalists. Yet, to the surprise of the Republicans, when the question arose a year later, the Court held that the act was constitutional (*Stuart* v. *Laird,* 5 U.S. 299). That decision, wrote William Rawle in 1825, shows that "party taint seldom contaminates judicial functions."* That decision, made in a day of stormy seas, got the Court off to a good start.

The volume of legal business at the Supreme Court level was very slight until after the Civil War. During the first sixty to seventy years, most of the time of a Justice was spent riding his circuit, the geographi-

*Charles Warren, *The Supreme Court in United States History,* Vol. I (Boston: Little, Brown, 1937), p. 272.

cal area described by Congress. Thus the Fourth was, in those days, the District of Columbia, Virginia, Maryland, North and South Carolina. John Marshall was the first Circuit Justice of the Fourth, and since then the Fourth Circuit has always been served by the Chief Justice. When John Marshall was riding circuit he was trying cases in the federal trial court in the Fourth Circuit.

Under President Ulysses S. Grant, Congress changed the number of Justices from five, as it was in the beginning, to nine; post–Civil War days gave rise to an increasing volume of work, and travel time was slower.

In 1891 Congress created a circuit Court of Appeals of three judges, each having only appellate jurisdiction (26 Stat. 826). The Justices of the Supreme Court stopped riding circuit, but each, as Circuit Justice, had certain duties to perform, such as considering applications for stays, for bail, for extensions of time, and so on. The Ninth was my circuit from the beginning; at first it included the seven Western states and was extended to Alaska and Hawaii when they were admitted. In my time no Justice sat as Circuit Justice in his Court of Appeals except Felix Frankfurter. His was the First Circuit (Massachusetts, New Hampshire and Maine) and he arranged it so he could sit on a case or two. In the early days a Justice who sat as Circuit Justice would also sit on the case if it came up on appeal. Today the Justice would excuse himself.

By statute there is an annual Judicial Conference in each circuit. In some circuits the conference was hardly more than an extended luncheon meeting. Such was true in the Second Circuit under Learned Hand. The Fifth Circuit (Alabama, Georgia, Florida, Louisiana, Mississippi and Texas) as well as the Fourth were a combined business and social affair.

A few Justices on the Supreme Court have been from the Fifth Circuit: Lucius Quintus C. Lamar, Edward D. White (who became Chief Justice) and Hugo Black. Hoover had nominated John J. Parker from the Fourth to our Court, but he had not been confirmed due to the opposition of labor. Owen J. Roberts was named instead, and took that seat, though in my view Parker was much the superior judge.

Hugo Black would never miss a Fifth Circuit conference. At first he was rather coolly received, the circuit judges considering him radical. In time they came to love him; and his annual custom was to give them a lecture, much in the same fashion as he had taught a Sunday School class in Birmingham, Alabama, for years.

Our conferences at the Ninth Circuit were more like social affairs. At the start William Denman was Chief Judge. He had a talented and attractive wife, Leslie Van Ness Denman, who researched Navajo folkways and wrote *Dance With Fire* (1952), an account of the Mountain Chant, a Navajo healing ceremony to ensure health and well-being and to eliminate evil from the mind and spirit. The Denmans entertained graciously in their home on Telegraph Hill in San Francisco, but he was a bit of a tyrant at the conference. First, district judges were tolerated, but not very welcome. Second, lawyers were neither welcome nor tolerated. Denman made them sit in the back where spectators at court trials sat, not in front of the bar. I thought district judges should be represented not only at the Judicial Conference of the circuit, but at the Judicial Conference of the nation (established by Congress) over which the Chief Justice presides. It is through that national Judicial Conference that most of the proposals for legal changes are made to Congress. Denman fought having district judges represented on it. The leader of the opposition was James Alger Fee, district judge from Oregon. Jim and I were old friends, way back to Whitman College days. He was a Republican, conservative, a bit of a martinet, but a real friend to a man in need.

He and Denman did not like each other. The breach occurred long before Denman had been named to the Court of Appeals. Denman, when he was a lawyer, had the habit of walking across the courtroom with an exhibit, shoving it under the nose of the witness, and like a sledge hammer, assailing the witness. Fee had a sensible rule that if a lawyer had a document to show a witness, he should hand it to the bailiff, who would take it to the witness. Denman rebelled at that rule, and at one trial when he was trying a case before Fee, he started toward the witness with a document. Fee stopped him. Denman took one more step and Fee said, "Counsel, if you move an inch more toward the witness you are in contempt of court and go at once to jail." Denman, white with anger, protested. Fee was adamant and said, "Counsel, you have a choice—either hand the document to the bailiff or go to jail." Denman handed it to the bailiff.

The two men were much alike—stong-willed, determined, resolute. At every conference they clashed. Denman, presiding, would make a statement, and Fee, protesting, would move his chair forward and ask, "So what?" Denman would repeat the statement and Fee would move his chair forward and again ask, "So what?" It always ended with Fee practically shaking his fist under Denman's nose.

Fee had adopted the practice of never having a cocktail or highball with a lawyer; he said it led to improper discussions by lawyers of cases. At one of those conferences, a judge tendered me a reception. Jim Fee, of course, attended but would take no drink. I asked the host if he could put me and Jim in a side room for, say, five minutes and send in a waiter with some bourbon, as there were matters I had to discuss privately with Jim. It was arranged, and Jim and I were soon closeted in earnest conversation. As if to make up for lost time, Jim was tossing off a few one-shot drinks. We soon rejoined the party and in about ten minutes I heard a ruckus at the far end of the room. I went over and there was Jim with his coat off, standing in the best pugilistic style, facing a lawyer and challenging him to fight.

Our Ninth Circuit conferences moved up and down the Coast from Seattle to San Diego, once in Missoula, and once in Reno. Then the local bar association took over and provided unique social gatherings. The Missoula occasion was actually at Glacier National Park, under the auspices of the then Chief Judge, Walter Pope, one of the best minds we had on the Court of Appeals.

We had a wide range of talent in the Ninth Circuit court system. Jacob Weinburger of San Diego held forth for many years as an outstanding judge. Other stout judges in the Ninth Circuit included Louis E. Goodman, who served as district judge from 1942 until his death in 1961.

In 1953 a House committee was looking into certain federal grand jury investigations in California. The grand jury had been impaneled by Judge Goodman, and he was subpoenaed by the committee and asked questions concerning his conversation with the foreman of the grand jury. The functioning of a federal grand jury, Judge Goodman asserted, was part of a "judicial proceeding," and the conduct of a federal judge in a "judicial proceeding" was beyond the competence of Congress to inquire into, except in impeachment proceedings.

Judge Goodman and his six colleagues on the District Court bench stated their views as follows:

> . . . The judges signing below, being all the judges of the court, are deeply conscious, as must be your committee, of the constitutional separation of functions among the executive, legislative and judicial branches of the Federal Government. This separation of functions is founded on the historic concept

that no one of these branches may dominate or lawfully interfere with the others.

In recognition of the fundamental soundness of this principle we are unwilling that a judge of this court appear before your committee and testify with respect to any judicial proceeding. The Constitution of the United States does not contemplate that such matters be reviewed by the legislative branch, but only by the appropriate appellate tribunals. The integrity of the Federal Courts, upon which life and liberty depend, requires that such courts be maintained inviolate against the changing moods of public opinion. We are certain that you as legislators have always appreciated and recognized this, and we know of no instance in the history of the United States where a committee such as yours has summoned a member of the Federal judiciary . . .

Eisenhower named Richard Chambers of Arizona to the Court of Appeals, and shortly thereafter Chambers became Chief Judge. He was nominally quite conservative, but enough of a skeptic to render some wise decisions. He was also an excellent administrator and managed the affairs of the circuit with finesse. There was a growing tendency among federal judges to ride herd on fellow judges. The famous case involving Chief Judge Stephen Chandler of the District Court for the Western District of Oklahoma (*Chandler* v. *Judicial Council,* 398 U.S. 74), in which Hugo Black and I dissented, is an illustration of how easy it is for judges to get a scunner against a judge who may be a bit of a nonconformist and take disciplinary action against him. Young Senator Joseph D. Tydings of Maryland was promoting legislation which would give panels of federal judges broad authority to discipline "culprits." Chambers was violently opposed to that kind of measure and made many trips to the capital to testify against it.

The regime of judges riding herd on "culprits" was ominous because of the conservative leanings of most federal judges. The unhealthy practice had developed of Presidents naming federal judges from lists endorsed by the American Bar Association. The ABA had many fine credentials; but it largely represented the big corporate and financial interests of the country. If we have corporate-minded judges, we should also have sharecropper judges and labor judges. A bunch of sharecropper judges would have no business "riding herd" on another judge any more than would corporate judges. But under the influence of the ABA our federal judges have become rather mediocre, conservative influences in the law.

Under our system, impeachment is the only disciplinary method against judges. This procedure has been made difficult because of our desire to have an independent judiciary. An independent judiciary has been the great rock in stormy seas, but with the tendency of Presidents to make American Bar Association appointments, our only hope as a people was that a President would make a mistake—Presidents do make mistakes. Holmes was a "mistake" by Teddy Roosevelt's standards. McReynolds was a "mistake" by Wilson's. Warren was a "mistake" by Eisenhower's standards. Chief Justice Donald R. Wright of the California Supreme Court was one by Ronald Reagan's standards; and Arlin M. Adams of the Third Circuit Court of Appeals was one by Mitchell's and Nixon's standards.

Men of conscience trained in the law are not easily tethered when given the sovereignty of judicial power.

I always felt that the business sessions of the Judicial Conference were on the long and boring side. The main contributions to the conference, it seemed, were from practicing lawyers who after Denman's time were most welcome and became active program participants. There were three days of conferences, the grand finale being a dinner for judges, lawyers and their wives. I thought they were becoming more like prayer meetings than joyous occasions. So once, when asked to say a few words, I told a story about a lawyer who worked hard to prepare a rather technical paper on Roman law. He went by train to another city to deliver the speech at a lawyers' and judges' dinner. When he unpacked his bag he discovered to his consternation that he had left his paper at home. He was so inexperienced in Roman law that he decided not to improvise, but to choose an ad-lib subject. He chose sex and talked for some twenty minutes on the subject, to the pleasure of the audience. A few days later, after he had returned home, his wife remarked that he had left his prepared speech at home and asked what he had used instead. "Oh," he said, "I gave them a talk on aviation." Later someone who had attended the dinner saw his wife and said, "Charlie gave us one of the most fascinating talks I have ever heard." "Amazing," replied his wife. "You know, to my knowledge he has only tried it twice. The first time he got sick to his stomach, and the second time his hat blew off."

Half of my audience roared; the other half was shocked. And thus ended a restorative effort at after-dinner speaking to judges and their wives.

At another dinner I was preceded by a quartet which had the finest first tenor I had ever heard. I said in my brief talk that if I could sing like that tenor, I'd gladly resign from the Court. I must have received several hundred letters in the next few weeks offering me singing lessons free.

Lyndon Johnson appointed a man by the name of William N. Goodwin to the District Court in Washington State. I had never met him before a dinner of the Judicial Conference. We both sat at the head table, and we had not been there long before he started baiting me. I still don't know what he had against me, but this night he was full of bourbon, and shoving back his chair, shouted at me in a voice that could be heard across the room, "Come on, you bastard, and fight!"

Thereafter Judge Chambers called him the Bad Goodwin. Alfred T. Goodwin, named by Nixon to the Court of Appeals, had been on the Supreme Court of Oregon and was later a federal district judge. Chambers called him the Good Goodwin.

Chambers had a sly sense of humor. He would try to make this statement near the beginning of a business meeting: "I am happy to announce that Justice Douglas, our Circuit Justice, is present. And I understand he will give room service on all applications for bail or for stays of execution."

Chapter XI

The Press

In time I wrote many opinions sustaining and defending the press. I, along with Hugo Black, was a strict constructionist who thought the First Amendment meant what it said when it commanded that Congress shall make "no law . . . abridging" freedom of the press. Black and I also felt that the same restrictions were imposed on the states when it was held that the First Amendment was applicable to them, as I have discussed, by reason of the Fourteenth Amendment—in a decision rendered by the Hughes Court, and in an opinion written by him in 1930.

My defense of the press did not stem from my personal opinion of its quality. It was, I thought, as depraved as it had been in Jefferson's time. My feelings, however, were like Jefferson's—that craven and abusive and self-seeking as the press is, a much worse press would result from governmental surveillance.

So far as accuracy of facts is concerned, in my time the magazine that consistently deserved the lowest grade was *Time.* It was the most inaccurate of all. I made that decision on the basis of the items reported of which I had personal knowledge. *Time* always misstated, exaggerated or manufactured facts in those instances. Eventually I stopped reading the magazine.

The *National Geographic,* for which I did numerous articles, failed for quite different reasons in fulfilling the press function. It had a special charter from Congress making it tax-exempt, and this tax exemption made it very timid of criticism. In 1954, for example, when the French still controlled Morocco, I photographed street scenes, showing children with open sores on their faces, the sores covered with flies. I also ran into the nationalist underground working for the return of King Mohammed, then in exile on Madagascar. Rebellion was boiling and I thought I could get the story, which in fact I did get for *Look.* But the people at the *Geographic* turned me down, saying they always told of the beautiful things that were happening, never the ugly ones. The king whom they were photographing was a stooge of the French, an opium user, and barely conscious an hour or so a day. The magazine produced a beautiful picture story on Morocco, but it was all unrelated to reality.

By the same token, the *Geographic* would not commission stories on Communist lands until and unless the story met State Department approval. The magazine, high-minded and supersensitive to its tax exemption, never, never told the story of the crumbling of an old feudal system. Thus it lost innumerable journalistic opportunities following World War II.

The most accurate reporting, to my knowledge, was on the financial pages of the New York *Herald Tribune* and in the *Wall Street Journal.* The record of the *Herald Tribune* was due largely to Robert Kintner, later a columnist with Joe Alsop and still later president of the National Broadcasting Company. Bob covered the financial arms of the federal government, including the Securities and Exchange Commission. He was smart, honest and accurate on his facts, whatever one might think of his conclusions. The high goals of the *Wall Street Journal* were largely set, in my time, by Barney Kilgore.

Another man in the same tradition was Palmer Hoyt of the *Oregonian* in Portland, and later, the Denver *Post.* He too was meticulous on facts; and when he became editor he launched a revolution in newspaper circles by taking editorial comment out of news stories and putting it on the editorial page. It was a sad reflection on the press that such a move was a revolution. But the American press by and large wrote its news stories to praise or lambast, to build up or cut down the person in the news. The news was slanted to meet the editor's predilections. Robert Lucas, who was with Hoyt on the Denver *Post* and later represented the Gannett clan in Washington, D.C., moved in the same fine tradition, and there were, of course, others.

There were not many real reporters in Washington. A real reporter, as I use the term, is someone who searches out the facts on his or her own. In the capital there were a few solid muckrakers, notably I. F. Stone and Drew Pearson. But most reporters followed the course of least effort and lived on government handouts or curried favor with high officials like J. Edgar Hoover for tip-offs or leads. Presidents, Cabinet officers or agency heads handed out tidbits to favored reporters. Much classified, even top secret, material was leaked in this way. Government's purpose was served and the reporter who reported faithfully, stressing precisely the right angle, could expect to be rewarded again.

The victim was the public, which did not know who the "undisclosed but reliable source" was. Full disclosure would have revealed the strategy being employed. Much of the disastrous build-up of public support for our activities in Vietnam was the product of these discreet "leaks" to the press.

The official line that was pushed by the government as respects Vietnam was often half-truths or distorted facts or plain lies, as the Pentagon Papers later were to show. The lie was often believed on the inside as well, leading men whose personal opinions differed from the official line to drop out of government or accustom themselves to working in a system that produces cyncicism and self-deceit. The fact that a Lyndon Johnson could have his way and mold the American mind as he did is as alarming as were Goebbels' techniques under Hitler.

Secrecy in the press concerning the real authority of articles is not the monopoly of newspapers. Even law reviews, supposedly erudite and objective journals, publish articles which professors and others are paid by an outside interest to write. The judge who cites them in his opinion may be the victim of a gross fraud, for the article on which he relies is the product not of scholarship, but of sly corruption.

The press is often the handmaiden of a special-interest group. Some articles it publishes are written by paid agents of men or by people with an ax to grind—for example, a dictator in the Caribbean or the Nationalist Chinese government on Taiwan. The public relations firms of special-interest groups prepare articles on current issues of public interest, say, pollution or medical care. Then they find an industry group to finance the projects and provide newspapers with special articles and editorials. One editorial, having a particular and favorable industrial slant, may in the course of a week or so appear in two thousand newspapers. The industrialists are not deceived, nor are the newspapers. The only people deceived are members of the reading public. The plague of the "hidden client" lies heavily on the newspapers. Ben Bradlee of the Washington *Post* says that by that practice "we demean our profession," for we let the papers be used "for obvious trial balloons and for personal attacks."

The Washington press had that character, no matter which the Administration, but Nixon gave the practice an evil twist. In his first term there was a nationally known newsman on the White House staff. As I will discuss, one of Nixon's first undertakings as President was to get me off the Court. He turned Spiro Agnew and Gerald Ford loose on me, but this "newsman" also played a role. He wrote stories about me based on wholly manufactured facts and peddled them to Washington newspapers. I knew about them because sometimes a newspaper—usually the *Evening Star*—being dubious about the facts, would try to verify a story by calling friends of mine, such as newsman Harry Ashmore, a Pulitzer Prize-winner then with the Center for the Study of Democratic Institutions at Santa Barbara. As a result, some of the "newsman's" plants were never printed, but the Nixon effort to use the press to destroy a man continued. David Brinkley, the television commentator, joined their forces. Nixon's staff had apparently started a rumor that I was tied up with some nefarious Mafia figures. I hadn't even heard of the characters, let alone did I know them. The press called my office, and my secretary was instructed to tell them that. Brinkley chose the episode to wind up his TV broadcast that night, stating what the charge against me was. Then, with a knowing look in his eye, he added, "Justice Douglas, when asked, replied that he knew nothing about the matter." The tone of voice implied that I knew plenty but would not talk. Brinkley exploited the use of innuendo in his broadcasts, proving Agnew's case that the mass media used TV to do in their target-people.

One of the saddest examples of a person who used this technique was Bob Allen, an old friend of mine. He printed stories about me that were totally made up, and he never once checked them. Bob Allen, husband of the outstanding journalist Ruth Finney, was, in his later years, "down at the heels" and struggling to keep his column alive. So the Nixon "newsmen" of the Washington world would feed him fabricated lies. I was greatly tempted to sue, but my attorney, Simon Rifkind, always vetoed it. A libel action would only publicize a column that few people read and catapult a miserable Bob Allen into national prominence. Yet in these discussions with Si Rifkind I began to realize that at times a libel suit is probably a substitute for a duel. Man's combative instincts are strong, as is his urge that a wrongdoer be called to account.

I have spoken disparagingly of the press, but in its exposure of the dirty deeds and tricks produced by Watergate, it lived up to its ancient tradition. Carl Bernstein and Bob Woodward, the reporters who dug deep, were brave and stalwart, for a Nixon would use any of his great powers to destroy an investigative reporter. The publisher of the Washington *Post*, Kay Graham, also had courage and guts, for her TV and radio licenses could have been revoked by Nixon at any time. But for the press, America might have suffered Watergate without any remedy. Jefferson would have been proud of the manner in which the press uncovered the whole Watergate scandal—wrongdoing that could really have done us permanent damage, shaking the very foundation of the republic.

Quite the opposite of the Bob Allens of journalism was Leonard Lyons of the New York *Post*. I do not believe he ever said an unkind or malicious word about anyone in his column. He sorted out his stories, leaving the ugly ones to the scavengers and making only light-hearted, humorous or gracious comments about people. Bob Considine of the Hearst group had an equally high standard, though he wrote a very different kind of column.

It was through Leonard Lyons that I met Walter Winchell, newsman, columnist and night-club devotee, and one of Lyons' competitors at Sherman Billingsley's Stork Club in Manhattan. Winchell made this his night headquarters, in the back room for very special people called the Cub Room. There he had table number 50, and to it came all the public relations men hoping to get him to use one of the gags or *bons mots* of one of their clients.

Winchell was famous for his diatribes against the famous and the great, giving no quarter. He posed as the great muckraker of the thirties and forties. When World War II arrived, Winchell joined the Navy and became a commander, and while in the service, continued both his column and his Sunday-night broadcast, the latter sponsored by a cosmetics firm. Criticism mounted over a naval officer profiting from a private enterprise of that sort while on active duty. Winchell came to Washington, D.C., greatly disturbed. During dinner at the Mayflower Hotel he told me that he was going to commit suicide and showed me the .45 Colt revolver in his pocket that he planned to use that night. I walked the streets with Winchell until the first streaks of dawn came over the city. I dissuaded him from suicide, promising that FDR would see him and work out the situation. I called FDR before eight that morning, and he saw Winchell before noon. What, precisely, transpired I do not know, except that FDR put his arm around Walter. Harry Hopkins arranged for Winchell to leave the states for a while, on a mission to South America. Winchell did just that, and the plane on which he traveled engaged a German submarine en route, earning Winchell a Silver Star.

Walter Winchell played a dramatic role in the New Deal. As FDR's charisma could not be transmitted without radio, so would his program have faltered without radio and Walter Winchell. About 90 percent of the population listened to Winchell's Sunday-night broadcasts—more people, probably, than listened to FDR. Winchell was the "hatchet man" who exposed, ridiculed and belittled the opposition. He took to Main Street, in language the common man could understand, the basic issues involved in the New Deal and a description of the characters representing both good and evil.

Winchell's Sunday-night broadcasts, at nine, started out with "Good evening, Mr. and Mrs. America and all the ships at sea." He spoke in a staccato voice. He coined words—Ratzis (isolationists), whodunit, fooff (pest), debutramp (debutante). He was so popular that NBC gave him a contract that was to pay him $10,000 a week for the rest of his life.

Everything went well for a while, until Winchell became piqued at some minor episode. He marched into the office of the president, Robert Kintner, full of complaints and threatening to cancel the contract. Kintner handed him pen and paper, telling him it was agreeable with NBC if Winchell canceled out. Winchell, still in a rage, wrote out a notice of cancellation and gave it to Kintner, who accepted it by initialing the document. Within a few weeks Winchell's lawyers were pounding on NBC's door, seeking to have the contract restored. But they were unsuccessful. Thus ended what had probably been the most remunerative contract ever signed until that time by a network for a radio broadcaster.

In the early years Joseph Alsop, soon to gain eminence as a political reporter, gave Sunday stag luncheons at his Georgetown house. Joe, a gourmet, was obese and had the sense to do something about it. He went into Johns Hopkins Hospital and lost the necessary poundage, paying the hospital and medical bills with a fee for an article that appeared, I believe, in the *Saturday Evening Post*. At these Sunday luncheons Joe had a few old friends and a few luminaries. It was like *Meet the Press,* with Joe serving in an active role as questioner. I remember young colonels, who later became generals, expounding on American naval, air and ground power. There were searching questions concerning FDR's next political move, the likely fate of a controversial bill before Congress and similar issues. But Joe's main interest was Churchillian. Joe saw America's power in military terms. Like Churchill, he was an aristocrat who had little concern for people except as foot soldiers to establish beachheads, pilots to bomb cities, and seamen to impose blockades. In his eyes we were even then moving to take over England's position in the global scheme of things. I do not say this critically or with a feeling of ill will. Joe was innately very conservative, but he was not a Goldwater or Reagan, or a John Bircher as the right wing emerged in later years. He was a champion of civil rights, a respecter of the aristocracy of talent, and a Tory in the best sense of the word. All of these qualities and attitudes which were evident in the late thirties came to full fruition in his writings on the war in Vietnam in the sixties. Joe's regard for the decencies of our civilization was always evident, as when he came to the defense of Hugo Black when he was cruelly hounded by the press because of his earlier and fleeting association with the Klan.

There were some great radio and TV men in my time, one of the ablest, one of the most forthright and fearless being Elmer Davis, who died in 1958. He was a Hoosier who became eminent as a newsman, a novelist and later as a free-lance writer. In 1939 he became a radio news analyst; he and Edward R. Murrow, another close friend of mine, covered World War II and brought its horrors and drama into American living rooms. Eric Sevareid, another friend, joined them in broadcasting the news of the Japanese and the Pacific. Their technique was never to sugar-coat bad news. FDR soon created the Office of War Information and made Davis the head of it, giving him the power to issue directions to all agencies of government with respect to their information services. In that role Davis made many powerful enemies; and many came to the fore when he resumed broadcasting at the end of the war.

Davis entered the lists in the campaign against McCarthyism and the technique of destroying men and women through innuendo and suspicion. Using the manufactured figures designed to show that Communists controlled the government, he exposed the fallacy of that propaganda. His motto was, "Don't let them scare you." He and Ed Murrow did more than any others to calm the fears of those who were led to believe that the Communists were about to take over the nation. They greatly honored the First Amendment and our basic premise that a man's beliefs are sacrosanct and that he has the right to express his ideas whether they are repulsive to people or in keeping with majority opinion.

The Black Silence of Fear swept the nation, the fear of being tagged as a Communist or blacklisted because one associated with Communists, real or imagined. During the peak of McCarthyism, some towns became closed societies, intolerant of ideas. In Los Angeles, for example, there was a forum featuring Eleanor Roosevelt, Robert M. Hutchins and myself as speakers. One winter all public halls and auditoriums except one were denied to the forum because the owners or managers of the properties did not want to be associated with these three particular lecturers.

Most newsmen were intimidated by this climate of fear, and Davis and Murrow were in the minority. Raymond Swing, whom I mentioned earlier, was another "great" in the Davis and Murrow tradition, as was Walter Cronkite, who at this same time was struggling to keep alive as a commentator in Los Angeles. He had difficulty getting sponsors because he was considered too liberal. He was kept on the air by my friend Seniel Ostrow, who manufactured mattresses and cherished the liberal tradition.

The journalist and correspondent Paul Harvey was of the opposite school, exploiting the innuendo to attack people and programs. Our newspapers were also running with the crowd. On the national front I could count only ten papers that stood up against McCarthyism—not a very good record for those who pretend to extol First Amendment values.

It is difficult to choose among the various contenders for the post of chief prostitute. The award probably goes to Westbrook Pegler, a clever writer who discovered how to make $75,000 a year through unmitigated falsehoods that tickled the fancies of right-wing readers. He described Eleanor Roosevelt as a madam of a whorehouse. By a stratagem he got into my office, only to write in a piece that my blue eyes could not conceal the Communist that I was. In time his column became so consistently extreme that his syndicate refused to print him. His life was a tragedy due in part to alcohol, but he was very talented and could have done many creative things with his pen.

The Court, I discovered, got very poor news coverage for several reasons. There were few reporters who made the history of the Court their profession. That is to say, the reporters were bright but uninformed men who were doing the best they could with complicated and technical material. Moreover, the appetite of the news services for spot news put tremendous pressures on the newsmen to write their stories in a few minutes and get them on the wires. The result was usually news stories which the author of the Court opinion would hardly recognize as descriptive of what he had written. That's why the public got strange and distorted views of the Court and its rulings. In the forties I pleaded with Henry Luce to give a few solid pages of his magazines to intelligent reporting of Court decisions. He made a feeble effort, but no magazine or newspaper was faithful to the task.

Frankfurter's drive was to get newsmen to study law at Harvard, and some did, notably Anthony Lewis, one of the ablest journalists of my time. Newsmen who study law usually become advocates of a particular type of jurisprudence that dominates the law school where they went, so they are apt to bring to their reporting the prejudices of one school of thought or another. Tony Lewis grew out of that stage; some never did.

One of the best men covering the Court in my time was Dillard Stokes, who worked for the Washington *Post.* He was accurate and meticulous as to details and neither pro-Black and pro-Douglas or anti-Frankfurter in his slant or prejudices. He had one trait, however, that cost him his job. At the end of each Term he put into tables the production of each Justice in opinions for the Court, concurring opinions and dissenting opinions. Frankfurter despised those columns, since they showed, truthfully, that he wrote fewer opinions for the Court than any other Justice. He ranted and inveighed against Stokes in the precincts of the Court, denouncing anyone who would even intimate that writing a few opinions was not equal to writing many opinions. "Cases are not fungible," he would shout. Finally he induced Phil Graham, his former law clerk and publisher of the *Post,* to remove Stokes from the assignment. It was rather sad, because Stokes had more insight into Court problems and more knowledge of Court history than any other reporter before or since.

The Justices had long proposed that headnotes be distributed with opinions to the press so that newsmen would have, in capsule form, the essence of each decision. Frankfurter vigorously opposed the move, claiming that the headnote would in time become the text, to the neglect of the opinion. But finally, in 1971, after he had left us, the headnote, prepared by the Court Reporter, was used, and it has measurably helped increase the accuracy of reports sent over the wires on opinion days. To aid the newsmen we gave up making Mondays the exclusive opinion days, handing down opinions throughout the week when the Court was hearing arguments. In this way the burden on newsmen was somewhat lightened. Yet by and large, mediocrity in reporting continued to be the norm.

The one reporter who stood head and shoulders above all others when it came to the work of the Court was Irving Dilliard of the St. Louis *Post-Dispatch.* To my knowledge, he read every opinion of the Court as long as he was on that paper's editorial page, and discussed and debated the merits of the decisions with the skill of a professor of constitutional law. That newspaper's editorial page therefore reflected the true issues before the Court. But it was the exception. Most editorials expressed the prejudices of the publisher, who was usually unenlightened on the history and background say of the Fourth, Fifth and Sixth Amendments. The editorial page was used as a club by the publisher against the Court; there was little insight concerning the substance of the Constitution even in the supposedly ethical *Christian Science Monitor.*

Of the press there were only a few who were strong in American history, the Bill of Rights, and the problems of a multiracial, multireligious and multi-ideological community. Besides Irving Dilliard there was Irving Brant, biographer of James Madison. Walter Lippmann was a third, and a fourth was Harry Ashmore, who came out of Arkansas. Most of the rest were pretenders who hung their news items on some bit of Americana, such as the flag. There were indeed few editors or columnists who tied current events to American ideals in the philosophic sense. Raymond Clapper, who died a tragic death in the Pacific in World War II, might have been a fifth. But his successor, Marquis Childs, cheapened the profession by using the Fourth Estate as a weapon in a shower of personal vendettas.

The American press, as I have suggested, is by and large a mimic, not an original research group. It prints handouts from government and from industry and expresses its opinions on those items. But the basic facts are seldom mined; the press does not have the initiative or the zeal to ferret out the original from the false or pretended. I will refer more to that when I write about Vietnam. Suffice it now to say that most of the "facts" disclosed in the Pentagon Papers were so well known in Vietnam that only a newsman's decision (or his paper's decision) to look the other way and parrot what the military told him, kept the American public from knowing full well what was going on there, at least during the sixties.

The key role in those years was played by the CIA. Yet there were no news stories out of Vietnam even by the New York *Times* to reveal (a) which members of the Saigon government were on the CIA payroll, (b) what the CIA rates of pay were, (c) how the CIA organized riots, (d) how much they paid those who shouted, those who carried banners, those who only marched. Considering that I knew about these things through my Vietnamese contacts, think how much more a newsman searching Saigon for the truth could have found!

In later years Americans were entitled to know these same facts about CIA activities in Laos and Cambodia. But few, very few, such facts filtered through until much later. The press was greatly remiss in our "war" in Southeast Asia.

Between 1959 and 1963 the New York *Times* had outstanding reporters in Vietnam: Tillman Durdin, Robert Trumbull, Drew Middleton, Homer Bigart, Jack Raymond, David Halberstam. Yet few of the vital facts ever found their way into print. Why this great, this enormous default? It is hard to believe, but I think it is true that in those years our press in Vietnam was as much under the thumb of the armed services as Russia's press is under the thumb of the Politburo.

The details were shown by Susan Welch of the University of Illinois in a paper she read in 1970 at the Political Science Association meeting. Three American newspapers—the New York *Times,* the Washington *Post* and the San Francisco *Chronicle*—prepared the American people for military intervention in Vietnam. The task was easy because Congress, the public and the academic community as well as the press knew little about Vietnam. The press was largely dependent on the Administration for its information and for its assumptions. Newsmen dutifully drew the picture of Ho Chi Minh as a "tool" of world-wide Communism, when many of us who knew Vietnam thought of him more as a Tito. They dutifully reflected the official line that Ngo Dinh Diem was a fascist, unsuited for his task to lead South Vietnam, anti-Buddhist and an oppressor. The *Times* at least had a reporter in Saigon who could have found out (a) that the U.S. official opposition to Diem was due to the fact that he bitterly opposed an American expeditionary force in Vietnam; (b) that many of the Buddhist protests, including some of the immolations, were CIA-arranged affairs; and (c) that the CIA role was to get the agitators to incite the military against Diem so that the police would move in and so that Diem could then be denounced as a bigot for engaging in "religious persecution."

One episode that took place in Geneva a few years later, in 1967, is symptomatic. The Center for the Study of Democratic Institutions held a *Pacem in Terris* conference there; and the Saigon government sent an official delegation to speak and be heard. Gene Gregory, our great Vietnamese expert, told me that the Vietnamese who headed the delegation was on the CIA payroll. As a result the Center—quite properly, I thought—refused to treat the delegation as accredited and disallowed it a chance to speak. James Reston of the *Times* covered the conference, and taking him aside, I told him in detail the CIA's role with that delegation, including the name of the Vietnamese man involved. Reston merely turned and walked away, and the *Times* never printed a word about the episode.

Yet, as the Pentagon Papers later revealed, the CIA's role in Vietnam was the key to our deep involvement. The facts could have conditioned the American mind to accept and acknowledge defeat long before disaster arrived.

The press is very sensitive to its own First Amendment rights, but it has done very little to promote First Amendment values. Spiro Agnew, as Vice President, continually berated the press because it had not been objective. To that Tom Wicker of the New York *Times* accurately replied that what Agnew was expressing "is a rather Marxist view of the news media, a view that the media really should serve the interests of the State. That is the element of the Agnew criticism that in too many cases we have failed to recognize."*

The role of the press is not to defend any institution or any party but to search for the truth involved in important public issues. Many of the "facts" lie buried in the files of the federal bureaus in Washington. The Freedom of Information Act of 1966 (5 U.S.C. 552) was designed to make those agencies open their files. They did not fully do so in my time. While sporadic efforts have been made and some court contests

Columbia Journalism Review (May/June 1971), p. 7.

ensued, the press at no time waged an all-out campaign to get at the truth. It was easier to "cover" the institutions, take their press releases and accept the "official" version as the gospel. The result was that, in my time, the people knew less and less what forces were behind the decisions of the agencies. If the press had done its job, the pitiless spotlight of publicity would have exposed the cancerous condition of our government and disclosed the powerful and evil lobbies that more and more dictate policies.

The press is a many-colored institution. Our stoutest segment is in the regional weeklies, our weakest is in the mass media. They are the weakest because they are supported by advertisers who sell their wares on television and radio. Advertisers do not censor in the crude sense of the word, but, in large measure, they control the mass media. No one selling beer wants to sell it on a "Communist" or "subversive" program lest the product itself acquire that association. So the information on public affairs offered by the mass media covers only a narrow segment of the spectrum of ideas. The long-run effect is to dispense either trifles or bits of controversies that act as sedatives. The mass media, in other words, do not and will not deal with explosive aspects of issues; they are not leaders in debate and ferment. They tend to echo only the philosophy of the Establishment.

Newspapers often compound the defect. The Newhouse chain was typical. It was out to make money, and only to make money. The papers it bought may have been great crusaders at one time, but the Newhouse management stilled their voices. They all marched in unison, dispensing either sensationalism or humdrum views, never crusades.

David Lawrence was one of the first men I met in Washington, and by then he was already a noted newsman. Though we were in some respects poles apart, we were good friends in those early years. Dave used to tell me how close he had been to President Woodrow Wilson. One night as we walked down Connecticut Avenue from the Mayflower Hotel he repeated his praise of Wilson, stopped for a moment, took me by the coat sleeve in a very friendly way and said, "You know, Bill, I am the only real Democrat left in this town. They all became something else." I wondered at the time if it was not Dave Lawrence who had become something else.

Dave had founded the *U.S. Daily,* a chronicle dealing with activities of the federal government. In 1946 he launched a magazine dealing with world affairs and called it *World Report.* In 1947 he merged the two into *U.S. News & World Report,* which soon had a circulation of about 2 million.

He always gave me a complimentary subscription, and I read the magazine regularly, especially the editorials and the articles on the Court. But in the fifties, when the hunt for "subversives" was on and the charge that one was a "Communist" was the most libelous statement a paper could make of a person, Dave Lawrence's magazine introduced into journalism a feature that probably helped circulation.

In those years, cases by the dozens appeared where a person was charged with being a Communist or that he had once been a Communist, or real Communists were tried for teaching Marxist philosophy. A Justice who ruled that individuals so charged were entitled to due process or First Amendment rights like any other person, or who ruled that only their acts, not their beliefs, were punishable under the Constitution and the Bill of Rights, was labeled "Communist" or "pro-Communist." Dave Lawrence's reporters made tables of our cases and rated Justices as 27 percent, 50 percent, 90 percent "Communist." I usually got a 90 percent rating in Dave's columns, and so did Hugo Black. One time, however, Hugo was rated 91 percent and I only 90 percent. I teased him about, saying I was sorry to see him outdo me. Hugo laughed as he replied that he was sure David Lawrence never intended to do Hugo Black a favor.

Arthur Krock, who came out of Louisville, was of the same vintage as David Lawrence. Krock was of the old school of journalism: fastidious, and dedicated to honesty and to the keeping of confidences. By the forties, few would call him "liberal." He had, however, been an FDR supporter until the Court-packing plan in 1937. He did not get along with FDR and was sure that FDR did not trust him. That is why, when he ran a small front-page box in the New York *Times* the day after Brandeis retired in 1939 saying that White House sources predicted that I would take the Brandeis seat, he asked me to mention to no one that he, Krock, had prepared the box. "It would kill your chances," he said.

FDR did have reservations about Krock, but what the basis for them was I never knew until FDR put it all in a nutshell when he told me, "Krock always finds something wrong with everything. If he went to the Louvre in Paris and saw the 'Mona Lisa,' he would praise her to the skies but then add, 'You know, of course, that she had a very ugly case of halitosis.' "

Felix Frankfurter despised Arthur Krock—I have no idea why. Every once in a while Felix would see a Krock column, snort and become truly indignant.

Arthur belonged to the Metropolitan Club, a place where the elite forgathered; he'd take me there for lunch occasionally. As we walked in I would usually say, "Arthur, the rich, conservative members of this club will probably cancel your membership because of your indiscretion in bringing me through these doors." He would always laugh, secure in his high-Episcopalian retreat.

Once in a while under Truman or Eisenhower I would come back from an overseas trip with a report of an imminent newsworthy event. When I did, I told Arthur about it, since, like all newsmen, he valued a scoop. When the story appeared, a White House spokesman would always denounce Arthur and he'd call me to ask what was going on. I'd reply that he was paying the price for being right; and he was right. One story I passed to him involved Harold Ickes, a New Dealer but at heart a Teddy Roosevelt Bull Mooser who eagerly sought out Eisenhower, spent time with him and decided that Ike would make the *ideal Democratic candidate.* When I asked Harold why he was so enamored of Ike, he went on at great length explaining that Ike, though a military man, was against war and would do more than anyone else to promote peace. "With him the Democrats can win," Harold would say. And Harold was also sure that Ike would land on the Democratic ticket. I ran into Arthur and told him the story, which he printed. And passionate denials came from all sides.

Probably the factor that separated the journalists of outstanding quality from the rest of the press was that they held the First Amendment in high regard and were not propagandists for one school of thought or another. They never cheapened the First Amendment in the fashion of some French and Italian newsmen to turn a penny either by manufacturing news or by mixing fact with fiction or fact with opinion so as to make the truth impossible to find.

Yet looking ahead, the days seem dark to me. Great wealth controls most of our news outlets. The conservative influence of the press will continue; a Society of the Dialogue, as espoused by the First Amendment, will be increasingly difficult to stimulate.

Chapter XII

The
Chief Justices

The Chief Justices under whom I served were Hughes, from 1930 to 1941; Stone, from 1941 to 1946; Vinson, from 1946 to 1953; Warren, from 1953 to 1969; and Burger, who was appointed in 1969.

My friend George W. Norris, for many years senator from Nebraska, strongly opposed the confirmation of Charles Evans Hughes as Chief Justice in 1930. Norris said:

> During the last five years he has appeared in 54 cases before the Supreme Court. Almost invariably he has represented corporations of almost untold wealth. . . . During his active practice he has been associated with men of immense wealth and lived in an atmosphere of luxury which can only come from immense fortunes and great combinations. Without charging Mr. Hughes in any way with being dishonest or unconscientious, it is only fair to say that the man who lives this kind of a life, whose practice brings him wealthy clients and monopolistic corporations seeking special governmental favor, it is reasonable to expect that these influences have become a part of the man.

> (72 *Cong. Record* 3373)

What Norris said about Hughes was true as a general proposition but his judgment would disqualify most men of wealth from sitting on the Court, for their holdings might generate in them hostility to reforms that touch the Establishment and its interests. But wealthy men are not necessarily captives of a class prejudice. Brandeis, one of the wealthiest, was a libertarian. Stone, who was affluent, had some of the same characteristics. William Howard Taft, who was Chief from 1921 to 1930, and Stephen Johnson Field, Associate Justice from 1863 to 1897, were different. But Hughes was not a prisoner of the clients he had served.

Hughes was first named to the Court by President Taft in 1910. He served until 1916, when he resigned to run for President against Woodrow Wilson. When Hughes was appointed to the Court, Taft in effect promised to make him Chief Justice to take the place of Melville Weston Fuller (Chief Justice from 1888 to 1910), who was not expected to hold that office long. The vacancy in the office of Chief Justice, in fact, occurred about six weeks after Hughes was named to the Court. At that point all the other Justices, except Holmes, prepared a round-robin letter for Taft saying that they did not want to have Hughes, the junior member of the Court, made Chief Justice. Taft therefore reneged on his promise to Hughes and named a sitting member of the Court, Edward D. White of Louisiana, as the Chief. Hughes returned to the Court in February 1930, after being named Chief Justice by President Hoover. He retired in June 1941.

Brandeis, who greatly admired Hughes, spoke to me at length about Hughes leaving the Court in 1916 to run for the White House against Wilson. "It is good that Hughes lost," Brandeis said reflectively, "not for any political reason, but it was in the best interests of the Court that he did not win." He went on to say that the Court should never become "the stepping stone" for ambitious men, and he emphasized that if Hughes had won, other men might try the same formula and get on the Court to obtain political preferment.

The Brandeis philosophy was similar to Melville Fuller's, who was asked in 1892 by President-elect Cleveland to become Secretary of State. Fuller declined, stating in a letter: "I am convinced that the effect of the resignation of the Chief Justice under such circumstances would be distinctly injurious to the Court. The surrender of the highest judicial office in the world for a political position, even though so eminent, would tend to detract from the dignity and weight of the tribunal. We cannot afford this."

After his defeat for the presidency, Hughes practiced law in New York City and later, between 1920 and 1930, he was a member of the International Court of Justice. Even when he practiced law he gave about one third of his time to civic and bar-association affairs. As a lawyer he argued before the Court almost as many cases as the Solicitor General's office, sometimes as many as four a week. He was a lawyers' lawyer, getting assignments from various law firms. In the twenties and thirties, when a dollar was a dollar and income taxes were nominal, Hughes would get $25,000 for preparing a brief and arguing the case. His practice covered a wide range, including union matters as well as financial and business problems, but he actually won only about half his cases because of the desperate plight of the causes of the clients. He would dictate briefs using a bevy of secretaries. Some would be typing while one was taking dictation. So, very quickly, Hughes had a complete copy, which he usually revised but once.

He used the same technique when he became Chief Justice. He was, I think, one of the leading Chief Justices. He was not a liberal in the populist sense; he was not a reformer. He had however, a keen sense of constitutional values, he was a protagonist of individual rights, and he had a nose for facts that told him when injustices were being perpetrated.

Hughes first made his great impact on me in 1920 when he protested the treatment of socialists by the New York Assembly. The socialists had been advised by the Speaker of the New York legislature that they had been elected "on a platform that is absolutely inimicable to the best interests" of New York and the nation. Thereupon a resolution was passed denying them seats, pending an investigation, the charge being not that these men had violated any law but that they were socialists. They were, in other words, outlawed because of their political beliefs and social philosophy.

Hughes protested to the Speaker as follows:

> . . . If public officers or private citizens have any evidence that any individuals, or group of individuals, are plotting revolution and seeking by violent measures to change our Government, let the evidence be laid before the proper authorities and swift action be taken for the protection of the community. Let every resource of inquiry, of pursuit, of prosecution be employed to ferret out and punish the guilty according to our laws. But I count it a most serious mistake to proceed, not

against individuals charged with violation of law, but against masses of our citizens combined for political action, by denying them the only resource of peaceful government; that is, action by the ballot box and through duly elected representatives in legislative bodies.

This letter rallied public opinion. The press denounced the tactics, as did the American Bar Association. Though the New York Assembly expelled the five socialists, anyhow, Hughes's protest stirred the conscience of America in a dark day of intolerance.

Those unfriendly to Hughes pointed to the speed with which he denounced the "sit in" strikes (see *NLRB* v. *Fansteel Corp.,* 306 U.S. 240). Yet he gave broadening scope to the Fourteenth Amendment by sweeping within it the First Amendment and thus making applicable to the states the guarantees of freedom of speech and of the press, and of the right peaceably to assemble. His were not easy decisions in the context of their times. In 1931 the freedom-of-expression issue arose in a case which involved the display of the Communist red flag as a symbol of opposition to the *status quo,* a statute whose words were "so vague and indefinite" as to permit punishment of fair and free political discussion (*Stromberg* v. *California,* 283 U.S. 359, 369).

The "peaceable assembly" case also involved Communists who had assembled in Portland, Oregon, in protest to raids on workers' halls and homes, to the shooting of strikers by Portland police, to conditions in the local jail, to the tactics of employers in breaking maritime strikes, and the like. Their conviction for criminal syndicalism was reversed, Hughes saying that "even subversives have the right to take part in a peaceable assembly having a lawful purpose" (*De Jonge* v. *Oregon,* 299 U.S. 353).

It takes more than two swallows to make a summer and more than two decisions to appraise a judge. Someone else will have to do the definitive work on Hughes; those who have tried so far have failed. As a living, active Chief, as an administrator, as the head of a federal system of law and justice, he had few peers. My admiration for him grew with the years.

Hughes was once described as being as undramatic "as an adding machine." He was indeed like a terrier after a rat—intent on cornering every fact. Hughes "believed in God but believed equally that God was on the side of the facts."

In preparation for speeches Hughes would put down, in longhand, a brief outline from which he would dictate a draft. Like his opinions, the draft would be revised but once. He would read it aloud several times and then deliver it from memory without text or even notes. William Gossett relates how Hughes, standing in Westminster Hall, London, as president of the American Bar Association in 1924, delivered flawlessly, from memory, a 5,000-word speech. He had a photographic mind.

I have seen him go through a sheaf of twenty or more legal-sized sheets turning each page as if he were merely counting the number of pages in the bundle. He was, however, reading each one, obtaining at a glance the gist of each sheet. He seemed almost ravenous as he ransacked records for the essential facts. His time on a case was spent mostly on the records, not on the briefs.

This knack of Hughes's in the area of facts worked wonders in the *in forma pauperis* cases. A federal act going back to 1892 gave every pauper the right to proceed in any federal court without payment of fees. But governmental accounting practice was awkward and the Court, at the suggestion of Brandeis, substituted instead a "special fund" to be made up of the fees paid by attorneys on admission to the Supreme Court Bar and to be administered by the Court. This "special fund" continued until the act of March 10, 1964, when legislation was enacted channeling all such fees into the Treasury and appropriating money for administering the 1892 act in the Supreme Court.

At the start of the seventies there were over 2,500 *in forma pauperis* cases a Term. In the time of Hughes there were few such cases. But he personally took every document addressed to the Court—whether typewritten or in a penciled scrawl—labeled it an "application for leave to file a petition" and reported each case to the Conference. To give an example of the need involved in such a case, once I was in the office, alone, before the staff came in. The Court's switchboard opens at eight-thirty, but I was usually in my office by seven-thirty. One day Mrs. Douglas promised me that she would call me at eight o'clock sharp on a family matter. I watched the buttons on my phone, and sure enough, at eight o'clock the light went on and I lifted the receiver. A lady's voice —not Mrs. Douglas'—said she had a call for me from Bowling Green, Kentucky. I asked her who was calling. She said, I thought, a Mr. Andrew Binke, whom I knew; so I told her to put him on. A man answered giving a different name—someone I did not know.

He said, "I am in jail. The sheriff let me out to make a call."

"Why are you in jail?"

"My wife put me there. I got out once but she put me back in."

"Why?"

"I don't know, but I need a lawyer; and in thinking about it, you are the only one I can think of."

"You need a good legal-aid lawyer. You can get one in Bowling Green."

"No lawyer—legal-aid or otherwise—will help me in Bowling Green."

"Then call Louisville. They have a fine bar, good legal aid, a fine law school, an active Civil Liberties Union."

"Okay. Thank you very much. Now I gotta go back in the cell and see if the sheriff will call Louisville for me."

Thus the waves of despair and poverty, and the feeling of helplessness, often lap at the very edges of the Court.

In Hughes's time, as now, the cases fell into three categories. First were applications by demented people, some of whom had been adjudicated. In the thirties, one repeated application came from Clarence Brummett, who wanted the Court to help him wage a war against Turkey (see *Ex parte Brummett,* 295 U.S. 719). Most applications came from prisoners. A third type came from indigent persons who had no counsel and knew nothing of federal procedure. In that type of case, Hughes would send for the record below and do the clerical work that counsel usually performs.

In the October 1928 Term, only nineteen *in forma pauperis* cases were filed, and none went to argument. Beginning in 1937, the list grew and grew until by 1945 the volume was sufficient to create a Miscellaneous Docket for *in forma pauperis* cases, and by 1948 there were several hundred cases on that docket. That, of course, was after Hughes's time. But in his day he used the Miscellaneous Docket to ride herd on the lower federal courts that had become lax in dealing with the problems of "undesirable" people.

Under Hughes, we started granting certiorari to review petitions filed by prisoners. The Ninth and Tenth circuits had developed the practice of resolving questions of fact as well as of law on *ex parte* affidavits (i.e., without hearing evidence from both parties). In 1941 we told the lower federal courts to put their house in order, so to speak, by following the statute and holding evidentiary hearings in such cases (*Walker* v. *Johnston,* 312 U.S. 275, 285). And we also held, in *Holiday* v. *Johnston* (313

U.S. 342), another Ninth Circuit case, that the hearing required was one before the district judge, not before a commissioner or master designated by the district judge.

Near the end of the Hughes regime, the Bob White case came up from Texas. Bob White, an illiterate Negro, was convicted of rape and sentenced to death. We denied certiorari in 1939. In 1940 he filed a petition for rehearing, adding an additional ground that his conviction was based on a coerced confession.

Hughes, smelling a rat, sent for the record and discovered ugly episodes involving police brutality leading to the confession. We granted the rehearing and reversed out of hand, citing recent decisions holding that state convictions based on coerced confessions violated the Due Process Clause of the Fourteenth Amendment.

Texas officials complained bitterly, sending lawyers to Hughes to tell him that he and the Court were arbitrary. Hughes, more astute than the Texas lawyers, suggested that the state of Texas file a petition for rehearing, which was done. So we granted the state's petition for rehearing and heard oral argument. In an opinion written by Black, we denied the rehearing, which meant that the case went back for a new trial (*White* v. *Texas,* 310 U.S. 530).

Black's opinion revealed all the horrible details surrounding the way the confession had been obtained, and Texas groaned because the manner of "Texas justice" was fully disclosed.

At the new trial, while Bob White was testifying in a Texas courtroom, the husband of the prosecuting woman entered the courtroom. On the rehearing, I had read the entire record and it seemed to me that the rape charge was concocted, that the woman was the promoter of the project and screamed only when she thought they were about to be apprehended. However that may be, when the husband entered the courtroom he proceeded up the center aisle, pushed open the gate leading to the bar, walked up to Bob White, whipped out a pistol and shot him dead.

The presiding judge dismissed the jury because the Bob White case had become moot. The husband was indicted, tried and acquitted six days later.

At his trial the *prosecutor* said:

> When the case was reversed it looked like the end of the row as far as the law was concerned. The state proceeded to trial again last week, knowing it would not have the use or benefit

of White's signed confession. The state's case would have to be based on circumstances which, without the confession, would have been insufficient to sustain a conviction. It was unfortunate that Mr. Cochran was forced to do that which was done. It was his wish that the law handle the matter. In my opinion the guilty party got justice, but it was unfortunate that it had to be at Mr. Cochran's hands. . . . If I were going into that jury room, I wouldn't hesitate, I wouldn't stand back a minute, in writing a verdict of not guilty. . . . I ask you to return a verdict finding Mr. Cochran not guilty.

And the Texas courtroom audience applauded.

The "nose" Hughes had for facts thus led to the unraveling of a Texas drama that is one of the ugliest blotches on the American standard of justice.

Hughes was, to use a phrase of Brandeis's, "a very efficient Chief Justice." He accomplished in four hours what it would take the average judge eight hours or more to do. He was very meticulous in every respect and most punctilious in the affairs of the Court. At that time the Court met at twelve noon and we always walked in not thirty seconds late or ten seconds late—but exactly at twelve. Hughes would be in his robe in the Conference Room by five minutes to twelve, and if one of the Brethren had not appeared by three minutes or two minutes to twelve, he would send a messenger down the hall to get him. One morning he was impatient because it looked as if McReynolds would be late. So he sent a messenger down to McReynolds's office, which was only a few steps away. The messenger entered, and being brought into the presence of McReynolds, began to tremble and shake. He bowed low and said, "Mr. Justice, the Chief Justice says you should come at once and put on your robe." McReynolds, looking up and calling the messenger by name, said, "Tell the Chief Justice that I do not work for him." McReynolds turned up in Court about thirty minutes later.

Gates, the Court barber at the time, would go out to the Hughes residence (now occupied by the Burmese embassy) every Sunday to trim his beard. Hughes had had the beard for years. At first it was a bristling red; now it was snow-white. It and his mustache gave him a Jovian appearance. Gates, my reliable informer, often told me that the "soil" out of which the Hughes beard grew was "very healthy."

Hughes, though severe and dignified in appearance, had a keen sense of humor. But for his strict Baptist upbringing he would have made an excellent end man in vaudeville. He loved to tell tales concerning the dry era of Prohibition when the wife of an Asian ambassador who sat next to him at a formal White House dinner was anxious for a drink and whispered in his ear, "Have you by any chance got a nip on your hip?" The idea of this august personage carrying a flask challenged the imagination.

Hughes also had a story about the lawyer who outfoxed his opponent when the case was still before a judge and undecided, by sending a present to the judge. His opponent chuckled when he heard about it because, knowing how upright the judge was, he knew the gift would prejudice the man against his opponent. But the rejoinder of his opponent was shattering: "You overlook one thing. I put your card in the package."

William Gossett relates how Hughes and his wife once stepped out of an elevator into the lobby of a New York City hotel. A woman waiting for the lift saw Hughes and his wife walk out and said in a hushed voice, "Oh, I thought you were dead." Hughes smiled and bowed, saying, "Sorry to disappoint you, madam."

Hughes loved Jasper National Park in Canada. He and his wife took a cottage there, and that's where he received his mail bags full of certioraris and where he did his summer work. They ate in the central dining hall. While they were waiting for the dinner bell on the porch one night, a bear approached their cottage.

"Mrs. Hughes was unreasonably nervous about bears," he later told me.

She arose and started to enter the cottage when he stopped her. "Sit down, my darling, and I'll take care of the bear."

The bear came closer, reached the steps of the porch and started up. Mrs. Hughes screamed.

"Don't be nervous," he admonished. Then he walked to the edge of the porch where the bear was climbing the steps.

"I summoned," he said, "all the dignity that I could command, and raising my hands, I shouted at the bear, 'Stop!' "

"What did the bear do?" I asked.

"What did he do?" he replied with a note in his voice that indicated disgust that anyone should wonder what happened. "What did the bear do? He stopped, of course."

One of the most touching episodes in his life occurred near the end when he and Mrs. Hughes entered a restaurant in New York City for luncheon. There were tears in his eyes as he told me, "The whole room became hushed as we entered. Then everyone stood up until we were seated."

As Gossett has related, Hughes was very much in love with his wife, who died shortly after their fifty-fifth wedding anniversary. To emphasize how young she looked he'd say in a teasing way, "Everyone says, 'I didn't know the Chief Justice had married a second time.'" And to family members he'd say, "Mother will live to be an old lady and will say to our children, 'I can't quite remember what the old man looked like.'" On their fiftieth wedding anniversary he wrote his wife a love letter: "Fifty years are all too short for such happiness. All I have I owe to you. If I could have my dearest wish, it would be that I should live with you forever."

Hughes, a great Chief Justice, was also a wise man. On June 30, 1941, as the robed line formed to walk into Court, he turned, raised his hand and said, "There will be a short conference after we rise."

All business had been transacted, nothing unfinished remained, so we all knew that some important announcement was to be made. Hughes was then seventy-nine years old. Though he had been ailing from stomach trouble, overall he seemed in good health.

As we took our seats at the Conference table, Hughes announced that at noon that day he had sent the President notice of his retirement. He then said farewell to us and spoke an affectionate word. With tears in his eyes he said, "I am sure I could continue a few years more and do the work." He was indeed a man of prodigious capacity, as I have said. "But," he added, "I have always feared continuing in office under the delusion of adequacy."

Hughes was eventually affected by a failing heart. The standard treatment in those days was digitalis, the drug obtained from foxglove. But Hughes like many others, including myself, was allergic to that particular drug. With it he would have lived some years longer. Without it, he died at the age of eighty-six, still very alert mentally.

Hughes, unlike many of us, did no work on the Bench, sending for few reports cited in argument and making few notes. He kept his eyes glued on the advocate, following his every word and only occasionally asking a question. He watched the clock like a hawk, never allowing an advocate to exceed his allotted time. His close attention, his complete absorption in the argument, and his Jovian appearance made the presentation tense and taut. The hearings were decorous, without a touch of the tyrannical, but they were not the free-for-all that occasionally took place under his successors.

Under Hughes, the Conferences were on Saturday and the assignments were made that same day. Hughes, however, tried to keep Cardozo's assignment from him until Monday. Cardozo, being a bachelor, had a very meager social life. Hughes knew that if Cardozo got an assignment Saturday night, he would work on it over the weekend. And Hughes thought Cardozo's health was too delicate for that kind of weekend work.

Later Chief Justices were not as prompt as Hughes in getting out assignments. Seldom were any made at the end of one week of argument, if another workweek was to follow. And even then the assignment would not come around until Monday or Tuesday.

The manner in which Hughes conducted the Conference annoyed Stone. Hughes, as I said, was most efficient. The Conference started at noon, and no matter how long the Conference List, we were usually through by four-thirty or five. The discussions were short; Hughes's statements were always succinct. He never interrupted to argue or debate, and he promptly took a vote when everyone had spoken his piece. This was irritating to Stone. Stone was, first, last and always, a professor who wanted to search out every point and unravel every skein. So he instituted the custom of having a rump conference at his house every Friday afternoon after Court. He would preside as the de facto Chief Justice and discuss all the cases to be decided the next day. Black never attended. Frankfurter, Roberts and I usually went, and sometimes Murphy joined us. This rump conference seemed to bring Stone satisfaction because he could express himself.

As he had opposed Hughes's nomination, my friend George Norris opposed Stone in 1925 when Coolidge first named him to the Court:

> If we fill the bench and high executive offices with men who have the viewpoint of special interests and the corporations, we will soon have put the common citizen under the yoke of monopoly, and will have put our Government in the hands of trusts and corporations.
>
> (66 *Cong. Record* 3053)

When FDR sent Harlan Fiske Stone's name to the Senate as Chief Justice in 1941, however, Norris was the only one to speak, this time saying that he recanted what he had said years earlier, and was voting for Stone's confirmation (87 *Cong. Record* 5618).

When Stone became Chief Justice, our Conference was never finished by four-thirty or five. We moved the starting time back, first to eleven and then to ten o'clock, but we still could not finish by six on Saturday. We would come back at ten o'clock on Monday and sit until five minutes before noon, and then go into Court for four hours to hear cases argued. We would again go into Conference at four and sit until five or six. Sometimes we still would be unfinished by the end of the day and have to go back into Conference at ten on Tuesday morning, and again at four in the afternoon on Tuesday. Once we even had Conference on Wednesday from ten to noon and from four to six—to finish up the previous Saturday's Conference List. Under Stone we were, in other words, almost in a continuous Conference. He believed in free speech for everybody, including himself. His insistence upon detail hastened his death. If there were twenty-two points in a petition for certiorari, he would discuss every single one of them. The work was grueling and it was just too great a strain for a man of Stone's age.

He showered Black and me with assignments of cases to write opinions for the Court. Each of us would write thirty or more cases a Term, but Stone was himself a prodigious worker.

Stone, like Hughes, never gave a Justice a new assignment until the old ones were liquidated. That meant that Frankfurter, who liked to hang on to cases for months on end before writing the opinion, wrote few opinions for the Court. For Term after Term, Frankfurter would write nine or ten opinions for the Court and no more.

Stone was a genial and affable man who for some reason did not like Black. But Stone and I had the special relationship of teacher and student that kept us very close during his entire service on the Bench. I remember once after a long discussion we finally voted and came out five to four, Stone being in the minority. Pointing down the table to me, he said, "Douglas, I can understand why my other Brethren have gone astray, but for the life of me, I cannot understand why you went with them." I replied, "Chief, all the law I ever knew I learned from you." He hit the table with his fist and said, "By God, you did not learn that from me!"

Out in Silver Bow County, Montana, there was a sheriff who got paid one dollar a day per prisoner for food. This chap padded the rolls with prominent names he gleaned from the papers, and Harlan Fiske Stone was one. The local authorities would do nothing about the matter. Finally the federal income-tax men moved in, starting a criminal prosecution for nonpayment of taxes. Stone's name, as well as the names of others, was brought out at the trial; and I never have seen a man more upset than Stone. Counsel for the sheriff saw it was time that the twelve jurors, good and true, put an end to the practice of the capital sticking its hand into local affairs. Sure enough, a verdict of not guilty was returned, although there was evidence that some $75,000 had been collected for "prisoners" like Harlan Fiske Stone.

Stone always brought his lunch from home and ate it in the dining room with the rest of us, who ordered from the cafeteria in the basement. His wife made a delicious crab chowder, and I noticed that a cup of it was usually in Stone's thermos.

Stone had long been overweight, and while he was abstemious as to hard liquor, he enjoyed food and wine. He boasted that blindfolded he could tell the vintage of any European wine. When he gave luncheons and dinners he reprimanded those who smoked—not on ethical grounds, but because, he said, one who smoked while drinking wine could not really enjoy the bouquet.

Stone had the worst handwriting on the Court, except possibly for me. There were no vowels or consonants, only many lines. It was a standing joke that if one dipped a fly in ink and let him crawl across a page, one had a fair replica of Stone's handwriting.

Stone had two sons, Lauson and Marshall. The latter was a mathematical genius and rated high in his father's opinion. Marshall's first volume on math was entitled *Linear Transformation and Helbert Space and Their Applications to Analysis.* At a formal dinner in his home, Stone once held forth at length concerning Marshall's achievement. With the book in his hand he turned to me and said, "I am so proud because there's not a sentence in this book I can understand."

Stone did not actually die on the Bench, but he did have a fatal stroke in 1946 while I was reading *Girouard* v. *United States* (328 U.S. 61), to which he had written a dissent. As I announced the decision I heard Stone mumbling, and when I finished I signaled Black to do something. He recessed Court and we carried Stone off the bench and put him down on the couch in the Robing Room. We then had a hurried Conference after we called the Capitol physician, and decided that since Stone was still alive, we should return and announce the remaining decisions; otherwise we might have had to put some cases down for rehearing.

Fred Vinson was Stone's successor. On June 6, 1946, I heard of his appointment on the radio as I was driving to Lyndon B. Johnson's home for dinner. There was of course a toast to Vinson; and after dinner Lyndon suggested that the guests excuse him, Speaker of the House Sam Rayburn and me while we went to Vinson's apartment to drink a toast to the new Chief Justice. He was not there when we arrived. His lovely wife, Roberta, greeted us, and she was in tears.

"Why are you crying?" I asked.

"I never wanted my husband to be Chief Justice," she wailed.

The truth was that Truman had asked Fred that afternoon how he'd like to be Chief Justice. Fred indicated he would not mind in the least. "Don't say anything about it," said Truman. "We'll see." So Fred, who had confided in Roberta about every major decision in their lives, did not call her. In about an hour, however, he heard the announcement over the radio and tried to reach her. He gave up after tracing her through several stops she had made. On her way home she heard it on the radio and started crying. The fact that she had not been consulted meant to her that Fred did not love her anymore.

"I never can go back to Fred," she kept saying.

It took several Scotch and sodas to quiet Roberta, and several more to honor Fred Vinson when he appeared. So we did not get back to Lyndon's party until very late.

Vinson, known as the "great oak" for his stands on the side of the Establishment, was an old friend. And the first day he spent at the Court as Chief Justice was a memorable one. Around five-thirty I went to his office, and after I was ushered in, he asked me, "What do you know?" I suppose that expression dates back to the precinct level of Louisa, Kentucky, where Vinson was born. In any event, it was his standard salutation.

We sat and talked awhile; then he looked at his watch and announced that in an hour he had to be at a black-tie dinner with Roberta. He pressed a button and when his secretary came in, he said, "Send for the Court car."

I did not want to miss this scene, as there was then no such thing as "the Court car."

Out of curiosity, I walked with Vinson down two flights to the garage, where we waited and waited. Finally there was a roar and a Ford pickup came around the corner. Vinson, as Secretary of the Treasury, had at his command nearly thirty cars, day and night. He pointed to the pickup and asked me, "What's this?"

"The Court car," I replied.

He climbed in, and as the pickup moved out of the garage, he turned to look at me. Never have I seen such a humiliated Chief Justice.

Vinson tried in vain to get a limousine for his new office. Yet, though he knew his way around the Hill and had a specially warm relation with Sam Rayburn, he never got the authorization.

Fred Vinson had a gentle voice and gentle manners, though underneath he had a resolution of steel. At Conference he very seldom raised his voice, but he would filibuster for hours to have his way on a case. One day Frankfurter kept baiting Vinson with barbed taunts. At last Vinson left his chair at the head of the Conference Table, raised his clenched fist and started around the room at Frankfurter, shouting, "No son of a bitch can ever say that to Fred Vinson!" Shay Minton and Tom Clark intercepted Vinson and held him until he had cooled off. Before the day was done, Vinson of course apologized.

In those days I spent almost every summer going into the farthest reaches of some continent. One day I went by Fred's office to say goodbye and to invite him to come along with me to Indonesia. "Fred," I said, "I know where there is one of the few living white rhinoceroses alive. We'll catch it just for you."

He laughed uproariously, and lighting a cigarette, said, "Bill, for you I'd do almost anything. But catching a rhinoceros? No! We have them right in the zoo near where Roberta and I live. Never have I gone to see one. Why should I travel around the world to see one?"

"Then let's go to Katmandu, strike north to the Tibetan border, turn east, cross Bhutan and come out in Assam, the headhunter country."

Fred replied, "The doctors say I am overweight, so they have me eating beefsteak three times a day."

"Come with me and you drop the beefsteak at once."

"Why?"

"Because where you and I would go we'll be physically ill and lose pounds like magic."

"My friend, you are forty-two years too late."

Embracing him, I said, "Fred, I'll pick you up on your reincarnation."

"Reincarnation!" he shouted as I waved goodbye.

Vinson was warm-hearted and easygoing. He was a happy party man, enjoying bourbon and branch water, bridge with Eisenhower at the White House, and all the amenities of social Washington. He had huge bags under his eyes and a very heavy paunch. Dr. George Draper, the physician I so respected, had seen him at a gathering and I asked what the medical appraisal was.

"He'll die soon of a heart attack," Draper said.

His death did come shortly thereafter, on September 8, 1953, when he was sixty-three. He had served as Chief Justice for seven years. I was one of the Justices who made the long train trip to Louisa, Kentucky, for the funeral.

While Vinson was Chief there was a rumor that he had a direct telephone line to his crony, Truman, in the White House. That was not true. Vinson, like Earl Warren, who succeeded him, had a private telephone line in his office that did not operate through the switchboard. (Later Burger got one for each Justice.) The only Justice in modern times who asked for a private line to the White House was Frank Murphy, and his request was not granted.

Earl Warren had been governor of California for eleven years and was still in that office when, in 1953, Eisenhower named him to the vacancy caused by Fred Vinson's death. In retrospect, Eisenhower must have been sorry, for Warren was not exactly Eisenhower's type.

Nixon, then Vice President, and William F. Knowland, then senator from California, were responsible for the nomination. Nixon went to Ike saying something like "You must get Warren out of California. He has control of the Republican Party machinery and we can't do business with him."

Knowland was, I believe, out of the country at the time, but he and Earl Warren were close. In 1945 Warren had named Knowland to fill the unexpired term of Senator Hiram W. Johnson, who died in office. And the Warren-Knowland ties went way back—to Knowland's father, who ran the newspaper when young Earl Warren was prosecutor in Oakland.

So, several years later, when "Impeach Earl Warren" signs went up around the country and Nixon fans complained about the Chief Justice, I always reminded them that Nixon was responsible for Warren's being there. "Let's give Nixon credit for something liberal and progressive," I'd say.

Warren, as Chief Justice, was as nonchalant as Hughes was meticulous. As we have seen, Hughes never opened Court a second before or a second after twelve noon. But Warren never once was on time and was usually a few minutes late. In Warren's day, Court convened at ten o'clock instead of at noon, a change promoted by Justice Brennan, who was an early riser and who was always at Court by eight. In contrast, Warren never reached Court until five minutes to ten and we were never on the Bench until three minutes after ten or later.

While Hughes had been fastidious when it came to dress, Warren was very casual. At the American Bar Association meeting in London he walked to the platform in a suit that looked as if he had slept in it. I was, however, proud of him, for he stood in contrast to the Britishers, who were dressed so formally and neatly that they all looked alike.

Under Warren we acquired more law clerks, as I have related. They were busy and productive writing memos, which meant they needed stenographic help. So we acquired a pool of stenographers who usually took no dictation but who did copying. Someone reported to Warren that I was sending manuscripts of books to the pool for typing. The story was false. As far as I know, nothing from my office ever went to the pool. When I started writing books back in the forties, I hired an outside stenographer and paid her with my personal checks. She was Mrs. Gladys Giese of Glen Echo Heights, Maryland, later succeeded by Linda, her daughter. Warren never mentioned to me the rumor of my use of the pool. Rather, he brought it up at Conference, not mentioning my name but saying that the pool was being used by a Justice to turn out books on which royalties were received. When it came my turn to talk, I explained what my working arrangements were. But there was an iciness in Warren's attitude reflecting utter disbelief.

Only one other time did Warren lose his composure at Conference and take out after a Justice. Warren had mentioned the possibility of appointing someone as Clerk of the Court; Frankfurter had gone to the man immediately to dissuade him, as Frankfurter had a competing candidate. Warren heard of Frankfurter's mission and in a loud voice denounced him at the next Conference and threatened to take reprisals if Frankfurter ever repeated such a mission. What reprisals a Chief could take against a Justice I never could imagine.

Each of us was a sovereign who had got to the Court on his own without help from any Chief Justice. And most of the time Warren was polite, considerate and friendly, handling the Conference with consummate skill. He had no monopoly on stubbornness. But when he felt strongly on an issue—obscenity or flag burning—he held forth at length.

When Warren first came on the Bench he asked Black to preside when cases were discussed. He did this because, having been out of law practice so long, he felt an initial inadequacy. Black performed brilliantly, and in a month Warren had taken over. But Warren soon developed a habit during a week of argued cases of discussing each case with Brennan prior to Conference. The two of them had, so to speak, a "mock" conference, just as Stone used to have under Hughes.

Warren, mindful of the needs of the Justices, had a steel plate placed under the wood paneling at the front of the bench so as to give some protection against gunfire. It was a protection which we all took lightheartedly until word came one day from the FBI that six members of the Klan planned to throw a bomb at the bench.

Warren was a stickler for the proprieties. When he resigned from the American Bar Association because he did not believe in some of its policies, the then president of the bar spread the rumor that Warren was dropped from the membership roll because of nonpayment of dues. Warren was furious and went to great pains to correct the record in correspondence with the bar. "Think what my grandchildren might think of me if these lies went unanswered," he said to me.

In the beginning of the Court, the Associate Justices received an annual salary of $3,500, the Chief Justice receiving $500 more (1 Stat. 72). That $500 differential continued through the years. It was symbolic of the fact that the Chief Justice is *primus inter pares,* a presiding officer with no more power or authority at the judicial level than any Associate Justice. The Chief had of course other duties: he was administrative head of the building, having supervision over the many employees engaged in policing the place, cleaning the place, taking care of the Clerk's Office, and the like. But his power to assign opinions made it possible for him to lighten his own tasks at that level when the administrative work piled up. And at times it did accumulate. The creation by Congress of the Judicial Conference in 1922 (42 Stat. 838) made the Chief Justice head of a group composed of circuit court judges (and later district judges as well) which was in charge of recommending and drafting legislation governing the federal judiciary and which supervised rule making in the federal system, and the like. The Judicial Conference met in Washington, D.C., and took nearly two weeks a year of the Chief Justice's time. The Chief was also a trustee of the National Geographic Society, the American Red Cross, the Smithsonian Institution and the National Gallery of Art. Yet in spite of the fact that his outside duties had increased over the years, the Chief Justice's salary remained only $500 above that of the others. Fred Vinson thought that was unjust.

On May 12, 1953, Senator Patrick McCarran introduced a bill that would have raised the salary of the Chief Justice from $25,500 to $40,000 and the Associate Justices from $25,000 to $35,000. Vinson reported back to the Conference and warmly defended the proposal which would place the Chief Justice on the same level as the Vice President and the Speaker of the House and increase the difference between the Chief and the Associates from $500 to $5,000 a year.

The debate was long and heated. Black and Frankfurter took the lead in opposing Vinson, and I shared their views. On May 18 Frankfurter sent each of us a strong letter containing his opinion, with which I am sure a majority of the Court agreed. And as I reread it years later, the bitterness of that 1953 conference was relived. In the end, Vinson promoted the proposal that McCarran espoused, but it somehow or other never was approved by Congress.

In 1968 a Commission on Federal Salaries reported a recommendation to increase the salaries of the Justices and to pay the Chief Justice $3,500 more than the others. Warren brought the proposal to Conference, saying he had opposed any increase for the Chief Justice greater than what the Justices received, but that the commission overruled him. Warren's point was that in the sweep of history, when tensions are great on the Court and personal animosities flare up, the salary difference is almost certain to be an additional irritant. In 1968 the Conference shared that view.

After Warren resigned in 1969, Warren E. Burger, the fifteenth Chief Justice, came from the Court of Appeals for the District of Columbia, where he had served since 1956. I did not know him well before his appointment. At the Center for the Study of Democratic Institutions at Santa Barbara, we had invited him out for a panel discussion on law and order. That was in 1968, and a summary of his discourse was printed in an Occasional Paper. He seemed to prefer the inquisitional legal system of the Continent over our accusatorial system. While he would not throw out the Fifth Amendment, he certainly would dilute it. He deplored the length of time it takes to review criminal cases here, as compared to England and other countries, overlooking the fact that the most conspicuous delays have been in state criminal trials in which the states themselves have not honored the federal constitution. This practice has meant that a person having been unconstitutionally convicted in a state court can, under our system, get relief through habeas corpus in the federal courts, which, of course, takes time. If we honored those state judgments, we would have "law and order" in the popular sense, but we would fasten on our people a harsh discriminatory legal regime.

Another indication of his judicial attitude was revealed at a Gridiron dinner. The Chief Justice had never spoken at these dinners, but Burger started the practice in 1970. In 1971, in an effort at humor, he said he did not mind dissents. "As a matter of fact," he said, "if I have four others with me on an opinion, let the defendant have four votes." But that night the retired Chief, Earl Warren, got the biggest applause.

When he was nominated Chief Justice, on May 21, 1969, Burger's espousal of these "law and order" concepts gave him easy clearance by the Senate Judiciary Committee, headed by James Eastland of Mississippi. There was much more, however, behind the Burger popularity. He had been an attorney in the Department of Justice from 1953 to 1956, when Nixon was Vice President; he was, in a real sense, Nixon's "hatchet man." It was Burger who argued the Peters case in 1955 (*Peters v. Hobby,* 349 U.S. 331) against one of Nixon's so-called Communists. Burger lost the case before our Court, but the case helped him establish his reputation in political circles in Washington, D.C., as a "safe" man.

The most prominent man at Burger's swearing-in—apart from the President—was J. Edgar Hoover, head of the FBI, who thought the world of Burger. Yet, curiously, the informed decision of *Chimel* v. *California* (393 U.S. 958) was handed down the same day by Justice Stewart. This decision greatly limited the right to search, incident to an arrest for which no search warrant had been issued. It was at the very next Conference that Burger announced that *Chimel* must be overruled.

Burger was extremely personable, and he honored good personal relations. His idea of the Court was different from that of many predecessors. He thought of the Court as a symbol of an authority which had best not be exercised. He announced in Conference shortly after he took office that the cases we should decide each Term should never exceed one hundred. He also announced from time to time the precedents we should overrule. *Miranda, Gideon, Chimel, Reynolds* v. *Sims* and many others were on the list, and he eyed closely the votes that might be marshaled to achieve that result. Burger worked hard on it, but what was going on under Burger had gone on before, and will go on again, as political realignments on the judiciary are made by oncoming Presidents.

Burger loved the administrative aspects of the office. He loved being Chief. He took our Conference Room as his office—and without consulting us. He was very concerned with security. For example, the police in the building were equipped with two-way radios, the police force was increased, entrances to the building were guarded, and briefcases of visitors were searched, though this latter practice is no longer in effect.

In the 1970 Term, Burger told us that word had come from the FBI that some important federal official, perhaps a Justice of the Court, would be kidnapped and held for ransom in exchange for the release of federal prisoners. I spoke up to say, quite selfishly, "Tell the FBI that the kidnappers should pick out a judge that Nixon wants back."

During his first year Burger got the Court's budget increased by $800,000, which included the salaries of three law clerks for each Justice at $15,000 a year, and a $40,000-a-year assistant to the Chief. This assistant was in turn to have an assistant, and each to have secretaries, messengers, and so on.

The Court budget continued to grow over the years. I talked with Speaker Carl Albert of the House about it, and he said that Congress had no real way of knowing what went on inside a big department of government. And except for a scandal, that was true. Congressmen and senators took Chief Justices on faith. But Chief Justices at times were as clever promoters of Parkinson's law as lesser bureau chiefs.

Burger seldom made assignments of opinions at the end of the week of argument, sometimes waiting for as long as two or even three weeks. Under him the work of the Court dragged and the production fell off, so much so that I once said in Conference it would be "news" if the Court announced any decision.

As Chief, Burger was entitled by tradition to assign opinions *if he was in the majority.*

Even though his views on the merits of argued cases were in the minority, at the beginning Burger often kept those cases for himself to write. That was true in *North Carolina State* v. *Swann* (402 U.S. 43) and the other school-busing cases argued at the start of the 1970 Term in which at Conference he kept the opinions for himself, though he was in the minority. As a result, months passed without any progress being made to obtain a consensus in the Court, and the opinion finally filed was not his but a compound of mine, Harlan's, Brennan's, Stewart's and Marshall's. Burger lost out on *Swann,* but in 1974 he regained all lost power in the Detroit school case, *Milliken* v. *Bradley* (418 U.S. 717), which resorted to busing *only* if there were illegal acts.

When Burger became Chief Justice he also brought before the Conference, once again, the El Paso Natural Gas Co. case. In 1957 the Department of Justice, under Eisenhower, had started a suit against El Paso for its illegal merger with another gas pipeline company. El Paso won in the District Court but lost before us (*United States* v. *El Paso Natural Gas Co.,* 376 U.S. 651), since it was in violation of the Clayton Act. Back the case went for divestiture (*Cascade Natural Gas Co.* v. *El Paso Natural Gas Co.,* 386 U.S. 129), El Paso having been required to get rid of the merged company. The District Court balked at the remedy. The next time, we ordered the Judicial Council to assign a new judge to the case. The new judge also balked at divestiture, and we redirected that remedy. This last opinion was written by Warren in 1969 just before he retired (*Utah Commission* v. *El Paso Gas Co.,* 395 U.S. 464), and after it we called him Super Chief.

When Burger became Chief he announced that he and Blackmun would vote to grant reargument. Under our rules, dating back to 1882, no Justice voted on a rehearing unless one of the Justices who had heard the case voted that it should be reheard. Burger argued that it was a poor rule and should be changed. Black replied that this was the worst possible case in which to change the rule.

In the first place, Richard Nixon's former law firm had been heavily involved in the case, and for Nixon's judges to pull his chestnuts from the fire would be scandalous. Second, a terrific lobby on behalf of El Paso Natural Gas had descended on Washington, D.C., headed by a man once counsel to malefactors of great wealth and now a malefactor in his own right. While a petition for rehearing of El Paso was pending, the lobbyist, not a counsel of record, descended on Justice Brennan in his chambers making arguments that certainly should never be made absent opposing counsel. He was so demanding on Brennan that Brennan stepped out of the case. Next he went to Black, whom he had known for years, and wanted to leave an economic brief with him. Black, mindful of all the proprieties, rose up in anger and banished his old friend forever from his office.

I put together a memo touching on all pertinent matters and saying it would be filed publicly once the petition for reargument was granted. It never was granted, and when denied, no dissents were noted, Brennan merely remarking that he took no part in the consideration or decision of the case. Thus did Burger and Nixon bring to the Court a whiff of the scandal of oil that had plagued Harding and his Cabinet fifty years earlier.

Burger's concern for law and order became apparent in April 1971 when the Vietnam veterans came to town. They sat on the front steps of the courthouse, singing songs and acting in an orderly way. Unknown to us, Burger sent orders from the Bench to the Marshal to disperse them, which was done. Then, on his orders, 113 were arrested, the police refusing, however, to arrest one veteran in a wheelchair who pleaded to be taken in with the rest.

When the Court learned about it the deed was a *fait accompli,* and some of us were very upset. Stewart told me he could not understand why the Chief had acted the way he did.

"It is simple," I replied. "One who comes to the Court must come to adore, not to protest."

Stewart shook his head with sadness.

I said, "That's the new gloss on the First Amendment, Potter."

The Court is and always will be a storm center of controversial issues. For to it come most of the troublesome, contentious problems of each age, problems that mirror the tensions, fears and aggressiveness of the people. It will be denounced by some group, whatever it does. Some may go so far as to say the Court acts lawlessly, the criterion being what the reader's idea of "lawful" is. When I say the Court has acted in a lawless way, I do not intend that meaning. What I mean to say is that the Court's jurisdiction to act in the run of "appellate" cases is prescribed by Congress through statutes and rules. By Article III of the Constitution the "appellate" jurisdiction of the Court is completely under the control of Congress. Congress has prescribed the requisite conditions that entitle litigants to proceed in federal courts. Ancillary to that, it has created judicial circuits and, for each circuit, has created a Court of Appeal. As we have seen, the circuits are geographical units and the Chief Justice is empowered to name a Justice of our Court as Circuit Justice.

While the Supreme Court is in recess, a Circuit Justice can take any necessary action on his own on cases that may arise. A stay denied by one Circuit Justice is often submitted to another, and he is authorized to grant where the first one denied. Such an action is taken reluctantly and not very often. But it is done at times.

When the Justices are not on vacation but in the city having regular Conferences, the custom, to control shopping around from Justice to Justice, is to submit the second request to the Conference. And at times when I have granted a stay or other order at Goose Prairie, Washington, during vacation, I extended it only to the date when the full Court met in October.

In the summer of 1973 a District Court in New York City stayed the Secretary of Defense in bombing Cambodia. The Court of Appeals granted the stay; and application was made to Justice Thurgood Marshall, Circuit Justice for the Second Circuit, to vacate the stay of the Court of Appeals. He denied it with a twelve-page opinion (*Holtzman* v. *Schlesinger*, 414 U.S. 1304). Application was then made to me in Goose Prairie. I set the matter for hearing in the federal courtroom in Yakima, and at the conclusion of the hearing wrote an opinion granting the stay on the basis that only Congress had the power to declare war (Article I, Sect. 8) and that no war had been declared. I stated that under the Fifth Amendment neither "life, liberty, or property" could be taken "without due process" of law.

In the Korean "war," though no declaration of war had been made, Truman nonetheless seized the steel mills in order to increase war production. The Court held that seizure unconstitutional. If "property" may not be seized by a President when war has not been declared, how can "life" be taken? I developed these ideas in a five-page opinion (*Id.* 1316) and entered an order (1) vacating the stay entered by the Court of Appeals on July 27, 1973, and (2) restoring the order of the District Court.

Justice Marshall had seen the order I signed containing those two provisions. The Clerk, Mike Rodak, had shown it to him. Yet Marshall falsely stated that "the only order extant in this case is the order of the District Court." He thereupon talked on the phone with all members of the Court except me and stayed the order of the District Court. That was *lawless* action, for only the Court could vacate my order reinstating the order of the District Court. For the Court to act, it must have a quorum of six (28 U.S.C. Sec. 1). Justice Frankfurter said in *Rosenberg* (346 U.S. 271): "Oral argument frequently has a force beyond what the written word conveys." That is doubly true of the Conference, in which Justices present opposing arguments face to face. Though the effect is usually to establish what the consensus is, rather than change the opinion of any Justice, Marshall's telephone consultation certainly gave no such opportunity. It was, moreover, as I have said, "lawless."

I filed another opinion in *Holtzman:*

> Whatever may be said on the merits, I am firmly convinced that the telephonic disposition of this grave and crucial constitutional issue is not permissible. I do not speak of social propriety. It is a matter of law and order involving high principles. The principles are that the Court is a deliberative body that acts only on reasoned bases after full consideration, and that it is as much bound by the law of the land as is he who lives in the ghetto or in the big white house on the hill. With all respect I think the Court has slighted that law. The shortcut it has taken today surely flouts an Act of Congress providing for a necessary quorum. A Gallup Poll type of inquiry of widely scattered Justices is, I think, a subversion of the regime under which I thought we lived.
>
> One Justice who grants bail, issues a stay of a mandate, or issues a certificate of probable cause cannot under the statutory regime designed by Congress vacate, modify, or reverse what another Justice does. The Court of course can do so—and only the Court—but when the Court acts it must have six Members present.
>
> Under the law as it is written the order of Mr. Justice Marshall on August 4, 1973, will in time be reversed by that Higher Court which invariably sits in judgment on the decisions of this Court. The order of August 4, 1973, in this case would be valid only if we had the power to agree by telephone that the rules framed by Congress to govern our procedures should be altered. We have no such power. What members of the Court told Brother Marshall to do on August 4, 1973, does not, with all respect, conform with our ground rules.

(314 U.S. 1324–1326)

When a Court acts "lawlessly" it is in a poor position to preach its "law and order" theme. I hesitate to say this, but I believe that some Nixon men put the pressure on Marshall to cut corners. Sad to say, he did so and thus emulated the "law and order" men during the Watergate period.

The Chief Justices with whom I served were a varied group. Each brought dignity and character to the office and distinguished the Court by his presence. There were many ideological differences between them. Warren was closer to Hughes than the others. Burger was close to Vinson. Stone was somewhere in between. But ideological clashes are no measure of "good" or "bad," and can flourish between men each of whom is equally dedicated to the Constitution. Those differences are inherent in our system and create no serious disorders within the Court. In my time the Brethren, though strenuously opposed on decisions, remained an amicable group. Each Chief Justice promoted friendly relations, even if he was never able to convince the irascible ones who often voted him down in Conference.

In the Rosenberg case (346 U.S. 273) Vinson on his own called the Court into a Special Term to hear argument on whether my stay of execution should be noted. As we assembled on the morning of June 18, 1953, Black (*Id.* 276) raised the point that the Chief Justice has no power to determine if and when the Court should assemble in a Special Term. Black spoke long and fervently. Frankfurter agreed with him, as did I.

Since, however, the Special Term had been called to pass on my stay, I stated I preferred not to vote on the issue. Burton, as I recall, agreed with Black and Frankfurter. The others were none too clear, though probably a fifth vote could have been summoned. Vinson was in a towering rage at the suggestion and finally no one pressed the point. Black, however, noted his dissent *(loc. cit.)*.

The Chief Justice has been given special powers by the Congress, as for example the custody and management of the courthouse (40 U.S.C., Sec. 13b, Sec. 13c, Sec. 13f). The quorum of six is provided by Congress. But nowhere is the Chief Justice given the important power to summon or not to summon the Court in Special Term. He has, on all Court business, only one vote. And it is good law, I think, that Black, Frankfurter and I propounded—viz., only a majority vote of the Court can determine whether (and if so, when) the Court should meet in Special Term. That seems implicit in 28 U.S.C. Sec. 2, which, after stating that the Term starts on the first Monday of October of each year goes on to say, "and may hold such adjourned or special terms as may be necessary." It is the Court that "may hold" such special terms, not the Chief Justice.

There are of course tensions in every group dealing with critical decisions in controversial areas. My own experience with diverse groups over long years on the Court made me smile as I read Justice Holmes's comment:

> I am on most friendly terms with all the judges, but I suspect that if I should be gathered to Abraham's bosom some of them would think it an advantage to the law, even if they missed a friend.*

Earl Warren died at eight o'clock in the evening at Georgetown Hospital on July 9, 1974. I went to see him at four-thirty and one look satisfied me that he would not be with us long. I talked with W. Proctor Harvey, our leading cardiologist, who was leaving Room 6103 as I entered and he said, "He's a very sick man." But though low in energy, the Chief was bright in spirit and very lucid. He held my hand, pulling me to the bed and asking me to be seated. He wanted to talk. He wanted to talk about the Big Case, the one argued July 8 involving Nixon's refusal to deliver tapes to Judge Sirica. He had no questions to ask, only views to espouse. I would not, of course, listen to an outsider, a volunteer who was seeking to trap me. But Earl Warren and I were long associated and he was still in the inner circle of the Justices. He plainly was dying and he wanted his views known. What he said was this:

"If Nixon is not forced to turn over tapes of his conversations with the ring of men who were conversing on their violations of the law, then liberty will soon be dead in this nation. If Nixon gets away with that, then Nixon makes the law as he goes along—not the Congress nor the Courts. The old Court you and I served so long will not be worthy of its traditions if Nixon can twist, turn, and fashion the law as he sees fit.

"As to you, Bill Douglas, if you are not perfectly satisfied with what is written, speak up. They are afraid of you because you are the conscience. Speak up. Do not fail. Then all will be well."

This speech exhausted him and he fell back on his pillow, breathing heavily.

*Holmes-Pollock Letters, Vol. II, p. 268.

I tiptoed out, not realizing I would never see him alive again. I had promised to return in the morning; soon he was gone.

He was in Georgetown Hospital because Nixon, as Commander in Chief, had denied him access to the superior facilities of Walter Reed Hospital, which he wanted to go to. The day he told me of the way Nixon had blackballed him at Walter Reed brought tears to his eyes. Not having any guile himself, he could not attribute guile to others. He had charity as well as integrity. He represented the America that was wholesome, not the America of the adventurers who used White House power for personal ends.

After Earl Warren's death, Warren Burger did a most gracious thing. He came to my office and proposed that we arrange for Warren to lie in state in our Great Hall foyer. I heartily approved and helped persuade the family. Technically it was not "lying in state," which could be done only for three days and with the assignment of four thousand troops. He would lie in state for thirty-six hours; and four guards would always be on duty.

On July 11 his casket was brought up the long front steps by nine husky police from our force, draped in the flag he dearly loved. The Court stood on one side, the family on the other. And after the prayers were read, we walked over to the family to express our grief. I put my arms around his wife, Nina, who burst into tears crying like a little girl; she was so crushed, so lonely, so frightened.

And then the public came to pay their respects—about ten thousand in the day and a half. This had never been done before for any Chief Justice, but Burger thought it was most appropriate not only for Chief Justices but for ordinary Associate Justices. He was indeed a man with a keen sense of the proprieties and with pride in the institution.

Four of Warren's former law clerks took turns standing by the bier with the guards. Flags were of course at half-mast. The weather was perfect—clear skies, mild temperature, a relatively low pollution count in the air.

The services were in the Washington National Cathedral at one o'clock on July 12. The members of the Court were honorary pall bearers. It was a tripartite religious service—Rabbi Alvin I. Fine, Archbishop Phillip M. Hannan, Bishop John T. Walker, Rev. Canon Jeffrey Cave and Rev. Canon C. Leslie Glenn.

Burial was in Arlington National Cemetery, the Court again serving as honorary pallbearers. Burger was presented with the flag from the casket, neatly folded by the Army pallbearers at the cemetery. Burger presented it to Mrs. Warren.

Warren clearly ranked with John Marshall and Charles Evans Hughes as our three greatest Chief Justices. He did not have the erudition in the law that the other two had, but he had an understanding of the needs of the common man as opposed to those in corporate and other high hierarchies. Earl Warren had a passion for justice, for "constitutional law and order." He was a man of great integrity. In his youth he had been a brakeman on freight trains in and out of Bakersfield, California. He had come up the hard way. His father, even in later years, was in charge of the huge heating unit in the Coronado Hotel in San Diego.

When he was governor, Warren had fervently espoused the program of evacuating and locking up the Japanese on the West Coast during World War II—an advocacy that he later regretted. As governor, he opposed reapportionment of the legislature, a measure he endorsed in the "one man, one vote" line of decisions by our Court (*Reynolds* v. *Sims*, 377 U.S. 533). As governor, he was a member of the three-man council filling vacancies on the Supreme Court and opposed the naming of Max Radin, my dear friend. I was shocked at the time and never discussed the matter then or later with Earl Warren. Reasons that appeal to governors do not always stand up under the pitiless scrutiny a man must give a problem when he takes the judicial oath.

Earl Warren had a capacity for growth, and under the impetus of the judicial oath he grew and grew. Two little—some would say picayune —cases illustrate his intense sense of justice. One came from Iowa, where burial in a "caucasian" cemetery was denied an Indian (*Rice* v. *Sioux City Memorial Park Cemetery*, 349 U.S. 70). Another case was *Hamilton* v. *Alabama* (376 U.S. 650). A black woman, Mary Hamilton, was on the witness stand. The judge kept addressing her as Mary. She refused to answer unless she was addressed as Mrs. Hamilton. So the judge held her in contempt and sent her off to jail. These rulings aroused in Earl Warren a deep protest.

He had a keen sense of proprieties; he never spoke ill of anyone; he loved his family. When Nelson Rockefeller was divorced he was outraged because of the impact this would have on the young children of the new Mrs. Rockefeller. He voted with disgust on cases involving obscenity. Hugo Black and I never liked obscenity either, but we believed that all utterances and all publications were protected by the First Amendment. Whether Earl Warren would in time have come to that conclusion no one knows. But "the sea of ethics," on which he believed the Constitution rested, in his view gave no sanctuary to any indecencies. That leaves room for highly subjective constitutional decisions. I say this not in criticism of Earl Warren but only to present his approach to problems that had been conditioned by his long life in American politics.

Earl Warren was a regular visitor to the Bohemian Grove, an exclusive club in California. I had been invited many times but always declined, for I knew I would chafe as a captive of an elitist group of men, most of whom I did not admire. Earl Warren always came back from these visits with a supply of good stories.

On one occasion Herbert Hoover, who was then over eighty, was there. He was asked why the public attitude toward him had changed. In the thirties he was the engineer who had "damned, drained, and ditched the nation"; now he was greatly honored.

"How come this great change?" he was asked.

Hoover's answer was, "I outlived the bastards."

That story came back to me as I left Room 6103, where Earl Warren lay dying. I recalled the huge billboard outside Odessa, Texas, that read: "Impeach Earl Warren." Those billboards were down; the public mind had changed; Earl Warren, a man of high principle and great integrity had also "outlived the bastards."

I had an interesting experience as the Chief's casket came down the steps of the courthouse and reached the flat plaza. At that instance a flight of pigeons flew low over it, and my mind returned to the Ganges in India when a funeral pyre started its float down the holy waters. At that instant a flight of birds swooped low over the scene, my Indian companion reminding me that that was the flight of the spirit of the deceased. I like to think that the spirit of Earl Warren is abroad in this land, quickening the conscience of our people.

Chapter XIII

The President
and the Court

Most Presidents name Justices who, they think, will vote the way they would vote. That is what I would do were I President. But it doesn't always work out: FDR was well known for "packing the Court" with his own nominees, yet his Court was noted for its conflicts and divisions. The mistakes of some Presidents are bitter ones, as, for example, Teddy Roosevelt's nomination of Holmes, who voted against Teddy on his big antitrust case (*Northern Securities Co.* v. *United States,* 193 U.S. 197).

Some Presidents have risen above politics and named outstanding "nonpolitical" judges. The examples in my time were the nomination of Hughes in 1910 by Taft and that of Cardozo in 1932 by Hoover. But Presidents usually play their politics with judicial nominations, seeking the person to fill a particular vacancy with his own short-range political program in mind. For example, William Howard Taft, as President, was personally very active in seeking out men for the Bench. He named six to the Supreme Court, most of them old friends: Edward Douglass White, Horace Harmon Lurton, Charles Evans Hughes, Willis Van Devanter, Joseph Rucker Lamar and Mahlon Pitney.

After he became Chief Justice he kept a watchful eye on candidates for his high Court: Learned Hand, a brilliant man, seemed destined to sit there, but Taft as Chief Justice got Hand deflected by stating that Hand on the Supreme Court "would ride herd" on Brandeis. Taft had opposed Brandeis when he was named by Wilson, since he was, in Taft's mind, a troublesome character. Taft later fumed over the way Holmes and Brandeis polished their dissents. It was bothersome to Taft that they were so meticulous in refining them as if they would someday become law. He found their dissents to be quite difficult to deal with when they so devastatingly challenged the majority opinion.

In modern times only FDR named more men to the Supreme Court than Taft. There were nine in all—if Jimmy Byrnes, who served for only about one year, is included, and if we count elevating Stone to be Chief Justice. His appointments, however, had consequences FDR obviously did not foresee.

Apart from Harold Burton, the kindest, friendliest, most polite and courteous Justice on the Court in my time was Stanley Reed. But like the Truman appointees, Stanley took a dim view of dissidents and revolutionaries, assuming a small-town stance when it came to the Bill of Rights. FDR probably named him because he felt that Stanley Reed would never strike down New Deal legislation. The difficulty with that kind of reasoning is that times change, and so do issues. The economic matters which seemed so overwhelmingly important to FDR were eclipsed in a year or two, and the country moved into new areas. It was in those new areas that Reed was out of place. The Vinson Court almost always had his vote against a civil rights issue.

Jimmy Byrnes was another FDR nominee who was also out of place in the onrush of new problems. Jimmy, segregationist *par excellence,* represented the plantation school of thought. McReynolds of the old Court, who became FDR's *bête noire,* was of the same school of thought. And Reed, who would feel insulted to be classified with those two, was very much like them except for one thing—he had an expansive view of the commerce power and was ready to sustain the assertion of congressional power in that field beyond the outer limits of McReynolds and Byrnes.

The Reed and Byrnes appointments reflect the political reality that, in FDR's time and in his political scheme, the South was an important ingredient—not necessarily the Old South of McReynolds, but preferably the New South of Hugo Black. But the South was essential. Joe Robinson, archconservative, was slated to fill the first Supreme Court vacancy. Reed and Byrnes were in the Robinson tradition.

The other FDR nominees were a varied lot, each of whom I liked and admired. They could not be typed, each being very much an individual. The ones I enjoyed most were Black, Murphy and Rutledge because, I assume, I was closer ideologically to them than to the others. FDR had, as I have said, little respect for lawyers and for judges. I think he enjoyed naming judges who would make the established order wince. That generally could not be said of his appointments to the District Court. He made a few distinguished nominations there, Simon Rifkind of New York being one, but by and large he let the city machines name the district judges.

Above that level, however, FDR named offbeat men. "Let's find someone who will upset the fat cats," he would tell me. And so he found Henry Edgerton of Cornell Law School and put him on the Court of Appeals for the District of Columbia. That's the way he found Wiley Rutledge for the same court, and the way he found Charles E. Clark of Yale for the Second Circuit Court of Appeals and Jerome Frank for the same tribunal. The list was a long one.

Doubtless the same ingredient in FDR's selection of men for the Supreme Court explains Hugo Black, Wiley Rutledge, Frank Murphy and, perhaps, me. But the naming of Frankfurter, Jackson and myself was propelled by another consideration as well—close personal friendship. Other Presidents have been likewise moved and such will always be the case.

Most Presidents have, I think, kept hands off the men they have named to the Court. FDR was very discreet in his relations with members of the Court whom he had named. An occasional civilian would say to me, "Well, I suppose you've got your orders from Roosevelt on how to vote on all those cases." I remember visits to Yakima when I would get these questions from the unreconstructed opposition. Once, out in the woods, Curtiss Gilbert, older brother of Elon, my boyhood friend, took me to task for knuckling under to FDR for deciding cases opposed to the Gilbert view, for being a mere puppet of FDR. There were plenty of people in Washington, D.C., to offer advice of that character. But FDR never did. His sense of propriety was much keener than Gilbert's; and he never breached it.

The only President who undertook to criticize my decisions was Lyndon Johnson, who one day in 1967, while in an ugly mood, denounced me to my face for my decisions under the First, Fourth and Fifth Amendments. Truman, of course, greatly resented the steel-seizure decision (343 U.S. 579), in which a majority of us held he had no power in peacetime to seize the steel mills. And at a stag dinner which Hugo Black tendered Truman in Black's lovely Alexandria garden, Truman, in good humor, teased the majority about it and praised Vinson for his "masterful dissent." But unlike Johnson's tirade, Truman's light-hearted criticism was in utmost good taste.

His conduct at the poker table seemed to me less so. Disaster followed me there. FDR used to have a $2 limit on every hand. Truman, who dealt first one evening, required every player to put in $10 to get the first card and $10 a card thereafter, plus $20 to fill his hand. So before the betting began, everyone had $70 in the pot. It was too rich a game for me. I played very few hands but then went around the table, looking at what the others had and watching how they played their hands. I was interested to see that Truman seldom had more than two pair and that even those with three of a kind or a full house would throw in their hands, letting Truman win. I was shocked at the patronizing attitude. Our strategy with FDR had been to do him in, if possible, and to gloat over a victory. Not so with those who played with Truman. He walked out of my house that night with $5,000 in winnings. I was so disgusted I never played another game of poker in my life.

Truman's appointees to the Court were Fred Vinson, Tom Clark, Sherman Minton and Harold Burton. Under Truman the Court sank to its lowest professional level until the Burger Court arrived. I speak, of course, from the viewpoint of one who believes that the judiciary should be alert to construe the Constitution and laws of the United States as providing a strong arsenal for protection of the individual, whatever his place in the spectrum of ideas may be. Most of the Truman appointees reflected the small-town attitudes of conformity more than the emerging urban consciousness of the need for diversity. Tom Clark was different in the sense that he changed. He had the indispensable capacity to develop so that with the passage of time he grew in stature and expanded his dimensions.

These small-town people were the stuff out of which the populist movement was fashioned. They would be called liberal on economic issues. I remember FDR's Vice President Jack Garner and his lectures to me on the menace of the Three M's: the Morgans, the Mills and the Mellons, who represented the power of Wall Street and Big Business as against the country bank and the small merchant. Their symbolic opposition to "bigness" reached all combinations where power was concentrated and used. Big unions were considered a menace; and I suppose that Vinson's antagonism toward John L. Lewis and the mine workers in *United States* v. *United Mine Workers* (330 U.S. 258), decided in 1947, was as emotionally charged as his decision in 1953 that the Rosenbergs (*Rosenberg* v. *United States,* 346 U.S. 273) had to die.

During the Mine Workers case, Vinson kept muttering that John L. Lewis was "gettin' too big for his britches." I am not at this point criticizing the exposition of the law that Vinson made as spokesman for the Court; nor was I any great friend of Lewis, who had been scheduled to blast my nomination to the Court in 1939, as I described in *Go East, Young Man;* rather, I criticize Vinson's complete dedication to finding or fashioning some law to put John L. Lewis "in his place," just as in earlier days the Court had worked hard to put Eugene V. Debs in his place (*In re Debs,* 158 U.S. 564).

Vinson, Clark and Minton were populist-type liberals. They were cut from the same cloth as Homer Bone, long-time senator from the state of Washington, who was a "giant killer" when it came to taking on a private utility company. But when it came to the Bill of Rights he was curiously the archreactionary. He carried on at great length about the Self-Incrimination Clause of the Fifth Amendment, to which he was bitterly opposed. He thought the police should have great leeway in getting confessions out of a suspect, even through the use of coercion. "Why should we worry about his 'liberty'? The lady who was raped and killed lost her 'liberty,' didn't she?"

That was also the Vinson and Minton philosophy. And, I suppose, at bottom it was the philosophy of Main Street. For I doubt that the Self-Incrimination Clause of the Fifth Amendment would ever have been adopted by the American people, at least since World War II. People never understood it; its meaning had been lost in the mists of history; it seemed to most people to be strangely out of place with the mounting crime rate. And I also suppose that at the root of the great cry of "law and order" reflected in the 1968 campaign, where Nixon, Humphrey and Wallace battled it out, was a dark suspicion that coercing people to incriminate themselves was not a horrendous practice, and that the crime wave that multiplied in the fifties, sixties and seventies was caused in part by court decisions construing the Fifth Amendment.

Yet when it came to the Equal Protection Clause, no one was more adamant than Minton in insisting on equality in the treatment of blacks. He was indeed one of the great mainstays in the early school-desegregation cases.

Minton was appointed to the Court in an unusual way. FDR named Jerome Frank to the Second Circuit Court of Appeals to fill the vacancy of Robert Patterson, who had resigned in 1940 to take an executive position and who ended up as Secretary of the Army. Jerry took the post on the understanding that he would resign if Bob wanted the old job back. But FDR died, and in the early fall of 1949 Wiley Rutledge died, leaving a vacancy on the Supreme Court. Tom Clark went to Truman and recommended that he name Patterson to the vacancy. Truman agreed to send Bob's name up the following Monday. Meanwhile Shay Minton, previously named to the Court of Appeals for the Seventh Circuit, flew to Washington and walked into the White House to see the President.

"What can I do for you, Shay?"

"Harry, I want you to put me on the Supreme Court to fill that new vacancy."

"Shay, I'll do just that," Truman replied.

And so Minton rather than Patterson became a Justice. By happenstance, Patterson died tragically in less than three years in an airplane crash at Newark, New Jersey.

It wasn't until 1965 that a close personal friend was again nominated by a President when LBJ named Abe Fortas, his lawyer and confidant for nearly thirty years.

Shay Minton was a great storyteller. While traveling with the Truman Committee of the Senate, Shay would turn to Truman when they landed at an airport or arrived by train and say, "Harry, should we go to the hotel and check our bags or go straight to the whorehouse?"

One day in Conference when we were discussing a railroad personal-injury case, Shay told a story of a like case in Indiana. The key witness was a brakeman, and on cross-examination the lawyers were trying to pinpoint his exact location at the time of the accident. It finally was settled that he was in the caboose. What was he doing? All he would say was that he was engaged in "railroad talk." He refused to elaborate. Finally, after being warned by the judge to answer or be in contempt, he replied, "Railroad talk? Oh, that means fucking and back pay."

Harold Burton was also on the Truman Committee, investigating waste in defense spending. That association and service in the Senate provided the basis for a warm friendship. Burton, ex-mayor of Cleveland and the first Truman appointee, was as conscientious a man as ever sat on the Court, God-fearing, and painfully slow in his work. He spent night after night, way after midnight, in his office. He was deeply religious and carried a high standard of rectitude into his daily life. He was a "law and order" man, reading the Bill of Rights as placing light restrictions on the police. Learned Hand once called the Bill of Rights "an admonition of moderation," not as specific commands. That was the Frankfurter view. And although Harold Burton did not articulate that position, that seemed to be pretty much the standard by which he judged cases.

He had a strong humanitarian impulse that shone through at odd times. A black man was placed in the electric chair for execution, but when the dose given him did not kill him, the authorities arranged to repeat the performance. The case reached the Court (*Francis* v. *Resweber,* 329 U.S. 459) and Burton wrote quite movingly in dissent for Murphy, Rutledge and myself against the second performance.

On the racial front, Burton was as much a stalwart as Minton. Truman named Burton, a Republican, because he liked him and liked his work on the Truman Committee during World War II. "The most conscientious and hard-working committee member I ever did know," Truman told me.

Truman seemed to like picking mediocre men. One reason may have been revealed in a few comments that he once made to me. By sheer chance he seemed to be very high or very low on the scale of emotions whenever I saw him. He would be either roaring with laughter and telling barnyard stories or deeply upset. A couple of times when I was alone with him in his White House office, he broke into tears. Once was when the problems of Korea and Red China were mounting high. MacArthur was urging him to invade Red China, and I was urging him to recognize the Peking regime. He turned nervously in his swivel chair and looked out the window for a moment, and then, facing me, broke down and cried, saying, "Bill, I'm only doing what I think is best."

On one occasion he tried to make a joke of his tears by telling me, "Don't shoot the old piano player. He's doing the best he knows how."

Another time he talked a lot about "these highfalutin people." Who they were I never knew. He kept saying that they came in and tried to "lord it over" him. And then came a revealing statement: "You know, Bill, you are one person I see who does not try to make me feel inferior."

I often wondered if the reason why he named people like Fred Vinson to the Court was in order to be surrounded by men whose stature did not exceed his own. That theory largely explains Nixon's appointments as well as a long list of Truman's. For example, Howard McGrath of Rhode Island narrowly missed being appointed to the Court by Truman. McGrath was a machine Democrat who was wealthy and not very bright. He was pleasant company and a kind man, but to my amazement, he ended up as Solicitor General from 1945 to 1946. He had as much qualification for that post as I would have as a brain surgeon. The points of law, the constitutional philosophy, the dimensions of prior decisions were much too complicated for Howard. His arguments in the job were not numerous, as he wisely left the presentation of most cases to his staff.

Howard despised the post of Solicitor General and desperately longed to be on the Court. He pulled wires and thought it was all arranged when Murphy died, in 1949. One day he was told by the White House to come over with Tom Clark to see the President. When the two walked in, Howard was confident that Truman would ask Clark, then the Attorney General, to send Howard's name up to the Senate as Associate Justice. To Howard's surprise, Truman told Clark he had decided to put him on the Court, and turning to Howard, he said that he would become Attorney General. Howard was so upset and disappointed—indeed so bitter—that he refused to say yes. Truman insisted, and Howard agreed to think it over.

"I'll give you two days," said Truman. And in time the party regulars, who had backed Howard for the Court, urged him to accept, which he did most reluctantly.

Brennan was another recess appointment made about three weeks before the 1956 election. Herbert Brownell, who was Ike's Attorney General, received a call from Ike saying, "Find me a Catholic real quick. Minton has retired."

It so happened that a few days earlier there had been a conference of state judges at the Department of Justice, presided over by Brownell. Arthur Vanderbilt, Chief Justice of New Jersey, was supposed to have attended, but because he was sick, he called Brownell to ask him if he could send a substitute. Brennan went to the conference in Vanderbilt's place, and Brownell was very impressed with his performance. As soon as Brownell heard from Eisenhower, he sent for Brennan and told him that he would recommend him to Ike. Brennan, completely bewildered, went home, only to read the next day that he had been named to the Court.

Brennan had strong New Jersey support. Sylvester Comstock Smith, Jr., general counsel to the Prudential Life Insurance Company and later president of the American Bar Association, though much to the right of Brennan, told Brownell he deserved the post—because he was a Catholic, a Democrat and a liberal.

Justice Burton, a Republican, was largely responsible for John Harlan's appointment. He admired Harlan's grandfather, the sole dissenter in *Plessy* v. *Ferguson,* which in 1896 held that segregation of the races in public facilities was constitutional—provided the separate facilities were equal. Burton thought it was time to revive that Harlan tradition, now that the Court had held segregation in public schools unconstitutional. There were many other promoters of John Harlan, but Burton led the list.

I am not sure how or why Potter Stewart was nominated. He was a distinguished Yale alumnus who came from a prominent Cincinnati family. His father was Chief Justice of Ohio, and Potter quite early went on the Court of Appeals, Sixth Circuit. Like Harlan, he was an extremely able lawyer and judge, but he was younger by twenty years and had some capacity for growth. Earl Warren exercised a measurable influence on Stewart, though Stewart and Harlan were the nucleus of the new conservatism on the Court.

Charles Whittaker of Kansas City was a protégé of Roy Roberts of the Kansas City *Star.* Roy, strong in Republican circles, got Charlie named to the District Court. In a year he got him named to the Court of Appeals. Hardly a third year had passed when Roy got him named to our Court—a phenomenon that caused the irrepressible Frankfurter to say, "We can get a judge from the District Court quicker than we can get a case from that court."

Whittaker, an affable companion, was, in his ideas, close to the Stone Age Man, General Curtis E. LeMay, who ran with George Wallace on the presidential ticket in 1968. Whittaker was the quiet recluse, not the extrovert that LeMay represented, but their viewpoint of the world and of law was very much alike. I speak from personal knowledge of both, as I served with Whittaker and knew LeMay when I was going through a long convalescence in the Arizona desert.

Neither FDR nor Ike named men who were alike. Only Truman and Nixon tried to name "peas in a pod." But all four Presidents must have been surprised and disappointed at the differences that soon developed between their nominees.

Kennedy's choice of Byron R. White had no ideological overtones, being based, I believe, on consideration for services rendered—White having managed Kennedy's campaign in Colorado and served as Deputy Attorney General in Bob Kennedy's Justice Department. White, the first former law clerk named to the Court, had served as one of Vinson's clerks in the 1946 Term. He had come out of Yale with the reputation of being a great "liberal." He was indeed the opposite, but his great legal ability went far to bolster Fred Vinson in his conservative opinions. William H. Rehnquist was destined to render the same kind of service to Burger.

Arthur J. Goldberg, Kennedy's other appointment, had sought the Court post. A few years later he allegedly asked to be moved from the Court to the United Nations, though in later years he vehemently denied this and called LBJ and denounced him for spreading the contrary story. Goldberg was an old friend of mine and an excellent judge, but I think that emotionally he belonged on the hustings or in practice. Adlai Stevenson, as Ambassador to the UN from 1961 to 1965, died of a broken heart, for policy was made in Washington, D.C., by the State Department, the Pentagon and the White House. Our UN Representative was a mere errand boy; that killed Adlai, and Arthur Goldberg later chafed in the role. He must have known that that would be his fate once he left the Court. Perhaps he longed for another public office or for law practice. Certainly he knew that at the UN he would be merely a Charlie McCarthy for Dean Rusk. I learned on my visits with him at the UN that official life there was also impossible. There were dozens of cocktail parties a week to attend and a dinner almost every evening. The people at the UN were, of course, highly protocol-minded; and the American Ambassador simply could not follow his own desires and take his wife to the movies.

LBJ's two nominees—Abe Fortas and Thurgood Marshall—were quite different, though not opposed. Marshall was named simply because he was black, and in the 1960s that was reason enough. At that time, few black people studied law, and those who did seldom reached the top. Marshall attained the pinnacle for conspicuous service in civil rights—not civil rights generally, but civil rights in the field of race. The public needed a competent black on the Court for symbolic reasons; none was needed to put the Court right on racial problems. Where would a black judge stand on mergers, on Sherman Act cases, on "Communists" in defense plants or schools, on public aid to parochial schools, on civilian control over the military, on the right of the police to search without a warrant, on whether being an "active Communist" can be made a crime? No one knows the answer. Being a black was no clue, for blacks, like Jews, Germans, English and others, can be reactionary. Moreover, a black reaching the top was likely to be anxious to prove to society that he was safe and conservative and reliable. That at least had been the history of most black appointees to the judicial posts.

I was too close to Fortas, ever since he was a student at Yale Law School, to be objective about him. He was bright, able and liberal. He had had a broad, active practice that included representation of offbeats and nonconformists, as well as corporations and conservative members of the community. He would have made an excellent Chief Justice. The points against him made at the hearings before the Senate Judiciary Committee were petty and irrelevant.

The "separation of powers," critics said, should have kept him from advising LBJ while a member of the Court. I refused that role under FDR basically because giving advice might well have disqualified me from sitting in many cases. When Johnson became President, I would time and again receive a message from him saying a columnist or journalist was off base on such and such a topic, and would I please send for him or to go New York to see him and put him straight. I, of course, never responded.

In December 1966 I was at Yale addressing the senior college class, and the long arm of LBJ was present. Undergraduates had voiced their protest against our policy in Vietnam and Johnson was trying to get those dissenters discharged from Yale or disciplined by Yale authorities. He seemed to neglect no device to try to force public unanimity with his views.

In the case of Fortas, there were no instances in which his consultations with LBJ in any way implicated cases coming to the Court. Moreover, there never has been a complete "separation" of executive and judicial functions.

While John Jay was Chief Justice, he also served as ambassador to England. While Oliver Ellsworth was Chief Justice, he served as ambassador to France. When John Marshall was appointed Chief Justice he continued to serve as Secretary of State under President John Adams. Unfortunately his dual service raises serious questions about the propriety of his participation in and writing of the famous opinion expressed in *Marbury* v. *Madison,* 5 U.S. 137 (1803). It was in that case that Madison was being sued as Secretary of State for his failure to deliver judicial commissions that had been left over by his predecessor in office, now Chief Justice Marshall. Having been responsible for these commissions during his tenure as Secretary of State, John Marshall would have been compelled to disqualify himself from sitting on the case were it to be brought today.

In 1877 there was an Electoral Commission of fifteen members appointed to resolve the presidential contest between Samuel Tilden and Rutherford Hayes. Five Justices of this Court—Nathan Clifford, William Strong, Samuel Miller, Stephen Field and Joseph Bradley—served on that commission. They rendered an eight-to-seven decision, giving the White House to Hayes. In my time, Robert H. Jackson stayed on the Court, receiving his full salary, while he served as prosecutor in the Nuremberg trials; Owen J. Roberts served as a member of the commission to investigate the Pearl Harbor disaster; and Chief Justice Warren served as chairman of the commission investigating the assassination of President John F. Kennedy.

Justices have at times advised Presidents. Certainly Brandeis did, and Frankfurter too. Whether their advice caused any collision with future judicial decisions which they had to make, I do not know. But if there had been such a collision, those men would have been the first to suggest that they not sit. All Justices I served with have been extremely sensitive to the matter of disqualification, leaning over backwards to observe the appearance of propriety as well as the proprieties themselves.

Another charge against Fortas was that he was paid fees for lecturing at American University. In the early years quite a few Justices were part-time lecturers on law faculties. In my time there was hardly a single Justice who did not receive some fee for some lecture. I traveled extensively around the world, financing my own way. Those were expensive trips and I recouped the costs through writing books and giving lectures. (My travel and other books amounted to over thirty.) I gave formal lectures, such as the Edge Lectures at Princeton ("America Challenged") and the Stokes Lectures at New York University ("Towards a Global Federalism"). I also spoke on college campuses to students and adults alike on a variety of topics—"Russia Today," "Red China v. India," "Communism in Southeast Asia," "Points of Rebellion" (dealing with the mounting internal tensions), "The Supreme Court in

American History," "Latin America Today," "Israel and the Democratic Front," and others.

Many Justices have held securities in business companies. Others have served as trustees or directors of institutions. Taft was on the Yale Board of Trustees for years. Burton, Jackson and others had similar outside connections. I, for some years, was a member of the Board of Overseers of Whitman College. If Whitman had been a litigant before the Court, I would not have participated in the case. If a Justice or his family held stock or bonds in a company before the Court, the Justice would take no part in the decision. In my time the disqualification was honored, even if the securities held were of a minuscule amount. Justices indeed leaned far backwards to avoid participating in some cases, as when a former client was a litigant or a former law firm was the advocate, even though the Justice had no monetary claim against the old client or old law firm.

A close relative who appeared as advocate would drive a Justice out of the case. Hughes never sat on a case argued by his son, Charles E. Hughes, Jr., who indeed resigned as Solicitor General when his father was confirmed as Chief Justice. Justice Brennan never took part even in considering a petition for certiorari prepared by the law firm with which his son, Bill, was associated. And Justice Clark retired so that his son Ramsey could become Attorney General.

What blocked Fortas in 1968 had blocked John Rutledge in 1795. He was named Chief Justice by President Washington while Congress was in recess. Rutledge made a speech criticizing the Jay Treaty, by which England and the United States had agreed to establish limited trade relations. The Federalists were riled and voted him down, 10 to 14, when the Senate convened. That vote, like the filibuster against Fortas, had nothing to do with Rutledge's fitness for office. He had become a symbol of what the majority disliked. Fortas was not disliked personally, but he was the symbol of the Court, which had encountered severe criticism because of its libertarian philosophy, and more important, he was rated as a crony of the discredited Lyndon Johnson.

Arthur Goldberg's resignation from the Court in 1965 set a strange series of events in motion which is worth summarizing here: it created a vacancy that Johnson filled by appointing Fortas. Then, when Warren retired as Chief Justice, in 1969, at the end of Johnson's term, LBJ named Fortas to succeed him. Because Fortas had been Johnson's attorney and close friend prior to coming onto the Court, the inquiry in the

Senate on his confirmation probed deeply into whether Fortas had continued to give Johnson advice while he was an Associate Justice. By that time Johnson himself had created a credibility gap of vast proportions; as a result, much of the antagonism against Fortas was merely a reflection against Johnson. In any event, Johnson withdrew the Fortas nomination as Chief Justice and shortly thereafter Fortas resigned from the Court altogether, for a variety of reasons which I will relate in another chapter (pages 357 ff.).

This gave Nixon, who came to office immediately after that, two appointments—Burger and Blackmun. Had Goldberg not resigned when he did but stayed on the Court, Johnson would have named Fortas as Chief Justice when Warren retired, and the Court, under Abe's direction and management, would have continued in the manner of the Warren Court. Fortas would then have come to the Court from private practice, and it would never have been a disability to have been a lawyer who was adviser to the President. A Justice as adviser to the Chief Executive is quite another matter. In that sequence of events, there would have been no vacancies on the Court for Nixon to fill until late in 1971, at the time of the deaths of Black and Harlan.

When Abe Fortas resigned, Nixon nominated Clement F. Haynsworth, Jr. of the Fourth Circuit Court of Appeals. Haynsworth, I thought, would have been a good judge on our Court. I think Hugo Black felt the same way.

It was at a Fifth Circuit conference that Hugo first met G. Harrold Carswell, first a District Court judge from Florida and then a member of the Court of Appeals. When Nixon nominated Carswell to our Court, a storm of protests was heard. But Hugo told me he thought Carswell would make a fine Justice. As the controversy over Carswell's confirmation mounted I kept asking Hugo if he'd changed his mind. No, he said, he had not. One must remember, Hugo said, that very few outstanding men have sat on the Court, that American politics was inclined to produce mediocrity in public office, and that though Carswell might not be a giant, he was competent. I had never met Carswell, and even after he failed to be confirmed, I only met him very casually and I never had a chance to visit with him. Nor had I ever read any of his opinions, except those circulated by the opposition. But as the days passed and his confirmation was hanging in the balance, I kept asking Hugo about the man. Finally he said this, "I really do not know much about him except I believe he is competent. Moreover, his wife and I have ended up partners at bridge. And if they move up here to Washington, D.C., Mrs. Carswell and I can beat any couple in town." Carswell failed to be confirmed by a slender vote and five votes were lost to him when Gerald Ford said that if the Senate did not confirm Carswell, the House would impeach me.

The problem of a Justice and his disqualifications sometimes appears in bizarre forms.

Telephone wires in Washington are commonly tapped; and I have at various times been morally certain that all Supreme Court wires were tapped. In the early days it was easy to recognize a "tap" by a recurring beep-beep sound. Later, more sophisticated methods were used, and even the most suspicious telephone users were not aware of what was happening.

During Hughes's terms as Chief Justice, he somehow discovered that our Conference Room was "bugged." He made a quick, intensive investigation and learned that two employees of the Court had been enlisted by a District of Columbia policeman to place a bug in the room. He ordered the Marshal to discharge the two employees "within the hour." They were fired; the bug was removed; the episode was given no publicity. Who the person or persons behind the policeman were we never found out.

When Warren became Chief Justice, he had the Conference Room, where the nine Justices discuss and debate the cases, "swept." That "de-bugging" operation was expensive, costing about $5,000; and there has never been an item in the Court's budget for such an expenditure. So Warren got the FBI to "sweep" the room. The problem was that those most likely to tap Supreme Court wires were the FBI, the CIA and the National Security Council; and it seemed probable that in the sixties not only our telephones but also the Conference Room were bugged.

The issue had arisen in a curious way. Albert Parvin, businessman of Los Angeles, read my book *America Challenged* and decided to form a foundation to further the ideas in the book. I became director of the foundation and its president. The foundation dedicated itself to promoting the training of democratic leaders in underdeveloped nations (see pages 365 ff.). I received a salary on the understanding that none of my expenses would be billed to the foundation, but would be paid by me personally. The portfolio of the foundation contained various securities, including a fractional interest in a mortgage on hotel properties in Las Vegas. A lurid Los Angeles news item carried the story that I therefore was tied to gambling interests, and the conclusion stated was that obviously therefore I could not sit in *Black* v. *United States* (385 U.S. 26), a case involving a gambler whose wires had been tapped by the FBI.

Both White and Fortas were out of the case. If I could be taken out, a six-man Court would be left. If an outsider had overheard the Conference discussions of this case he would have realized that if seven sat, the case would be decided four to three one way or the other. Thus, our vote on October 14, 1966, to set the case down for rehearing had four in favor (Brennan, Clark, Douglas and the Chief) and three opposed (Black, Harlan and Stewart). If I was out of the case, a Court of six would probably end up equally divided. Only one who had access to the privacy of the Conference Room would have known that I was the key person in the case.

Convinced that our Conference Room was bugged and that the Los Angeles news story was inspired by the FBI, I wrote a separate opinion in *Black* v. *United States:*

> There has been a studied effort made to drive me out of this case. Vicious articles have been printed by the press carrying libelous innuendoes that link me with this petitioner, with the underworld, and with others associated with him. I have no acquaintance with petitioner and no connection whatsoever with him, with his associates, or with the underworld.
>
> I file this separate opinion because this is not the first time that powerful forces have tried to drive a Justice out of a particular case.
>
> The integrity of the Court is one of the Nation's choice traditions. That integrity cannot be maintained if one of us, qualified to sit by all moral and ethical standards, allows himself to be driven from sitting in judgment on a case.

I was dissuaded by some of my Brethren from filing this opinion, but I remained convinced that that was the truth of the matter.

In the sixties, no important conversation or conference in Washington was immune from wiretapping or electronic surveillance. By 1974 hearing rooms at Congress were being bugged. Some of these broadcasting devices enabled a person sitting in a car a few blocks away to hear the secret testimony of witnesses given in "closed" sessions. The

CIA, before sending officers up to Congress to testify, had the room "swept," but the clandestine electronic ears in Nixon's days were everywhere in Washington.

It was common for committees of Congress to make public only the total sums appropriated for the intelligence activities of the CIA, the Defense Intelligence Agency, the National Security Agency and the separate intelligence units in the Army, Navy and Air Force. In late 1973 a new national intelligence agency came onto the federal scene. It was called the National Reconnaissance Office, and not even Congress knew what it did.

Secrecy proliferated under Nixon. The people, who are the sovereigns, knew less and less about their government's operation. Under the cloak of secrecy, high crimes and misdemeanors were committed. Secrecy—whether in terms of budgetary expenditures or in terms of documents marked "Secret"—covers the tracks of a bureaucrat for at least ten years. These are extremely convenient devices to cover the tracks of irresponsible agents. I had a "Secret" stamp at the SEC, but I do not believe I ever used it.

On March 10, 1969, the Court handed down an opinion in *Alderman* v. *United States* (394 U.S. 165) and related cases in which defendants or their attorneys in criminal cases had had their wires tapped and been put under some kind of electronic surveillance. That kind of surveillance had previously been held to be a "search" and "seizure" within the meaning of the Fourth Amendment; and the exclusionary rule, first announced in 1914 in the *Weeks* decision (232 U.S. 383), had been ruled applicable to statements intercepted, as it had been to documents seized.

Black, who did not think the Fourth Amendment was applicable to wiretapping or electronic bugging, dissented. Harlan and Fortas wrote separate opinions, concurring in part and dissenting in part. They had slightly different views as to standing of aggrieved persons to complain. Harlan and Fortas also thought that all "national security" cases should be exempted—each, however, defining that category in somewhat different terms.

But all eight sitting Justices (Marshall took no part) agreed with the heart of the ruling in *Alderman* that where the Fourth Amendment is applicable, the prosecution should be required to hand over to the defense the records of all conversations in which the accused played a part. The Court rejected the counterproposition that all these tapes be handled in *in camera* proceedings by the District Court.

Sometime later I learned from court sources that the announcement of the decision resulted in a long series of conferences between the Department of Justice, the FBI and the CIA. On March 12 it was apparently decided by these agencies that someone representing John N. Mitchell, the Attorney General, should pay a visit to Chief Justice Warren. It was then decided that perhaps that was not appropriate. So it was suggested that the public relations man from Justice, Mr. Jack Landau, should go and see Justice Brennan, with whom he had a slight acquaintance.

Justice Brennan immediately brought him in to the Chief Justice because what Landau had to say pertained to the Department of Justice's threat that something terrible would happen to the Court unless it changed its ruling in the Alderman case. This is the first instance in the memory of anyone connected with the Court in which the executive branch has made actual threats to the Court.

Specifically, Landau warned the Chief Justice that the Justice Department would get laws passed by Congress which would change the rule of admissibility of wiretaps and the processing of them during a trial, or that it would get a law passed which would take away from the Court appellate jurisdiction of any case involving the constitutionality of wiretapping.

The Chief Justice told Landau that the way to present the views of the Department of Justice was through a petition for rehearing, and that the Court would consider not the argument advanced by the Attorney General and his deputy, Richard G. Kleindienst, and Landau, but only points of law that they might present in the petition for rehearing. Landau replied that the Solicitor General was hard at work on a petition for rehearing and that it would be filed soon. Warren said that the political considerations Landau was talking about were wholly irrelevant to any decision the Court would make.

It came out in the discussion that either the FBI or the CIA had been tapping all of the embassies in Washington—i.e., 109 of them. (Later, in a telephone call, Mr. Landau reduced that figure from 109 to 46 active continuous taps, as distinguished from those made occasionally.) The embarrassment to the executive branch was the public disclosure of the fact that it had been tapping embassies. This disclosure, however, was not made by the Court but, eventually, by Fred Graham in a New York

Times article that appears to have been planted by Kleindienst.

None of the horrible fears and imaginary difficulties which Graham's article foresaw were adverted to even indirectly by the Solicitor General when he argued the case. And the fact, of course, that the embassies were bugged had nothing to do with the legal nature of wiretapping. Apart from national security cases—which were very few and far between—the wiretaps involved a miscellaneous run of crimes including the so-called draft evasion by Cassius Clay, later known as Muhammad Ali. The fact that it was an embassy wire that was tapped had no bearing upon the Fourth Amendment problem of whether there should be disclosure or nondisclosure to the defendant, usually an outsider with no embassy connection.

Landau and Graham claimed that the Court was split. They were wholly misinformed, as all eight of us thought seized conversation, like seized papers, should be disclosed at the trial to the accused. Apparently the Department of Justice had not read the decision very carefully.

It seems pretty evident that Kleindienst, and perhaps Mitchell himself, wanted to give the Court as much trouble as possible.

The Chief Justice called a Special Conference on March 17; and I inquired whether he had asked Landau about the bug which I am sure existed in our Conference Room. Warren said no, but he had asked whether his own office was bugged, and Landau, expressing great surprise and astonishment, held up his hands and said certainly not.

Warren handled the matter with ease and delicacy. Hughes would have stood up at the start of the talk, beard bristling, and leveling a finger at Landau, would have thundered, "Young man, you will be cited for contempt of court."

It was not only the Nixon Administration that attempted to influence justice. Tom Corcoran, who had been FDR's "hatchet man," remained an active lobbyist. His technique was to work "underground," processing applications through administrative agencies by contacting key staff members and bringing political pressures to bear upon the agencies themselves. That's how he appeared in one case, which was before the Court several times. Interestingly, when he tried to get Justice Brennan to act in this case, he said that if the Court did not allow the merger he was advocating, he'd get a bill through Congress that would approve it. In March 1971 that bill was introduced in the Senate.

• • •

The Administration had attempted to erode the constitutional guarantees which had been reinforced by the Court since Hughes was Chief Justice. Hughes did not initiate the incorporation of the Bill of Rights into the Due Process Clause of the Fourteenth Amendment. That started in 1897 in *Chicago, Burlington & Quincy Railroad Co.* v. *Chicago* (166 U.S. 226) when the Court held that the Just Compensation Clause of the Fifth Amendment was applicable to the states. But he did hold for the Court in 1931 that the First Amendment was applicable to the states (*Stromberg* v. *California,* 283 U.S. 359). Under Warren, more and more provisions of the Bill of Rights—originally applicable only to the federal government—were by reason of the Fourteenth Amendment held applicable to the states. They included the right to counsel (*Hamilton* v. *Alabama,* 368 U.S. 52; *Gideon* v. *Wainwright,* 372 U.S. 335; *Argersinger* v. *Hamlin,* 407 U.S. 25). They also included the right to confrontation with the person making the accusation (*Pointer* v. *Texas,* 380 U.S. 400); the Self-Incrimination Clause of the Fifth Amendment (*Malloy* v. *Hogan,* 378 U.S. 1; *Mapp* v. *Ohio,* 367 U.S. 643); and the right to the Protective Procedures of the Bill of Rights when it came to custodial interrogation of suspects, including the Self-Incrimination Clause of the Fifth Amendment and the Right to Counsel provision of the Sixth (*Miranda* v. *Arizona,* 384 U.S. 436).

These enlargements of constitutional guarantees—started by Hughes and completed by Warren—drew the fire of people in power. They came down on the side of adhering to due process of the law at a time when Nixon's cry was for "law and order." Nixon's judicial appointments were made with that aim in view, but his actual aim was to cut down constitutional protections and to make it easier for government to move against alleged offenders.

Although "due process" is not defined in the Constitution, the guarantees of the first eight Amendments—originally applicable only to the federal government—are pretty sturdy standards for due process. Why not apply them to the states through the Fourteenth Amendment? It was far better we do that than leave due process to be defined according to the predilections of individual Justices. That was Black's position and mine. That was the position that the Burger Court steadfastly rejected.

The Nixon program, if honestly embraced, should have included a national debate on constitutional amendments. If government was to be all-powerful, if the individual was to be further submerged, the Bill of Rights should be revised. Lifelong appointments to the Court were not the way to do it. The predilections of the Justices often reflected jaundiced and parochial views. If we want a more powerful government, we should go to Russia, Eastern Europe or Spain and study contemporary models. Do we want torture used in prisons? Do we prefer holding men and women incommunicado, as in Russia, for nine months? Do we want the privacy of homes and offices broken down by electronic surveillance? Whose homes? Despised minorities or the affluent people as well?

These are large problems all covered in the Nixon days by "law and order" camouflage. Behind the Nixon drive for conformity was a hearty disrespect for the First Amendment. Suppression of a critical press became a dominant theme in the Nixon-Agnew line of attack.

As noted, the First Amendment was made applicable to the states in an opinion for the Court by Hughes in 1931 in *Stromberg* v. *California.* Hughes reasoned that "the conception of liberty under the due process clause of the Fourteenth Amendment embraces the right of free speech" (*Id.* 368). The First Amendment reads:

> Congress shall make no law respecting an establishment of religion, or prohibiting the free exercise thereof; or abridging the freedom of speech, or of the press; or the right of the people peaceably to assemble, and to petition the Government for a redress of grievances.

As the Fourteenth Amendment has been construed since *Stromberg,* it now must be read as saying *"Government* shall make no law . . ."

The philosophy of the First Amendment has been embraced across the globe by men and women of various faiths. I never knew Gandhi, but he was one of my heroes. I devoured all he wrote. I always place flowers on his grave when I visit India. Gandhi was inspired by Thoreau's essay on civil disobedience, which may be summarized as follows: the refusal to obey certain governmental policy characterized by the employment of such nonviolent techniques as boycotting, picketing and nonpayment of taxes. Thoreau withdrew from society, lived alone on an isolated pond, and once refused to pay a tax. For that he submitted himself to arrest and went to jail. Gandhi's civil disobedience was likewise peaceful. It was, however, much more effective. Gandhi's tactics were largely instrumental in summoning 400 million people to one great overwhelming cause and in peacefully toppling a colonial regime.

Alexander Solzhenitsyn asked his people to take no action against the government but only to stop cooperating. By not participating in spreading "the lie" that the Soviets do not have camps for political prisoners or a secret police, "we commit," he said, "a moral action, but not a political one, which is not criminally punishable." Solzhenitsyn, apparently, adopted an essentially Gandhian approach.

The philosophy of the First Amendment marks a bold venture, judged by the problems of this troubled world. It is bold because ideas are dangerous—more dangerous than guns. Ideas unite people; they pass over borders in spite of the battalions that guard those borders. They live on and on—throughout time. Many still walk to the measure of the ideas of Zoroaster, Buddha, Jesus, Mohammed and other men and women with powerful concepts in religious, political or educational work. So when we honor Gandhi, we honor the best in Eastern and Western civilization—the power of the mind and the right of the mind to be free—to consider, believe and speak what one thinks is the truth.

Early in 1974 Solzhenitsyn was deprived of his citizenship and exiled for the publication of *The Gulag Archipelago*, which depicted the conditions in Russia's prison camps.

Early in 1974 Miklos Haraszti was convicted of distributing his book exposing working conditions in an Hungarian tractor factory. The "crime" was incitement against a fundamental institution of the Hungarian state—the wage system. The main complaint of the book was apparently aimed at the "piece rate system" said to be "a capitalist creation" of the Hungarian government.

Those in power are easily upset, for they have a low tolerance for criticism. The police, bent on maintaining the status quo, usually arrest the speaker, not the hecklers. Those who are the dissenters, those nonconformists who plead for a different order, a more humanistic philosophy, a less materialistic approach often walk in solitude.

What Solzhenitsyn said about lies and falsehood came early in 1974 after the Watergate horrors were fairly well disclosed. Solzhenitsyn did not write about them but about his own nation's problems. There is no downgrading of a First Amendment in Russia, for she never had one. We did downgrade it; and it was the main Nixon target when he dogged reporters, investigated dissident groups, put critics on his "enemies" list for IRS probes, tried to manipulate the FCC to cancel radio and TV licenses that were in hands unfriendly to him.

Some people on this side of the water were quick to denounce Solzhe-nitsyn, saying that at heart he believes only in a society run by techno-crats and theologians. That is irrelevant to First Amendment values. For free speech opens up the entire spectrum of ideas, some congenial to us, some hostile. It is indeed at war with the values inherent in the First Amendment to say "Believe as we do—or else."

Solzhenitsyn, who received the Nobel Prize in 1970, was never al-lowed to deliver his acceptance speech, which contained these pas-sages:

> We shall be told: What can literature possibly do against the ruthless onslaught of open violence? But let us not forget that violence does not live alone and is not capable of living alone: It is necessarily interwoven with falsehood. Between them lies the most intimate, the deepest of natural bonds. Any man who has once acclaimed violence as his method must inexorably choose falsehood as his principle. At its birth, violence acts openly and even with pride. But no sooner does it become strong, firmly established, than it senses the rarefaction of the air around it, and it cannot continue to exist without descend-ing into a fog of lies, clothing them in sweet talk. It does not always, not necessarily, openly throttle the throat; more often it demands from its subjects only an oath of allegiance to false-hood, only complicity in falsehood. . . .
>
> Let that enter the world, let it even reign in the world—but not with my help. But writers and artists can achieve more: They can conquer falsehood.

On February 12, 1974, on the eve of his expulsion from Russia, Solzhe-nitsyn said: "So in our timidity, let each of us make a choice: Whether consciously to remain a servant of falsehood—of course, it is not out of inclination, but to feed one's family, that one raises his children in the spirit of lies—or to shrug off the lies and become an honest man worthy of respect both by one's children and contemporaries."

We cannot impose a regime of civil rights on another nation, but we can speak up and make our own moral position clear. The Soviets tend to believe that what is not reported in their press, what their people do not know, never has happened. That is why talking about it frankly and earnestly helps make an oppressor face up to what really has happened.

William Faulkner, on receiving the Nobel Prize in Stockholm on December 10, 1950, made an acceptance speech which contains a profound reflection on First Amendment values:

> I feel that this award was not made to me as a man but to my work—a life's work in the agony and sweat of the human spirit, not for glory and least of all for profit, but to create out of the materials of the human spirit something which did not exist before. . . .
>
> Our tragedy today is a general and universal physical fear so long sustained by now that we can even bear it. There are no longer problems of the spirit. There is only the question: When will I be blown up? Because of this, the young man or woman writing today has forgotten the problems of the human heart in conflict with itself which alone can make good writing because only that is worth writing about, worth the agony and the sweat.
>
> He must learn them again. He must teach himself that the basest of all things is to be afraid; and, teaching himself that, forget it forever, leaving no room in his workshop for anything but the old verities and truths of the heart, the old universal truths lacking which any story is ephemeral and doomed—love and honor and pity and pride and compassion and sacrifice. . . .
>
> Until he relearns these things he will write as though he stood among and watched the end of man. I decline to accept the end of man. It is easy enough to say that man is immortal simply because he will endure; that when the last dingdong of doom has clanged and faded from the last worthless rock hanging tideless in the last red and dying evening, that even then there will still be one more sound: that of his puny inexhaustible voice, still talking. I refuse to accept this. I believe that man will not merely endure: he will prevail. He is immortal, not because he alone among creatures has an inexhaustible voice, but because he has a soul, a spirit capable of compassion and sacrifice and endurance. The poet's, the writer's, duty is to write about these things. It is his privilege to help man endure by lifting his heart, by reminding him of the courage and honor and hope and pride and compassion and pity and sacrifice which have been the glory of his past. The poet's voice need

not merely be the record of man, it can be one of the props, the pillars to help him endure and prevail.

The First Amendment always seemed to Hugo Black and me to be a "preferred" guarantee of the Bill of Rights. That idea was often ridiculed. But it is "preferred" because when it says "no law," that is in terms absolute and quite unlike the word "unreasonable" search or seizure in the Fourth Amendment or "speedy" trial in the Sixth or "excessive" bail in the Eighth. The values the First Amendment protects are necessary in a multiracial, multireligious, multi-ideological society of the kind we profess to be. The First Amendment sets us apart from most other nations. It marks the end of all censorship, it allows the ability of the mind to roam at will over the entire spectrum of ideas, and the sanctity of one's beliefs. It—not our bombs or air force or missiles or manufacturing skills or merchandising methods or GNP—sets us apart. A symbol of our health is the respect we show to First Amendment values. It was the great welling up of those values that led to the tragic demise of the Nixon Administration, which, like no other in my time, had sought to level First Amendment rights.

Chapter XIV

Six Presidents

Franklin D. Roosevelt

As I have mentioned, soon after I came on the Court, FDR began to call me, asking me to take one assignment after another. One summer he had several jobs for me as an administrative assistant at the White House. In June 1942 he asked me to spend the summer there. My job would be to knock department heads together so as to (a) expedite decisions and (b) resolve conflicts or differences of view.

I talked with both Roberts and Black about it and they agreed that I should decline the invitation. Hugo said, "If you do an effective job, you will get into a first-class row with some vested interest in twenty-four hours. If you don't get into a row, you'll be a flop."

I wrote FDR that "since last December I have often thought that I should enter the Army or the Navy. Except for such a major war move, I thought I should stay on the Court." I added: "I am inclined to the view that any real undertaking on my part to iron out difficulties between department heads who have authority and who in many instances have a real hostility would not prove to be helpful and might injure the Court."

My countersuggestion to FDR was that he designate for the job three or four men on a permanent basis with definite authority and responsibility, adding that they might be able to do "what department heads ought to do on their own 90 per cent or more of the time without any intercession."

Advising a President while being a Justice leads to complications, as Abe Fortas and many other Justices have discovered. The norm is not necessarily a true separation of powers, for every Justice is part of the town, of the nation, of the world, and is bound to play more of a role than that of passive onlooker. The difficulty lies in the disqualifications that may arise when future cases are before the Court. I saw that problem enveloping my projected advice to FDR and I therefore never undertook to serve in that role.

In my day I felt there was no room for a Justice in the executive branch. So I rejected all of FDR's requests for advice except one—to serve as a committee to recommend a person to head up the Office of Manpower. Sidney Hillman, Paul McNutt and others were vying for the job, and I gave FDR the benefit of my views. He kept coming back, again and again, with other jobs. I saw him often, played poker with him, helped him on speeches, but I declined his overtures to put me to work in the White House, as I did not think I should undertake that work unless I resigned from the Court.

Finally, on a hot September night in 1941, he asked me to do just that. I was at the rodeo in Pendleton, Oregon, when a resourceful White House operator tracked me down; I took the call in a phone booth and heard FDR say that the Court was not the place for me. I must resign.

In September 1941, FDR had in mind the creation of the War Production Board, which actually took place on January 16, 1942. In the meantime an office was vacant—Coordinator of National Defense Purchases, established by the Counsel of National Defense but soon to be transferred to the Executive Office of the President. FDR wanted me to take it over and create what in time became the War Production Board. Bernard Baruch had recommended me, the President said, and I must do it.

"Is this a draft—a real draft, Mr. President?"

"A real draft," he replied.

"Then I'll do it."

"Wonderful," he boomed back. "Call me the minute you get here."

I was back in Washington in a week and reported to the White House operator. I was sick at heart, for I did not want to leave the Court, but the Old Man could not be denied. No White House message came that day and none the next. None came that week. Soon I picked up a morning paper to read that Donald Nelson had been named for the office. I was greatly relieved. FDR never mentioned the matter when I saw him next. He looked like the cat that had swallowed the canary; but he never told me what had happened. The technique of complete silence was one of FDR's accomplishments.

I soon learned that Harry Hopkins, whose star was rising, had persuaded FDR to make the switch from me to Donald Nelson. Harry Hopkins was a sick man; and the sicker he got, the closer FDR pulled the man to him. Dr. Draper thought it was the "identity" FDR felt for Hopkins, both being invalids and both getting worse. While FDR's general level of health was good, he walked less and less. "The braces kill me these days," he would say. He was putting on weight; and his lack of leg exercises practically immobilized him.

Harry Hopkins was very much in the center of White House activities by 1941. He was indeed a physically sick man, his face being that of a cadaver at FDR's funeral. He had great personal ambitions—to succeed FDR. He was therefore instinctively jealous of anyone whom FDR liked. Warfare around a throne has always been acrimonious. Harry, whom I liked, saw me as a rival—which I was not in terms of personal ambition; but he treated me accordingly. He must have gloated over his shunting me aside and replacing me with Don Nelson. He and I never discussed the episode, though I always felt grateful for Harry's decapitation of me for that job, since it was one of the most thankless of them all.

When war came, on December 7, 1941, I was giving a luncheon at my home. Dr. Draper was there, and so was Henry Wallace. As a matter of fact, I had seated them at the same cardtable, as Draper had been curious about Wallace. Draper's opinion of Wallace, I later found out, was very revealing: "I'd keep him on the faculty but I'd never make him Dean." Which in Draper language meant that Wallace as an idea man was outstanding; as an administrator, not very good.

Robert P. Patterson, former federal judge and now Undersecretary of War, was also there. It was about one o'clock when my butler, Rochester (after whom Jack Benny was to name a famous radio and movie character), whispered to me that Judge Patterson was wanted by the White House operator. Bob shortly returned and told us he had an announcement to make. The room became silent and he said, "The Japanese have just attacked Pearl Harbor." Then he quickly left for the Pentagon.

FDR had been alarmed when Hitler became Chancellor on January 30, 1933; and I always thought that FDR's recognition of Russia on November 16, 1933, was the first conscious power move on his part in reaction to Hitler. It did indeed lay the basis for the final combination that was fatal to Hitler. I think that the prospect of a global engagement began to take definite shape in FDR's mind no later than 1937. His well-known "quarantine" speech, in which he denounced international terrorism, was made in Chicago in October 1937, and his "dagger in the back" speech on the Italian invasion of France was made in Charlottesville in June 1940. FDR in those three years often talked of "neutrality," but he was, as Rex Tugwell once put it, "the least neutral of all Americans." In 1937 the Ludlow Resolution, a proposal to require a popular referendum before Congress could declare war, was debated. It was defeated in the House in 1938 by a vote of 209 to 188 after FDR had sent a message that "it would cripple any President in his conduct of our foreign relations, and it would encourage other nations to believe that they could violate American rights with impunity."

My view of the conduct of foreign affairs is that the Constitution provides that it is Congress which has the power to "declare war" and that all diplomacy, short of that, is under the guidance of the President. That was my interpretation in 1937 when the Ludlow Resolution was debated as it was my view during the Nixon Vietnam war.

Hitler annexed Austria in March 1938, and then, after the "peace in our time" accord with the British Chamberlain government, took Czechoslovakia. The year 1939 saw Poland invaded. I was at the Polish embassy that night, and the Polish ambassador, both proud and valiant, took me aside to assure me that this was Hitler's greatest error, that the Polish army would cut the Germans to ribbons. I raised a glass to Polish victory but left the embassy with a heavy heart.

FDR's policy in these years and continuing into 1940 was to help the victims of the aggressors. He still talked of the defeat of Hitler by means "short of war"; and in 1939 he had, I think, a hope that Mussolini could be persuaded to stay out of war.

Throughout 1939 and 1940 he talked peace, peace, peace. Yet, as Hitler invaded nation after nation, he denounced those acts of aggression.

In 1939 he had proclaimed the neutrality of the United States in the war between Germany and Poland, France and the United Kingdom. In 1940 he was urging that we build up our armed defenses; and he was releasing surplus stocks of airplanes, artillery and munitions to Great Britain. In 1940, while dedicating the Great Smoky Mountains Park, he spoke mostly of the dangers of aggressive war. On December 29, 1940, he told the nation, "The Nazi masters of Germany have made it clear that they intend not only to dominate all life and thought in their own country, but also to enslave the whole of Europe and then to use the resources of Europe to dominate the rest of the world." It was then he declared we should be "the great arsenal of democracy."

On the Fourth of July of that year, he had warned the country that "the United States will never survive as a happy and fertile oasis of liberty surrounded by the cruel desert of dictatorship." On August 14, 1941, came the momentous Atlantic Charter announcing the new enduring compact between this country and England. And the next day came the joint Roosevelt-Churchill message asking for a Moscow conference. On September 1, 1941, he stated, "We shall do everything in our power to crush Hitler and his Nazi forces." On September 11, 1941, he told the country again about the Nazi danger, saying, "When you see a rattlesnake poised to strike, you do not wait until he has struck before you crush him." On October 13, 1941, he announced that aid was being rushed to Russia.

On December 6, 1941, he sent word to the Japanese ambassador, saying that the concentration of Japanese forces in Vietnam was the cause of great concern and asked for their withdrawal. Then came December 7, "a date which will live in infamy," and the declaration of war on December 8.

These are merely the well-known highlights of Roosevelt's policies toward the growing war. In between were dozens upon dozens of measures taken by FDR, building a mosaic of civilian and military agencies, all equipped with power to deal with the pressing problems of war, should it come. So, despite the Pearl Harbor disaster, we were, thanks to FDR's foresight, well prepared.

FDR did not cut many constitutional corners. He recognized that the source of his power was Congress. In his first inaugural he said, "I shall ask the Congress for the one remaining instrument to meet the crisis —broad Executive power to wage a war against the emergency, as great as the power that would be given to me if we were in fact invaded by a foreign foe."

In 1941 FDR did impound money appropriated by Congress for the building of highways to offset the increase in military expenditures (87

Cong. Record 66), which aroused some critics (8. Doc. No. 152, 77th Cong., 1st Sess.), as did later impoundments by FDR.

He did by-pass Congress in 1940 when he made a deal by which, in exchange for our destroyers, England gave us bases in the Atlantic. But he acted in reliance on an opinion of his Attorney General (39 Op. A.G. 484), and after consulting with Democratic and Republican leaders in Congress. The Lend-Lease Act was debated and passed by Congress. His earlier proposal to reform the Supreme Court was submitted to Congress.

FDR was criticized and denounced for starting a "presidential war" against Hitler—an alleged precedent for the later "presidential war" against Vietnam. All of FDR's sympathies and prejudices were for England's cause. He could not constitutionally have reacted otherwise. Hence, after close consultation with Churchill he started a vast rearmament program into which we had committed about $100 billion before war was declared.

To trace the further legislative and executive actions involved—in 1940 Congress authorized construction of plants for national defense and authorized the government to take them over for operation (54 Stat. 712). Then FDR sent American ships into the German U-boat zone, and this led to armed clashes between our vessels and Hitler's. But FDR did get Congress to modify the old Neutrality Act, passed on November 4, 1939, which was aimed at making it unlawful for any American vessel to carry passengers or materials to any foreign state at war, save for specified exceptions. Under this act FDR, by a series of proclamations, described the combat zones under the ban of the act. On May 27, 1941, FDR proclaimed an "unlimited national emergency" which required that the country put its defenses "on the basis of readiness to repel" any acts of aggression toward any part of the Western Hemisphere. On November 17, 1941, Congress amended the Neutrality Act so as to lift the ban on shipment of materials to nations at war and to authorize the President during the declared emergency to arm any American vessel.

Congress, prior to December 8, 1941, did not declare war on Germany or Japan. It was, however, active in authorizing the establishment of defense posts far from our shores and in readying America for any assaults. These preliminary moves by both FDR and Congress, in the eyes of some people, amounted to an undeclared war. I never thought it was. They involved a readiness to risk hostilities, but they never committed America to an all-out undertaking to destroy Hitlerism. A declaration of war would envisage a total effort against another power —the kind which the "presidential war" in Vietnam launched. FDR certainly believed in a strong presidency, but it was not a secretive one. He held press conferences twice a week, even through most of the war. He believed in participatory democracy and was constantly in touch with diverse people with diverse views, seeking enlightenment for himself and a consensus among the people.

I had a little to do with these policy decisions. During these days FDR would mull over his problems in the evenings, and he used me as a sounding board. The ugly character of the Nazi regime was a recurring theme as the persecution of the Jews loomed larger and larger. Those barbaric acts and the barbaric quality of the Nazis themselves were the main forces shaping FDR's policies.

I saw FDR on December 8, 1941, and he was indeed greatly relieved that the long period of waiting was over. I think that by the fall of 1941 he had hoped we would get into the war and throw our massive weight against Hitler and the Japanese. I think he would have asked for a declaration of war before December 8, 1941, if he could have managed it politically.

That day as I left the White House I realized that an armament program leads irresistibly to war. The reasons are partly subconscious perhaps. In any event, the pressures mount to use newly collected weapons and manpower. The military are bent on flexing their muscles; a theater of war is a place where promotions come fast.

The presence of a big whopping military establishment puts immeasurable pressures on Presidents, senators, congressmen, Cabinet officers. They begin to think more and more in military terms. The mass media are attracted to shining armor, like flies to honey. In time the nation is saturated with military news, military hopes, military thinking.

Preparedness, I realized that December day in 1941, no more stops war than the death penalty stops murders. Man is basically predatory, and preparedness excites the base instincts that propel man to killing.

As war settled on us, Washington was filled with interesting and often strange travelers. One was Robert Watson-Watts, the Britisher who invented radar. He was a short, round-faced man who spoke quietly and intently. I met him first at Jim Forrestal's for dinner. He was virtually ecstatic now that the German bombers could be detected when they were miles from England.

Clare Boothe Luce, later to be ambassador to Italy, came home shortly after New Year's saying, "I simply had to have Christmas with the boys"—meaning of course the U.S. Army. Jim Forrestal was having a stag cocktail party at his home when she arrived. Up she came and went around the circle greeting each of us warmly. But when she came to her husband, Henry, she said, "What, are you here?" and quickly passed along.

In the spring of 1942, Harry Hopkins went to London with General George C. Marshall and his staff to persuade the British that a cross-Channel invasion should take place in July 1943. They had tough sledding but finally obtained agreement; and their return home set in motion vast planning. But in the summer of 1942 the British sent Lord Louis Mountbatten to Washington. For two weeks FDR's old friend tried to talk him out of the project. Then Churchill arrived and continued the campaign against a 1943 cross-Channel invasion, pleading for a 1944 date instead and urging that late in 1942 a North African movement be launched. Once the Germans were driven from Africa, then southern Italy should be invaded with victorious British-American armies pushing on to Belgrade and Warsaw. From the British point of view, the strategy made political sense, for the British people, long hammered by German air power, would get a respite as the battles were transferred to new sectors. Moreover, with both sides of the Mediterranean under Allied control, the life lines of the Empire would appear safe, and the alarms and discontents mounting in India and Australia on one end and South Africa on the other would be quieted.

The American Chiefs of Staff were utterly opposed and the arguments continued far into one June night. But FDR was our prime compromiser and Churchill won in part. He got the North African campaign and a deferment of the cross-Channel invasion, and later he persuaded FDR that we should take Sicily and go up the long boot of Italy. His plan for a Belgrade–Warsaw route was rejected, since both we and the Russians were opposed to it.

As the story of Churchill's successful invasion of the White House spread, I began to realize that, right or wrong, the British knew geopolitics much better than we. They thought in global terms—of marches and countermarches and the fate of the Empire. We had become isolationist by reason of our preoccupation in leveling our own continent, and when we did develop people who were global experts, their views were shocking to us because the world was much less orthodox than we had imagined. The British knew all this and, knowing, thought always in terms of how and when and where to use their military power. I saw Americans beginning to take the same stance:

"We must take up where the British leave off."

"But for the British Empire, where would the world be today?"

"If the British navy had not been sailing the seas, we would not have had the peace and quiet to develop our own civilization."

These were the dominant thoughts of the Americans of my vintage. They believed, even after the atomic bomb, that military might was the kingpin holding civilization together. They had not begun to think in terms of law as an alternate to war. The Churchillian attitude was contagious. There would be bloody wars, but that is the white man's burden and the white man would of course come out on top.

There never was a "credibility gap" when FDR was in the White House. Feeling as he did that we would be drawn into the European maelstrom, he undertook to educate the people. But he never played tricks on them, nor did he give them false figures or pretend one thing while doing another. He tried to get the people to see the needs and the dangers, but he never manufactured facts, nor used verbal razzle-dazzle to create false issues and to utter half-truths. He did, however, have a high regard for human rights and knew that they were in the crucible.

The route he traveled was indeed a delicate one, for there was still a hard core of isolationism in the country and he had to educate the people on the menace of Hitler. Many voices helped him in that cause, particularly those of Winston Churchill and of Edward R. Murrow and Raymond Swing, whose factual radio reporting out of a bombed and battered London helped condition the American mind to the world of reality. And so far as the written word was concerned, no one had deeper insight and understanding than Dorothy Thompson, one of the first to give us a picture of the anatomy of Nazism.

FDR had resolved that the world should be rid of unilateral military action. During the war he talked with me many times about Woodrow Wilson and his ill-fated League of Nations. He talked about Wilson's mistakes. FDR thought that if we were to have collective security, the plans for it must be laid in advance of victory. He desired to capitalize on the spirit of unity and cooperation, dominant in wartime between the Allies, to lay the foundation of a new world agency providing for collective security.

"We'll call it the United Nations," he said.

And so he arranged the Dumbarton Oaks Conference, where the delegations of the United States, the United Kingdom, the Soviet Union and China met during 1944, completing their conversations on October 7. Their proposals outlined the general structure of what later became the United Nations, and they received FDR's blessing on October 9, 1944:

> This time we have been determined first to defeat the enemy, assure that he shall never again be in a position to plunge the world into war, and then to so organize the peace-loving nations that they may through unity of desire, unity of will, and unity of strength be in a position to assure that no other would-be aggressor or conqueror shall even get started. That is why from the very beginning of the war, and parallel-ing our military plans, we have begun to lay the foundations for the general organization for the maintenance of peace and security.

Dean Acheson, as Undersecretary of State under Cordell Hull, lob-bied the Senate for approval of the UN Charter. But he said in 1970, "I never thought the United Nations was worth a damn. To a lot of people it was a Holy Grail, and those who set store by it had the misfortune to believe their own bunk." But whatever its limitations, it was a step toward a Rule of Law—man's only hope for escape from total annihila-tion.

As the war progressed, missions came and went, all secretly. Harry Hopkins became a courier between FDR and Churchill and he ex-ecuted his assignments faithfully. I saw FDR frequently at night. He maintained that I made the best dry martinis of anyone in town. He liked them dry—six to one—and very cold, with lemon peel. After dinner we would often see a movie, usually alone, sometimes with others. One night William Bullitt, who had been our first ambassador to the Soviet Union, was there holding forth on the need to set up democratic underground organizations in Eastern Europe, a proposal that FDR vetoed.

Another night FDR sketched the architectural design for the Bethesda Naval Hospital, and the structure, as built, largely followed that design. Another night FDR talked of his successor. He was thinking of the election in 1948, for he had, I think, no premonition of his early demise. I asked him what men had emerged in the war effort who were of presidential caliber. After a long silence he replied, "George Marshall is the best of all who have crossed the screen." He went on to extol Marshall's many virtues and to explain why he thought he had the stature to lead the nation in the postwar world and deal with the multi-ideological problems that were certain to arise.

William (Wild Bill) Donovan, for whom I had once worked on a bankruptcy investigation, was then head of the Office of Strategic Services under the Joint Chiefs of Staff and was recruiting men for it. He came to see me, inviting me to resign from the Court, go to a training school and serve in the Asian theater. I was then too heavily committed, emotionally and otherwise, to the Court to leave it.

Admiral William F. Halsey was in town from the Pacific making speeches that caused the audiences to howl when he called the Japanese "yellow-bellied bastards." Admiral Chester W. Nimitz was going silently and efficiently about his business, and General Carl (Tooey) Spaatz was thrilling the nation with his aeronautical wonders. General Dwight D. Eisenhower was home on personal business. Admiral William D. Leahy at the White House was a strong and steady influence. I knew them all except Eisenhower, and admired each one for his particular talents. It was a great team that FDR had assembled.

But even the great were bogged down in paperwork. Memoranda were produced in greater numbers than bullets. They flooded the departments. On one of my regular lunch dates with Forrestal, I said, "Why don't you write a two-page memo and put in between the two sheets a half-dozen pages of the same size containing excerpts from the *Odyssey* or *Iliad*?"

The next time I saw him, Forrestal was laughing when he told me that he had done it and "the whole thing came back initialed by everyone, including George Marshall."

As the months passed, the alphabetical agencies multiplied and people poured into the capital to work for the government. Office space was at a premium. One day at lunch, FDR was talking about it. I suggested that he move the Supreme Court to Denver, Colorado. I pointed out that Denver is not far from the geographical center of the United States—a point north of Rapid City, South Dakota, not far from the Wyoming line. With the Court in Denver he could put hundreds of tables in the hallways of the court building in Washington, creating a regular assembly line for memoranda and other paperwork.

He pretended to think the idea was excellent but added, "How can I keep my eye on you all if you are way out there?"

The war produced a great spate of litigation.

War in the constitutional sense is more than a state of hostilities. As I discuss elsewhere, in the sixties Johnson carefully avoided asking Congress to declare "war" against Vietnam. Yet editors and people generally talked loosely about the "war." Some said that those who dissented against our Vietnam policy were guilty of "treason."

When does dissent become treason? Article III, Sect. 3, of the Constitution defines "treason" as follows: "Treason against the United States, shall consist only in levying war against them, or in adhering to their enemies, giving them aid and comfort."

This comes into play when there is "war," and "war" comes into being by a "declaration" by Congress, as provided in Article I, Sect. 8. The difference between "war" and a state of hostilities is tremendous —as constitutional students know.

So it is a form of illiteracy to talk about "treason" and "war" in the constitutional sense, when speaking of those who voiced their dissent against our Vietnam policies.

But the objection goes even deeper. Proof of "treason" requires proof of "overt" acts. Jefferson, who fought bitterly to exclude "constructive treason" in the old English sense from our Constitution, would turn in his grave at the suggestion that speech could be an "overt" act.

Sedition, of course, is quite a different thing. Whether speech alone could ever qualify is a very moot question. It was so condemned in one case in which "war" had been declared and was in process.

It was condemned in another case in which there was a "conspiracy" to teach the noxious creed even though there was no "war" in existence. But there were qualifications originally stated by Mr. Justice Holmes in the "clear and present danger" test.

The terms "treason" and "war" as used in the Constitution are words of art. The truck drivers and field hands of the nation cannot be expected to understand subtle constitutional nuances. But news editors who mold public opinion have a special trust, a special responsibility not to misuse terms.

The war power is a pervasive one. As Hughes once wrote: "The power to wage war is the power to wage war successfully." People are regimented in ways that defy peacetime notions of liberty. Property is controlled and regulated in fashions severe by normal standards. Great restraints are permissible, for the very life of the country is at stake.

When Tomoyuki Yamashita, the Japanese general, was captured and an American military tribunal was named to try him for violating the law of war—letting his troops commit atrocities against the civilian population and prisoners of war—we held that no constitutional questions were presented (*In re Yamashita,* 327 U.S. 1). And when an Allied military court was set up by MacArthur in Japan to sit in judgment on alleged Japanese war criminals, our Court held we had no jurisdiction even to entertain a petition for a writ of habeas corpus on behalf of a prisoner held or tried by that tribunal, since it was multinational in character, not solely American. But I felt and still feel that the Court had jurisdiction over the American member of that tribunal, since he was bound by the American Constitution.

The Japanese cases are another illustration of the way in which a state of "war" affects civil rights. Those cases are little understood. They reached the Court in 1943 and 1944, but they arose in 1942 when no one knew where the Japanese army and navy were. Actually they were starting their invasion of Malaya and Burma. But our Pacific defenses were so slight at that time that, as I have mentioned, the Pentagon advised us on oral argument that the Japanese army could take everything west of the Rockies if they chose to land. Evacuation of the entire population would of course have been permissible by constitutional standards pertaining in time of war. Was it constitutional to evacuate only citizens of Japanese ancestry? That was an issue hotly contested both in the curfew case (*Hirabayashi* v. *United States,* 320 U.S. 81) and in the evacuation case (*Korematsu* v. *United States,* 323 U.S. 214).

The Pentagon's argument was that if the Japanese army landed in areas thickly populated by Americans of Japanese ancestry, the opportunity for sabotage and confusion would be great. By doffing their uniforms they would be indistinguishable from the other thousands of people of like color and stature. It was not much of an argument, but it swayed a majority of the Court, including myself. The severe bite of the military evacuation order was not in a requirement to move out but in the requirement to move out of the West Coast and move into concentration camps in the interior. Locking up the evacuees after they had been removed had no military justification. I wrote a concurring opinion, which I never published, agreeing to the evacuation but not to evacuation *via* the concentration camps. My Brethren, especially Black and Frankfurter, urged me strongly not to publish. "The issue of detention is not here," they said. "And the Court never decides a constitutional question not present." The latter was of course not true, as John Marshall's famous *Marbury* v. *Madison* (5 U.S. 137) shows. In that landmark case, Chief Justice Marshall established the concept of judicial review of congressional acts by declaring section 13 of the Judiciary Act of 1789 unconstitutional. He did so in spite of the fact that the question brought before the Court was not the constitutionality of the act, but whether or not Secretary of State Madison should be compelled to deliver the judicial appointment papers left over by his predecessor in office. Technically, however, the question of detention was not presented to us. Yet evacuation via detention camps was before us, and I have always regretted that I bowed to my elders and withdrew my opinion.

On the same day that we decided the evacuation case we held that there was no authority to detain a citizen, absent evidence of a crime (*Ex parte Endo,* 323 U.S. 283). Meanwhile, however, grave injustices had been committed. Fine American citizens had been robbed of their properties by racists—crimes that might not have happened if the Court had not followed the Pentagon so literally. The evacuation case, like the flag-salute case, was ever on my conscience. Murphy and Rutledge, dissenting, had been right.

The "war power" as a source for economic regulation appeared in many cases—seizure of coal mines, rent regulation, price control, rate regulation, rationing of supplies, and the like. Even the states were held subordinate to the war power as when they sought to make sales at prices in excess of those Congress had set (*Case* v. *Bowles,* 327 U.S. 92). And Congress—which has long been held not to have power to legislate for the "general welfare" in our federal system (*United States* v. *Butler,* 297 U.S. 1)—was conceded the right even to fix rents in areas where the war effort had resulted in housing deficits (*Woods* v. *Miller Co.,* 333 U.S. 138).

The cases were not myriad but they were numerous, and from them comes the story that the "war power" is a broad, pervasive, concurrent power which gives Congress authority to do things it would never dream of doing in days of peace.

FDR did have a lingering grudge against the Court as an institution. He never really got over the defeat of his Court-packing plan. He mentioned it again when I proposed that the Court move to Denver. This time he asked why lawyers were so conservative, why they turned out to be stodgy judges. He mentioned no names, but he obviously had been disappointed at some of his own judicial appointees. I told him that there was nothing in the Constitution requiring him to appoint a lawyer to the Supreme Court.

"What?" he exclaimed. "Are you serious?"

I answered that I was.

He lit a cigarette, leaned back and after a moment's silence said, "Let's find a good layman." He became expansive and enthusiastic and held forth at length, going over various names.

"You'll have to pick a member of the Senate," I said. "The Senate will never reject a layman as a nominee who is one of their own."

His face lit up and he said excitedly, "The next Justice will be Bob La Follette." There was no vacancy then, and none occurred before FDR died. But a plan had been laid to shake the pillars of tradition and make the Establishment squirm by putting an outstanding, liberal layman on the Court.

As the years passed, the unpopularity of Henry Wallace grew. Though he, as Vice President, was President of the Senate and presided over that body, he had few friends there. He was never a hail-fellow, nor much of a mixer. By and large, he stayed aloof and remote. While he had a popular following in the country, he had few political friends in Washington. That feeling about him became a powerful factor in rejecting him for renomination in 1944. Everyone close to FDR knew that the President was a sick man. Some of us close to him thought he had suffered a slight stroke, though Ross McIntyre, his physician, denied it. Many of us felt he would not live through another four years. So the sentiment grew that Wallace must go and a new running mate be selected.

There was a mounting sentiment for me as FDR's running mate in 1944. I did nothing to encourage the movement and indeed did not covet the job. I had many talks with my friend Senator Frank Maloney about it. He was going to the convention and wanted to make the nominating speech, but I gave him a letter of refusal to be read at the convention in case some of my exuberant friends put me in nomination.

Frank said with all of the emotion an Irishman can muster, "They simply won't take Wallace. And Truman? Who is he? My colleague of course. But he's nobody. If I put your name before the convention, there would be a stampede."

Once, as June 1944 came near, Ed Murrow and Eric Sevareid came to see me. They wanted "the word" from me. They were friends and would treat the news discreetly—my resignation to run for Vice President as soon as the Court adjourned. But I shook my head.

Some of my friends were indeed dead serious about making me FDR's running mate. Henry Hess, later U.S. Attorney in Oregon and a famous trial lawyer, had a nomination speech which I had difficulty avoiding. He was an old friend and I loved him like a brother, and I could not get through his head that politics was not my bent. George Killion of California, later president of the U.S. President Line, was another unquenchable character with only that one mission in life.

Cal Cook of California was a third. I had known him at Whitman College and he was in the outer ring of Governor Culbert L. Olson politics in California. He was at the time in the dry-cleaning business and flew north, tracked me down in Oregon, and walked the trails there, trying to convince me to take the plunge.

On the way West that summer I had stopped in San Francisco for a few days to see Max Radin, the professor of law at Berkeley who selected my law clerk for years. I greatly enjoyed Max's scintillating mind, and it was refreshing to be exposed to him after a stodgy winter in the capital. On this 1944 trip Max gave me a stag dinner at a famous restaurant noted for its pheasant. Phil Gibson, Chief Justice of the California Supreme Court, was there; George Killion, Earl Warren and Cal Cook were also present. We had a special dining room with no other people within shouting distance. I left early, at about ten o'clock, as I was rising at dawn driving north. I had checked my hat and coat in the lobby of the restaurant near the entrance. I presented the check, waited a moment for the two articles, left a tip in a saucer and turned to leave. At that instant a flashlight bulb went off. To my right was the photographer; to my left was a blonde I had never seen. Where the two had come from I do not know. But it obviously was a frame-up to give WOD some nasty publicity. Cal Cook, who had followed me out, jumped the photographer, knocked him down, seized his camera and actually crushed it with his feet. He then called a cab for me, muttering some obscenities about the San Francisco press.

There were others in Washington—Abe Fortas and other SEC allies —who were really a stout band of campaigners for me; and if politics had been my dish, I'd have had as backers men who would have walked the last mile. I was grateful; I was impressed by their sincerity; my old analyst Dr. Draper thought it would be the best thing possible for the country. But the truth is, I never had the Potomac Fever and could not be excited about catching it.

Later I tried to get a copy of the longhand note refusing the nomination which I had given Frank Maloney. He had died prematurely; his wife, Martha, shortly following. They left a son, Bobby, who had all of his father's papers in a trunk. But by the time I caught up with Bobby the trunk had been in a flood and all the papers destroyed.

Despite my supporters, my decision was made—to stay on the Court. I thought that if a member of the Court were going to get into the Convention struggle, he should resign from the Court, as Hughes had done in 1916.

After the Democratic National Convention in 1944, which was held in Chicago, I learned that FDR had preferred that I run with him. I did not know it at the time; he had never broached the matter to me. But Grace Tully, who was then his secretary, tells how he dictated the famous letter on his railroad car in the Chicago switchyards. He did not repudiate Henry Wallace, as he did not want to alienate that bloc of votes. But he did not prefer Wallace and knew that the pros would never accept Wallace. This was true, for FDR was failing and those on the inside knew that the Vice President would likely take over before 1948. The pros kept demanding that FDR give them a clue as to his wishes. Finally he dictated the letter to Grace Tully saying he would be happy to run "with either Bill Douglas or Harry Truman." She gave the letter to Bob Hannegan, who was chairman of the Democratic National Committee and was Truman's manager at the 1944 convention. Hannegan was so upset over the letter that he turned the names around before he released it to the convention. So the convention delegates believed that Truman was FDR's first choice. I was at my cabin in the Wallowa Mountains of Oregon, miles removed from telephones and roads, and knew nothing of those shenanigans. An FDR "draft" would have been difficult to resist. I am glad I never had to face up to it in 1944.

That fall I met Bob Hannegan at a cocktail party. Bob was jubilant over the way in which he had steered Truman through the convention, and he laughed when he said, "Bill, we really did you in."

I put my arm around him, for I greatly liked him, and said, "Bob, if I ever did run for anything, I'd want you as my manager." In spite of Hannegan's great effort on Truman's behalf, when Hannegan died a couple of years later, Truman didn't go to his funeral because Hannegan's questionable financial dealings had come to light in the meantime.

After the returns of the 1944 election were in and the year 1945 approached, FDR faded quickly. The look of death crept into his face. He was pallid and listless. In January 1945 I sent him a birthday present, a martini mixer. As I have mentioned, he liked his martinis dry and very cold, and the perennial problem that I, his bartender, had was to make sure they were not too "watery." This particular gift solved that problem, for the ice was in a separate chamber in the center of a bowl whose walls were an excellent transmitter of cold. Off it went and back came the message:

> Dear Bill:
> Ever so many thanks for that fine birthday gift. I haven't seen anything like it in a very long time, so it is particularly welcome. I look forward to "launching" it soon and you were good to think of me! With my warm regards,
>
> As ever,
> Franklin Roosevelt

This note was written March 22, 1945. I lunched with him a few days before he died. He had always dominated the table, tossing bits of conversation to each person. This day he tossed nothing to anyone. I kept up a chatter, and he would raise his head to nod concurrence. But then he would drop his head and stay utterly silent as he consumed his food like an automaton. All the Rooseveltian gaiety, humor, deviltry, laughter, teasing, taunting had gone. The man was alive but doomed. I could hardly see him for my tears when we shook hands and said goodbye. I knew I would probably never see him again, for he was leaving that day for Warm Springs, Georgia.

When he died he was with Lucy Mercer, whom I did not know. Apparently, he had fallen in love with her when she was Eleanor Roosevelt's social secretary. At that time FDR was Assistant Secretary of the Navy under Josephus Daniels. George Draper had told me the story years earlier and had related how there was a showdown between FDR and his wife over Lucy Mercer. According to Draper, Eleanor was ready to leave her husband unless the ties with Lucy were broken. FDR's friends advised him to break them—if he wanted a political future. In those days divorce was an ugly word, and a person tarnished by such an event was deemed ineligible for public office. By and by the public mood changed, but at the time FDR bowed to it and gave Eleanor the necessary reassurances. But as Joe Kennedy once remarked, "An association so old and so intimate as that one simply could not be completely broken."

April 12, 1945 . . . I was alone in the late afternoon driving my car west on Constitution Avenue. A friend pulled alongside, sounded his horn and pointed to his radio. I turned mine on and out of the ether came the stark news—FDR had just died. I parked the car and walked for hours, trying to adjust myself to the great void that his death had created.

On April 14 the Court was at Union Station to meet the funeral train coming north from Warm Springs, Georgia. We followed the funeral cortege. Soldiers marched; great horses pulled the casket majestically up Pennsylvania Avenue. The multitudes lined the street. All was silent except for the distant sound of muffled drums, the scuffing of the feet of the soldiers, the sound of the horses' hooves, the impact of steel-rimmed wheels on the pavement, and the quiet sobbing of the spectators.

People loved FDR. He was the one who had banished Fear. Now that he was gone, Fear had returned to their hearts—and the people wept without restraint.

The Court, including former Chief Justice Hughes, attended the service in the East Room of the White House, and on Sunday, the fifteenth, the Court went by train to Hyde Park. FDR was buried in his garden behind a ten-foot-high hemlock hedge that was one hundred and forty years old. The peonies were just coming out; the pansies were blooming in all their glory.

Here was the house where FDR's mother had planned to keep him tethered as a stamp collector after polio had paralyzed him. Here was the scene of his greatest personal victory.

There were the customary twenty-one salutes—and Fala, his constant companion, barked at each one. As I watched and listened, the words of a New Hampshire lawyer came back to me. I had spent the summer of 1932 in that state and felt the mounting heat of the campaign as September arrived. One day in Wolfeboro I asked a prominent lawyer how the national election was progressing. Shaking his finger, he said, "America will never put a cripple in the White House."

Then I remembered Draper saying, "Franklin, it's your head and your heart, not your legs, that are important. Your head and heart can put you in the Governor's mansion in Albany and in the White House. Franklin, people will remember you for what you are, for what you do —not for your legs."

People around the world knew this instinctively. FDR heralded the strength of the spirit of man over all his handicaps.

His life had become the symbol of a cooperative world regime founded on unity in diversity, mutual help and friendship—the symbol which we rather quickly dissipated by making the Cold War our new crusade. That is one theme of this book—to show why it was that my generation became politically bankrupt.

FDR gave the nation the kind of leadership I admired. We seemed to lose stature and greatness in his passing, becoming petty and greedy and small where we had known magnanimity, altruism and humanism.

On October 21, 1944, looking ahead to the end of World War II and a new world order, FDR said that it "must depend essentially on friendly human relations, on acquaintance, on tolerance, on unassailable sincerity and good will and good faith."

Truman was to take a different stance. In August 1945 he dropped our atomic bombs on Hiroshima and Nagasaki—civilian targets. By that act he introduced America to the world in a new image—a modern Genghis Khan bent on ruthless destruction.

During World War II Churchill told FDR, "You are concerned to what extent you can act without the approval of Congress. You do not worry about your Cabinet. On the other hand, I never worry about Parliament, but I have continuously to consult and have the support of my Cabinet."

There is not, in our system, any mechanism *within the executive department* to check the President from making important decisions. FDR chose his Cabinet to represent the complex forces that elected him. He had conservatives in the Cabinet—Cordell Hull and William Woodin. He drew from the liberal wing of the Republican Party, taking Henry Wallace and Harold Ickes. Frances Perkins and Harry Hopkins represented the New Deal. His Cabinets represented more of a cross section of the American people than any of the other Presidents under whom I served.

FDR did not rely on the members of his Cabinet as a "think tank." He often used them to send up "trial balloons" to test public reactions to an idea with which he toyed. At times he would have them send up a couple of trial balloons inconsistent with each other.

But his main concern was with Congress. Every President is leader of the nation, as well as of his party. FDR knew that he had to receive support from both parties in Congress to get most measures through. On domestic issues he worked with such liberal Republicans as Senators Robert La Follette, Charles McNary and George Norris. On international issues he worked with such Republicans as James Wadsworth in the House, and Warren Austin and Henry Cabot Lodge, Jr., in the Senate. As war neared he put Henry Stimson and Frank Knox, stout Republicans, in the Cabinet, thus strengthening his ties to Republicans on the Hill.

When Churchill asked FDR for fifty of our destroyers in 1940, FDR hesitated to act without approval of Congress. He hesitated to ask Congress, for it promised to be a bitter controversy. His friend Charles McNary, for example, said he could not support the proposal in the Senate, but hoped FDR would find legal grounds for acting without the approval of Congress. Many conservative lawyers had taken the position that FDR could make the transfer under existing acts of Congress. There included Dean Acheson, George Rublee, Thomas Thacher (Hoover's Solicitor General) and C. C. Burlingham, friend of Felix Frankfurter and a former president of the Bar of the City of New York. So FDR went ahead on his own—and survived. The only time I recall when he did not carefully scout Congress before taking controversial steps was when he announced his Court-packing plan in February 1937. But that can be attributed to his excessive flush of success in the 1936 election.

More than any of the other Presidents, FDR sought to inform and educate Congress, as well as to coax, cajole or threaten Congress. He knew that as a democratic leader, he could never be too far ahead of the people, nor too far behind. On the issue of war, he wanted a united country. He had many opportunities prior to December 7, 1941, to call for a declaration of war, but on those occasions he felt that a request for a declaration of war would divide the nation. And of the Presidents with whom I served, FDR was the most principled and had the greatest integrity in the political and constitutional sense, for never would he cross the bridge from peace to war by any connivance such as was used in Vietnam some twenty years later.

Harry S. Truman

I knew Truman socially and liked him. His Truman Committee of the Senate, investigating the war effort, was doing excellent work. He was a quiet, serious-minded man. He had common sense and courage and a salty nature, and in 1944 I thought he would be an excellent running mate for FDR.

I began to have doubts about Truman, however, as the years went by. In 1947 Truman asked me to take Harold Ickes' place as Secretary of the Interior. He invited me to lunch at the White House and we sat for an hour or more discussing the problems of Interior. He sketched the situation in very glowing terms. But having been active in the conservation field, I felt I knew more about Interior, its drawbacks, its heavy-handed bureaucracy, its tie-in with the Establishment, than he did. I also knew about the two great polluters among its agencies—the Bureau of Reclamation, which tainted our rivers with salt, and the Bureau of Mines, which allowed coal operators to fill our streams with sulfuric acid. I trusted Truman on most domestic issues, but not those of Interior, so, convinced that I would be cast to the dogs, I told him I would not be interested. I went on to say that there was one way to get me into the Cabinet if he was anxious to have me. He asked me what that was, and then I told him: Secretary of State.

At the time, Dean Acheson held that post. I had known Dean for some years. When I was reorganizing the New York Stock Exchange, he was representing it. When, in 1937, I launched my SEC investigation of the Richard Whitney scandal and put Gerhard Gesell in charge, we were opposed by Acheson. Though Acheson was an able lawyer, he talked with a "holier than thou" attitude, and that is why he was often dubbed the "Episcopal priest" in legal circles. He made a fortune representing the Establishment, and he served it well and honorably. The outstanding characteristic of the man's mind was its completely negative character. As Jerome Frank once said, "Dean thinks in terms of retreat. If we can't hold this line, we will withdraw to this other one, and so on."

That defensive attitude robbed him of creativeness. His philosophical tendencies aligned him with the Establishment, which, at home and abroad, represented the status quo. The status quo in the United States is tolerable for most people. Abroad it is largely intolerable for all except the few who own and rule the country. This negative attitude of Acheson characterized our foreign policy. We were engaged not in reform, not in revolution, not in promoting liberal governments, but in defending the status quo. Under Acheson and Truman, the nation set its foot on the dreary path that it was to follow for the next decades.

Thus, America was already becoming the most suspect and most hated country on this planet. I thought that the office of Secretary of State afforded a signal opportunity to change that tide of events. So I told Truman that although I had no desire to leave the Court, if he offered me that post, I would probably find it irresistible. My suggestion was met with stony silence.

The next year, 1948, I was deep in the Wallowa Mountains in Oregon when I got a message through the Forest Service that I was wanted on the telephone. I went to the nearest phone, which was rather ancient and rickety, the telephone line being strung through many miles of forests and suspended from trees. I could barely hear Truman's voice from Washington. I gathered he wanted me to be his running mate in the 1948 campaign, but it was impossible to conduct a conversation on that phone. Moreover, all along the line there were probably a dozen people listening in. So I asked him if I could call him back on Monday morning, this being Friday afternoon. He said that was agreeable, so I packed my bag and drove to Portland, putting up at the Benson Hotel, where I stayed in my room for two days in prayerful consideration of his offer.

I talked with friends in Portland and there were dozens and dozens of telephone calls from people, some of whom wanted me to do it, and some of whom thought it would be silly. I was tempted to accept because I thought perhaps as Vice President I could have a voice in foreign policy, an idea I later learned to be utterly foolish. In spite of the gloomy prediction of Truman's chances, I thought at the time he could and would win. But I finally decided against it because, on balance, I concluded that my place was on the Court.

As I have mentioned, Justices Frank Murphy and Wiley Rutledge were warm, close personal friends of mine. We did not always agree, but those two, plus Hugo Black and I, had a fairly broad consensus, especially in the field of civil rights, which loomed larger and larger as the postwar witch hunt gained momentum. The Cold War was settling on us and intolerance of the nonconformists was increasing. It seemed to me that only very special reasons would justify breaking up that foursome. For in those days we often commented that with one more like appointment there would be five and the Court would enter the Golden Age. The five were to appear, however, only some years later.

It was with this in mind that I called Truman from Portland on Monday morning and told him of my decision. He rather gloomily answered, "We'll try to get along."

The foursome I desired to protect did not last long. Frank Murphy died on July 19, 1949, and Wiley Rutledge died two months later, on September 22.

The movement to make me the Democratic nominee for President continued after 1948. I played no part in this, nor did I have any desire for the office. My decision had long been made to stay on the Court. But the emotional drive behind the movement was strong, as indicated by a letter I received from my old, old friend, Rabbi Stephen Wise, who died in 1949. This letter, dated November 8, 1948, reads as follows:

> Perhaps I should not trouble you about this trifle, but I am very proud about it. In Ridgefield, Connecticut, where my son, Jim, lives and where his son, bearing my name, voted, the latter wrote in your name instead of voting for any of the candidates. He had been a member of the Douglas Committee at Harvard. He is a war veteran, a Harvard graduate, and now he is in the School of Business Administration. I may not be here in 1952, so I want you to know how glad I am that a Stephen Wise will represent me—that a Stephen Wise, my own son's son, will represent me in taking you off the Supreme Court and putting you into the White House.

Truman was a man of lesser stature than FDR, but I did relish his company. He enjoyed most of all being with his staff at lunchtime, and he often asked me to join them. Table talk was never serious but always relaxed, with much storytelling. Truman, unlike FDR, always told stories—off-color stories and most of them barnyard stories.

Before he took office he told John Snyder, an old friend from Missouri, that if he ever should become President, he'd make John his Secretary of the Treasury. John protested, saying he was not qualified, but Truman said inexperience did not matter. "If you have a technical problem, get an expert to give you a memo."

"What if I don't agree with what he recommends?" asked John.

"Then hire another expert," said Truman.

When Truman took office in 1945, he held a staff meeting at eight o'clock every morning. Those present were John Snyder and Major Harry Vaughn, the President's military aide. Truman would open the meeting by asking, "What shall we do today?"

I was very fond of both Snyder and Vaughn, but if Truman had had the Secret Service pull any two men off Pennsylvania Avenue and send them in, Truman would have received better advice. What saved Truman was the fact that Clark Clifford was his naval aide. Clark got wind of those critical morning sessions and tactfully wormed himself into them. Clark, a most astute and competent man, soon had the early-morning meetings under control, resigned his Navy post and became Truman's right-hand man.

Truman had a nondescript Cabinet; one of the few men of stature who was there permanently was Dean Acheson. Another man of stature was James V. Forrestal, Secretary of Defense, whom Truman squeezed out to make room for a nice but basically third-rate man, Louis Johnson. Harold Ickes was inherited from FDR. He and Truman did not get along, I believe, because Ickes looked down on the President. So Truman squeezed him out, and as I have related, asked me to take Ickes' place. Since I declined, J. A. Krug was named to fill Ickes' shoes; and Interior continued under the control of large vested interests.

FDR had been his own Secretary of State; Truman was not. Dean Acheson pretty much called the signals on foreign affairs, though it was Truman who took the lead in recognizing Israel. (More accurately, Clark Clifford took the lead on that issue.) Truman would give me lectures on the problems of the world, taking me over to the big globe in the Oval Office and explaining the history and present plight of the area I planned to visit at any particular time. I always thanked him, but I always realized his abysmal ignorance of what actually went on in the world.

One alarm that Hugo Black and I felt was the manner in which Truman militarized the nation. Military men were everywhere; the White House thought largely in military terms when foreign affairs were up for discussion. The Truman Doctrine, announced in 1947, resulted in our sending a military mission to Greece to help that country against Communist guerrillas. I was in Greece at the time and saw what was happening and why that military mission served a real need. But the Truman Doctrine developed inexorably into a program of American military intervention, first in Korea, then in Vietnam and then the Dominican Republic. Truman had nothing to do with any but the Greek and Korean adventures, but he greatly conditioned the American mind to think in terms of military solutions to problems of Communism.

He did more than that, of course; he sponsored the famous Point IV program to give U.S. financial aid to increase agricultural production in benighted nations. It worked, but not in the way he intended. The program increased the decay in most nations for the simple reason that sharecroppers got no benefits, only the landlords. Sharecroppers were already paying up to 95 percent of their crop as rent. The beneficiaries were the rich people, many of whom lived luxuriously in the United States. As a result, I made many speeches stating that what we needed was Point V—in essence a loan or a grant of funds only to those countries with a land-reform program that would give their peasants at least a slice of the good life which we bestowed upon landlords.

Truman was not an idea man. He boasted in private to me what a good politician he was. And he was very able at the grass-roots level, as his brilliant and dogged campaign against Dewey proved. At every whistlestop he made a speech and at the end he asked, "Would you like to meet the missus?" A cheer would go up, and Harry called Bess to come out and take a bow. Bess was a lovely lady in every sense of the word. She was the one who kept Harry honest. She was modest and retiring, but one of the best First Ladies ever in the White House. Eleanor Roosevelt, Jackie Kennedy and Lady Bird Johnson outshone her in public events, but Bess was sterling to the core.

Harry Truman's instinct on domestic issues was populist and he had the common touch. But when he was abroad meeting with the great conspirators of the world I would shudder; and when he had James F. Byrnes at his side, I shuddered more and more. For Jimmy, like Harry, was a genius at precinct politics, but in terms of Spaceship Earth, they were both quite ignorant.

Dwight D. Eisenhower

I knew Ike casually; and I liked him as a human being. His smile and his simple frontier approach to complex problems made him as American as apple pie. Like Truman he was a good President (which in the Nixon years began to look like a tremendous achievement) but he was not a great one. Someone once said that Ike was "the average American raised to the nth power." That is approximately accurate.

Eisenhower's campaign slogan was "Let's clean up the mess in Washington," and it appeared as if the questions of bribery and corruption in government would be a primary target for his Administration.

Those who take public office are commonly surfeited with gifts. I received many cases of liquors in my first weeks on the Court and promptly returned them. Gifts from friends with no axes to grind are of course different. Presidents are surfeited with presents. Truman received many, many cases of whiskey. A Tennessee group—respecting the man—gave me a case of Jack Daniel's whiskey to give Truman. I promised to deliver it, which I did. But as I went out of the door with the bulky package under my arm, Pete Haynes of East Tennessee said to my friend John J. Hooker of Nashville, "It's like sending lettuce by a rabbit."

It is ironic that Ike's Republican Administration, under the inspiration of Richard Nixon, made a searching investigation of everyone of any importance in the prior Democratic Administration from Truman on down, looking for misfeasance in office. Clark Clifford was investigated for months. John Snyder, who had been Secretary of the Treasury, was investigated for three years. He was from St. Louis, and they summoned a grand jury in that city to go through the life history of John Snyder. The grand jury returned "no true bill." Not satisfied, they summoned a second grand jury and combed through all the records another time. The second grand jury, like the first, returned "no true bill." Still not satisfied, the Department of Justice went to Omaha and impaneled a third grand jury. Once more the grand jury returned "no true bill" and at long last John Snyder was relieved of the sword of Damocles.

The Nixon technique was "search and destroy," and every personage connected with Truman was probed for indictment by a grand jury. The only results were two puny "offenders"—Lamar Caudle of the Tax Division of Justice and Mat Connelly, Truman's appointment secretary. They were charged with a conspiracy to keep a man named Sachs from being criminally prosecuted for income-tax deficiencies. They were convicted and sentenced to two years each and fined, and on appeal their convictions were sustained. When the cases came to the Court in 1958, my review indicated that the evidence was so thin that we should grant certiorari. But the Court denied the petitions on March 31, 1958, I noting my dissent (356 U.S. 921). Caudle and Connelly went off to prison, and Nixon succeeded in "tarnishing" Truman a bit.

Eisenhower had denounced the ethics of Truman's Administration and had promised in 1952 that his would be as "clean as a hound's tooth." The first scandal of his own Administration broke around Sherman Adams, former governor of New Hampshire and a man I knew and respected. Adams had long known Bernard Goldfine, who owned a Boston hotel and on a dozen or so occasions during a six-year period had put the Adamses up there free of charge. Goldfine had also given the Adamses a rug, and Sherman Adams a vicuña coat and a suit made to order. Adams was Eisenhower's chief of staff at the White House and Goldfine was in trouble with the Federal Trade Commission over alleged mismarking of cloth. Goldfine got Adams to make one or more appointments with the FTC to see Goldfine about his complaints. Beyond that, he apparently did nothing, but doing that much from the command post in the White House meant exerting powerful leverage. So Adams had to leave. But his improper conduct was quite minor compared to what Eisenhower himself did. Lavish gifts were bestowed on Eisenhower—Sherman Adams' boss. Eisenhower's farm at Gettysburg received tens of thousands of dollars in the form of livestock and machinery and money. The press was discreetly silent as to the list of donors. I knew some. One indeed was on the boards of directors of some forty big corporations, each of which did a huge business with the government. What a potent alliance with the White House!

Eisenhower was certainly not a crook. He was only insensitive to the implications of these massive gifts to him from key men in the Establishment.

Eisenhower's Secretary of the Treasury from 1953 to 1957 was George M. Humphrey. He came to Washington from the M. A. Hanna Company, with which he had been associated as general counsel from 1917 to 1929, president from 1929 to 1952 and chairman of the board until late in 1952, when President-elect Eisenhower designated him Secretary of the Treasury. The price which he set for nickel served a dual purpose —to protect the Treasury and to protect Humphrey's interests. But the press, while eager to print any story about refrigerators or whiskey or mink coats which the Truman entourage may have received, was careful never to expose the subtle machinations of Humphrey which made millions for his empire. In those days the going philosophy was, "What's good for the country is good for General Motors and vice versa."

What follows is not the product of my own original research. It is from the Report to Congress by the Comptroller General of the United States, dated April 1961.

On January 16, 1953, five days before George Humphrey was sworn in as Secretary of the Treasury in the Eisenhower Administration, three nickel stockpiling contracts were signed by the federal government with the M. A. Hanna Company and two of its subsidiaries, the Hanna Mining Company and Hanna Nickel Smelting Company. Humphrey and his family were major M. A. Hanna shareholders and in Senate Finance Committee testimony on June 20, 1957, just before Humphrey's resignation, it was established that he had continued to hold his stock throughout his tenure at the Treasury. In his capacity as Secretary, Humphrey was a statutory member of the Defense Mobilization Advisory Board, which helped to make policy on stockpiling.

The Hanna nickel contracts were entered into pursuant to the Defense Production Act of 1950, legislation designed, among other things, to stimulate the increased production of strategic materials. Nickel was in increasingly scarce supply from the outbreak of the Korean "war," and the United States had no producers of any consequence. Hanna had obtained the mining rights on the only major U.S. deposit at Riddle, Oregon, during the 1940s, but lacked an economical extraction process. Hanna's principal mining activities were in iron ore and coal.

By early 1952 the nickel shortage had become so acute that the federal Office of Defense Mobilization adopted a nickel-industry expansion program, offering guaranteed loans, advances and purchase contracts as incentives. Shortly after announcement of the nickel program, Hanna informed the government of its leased property at Riddle, and subsequent negotiations culminated in the contracts signed January 16, 1953.

According to the April 26, 1961, General Accounting Office Audit

Report to Congress, these contracts were drawn on Hanna's terms and accepted by the government "despite indicated high costs and uncertainties caused by lack of adequate testing, which would ordinarily warrant the complete rejection of the proposal."*

Contract DMP-49 with the Hanna Mining Company (known as the Hanna Coal and Ore Corporation until 1958) provided that the company would develop its leased nickel-bearing deposit at Riddle, Oregon, to mine the ore and to sell it to the government at fixed prices. The contract provided a basic fixed price of $6 a ton, including profit, and subject to escalation in case of increased base costs. The "examination of records" clause of the mining contract was so drawn as not to permit the government to have access to Hanna Mining's financial statements and cost records pertaining to operations under the contract.

The new company was to construct a smelting facility at Riddle, purchase the ore from the government at the same price the government paid Hanna Mining for it and process the ore into ferronickel for sale to the government.

The agreement was for the government to purchase the ferronickel at a price that included the cost of smelting and the cost of the ore, but did not include any profit to the smelting company. This arrangement was made at the Hanna group's insistence, for income-tax purposes, since all profits were included in the sales price of the ore paid to Hanna Mining, and the unusual separate contract feature made available a greater depletion allowance than would have been obtained if the mining company had sold the ore directly to the smelting company.

Contract DMP-51 provided for the M. A. Hanna Company, as agent for the government, to sell the government's ferronickel to industrial users and receive a sales commission one fourth of 1 cent per pound. In the event that ferronickel could not be sold to industrial users, the government was obligated to purchase for stockpile all ferronickel produced under the terms of the contract.

Development of the Riddle mining facilities was begun in March 1953, and substantially completed by the end of 1955. Actual costs totaled $3.5 million, including $441,000 for Hanna's exploration and research from the time of leasing the nickel property in the 1940s. The completed smelting plant cost approximately $22.8 million, including interest during the construction and break-in period.

*Page 9 of the above-mentioned report.

The price paid by the government to the smelting company was not based on the market price of nickel, but on production costs, including the cost of ore. Likewise, the government's resale prices for ferronickel to industry were based not on the market price of nickel, but on the prices paid by the government for ferronickel, well above its market price. From 1955 until the latter part of 1957, because of the shortage of nickel, most of the smelting company's output moved to industrial users at the premium prices. Expanding supplies and a slowdown in the economy then dried up the ferronickel market, and the government was obliged to stockpile the smelting-company output, which was then approaching peak capacity of more than 20 million pounds per year.

On April 1, 1961, just before the publication of a General Accounting Office Audit of the nickel-stockpiling contracts, Hanna exercised its right to take title to the smelting plant from the government on payment of the salvage value of $1,721,563. At the same time the contract for delivery of the remaining 20 million pounds of nickel was renegotiated at a price of 58.77 cents per pound of contained nickel, with delivery to be completed by June 30, 1965. The new price was based on the operating costs of the smelting plant, including, as before, the cost of the ore.

Three weeks later, on April 26, 1961, the U.S. Comptroller General transmitted the General Accounting Office's Audit to the House of Representatives and the Senate, concluding that "these contracts presented Hanna the opportunity to (1) utilize nickel deposits which it has controlled since 1943, and on which it had spent over $440,000 prior to the government's nickel expansion program, (2) recover these prior costs through contract operations, (3) develop and prove a process for the production of ferronickel at no cost to itself, (4) acquire facilities established solely for the production of ferronickel under the contract at a nominal cost to itself, (5) develop a commercial market for its product and (6) become the only significant producer of nickel in the United States using domestic ore deposits."*

By this time the Korean crisis had passed and there was no longer a shortage of nickel and other strategic materials. The government was considering ways and means to dispose of its stockpiles while still adding to them under contracts dating back to the early 1950s. Corporations holding government stockpiling contracts became restive to get out of

*Page 4 of Audit Report.

them when market prices of the contract materials exceeded government prices, but eager to comply with them when market prices fell below government prices.

Thus, early in 1962, Hanna was holding discussions with the government with a view to terminating its supply contract and also being designated as government selling agent for at least part of the government's nickel stockpile. Also in 1962, the U.S. Senate authorized a special investigation of stockpiling, and the Senate Armed Services Committee referred it to a newly impaneled Subcommittee on the National Stockpile. The investigation of the Hanna nickel contracts became explosive when George M. Humphrey, whom the subcommittee had not anticipated calling, insisted on appearing as a witness. From his testimony it became clear that he personally had made the final decisions on the contracts, and had insisted that they be signed just before he became Secretary of the Treasury. The subsequent subcommittee report concluded that Hanna's profits on the combined mining-smelting contracts were in the vicinity of $86 million from 1953 to 1963, with the government doing the financing and assuming all of the risks. The report pointed out that Humphrey had returned to the M. A. Hanna Company as honorary board chairman, upon leaving the Treasury in 1957, and his son Gilbert W. Humphrey was chairman of the board.

Publication of the subcommittee report, including verbatim portions of the Humphrey testimony, led to Senate suggestions of perjury. While the Justice Department ultimately decided not to pursue the perjury aspect, it did file a civil suit against Hanna, which was obliged to repay a total of $560,633 in principal and interest, over and above an earlier repayment of $63,525.

Taking a key part in all negotiations with the government, the drafting of the nickel contracts, subsequent amendments to them and their final cancellation was the long-time Hanna-Humphrey law firm, Jones, Day, Cockley and Reavis. After the contracts had been signed and Humphrey had taken office as Secretary of the Treasury, he soon installed Jones, Day partner H. Chapman Rose as Assistant Secretary, and later elevated him to Undersecretary. Rose returned to his private practice not long before Humphrey's resignation. Rose's brother and law partner Nelson became chief counsel to the Internal Revenue Service. Humphrey's son, Gilbert, practiced law with Jones, Day for two years before beginning his business career with the M. A. Hanna Company in 1948. The Roses have remained prominent in Republican politics, and Chapman's son Jonathan Rose was listed as special assistant to the President in 1972.

Starting with Eisenhower and continuing through Johnson and Nixon, feelers went out from big companies for "experienced" men in government who would like to be earning one million dollars a year in a couple of years. The men wanted were those who knew the "ropes," who had "influence," and could make the corporate path easy in Washington, D.C. This was one of the most insidious, corruptive influences which I witnessed during my forty-odd years on the Washington scene.

Another Eisenhower Administration incident involved the so-called Dixon-Yates controversy, which came to the Court in 1960 (*United States* v. *Mississippi Valley Generating Co.,* 364 U.S. 520). The case involved an old conflict-of-interest act which dates back to 1863. Until its recodification, the act (18 U.S.C. 434), provided that anyone who acted, directly or indirectly, as an officer or agent of a business could not at the same time conduct transactions with that business as an officer or agent of the United States government.

The Mississippi Valley Generating Co. had a contract to build a power plant for the Atomic Energy Commission. The contract was terminated because in its negotiations the government had been represented by a "dollar-a-year" man who was working for the Bureau of the Budget and, at the same time, was an active officer of an investment banking company. He had worked arduously on the project, furnishing cost estimates from his investment company and only stopped acting for the government (but without resigning) shortly before his company was retained by the sponsors as financial agent.

The case was a cause célèbre in Washington, for, by the sixties, government—due to the naïveté of Eisenhower—had become the happy hunting ground for the financial elite. Petty gifts for the Connellys and Caudles under Truman were as nothing compared to the huge trophies which merchants of finance sought when Eisenhower admitted them to the forbidden preserves of the federal government. In holding that the contract in the Dixon-Yates controversy was unenforceable, we said through Chief Justice Warren:

> As we have indicated, the primary purpose of the statute is to protect the public from the corrupting influences that might

be brought to bear upon government agents who are financially interested in the business transactions which they are conducting on behalf of the Government. This protection can be fully accorded only if contracts which are tainted by a conflict of interest on the part of a government agent may be disaffirmed by the Government. If the Government's sole remedy in a case such as that now before us is merely a criminal prosecution against its agent, as the respondent suggests, then the public will be forced to bear the burden of complying with the very sort of contract which the statute sought to prevent. Were we to decree the enforcement of such a contract, we would be affirmatively sanctioning the type of infected bargain which the statute outlaws and we would be depriving the public of the protection which Congress has conferred.

(364 U.S. 520 at 563)

Eisenhower was a great father figure. How good a general he was, I do not know. I knew Walter Bedell Smith, Eisenhower's overseas executive officer in World War II. My impression was that Eisenhower was "great" in the military sense, largely because of Bedell Smith and secondarily because he had the knack of getting opposed people working together in unison. My impressions may not have been reliable, because I was not close enough to the military situation to have an independent judgment.

I personally liked Eisenhower very much. He and I were often patients at Walter Reed Hospital at the same time. He, of course, had the palatial suite in Ward 8 and I was in an ordinary room down the hall. Dr. Elson, the Presbyterian minister, came daily to pray with and for Ike. He'd go right by my door and once I whistled at him. He stopped and chatted but never prayed for or with me. He seemed to me to be obsessed with a duty to succeed and save Ike. But Ike and I would meet occasionally and engage in pleasant talk.

Walter Reed built a balcony on Ward 8 where Ike could get a bit of fresh air. One Fourth of July I was a patient, though ambulatory. It was during Ike's final illness and he was bedridden. I ordered fireworks, which by D.C. law could only be "sparklers." I was joined by Mamie Eisenhower, and the two of us, plus an aide and a nurse or two, celebrated that evening on Ike's balcony.

I never thought Ike was the important figure General George C. Marshall was. Marshall was a man of great dimension—calm, methodical, wise. I saw him only on social occasions but quite frequently we would end up in a corner, talking about FDR, the war and international problems. One evening he said in confidence that he had been walking down Constitution Avenue at night and was astounded to see Ike coming toward him. Eisenhower was then stationed in England, the war was on, and Ike was AWOL. Marshall demanded to know why Ike was in Washington. Ike told him he had come back to arrange a divorce so he could marry his aide, Kay Summersby.

Marshall, in relating the episode to me, became even more angry. He had been responsible for Eisenhower's selection as head of our European forces and was stern with him. "I told Ike to get back to London that very night or I'd bust him."

In later years Harold Ickes came to me excitedly saying he had met Ike when Ike was president of Columbia and he was convinced that Ike wanted "fewer" wars than any other man, that he was against "war," that he was at heart a real Democrat. I told Harold Ickes that he was a romanticist, but Harold was sure Ike could be induced to head the Democratic ticket in 1952, and he kept plugging for him until Ike proclaimed his Republican faith.

Walter Lippmann summed up Eisenhower's popularity very aptly to me as 1960 approached: "But for the Twenty-second Amendment [restricting the President to two terms] Ike could be re-elected even if dead. All you need do would be to prop him up in the rear seat of an open car and parade down Broadway."

Dwight Eisenhower was indeed the father figure that Americans seem to cherish in their President. And the father figure is only a shade removed from the image of king which has plagued mankind throughout history. It seems to be the nature of people to believe in the false security which the father image instills.

John F. Kennedy and His Family

I have related in *Go East, Young Man* how Joseph Kennedy brought me to Washington to work for the Securities and Exchange Commission. That was in 1934, when Joe had a home in Maryland, a rather spacious place accommodating a large family. I knew all the boys—except for

Joe, Jr., who was the eldest—and their sisters. At the start these acquaintances were casual; Jack Kennedy was seventeen years old, Bobby
nine, and Teddy just an infant when I came to Washington.

Joe had a permanent residence at Hyannis and also a winter home in
Palm Beach. I visited them both frequently. He was a very generous
man and would usually call or write me and say that he had left an
airplane ticket for me at such-and-such a counter and I should pick it
up and come down and see him. On these visits, as the years passed, I
came to know his daughters Kathleen, Eunice, Pat and Jean quite well.
I was perhaps closer to Kathleen than to anyone else. Eunice liked me.
Pat was, I think, afraid she was stuck with me, and Bobby wanted me
to marry Jean. But though I admired them all, I never dated any of
them. It would have surprised Joe to know that his friend who took a
freight train across the country to law school could never marry a rich
woman. The barrier was too great for me to surmount; and I never
allowed it to be tested by becoming intimate with any of these wonderful Kennedy women.

Rose Kennedy, a very devout Catholic, was shocked when Kathleen
married a divorced man, a Britisher. Some months later I was at their
Palm Beach home when the news came that Kathleen and her husband
had been killed in an airplane accident over France. Rose, of course,
was greatly depressed but summed up her feelings by saying that she
was convinced that "the Lord had ordered it that way in view of Kathleen's sin."

When Jack went to Choate, he was a most attractive chap but rather
scatterbrained. When he finished Harvard, he had all the earmarks of
a playboy. I was with him at Palm Beach when he decided he would
run for Congress and I sat in on the Kennedy family discussions concerning the strategy. Rose and her daughters decided to put on teas in
every parish in Massachusetts, and they did. Jack, the only male present
at these affairs, carried off each event with grace and charm, and word
of his popularity spread. Then, when he reached the House, he really
did nothing of any importance.

I was again with him at Palm Beach when he decided to run for the
Senate. He asked me what I thought and I told him I was for anything
he wanted to do, but the first thing I thought he had to do was to
establish some solid record of achievement in the House. Despite my
advice, Jack went into the campaign and won handily. As a senator he
was as nondescript as he had been as a congressman.

Jack was indeed a playboy in public office up to 1958. In 1958 he and Joe and I had had many conversations on the question of whether Jack should run for President in 1960. To do so meant a complete change of character and a complete redesigning of his public image. Joe was a great manipulator, and had already decided that Jack should be President.

The discussion went back and forth—Jack was hesitant and then convinced, and then not sure, and so on. One day Joe came across the Hill from the Senate Office Building to my chambers and said, "Bill, the great decision has finally been made. Jack is going to go for the presidency. You can bet your ass on that." I asked if he was certain. He repeated, "You can bet your ass on it." I saw Jack a few days later to talk to him about the matter. There was already a change in him. He had become serious about a lot of things. He was shaken up. He was assuming a public pose and posture he had not assumed before.

Joe told me he was going to provide Jack with a private Convair and pilot and crew so he could go any time, night or day, anywhere. And that is the way he worked it out.

There was amazement in the Kennedy family when Jack took the West Virginia primaries away from Hubert Humphrey. But the campaign had been thorough in every detail. For example, on the day of the election Joe rented every automobile in every rental agency in West Virginia. He had people picked up at every house and driven to the polls and then taken home. And if they voted right, Joe saw to it they got a bottle of whiskey. Jack won handsomely, and I was surprised and delighted at the transformation in him.

At the convention in Los Angeles, Lyndon Johnson became more and more confident that all he had to do was wait in the wings to be summoned. So the quick nomination of Jack Kennedy was a terrible blow to him.

I saw much of Jack while he was President, but I never asked him for favors, nor did he give me any assignments. He talked with me about a vacancy on the Court. As I have related, I suggested Skelly Wright of Louisiana, but Jack decided otherwise.

I talked to Jack frequently about conditions in Iran and the corruption that was rampant. Then, when he entertained the Shah at the White House when he was here on an official visit, Jack concluded that the Shah was corrupt and not a person we could trust. Nasser Khan of the Ghashghais, a Persian tribe, had met Robert F. Kennedy, then

Attorney General, and as a result of that contact and my conversations with Jack, the Kennedys became interested in the problems of Iran. The idea was to withdraw American support from the Shah, causing his abdication, and to put his son on the throne and establish a regency around him. (That regency, in fact, had already been selected.) Whether Jack Kennedy would have gone through with the proposal, I do not know, but it was under active consideration at the time of his death.

I talked with Jack frequently about the growing crisis in Vietnam. I had introduced Ngo Dinh Diem to Jack, and my continuing visits to Vietnam had given me an emotional and intellectual investment in its problems. I saw that Jack was becoming more and more military-minded in his approach to Vietnam's problems; and I detected a growing doubt or suspicion about Ngo Dinh Diem. I almost asked Jack on one visit to send me to Saigon to make a report. But being on the Court, I never actually broached the matter. I perhaps had little distinction in foreign affairs. But I was distinct in one respect—I never traveled abroad at Uncle Sam's expense. I almost went to Saigon on my own to talk with Ngo Dinh Diem. But to my regret I did not do so, and we killed him.

Jack Kennedy, like Truman and FDR, was more dependent on an inner circle of advisers than on his Cabinet. Since he wanted to be his own Secretary of State, he chose Dean Rusk, and with a flair for the academic, surrounded himself with elitist scholars.

When LBJ was Vice President, he thought Jack was making too public his fondness for military might. True, Jack enjoyed the maneuvers of the Atlantic Fleet, for ships and water were part of his heritage, but I never dreamed he would lead us into the Vietnam "war." He did send a great military mission there, but the expeditionary force came later, under LBJ.

Jack was responsible, at least by default, for Diem's assassination. The man in the American embassy in Saigon who gave the signal was Henry Cabot Lodge (whom Jack had defeated for the U.S. Senate). Diem was not sufficiently servile to Pentagon demands; he was committed to rejection of any foreign expeditionary force. So he had to go. Jack's acquiescence was a tragic dereliction. Diem was the one barrier protecting America against the designs of the Pentagon. In reflecting on Jack's relation to the generals, I slowly realized that the military were so strong in our society that probably no President could stand against them.

The same month Diem died, Jack died, both assassinated. November 1963 was a dark month for me. The news of Jack's death came by a note to Earl Warren while we were in Conference. The old Chief read the message to us and then broke down and wept, tears running down his cheeks.

The Kennedys were to suffer great tragedies. Joe, Jr., was killed in World War II. Kathleen died in an airplane crash in Europe. Joe Kennedy, my mentor, suffered a severe stroke that left him a cripple and speechless. John F. was assassinated while President. Bobby was killed in June 1968 while campaigning for the Democratic nomination for President.

Though I knew Bobby Kennedy when he was a small boy, I lost track of him when he went to prep school and to Harvard, seeing him only occasionally on visits to his father's home either at Hyannisport or West Palm Beach. Those contacts mostly related to his football endeavors. He was a man of small stature, very vigorous, very aggressive, and more like his father than either Jack or Teddy, who more resembled their mother.

Bobby, being small in stature, was always overcompensating—a rather natural consequence of being the smallest of the four brothers —at least two of whom were quite tall and rugged.

I came to know Bobby intimately later, when he attended law school at the University of Virginia and induced me to come down and give a talk or two to student groups. Once he had entered the stream of the law, he kept rather close contact with me.

He threw himself with great vigor and intensity into the 1960 campaign on behalf of his brother. And when victory came, he had an important decision to make. I remember the lunch that he and I had at the Supreme Court, when he was debating whether or not to join the Cabinet as Attorney General. I told him I thought he would make a fine Attorney General, but that at some juncture in his life he should start a course that was wholly independent of Jack. While he had made an enduring contribution to Jack and Jack's future, my thought was that it was now time to think of himself. We reviewed at length various possibilities open to him. He did not want to practice law. Business had no appeal to him. He had no desire to teach law. He thought he might perhaps be happy heading up some foundation, but about that he was not sure. So by the time he left my office, he had made up his mind to be Attorney General.

In the months that followed, I saw him often at the Department of Justice. He was, in fact, a shirt-sleeve Attorney General, passionate and determined to carry through on things on which he felt a deep conviction. One of those that soon came to the surface related to the Iranian students.

That requires a word of explanation:

In 1955, when I had finally got a visa to visit the Soviet Union, Joe Kennedy telephoned me and asked if I would take Bobby to Russia with me. He said, "I think Bobby ought to see how the other half lives."

I told Joe that I would be happy to take his son. Joe was a crusty reactionary and a difficult man, but he was very fond of me and he cared a great deal about his boys. He had big plans for Bobby and probably thought that the Russian trip would be important in his education. Our plans were to go first to Iran and catch a boat on the Caspian Sea that would take us to the Russian port of Baku. So Bobby and I set up a rendezvous in Teheran. That was an old stomping ground for me, and I introduced Bobby to that country.

In a few days we took a cab and made the long drive from Teheran across the Elburz Mountains to the port of Pahlevi, where the Russian boat, which carried both freight and passengers, awaited us. This journey in Russia and Siberia took about seven weeks and at almost every stop and at every introduction, Bobby would insist on debating with some Russian the merits of Communism. The discussions were long, sometimes heated, but as I told Bobby, they were utterly fruitless because he could no more convince them than they could convince him. He had, however, a crusading attitude toward Russia at that time.

Everywhere he went, he carried ostentatiously a copy of the Bible in his left hand. And he spent his time on the planes not going over Russian agricultural or industrial statistics, but reading the Bible. The strain on him was considerable, so when we had reached our farthest point east, Novosibirsk, and started back, he became very, very sick. I felt his forehead and was sure that his temperature must be at least 105 degrees. We got off the plane at Omsk and went immediately to a room which our interpreter had reserved for us at the airport. I told Bobby I was going to call a doctor. He said he would have nothing to do with one because Russian doctors were Communists and he hated Communists. I told Bobby I had promised both his father and his wife, Ethel, that I would bring him back in a safe and sound condition and that whether he liked it or not, I was getting a doctor.

I put Bobby to bed and then, unknown to him, I sent for a doctor. After a while a thirty-year-old lady, dressed in white, arrived and I ushered her into Bobby's room. He was by then delirious and quite unaware of what was going on.

The Russian doctor sat by his bed for at least half an hour, merely watching him. When she came out to see me, her first words were, "Our patient is very disturbed." How right she was; for nearly two months he had been on a veritable crusade that was charged with great emotion.

The doctor said she needed antibiotics and would shortly return with them. But I brought out my medical kit, where she found what she needed and proceeded to give Bobby massive doses of penicillin and streptomycin.

I canceled all engagements and travel plans and stayed in Omsk for four days. What impressed me was the Russian doctor. That dear lady never left Bobby's room for thirty-six hours. When she emerged, her eyes were bright and she said, "Now he'll be all right."

She would accept no fee for her services, no gratuity; and she left as graciously as she had appeared. Bobby was confined to his room and to a strict diet for another two days, and he was still wobbly when he climbed aboard the plane for Moscow.

So my first impression of Siberia was one that inspired warmth and gratitude. A competent, faithful doctor had saved Bobby's life. It was an act of kindness that conditioned my future attitudes toward a land that by tradition was ominous and forbidding.

As a result of this rather extensive and arduous Russian journey, I began to see a transformation in Bobby. That is why I said in later years that I thought he had a real capacity for growth. He seemed to understand the plight of the miserable sharecroppers in Iran. And in spite of his violent religious drive against Communism, he began to see, I think, the basic, important forces in Russia—the people, their daily aspirations, their humanistic traits, and their desire to live at peace with the world.

This appeared in various forms as his political life flowered. The first example was when he was Attorney General. He called me to tell me that the Shah of Iran had insisted that the United States send back to Iran thirty Iranian students in and around the Washington area who were Communists. The Iranian ambassador dutifully took the message to Secretary of State Dean Rusk, who called Bobby and directed him to pick them up and have them deported. Bobby asked me what I thought he should do. I told him that I doubted that there was one Communist in the whole carload of Iranian students in this country, and that before he did anything he should have each of the thirty individuals checked by the FBI. The game of the Shah was obvious—to try to still the mounting opposition against him at home and control Iranians abroad by executing dissenters. A month later I got a rather jubilant call from Bobby, saying he had received the FBI report and that none of the thirty was a Communist. Therefore he told Rusk to go jump in the lake. That episode marked the beginning of his great interest in overseas activities and events.

In one of our conversations we got around to the idea that perhaps the next move he should make in his brother's Administration was to become Secretary of State in place of Rusk. He said he thought this might be difficult to arrange, but I said I would be happy to talk to Jack about it. Bobby seemed pleased, and I did talk to Jack. Although he made no promise, he not only indicated a great interest but considered it something quite feasible, come 1964.

When Bobby grew up, the Kennedy household was always filled with VIPs, from politicians to priests to actors and musicians from the stage and screen. It was Joe's idea to expose his young brood to men and women of accomplishment, hoping, I think, that their elements of greatness would be seen and studied by the children.

When Bobby acquired his own family, he continued that practice. He became, for example, a friend of John Glenn, our first astronaut, and Glenn was a frequent house visitor. General Maxwell Taylor also was worked into the household group.

James Whittaker, who had climbed Mount Everest, became a family companion. Bobby wanted me to teach his son David how to fly-fish. So I helped arrange a camping trip up the Elwah River on the Olympic Peninsula in my home state of Washington. Since this river is within the Olympic National Park, park officials came along. Bobby and I hiked the twelve miles from road's end, and the others went on horseback. A rather elaborate camp with tents, cots and portable toilets had been set up for the Kennedys, and a hostile Seattle press made much of that fact.

The Elwah is a cold, clear stream, ideal for trout, and I did my best with David, who was an instinctively excellent fisherman. I taught Dave how to float a dry fly and how to stimulate a nymph with a wet fly. I taught him to study the water for bug hatches and try to match the hatch with a fly of his own. I even tried to teach him the roll-cast, which the fisherman casts forward without bringing the line over his shoulder. As I performed my role of instructor, I began to wonder if this is the best way to bring up children. A boy raised in that environment has few chances for discovery on his own. To be taught how to do everything has, of course, its advantages, but on the other hand, when a boy secretly discovers a technique on his own either by observing an expert or by trial and error, he has been through a permanent and abiding experience. Or so it seemed to me. Yet Bobby's own life was probably greatly enriched by the way his father, Joe, and his mother, Rose, managed the family life. One result was that he was never overawed by greatness and was always at ease whether his companions were dukes or peasants.

Ted Kennedy, in a letter to Bobby's children after Bobby's death, said this about him:

> Most of all I shall remember our walks through the park from the Senate floor to the Senate office building in every kind of weather. He would suggest that I speak at an early morning assembly at a local high school here in Washington, urging the students to stay in school and continue their studies. He would remind me to give whole-hearted support to a fund-raiser to be held in Boston for Cesar Chavez' farmworkers. He would tell me of a recent trip to the Mississippi Delta, describing the extraordinary conditions of hunger, malnutrition and poverty he saw, and he would talk about the forgotten Indians in our country, and the injustices and indignities they suffered. These moments of conversation as much as any speech he made revealed his deep feeling and passionate concern for the forgotten American.

Rose had more sustaining power than anyone I have known. Her trust in God carried her through all the tragedies. She walked indeed as one of the noblest women of my generation; and her spirit carried over to Jackie, widow of Jack, and to Ethel, widow of Bobby.

On April 17, 1964, I had been on the Court for twenty-five years; and as the Court opened on April 20 the Attorney General, to my surprise, addressed the Court. He spoke without notes and with a feeling that touched me deeply. What Bobby Kennedy said was in part as follows:

> I would also like to add a brief personal note. I think it was my father who was responsible for bringing Justice Douglas to Washington a number of years ago, when I was about six years old [actually he was nine]. He came on the Court when I was thirteen, and I remember that bright day even now. He has been a great friend of our family for many years.
>
> I also remember vividly my trips with him around the world —not merely because of what I gained personally, but primarily because I witnessed the way in which he presented a picture of the United States to the people of other countries. He was a man who was able to tell them, in ways they understood, of our views and beliefs. He could speak with wisdom of our laws and explain our system of government. He could talk to them also, in everyday terms, of many other matters in which they were deeply interested—how much cotton was produced per acre in South Carolina or how much wheat in Nebraska. The many who have seen him in his travels, read his books, and heard his friendly words have been moved and inspired.
>
> He has been a great credit not only to this Court, but as a citizen of the United States and of the world.

On June 6, 1968, I was only one day out of open-heart surgery and was very weak. My radio under my pillow interrupted the musical program to announce that Bobby had been assassinated in California. The news was as shocking to me as the trauma of the surgery had been. I was so incapacitated that I could not even call Ethel. In a few days I managed to scribble a note of sympathy to Ethel and the children. But I could only follow by radio the news of the funeral and the awful aftermath of the new tragedy. Bobby, I thought, was on his way to becoming President; and if he had lived, he would have healed the nation's wounds and assuaged the dissensions rather than tear the nation apart as Nixon did.

When the threat of my impeachment was being made in 1969, Senator Strom Thurmond attacked me on the floor of the Senate, demanding that I resign.* The day was June 9; and Ted Kennedy, whom at that time I knew only casually and with whom I had never discussed the matter of Thurmond's complaint, rose to his feet to defend me. Thurmond's charge was that I had been connected with a Dominican committee when I was helping the Parvin Foundation run a literacy program in the Dominican Republic. I was connected with the group but it was not Communist; rather, it was trying to bring the non-Communist left into Latin American affairs. It failed because it turned out to be CIA-infiltrated; and the CIA affiliation was the kiss of death.

The story is relevant here only as a token of the Kennedy loyalty to a friend under public attack. Ted did only what Joe or Jack or Bobby would have done. The Kennedys were intensely loyal people. That was the Irish in them—the courage and fierce devotion that would bring them to their feet in defense of a friend.

Later I thanked Teddy for his spontaneous response to Strom Thurmond's attack. By then he knew that my response to an attack on him would be instantaneous. And he, like his father and his brothers, knew that a Justice, like a priest, may be fiery and courageous, and yet ethical.

Lyndon B. Johnson†

I was destined to serve under several Presidents and as the scroll of history unwound, it seemed clear to me that if the press remained free and the First Amendment flourished, no President could permanently harm this nation. Yet when I came to Lyndon Johnson, and then to Richard Nixon, I had more serious misgivings than ever before.

Lyndon B. Johnson and I arrived in Washington, D.C., at about the same time—1934 or 1935. He was head of the National Youth Administration in Texas, I was a special investigator for the Security and Exchange Commission. He was tall, gangling and garrulous. We struck up

---

*115 *Cong. Record*, Pt. 11, p. 15203.
†The first completed version of this section was stolen from my office between October 4 and November 15, 1968. No one outside the office staff presumably knew that there was such a chapter. In those days when wires were continuously tapped and public institutions such as the Court were under electronic surveillance, word of the existence of a chapter such as this one could spread quickly. This version re-creates the original text to the best of my memory.

an instant friendship, which, through various ebbs and flows, endured —with some qualifications—until his death in 1973.

I acquired great respect for Lyndon. I came to have an understanding of him, and with it, a greater insight.

First, there was the basic yearning of the man—he had to be loved. It never became so apparent to me as it did the day he took me on a tour of his ancestral home in Johnson City, Texas. The main emphasis was his mother and her love of him. This developed, in his life, to a desire to be loved by everyone, in the manner he imagined FDR was loved by people. When his mother passed on, her place was taken by Lady Bird, one of the loveliest women I have known. It was her strength and wisdom that carried insecure and frightened Lyndon through the later crises of his life. But it was this yearning to be loved that led him to the unprincipled associations and projects overseas. He threw his arms around every dictator in the world for the adulation it brought him.

Second, he had a barnyard quality in his personal talk.

Third, his passion for power encompassed money. He and Lady Bird came to Washington originally bringing with them about $20,000. Lyndon ran that sum up to at least $20 million by the time he left the White House. His fingerprints will be found on no documents; his footprints never appeared. Telephone logs never recorded what he said, for he spoke through stout allies, like Sam Rayburn, to stout bureaucrats, like Laurence C. Fly of the Federal Communications Commission.

All in all, he was a lovable, complex man. He was the best storyteller in Washington; and virtually every minute of every hour at a reception or dinner in the capital would be dominated by him.

In the early years his dinner parties were informal, friendly affairs presided over by Lady Bird. The cocktail party of the evening always lasted long so that their two little girls could be put to bed before dinner was served. Lyndon seldom had a stag party in his home, though he went to many. At these parties he not only tried to be abstentious but refused to make a speech or say a few words if he had had a drink. When I went on the Court, my brother Arthur gave me a stag dinner at the Statler, inviting Lyndon. I glanced at the list of speakers as I left the table for the men's room and noticed that Lyndon was next. Meeting him in the men's room, I told him so. He flushed, became angry and resentful, and said he would not return to the table. I repaired the breach with the toastmaster, and Lyndon remained an honored though silent guest.

Lyndon was the only man elected to office campaigning for FDR's Court-packing plan. He was naturally proud of his achievement, and being gregarious, he quickly widened his circles in Washington. He cultivated them as well, never ceasing to campaign at some party or dinner.

Once, when he was in an expansive mood in the late forties, he undertook to tell me how I should go about becoming President. His free advice was, in fact, not personal; rather, it was directed at the mythical man who aimed to become President; and I thought at the time that he was really talking about himself.

"You've got to do it through Sam Rayburn!" he said with a huge exclamation point. "Be with Sam every late afternoon for bourbon and branch water. [Sam had a hideaway office in the Capitol where the faithful forgathered late every afternoon.] Absorb as much of Sam's wisdom as you can. Sam represents the sanity and conservatism of the common people of this country. Shake off all those isms and leave the left-wingers to themselves."

That was the basic strategy LBJ employed. In 1960 Sam headed up the "LBJ for President" committee, by which time LBJ had parroted the Sam Rayburn philosophy to such an extent that Sam really thought LBJ was "my boy."

Dick Neuberger (Senator Richard L. Neuberger of Oregon) was an old friend of mine and a distinguished journalist. He loved the outdoors and used it over and again as a theme for his many articles. We floated the Deschutes River together, fishing for redsides. He was a frequent visitor at my tamarack cabin on the Lostine River in the Wallowas of eastern Oregon. Once he and I, together with Chet Bennett and Wade Hall of the U.S. Forest Service, took a hundred-mile horseback trip across the Wallowas in three days so that Dick could write an authentic inside story of the wilderness problems of those mountains. He and his wife, Maurine, had been an inspiring team in the Oregon legislature, and then he went on to the U.S. Senate, a journalist turned successful politician. There he promoted conservation and beautification programs, his anti-billboard legislation being prominent. He died of cancer in 1960 and his funeral was in Portland on March 13. I had despaired of attending, as the air fare was prohibitive and slower methods of transportation were impossible because of the Court's schedule. But Lyndon B. Johnson, Majority Leader of the Senate, had his secretary call me to say that Eisenhower had lent his official jet plane to the congressional delegation and that there was room for one Justice. So in that manner I crossed the continent and paid my respects to Dick's memory.

We were in the air nine hours that day—five going West and four returning. Of those nine, I spent eight hours talking with Lyndon. The words "talking with" are not quite accurate; "listening to" would be more precise, for conversation was almost impossible for Lyndon. He always took the lead and held forth with few interruptions. During this eight-hour talk, his theme was "My First Hundred Days in the White House." He was as sure of the Democratic nomination as he was that the plane would make a successful round trip. He was equally certain of victory in November. The nomination and the election were minor events and they would be handled. "Now is the time to lay out a program of action after the inauguration."

I would interrupt to say he did not have a chance of being nominated. That remark, which I repeated over and again, irritated him and he always rejoined, "My troops won't panic."

His "troops" were the Southern delegates—perhaps 220 strong.

"Where is your labor support?" I would ask. "Where is your Negro support? . . . Where is your farmer support? . . . Where is your independent support?"

He pooh-poohed, with great emphasis, any need of that kind of support.

I asked Lyndon if he was interested at all in sounding out labor, for example, on whether it would be behind him. He obviously was also embarrassed at the very thought that I might become associated with his campaign, not because I was a member of the Court but because I was too far "left." Later, out of curiosity, I saw some of my labor friends and sounded them out. They were against LBJ; they did not trust him (at that time); they thought, as the blacks also did (at that time), that he was too much "Establishment." My labor friends turned out to be Kennedy fans, news that Lyndon could not believe.

In that eight-hour talkathon, Lyndon moved me in and out of his mythical Cabinet. For a half-hour or so I was his new Secretary of State —"a man who knows more about the world than any American." His strategy was clear—none of his competitors had a chance. He ridiculed Stevenson. Kennedy would fall flat on his face; Symington was pathetic

—and so on. It was clear that he sincerely believed that those three main contenders would get hopelessly tied up in their struggles and finally by the tenth ballot "turn to Daddy." So the quick victory of Kennedy in the first ballot of the Convention was a crushing blow to Lyndon. For, after all, he was "Daddy" and the rest were by his lights only "upstarts."

Kennedy wanted Jackson or Symington as his running mate and had all but agreed to offer the vice-presidential nomination to one of them. In this regard, Clark Clifford was manager for Symington's candidacy, and Bobby Kennedy favored Jackson. But friends of Lyndon suggested that to prevent a breach, Jack should offer the vice presidency to LBJ —which, they assured him, Lyndon would refuse. Jack agreed and to his surprise ended up with a running mate whom he despised and mistrusted.

I was not convinced that Lyndon was implicated in the Kennedy assassination, though that was a common theory. He was, however, such a prime suspect that it was imperative for him to set up an independent commission to investigate the matter. The chairman would have to be a Republican; and the ideal chairman was the Republican Chief Justice, Earl Warren. Lyndon sent emissaries to the Chief to persuade him to accept. The Chief naturally rejected the offer instanter. So Lyndon called him over and "sold" him on the project.

When the Chief reported the matter to the Court, some of us asked why he had agreed to do it. I urged him to go back to LBJ and refuse to serve. I said, "It's like asking a girl to marry you. You can just tell her the next day that you've changed your mind." The Chief said he felt it would create hard feelings to decline now, so he stayed with it. From his reply I gathered that Lyndon had used innuendos relating to a "Communist plot" that perhaps reached deeply into government. As Jim Bishop relates in *The Day Kennedy Was Shot,* the Secret Service did suspect there might be a plot to destroy the leaders of this country, starting with Kennedy and going on to LBJ, John McCormack and Carl Hayden, the next three in line of succession. Thus, they had isolated LBJ in a remote corner of the emergency room at Parkland Hospital, Dallas, and then rushed him to the plane that took him back to Washington.

So the Chief accepted the chairmanship, reluctantly, and I think he regretted it before he had returned across town. However that may be, he and his commission did a very creditable job. The Chief kept the

Court from becoming involved in the commission as such by not using the Court building for the hearings and conferences; and by not employing any Court personnel in the investigation or hearings or in writing the report.

Warren told me that the CIA, the FBI and Congressman Gerald Ford were looking over his shoulder at the commission. One day Ford came in and told him to fire Joe Ball, counsel for the commission. When Earl Warren asked why, Ford told him it was because "Ball's associations are definitely pro-Communist."

Earl Warren had known Joe Ball for years. He was probably the ablest attorney in California, whose only sin was that he'd worked for Pat Brown against Nixon in the California elections.

Earl Warren told Ford, "I'm not going to discharge a man on the basis of rumors, like the McCarthy committee did for years. I'll only discharge him after a full hearing where he has a chance to hear charges against him and defend himself."

Ford didn't agree, and Earl Warren refused to discharge Ball. Though a progressive, Joe Ball is in fact very much a man of the center, and he is a superb trial lawyer.

The Chief Justice had ample precedent for undertaking the assignment on the commission. Associate Justice Robert Jackson had, as we have seen, taken leave for a full Term to act as prosecutor at the Nuremberg trials. Owen Roberts had headed up a committee to investigate Pearl Harbor. Those men lost time in Court work, but Earl Warren never lost an hour.

LBJ's years on the Hill had given him insight into the personalities, tastes, weaknesses and points of resistance of every congressman and senator with whom he had sat. Once the years passed and new faces appeared, his magic manipulation of that body of men would cease, for he would then be as much of an outsider as was FDR. But at the beginning, knowing each one and his foibles, he could, by cajoling, teasing, threatening, bribing, flattering, cursing, confiding, get about what he wanted.

He knew the senator who was the procurer of women for those who were headed for Florida. The going rate was $3,000 a month. How much "the girls" got, and how much the senator retained, I do not know.

Lyndon knew the ones who had made money by appropriating campaign funds.

He knew where the "bodies" were buried.

He knew when an approach through the wife or through the mistress would be best.

He knew how some shuddered at being photographed with him and how others considered it a great prize. Lyndon arranged for a photographer to be present at all his White House conferences or appointments. The guest—if he had pleased the President—would shortly receive a photograph showing him and the President and bearing an inscription appealing to his vanity. If the guest had not pleased the President, the photograph would arrive without an autograph.

In 1967 Congress authorized a special board to settle a bitter railway labor controversy. LBJ named a five-man committee, headed by Senator Wayne Morse, to resolve the crisis. On September 15, 1967, the committee rendered its decision, which, in the main, recommended the wage increase that the carriers had offered.

After it was all over, LBJ told me the background of the episode. He spoke sarcastically to downgrade those who he knew were my friends —Wayne Morse, Ernest Gruening, William Fulbright—the men who had fought him on foreign policy.

"I decided to make Wayne chairman. First I told him that I had read in the paper his statement that it was too bad Goldwater had not been elected in 1964, for the Republicans would be saddled with Vietnam. I said that if Goldwater had been elected I would not be honoring Wayne Morse with this call. Wayne is a vain man, and when I told him I had drafted him for the railway labor job, I said, 'Wayne, all the labor law I ever knew I learned from you. You are my teacher.' With that buttering up, Wayne took the job. Now, I knew it was a decision he'd have to make against labor. He's coming up for re-election in 1968. I knew his assignment would defeat him in that election. You just wait and see. And then tell me who the smartest one is—Wayne or LBJ?"

Morse was indeed defeated in 1968, and labor was in large part against him. LBJ's prediction was probably accurate. The point of the story is the Machiavellian character of LBJ, whose earlier years had been spent in spotting every man's weakness and then exploiting that trait to LBJ's political advantage.

LBJ gave us "consensus conservation," which was designed to gain support from everyone and please all people. This was not the "conservation" of Theodore Roosevelt or of FDR. Under them the Establishment did not get what it wanted. Under LBJ the Army Corps of Engineers and its dams never waxed stronger. Under LBJ the billboard industry scrapped most of our highway beautification program. Under LBJ water pollution was condemned, but industry had pretty much its own way when it came to cleaning up our rivers and lakes. "Consensus conservation" was the formula whereby LBJ gave the heritage of America away to the fat cats and the official vandals who have despoiled us.

Johnson, who coined the phrases and spoke for legislation that would have made him the greatest "conservation President" of all time, actually played politics with our resources, talking about the good earth as he would about motherhood and the flag, but winking at the Establishment while it took what it wanted.

He talked about the "new conservation" that brought "nature closer to the people." What he meant by this he explained when he dedicated the Percy Priest Dam in Tennessee. That dam made a 420-mile lake where nearly half a million people could boat, camp, hike and swim. The dam destroyed the river, where people could also boat, camp, hike and swim. But somehow or other a man-made reservoir was thought to be more valuable than a river. The Corps of Engineers, the Bureau of Reclamation, and TVA destroy river after river. The dams will in time silt in and be useless, the rivers will be gone forever, but the money spent in building the needless structures looks like a means to "progress" and people cheer.

When Arthur Goldberg resigned from the Court to head our United Nations delegation, Johnson wanted Abe Fortas, his old friend, confidant and legal adviser, to take Goldberg's place, and he asked me to talk with Abe. I did so and received a firm refusal, as Abe's personal affairs would not permit him to leave private law practice at that time.

Sometime later I heard over the radio a flash announcement that Abe was appointed. I got in my jeep and headed from Goose Prairie, Washington, our residence, to Yakima to reach a phone. En route I was flagged down by the Forest Service, through whom Lyndon had sent a message. When I got Lyndon on the phone he told me what had happened. At 11:45 A.M. he had Abe in his office doing final editing on a Vietnam announcement Johnson was to make. At 11:55 they finished and at 11:59 they walked to the door that opened on a press conference. Lyndon asked Abe to be present while he read the Vietnam statement, and Abe agreed.

With his hand on the doorknob, Lyndon turned to Abe and said, "Before announcing this statement, I am going to announce your appointment to the Court."

Abe was taken aback, saying they had been over that many times and his answer was still in the negative.

Turning full face to Abe, Lyndon said, "This Vietnam statement that you approved says fifty thousand more boys are going to Vietnam—perhaps to die. No one is ever going to shoot at you on the Court. Tell me, how can I send them to battle and not send you to the Court?"

Abe was silent a second and finally said, "Okay, you win."

When Lyndon told me the story over the phone, I said, "You bagged a good Justice, Mr. President."

What I have said so far puts LBJ in a poor light because he used people's frailties for petty or perhaps venal causes or employed them, as in Abe Fortas' case, to ambush a man. Yet as David S. Broder points out in his book *The Party's Over,* though Lyndon had powerful capabilities of persuasion on a person-to-person basis, he did not have them so much at the mass level. His technique was to use every representative of a group whose support he wanted as a convert. The persuasion was not across the room or at arm's length. It was nose to nose, with Lyndon putting on his hypnotic pressure. He was an amazing stunt man who personally went after every man or woman he needed in his political corner and worked him or her over to a fare-thee-well. Broder attributes this technique to LBJ's rise to power in the one-party state of Texas. Whatever the cause, it was person-to-person salvation administered by a most astute advocate. But his talents in this regard were limited. He could not sway the masses the same way. That is why, when those he had sold on the Vietnam war began to retreat, he was a lost soul. That is why he decided not to run again. Knowing the man and loving him for all his great points, I became physically ill to see his world collapse publicly on TV. He wanted to be loved by all, and when they left him on the war issue, it was a crushing, brutal, although inevitable and necessary, blow.

The Atomic Age drastically limits the use of force. It indeed calls for alternatives. The only known alternative is law. I thought perhaps I could get Lyndon to see that when I tried to induce him to speak at the opening of the *Pacem in Terris* convocation in New York City in February 1965. The theme was taken from Pope John's well-known encyclical; it was one in a series of conferences sponsored by the Parvin Foundation and arranged by the Center for the Study of Democratic Institutions of which Robert M. Hutchins was the head, I then being chairman of the board.

Lyndon at once panicked at the thought of making such a speech. I said that he could lead the nations of the world into a regime of law or at least call a working conference which would have that as an aim. He dodged, ducked and evaded the proposition, changing the subject and finally shunting me off to the staff that was instructed to sabotage me politely.

LBJ finally sent a letter: "I have no doubt that such a discussion, under private auspices, of the problems of peace will provide a major contribution to the greatest single problem of our time." But then came the typical abrasive tactics of LBJ; unofficial gatherings like this, he said, might be disruptive of official peacemaking efforts; this group was infringing on an area properly reserved for professional diplomats; it was attempting to exploit the President's prestige on behalf of a private group some of whose members were critical of his policies. (Later, when the 1967 *Pacem in Terris* conference was held in Geneva, the campaign of LBJ against them continued.)

By the time of the 1965 conference the bombing of North Vietnam had started, and that bombing under the direction of LBJ provided an obbligato to all *Pacem in Terris* efforts. We decided, however, that since Vietnam overshadowed all *Pacem in Terris* conversations, North as well as South Vietnam representatives should be invited—that one should not be invited without the other. They both promptly accepted. Our group, working through the State Department, even managed to get permission to invite Ho Chi Minh himself—a man whom two of our group, Harry Ashmore and William Baggs, had met in Hanoi, where they interviewed him on the matter. LBJ's State Department cleared a letter of invitation, which he surely knew about. Ashmore signed the statement and mailed it. The condition included was Ho Chi Minh's— i.e., that while the conference continued, neither side would use the occasion to improve its military position.

Our hopes were high that at last conversations might start. We were soon disillusioned. LBJ had sent a secret message to Ho Chi Minh on February 2, 1965, which reached Ho Chi Minh before ours did. LBJ's letter set forth as a condition for cessation of bombing the most stringent demands yet made: advance assurance that Hanoi would halt all infiltration of troops to the South by land or by sea. There was, of course, no promise that the U.S. build-up in South Vietnam would also cease or that our troop movements to that country would stop. LBJ's letter stated further:

> If you are able to accept this proposal, I see no reason why it could not take effect at the end of the New Year, or Tet, holidays. The proposal I have made would be greatly strengthened if your military authorities and those of South Vietnam could promptly negotiate an extension of the Tet truce.

LBJ took note of public statements suggesting that

> you would be prepared to enter into direct bilateral talks with representatives of the U.S. Government provided that we ceased "unconditionally" and permanently our bombing operations against your country and all military action against it. In the last day, serious and responsible parties have assured us indirectly that this is in fact your position.
>
> Let me frankly state that I see two great difficulties with this proposal. In view of your public position, such action on our part would inevitably produce world-wide speculation that discussions were under way and would impair the privacy and secrecy of those discussions. Secondly, there would inevitably be grave concern on our part whether your Government would make use of such action to improve its military position.
>
> With these problems in mind, I am prepared to move further toward an end in hostilities than your Government has proposed in either public statements or through private diplomatic channels. I am prepared to order a cessation of bombing against your country and the stopping of further augmentation of United States forces in South Vietnam as soon as I am assured that infiltration into South Vietnam by land and sea has stopped.

The key passages in *our* State Department–approved letter had read:

> In our several discussions with senior officials of the State Department . . . they emphasized that the U.S. remains prepared for secret discussions at any time, without conditions, and that such discussions might cover the whole range of topics relevant to a peaceful settlement. They reiterated that the Geneva Accords might be the framework for a peaceful solution.
>
> They expressed particular interest in your suggestion to us that private talks could begin provided the U.S. stopped bombing your country, and ceased introducing additional U.S. troops into Vietnam. They expressed the opinion that some reciprocal restraint to indicate that neither side intended to use the occasion of the talks for military advantage would provide tangible evidence of the good faith of all parties in the prospects for negotiated settlement.

The State Department–approved letter was not published in the press at the time LBJ's statement was. This deliberate dissembling, whereby LBJ's right hand vetoed what LBJ's left hand was doing, was typical of the actions which created the enormous credibility gap.

A couple of years later we still hoped that Ho Chi Minh might attend the May 1967 Geneva conference, but on May 19 we received Hanoi's formal cancellation.

By April 1967 the South Vietnamese had been protesting Ho Chi Minh's presence in Geneva. Premier Nguyen Cao Ky himself announced in Saigon that he would demand a boycott of *Pacem in Terris II* on the ground that Ho Chi Minh had been invited and Ky had not. The State Department expressed its concern, and all parties were again assured that Saigon would be represented if Hanoi or the National Liberation Front (NLF) was, but would not be invited to participate alone. Invitations stipulating this condition were dispatched to two South Vietnamese whose names were supplied by the State Department: Ky's foreign minister, Tran Dan Do, and Dang Duc Khoi.

Soon we had evidence that LBJ and the State Department were using this contrived South Vietnamese issue to undermine the convocation. In Berne the U.S. ambassador, John S. Hayes, complained that in submitting the first invitation to Hanoi we had given Ho the option of blocking Saigon's participation by withholding his own; he did not seem to be interested in the explanation that this also worked in reverse, since Saigon could block Hanoi in the same fashion. And in Geneva we began to cross the trail of Roger Tubby, the U.S. ambassador to UN organizations, who was busily running down the convocation all around the diplomatic cocktail circuit.

The Saigon issue had its repercussions in Eastern Europe. Although the conditions for the Southeast Asian panel had first been discussed at the Geneva planning session and all developments had been covered with the Eastern-bloc foreign ministries, we began to receive sharp questions about the South Vietnamese role, particularly from the Soviets. They were assured repeatedly that unless both Vietnamese belligerents joined the panel, neither side would be permitted to address the convocation. This condition, incidentally, was rejected by NLF representatives in Prague and Moscow, who demanded that Saigon be barred as the price of NLF representation. Our refusal to do so terminated that negotiation.

Finagling over South Vietnamese representation continued during the convocation. As soon as we received Hanoi's cancellation we cabled the South Vietnamese foreign minister to inform him that we were withdrawing his invitation pursuant to our prior understanding. The response was that he had already departed for Geneva, even though this was a good week ahead of time. Tran Van Do and Dang Duc Khoi arrived in the company of the ranking public relations expert from Saigon's Washington embassy, politely forced us to reject his demand that he be allowed to address the convocation from the floor, and neatly created the kind of free-speech issue that is guaranteed to draw a glandular response from the American press.

LBJ's Administration was largely successful in implanting in the American media the notion that the *Pacem in Terris* convocation was deliberately and suspiciously loaded against the United States. The public, official position in Washington was initially benign, then neutral. It was not until May 23 that the State Department conceded to the Associated Press that the Administration had in fact decreed a "hands off" attitude for *Pacem in Terris II.*

After that, the wraps were off and the effort to discredit the convocation was carried openly into the halls at Geneva. A State Department "observer," Frank Siverts, took up a post in the press room where he could exploit such contrived items as the South Vietnamese protest and knock down any suggestion that anything of consequence was, or possibly could be, going on in the hall.

This public relations countertechnique is most effective with spot coverage. The ordinary reporter, trying to summarize hours of serious, complicated talk in a few hundred words or a few minutes of television exposure, is at a hopeless disadvantage even if he has an adequate background for the assignment, which he usually has not. Most of those charged with the daily file from Geneva proved to be vulnerable to a persuasive young State Department foreign policy expert standing by with handy interpretations as they were jammed against their deadline by the relentless flow of words.

In Geneva both Mrs. Douglas and I received, first, pressures, and then, denunciation for not letting the South Vietnamese delegation be heard. But we all refused to turn the conference into a propaganda center for one group only. While we were still interested in dialogue, LBJ was interested only in a "consensus" that approved his project or plan.

There were important consequences following the crossing of LBJ's path by the Center. The Center was a foundation dependent on tax-deductible gifts for its support. LBJ turned the Internal Revenue Service loose on the Center in an effort to deprive it of this tax immunity. Though the tactic did not succeed, the obvious lesson was that anyone who dared cross LBJ's path was in danger of paying a heavy price.

The Vietnam "war," in the end the political undoing of LBJ, early became a real obsession with him. Our intrusion in that country's problems never had the solid backing of the American people, and at no time did Johnson ever dare go to Congress asking for a declaration of war. The whole martial regime which flourished in his Administration squeaked through crisis after crisis. Even the courts, unfortunately, refused to touch the issue because it was too "hot" politically, in the sense that to consider the matter would mean a head-on collision with the Chief Executive.

LBJ—like Nixon after him—always spoke of peace and emphasized how peaceful the intentions of Americans in Vietnam were. That, of course, was fraudulent talk. Almost every day of the Johnson term brought an escalation of the war effort. Many nations, at his instigation, worked on the Vietnam peace problem, but little did they realize that he was making each of them a patsy, since he had no intention of settling the war or coming to terms with Hanoi.

One of the best potential intermediaries in this affair was Moscow, which had maintained a very close working relationship with Ho Chi Minh. Moreover, unlike the Chinese, the Russians were not suspect in the eyes of the Vietnam people. The Indian ambassador in Moscow generated many conversations with the Russian foreign office about the end of Vietnamese hostilities, and those messages would in time be transmitted to the Indian embassy in Washington. During many of the critical times in question, the top Indian official in charge in Washington was the minister, Dr. P. K. Banerjee, who was an old friend of mine, and one of the ablest and finest men I ever knew. He would quite often make a trip across town to see me and give me a report.

In December 1966 he came and relayed the message from the Russians that Ho Chi Minh was ready to sit down any day and talk with President Johnson, with a view to putting an end to the hostilities and resolving the differences between the two countries. Dr. Banerjee normally would have gone first to the State Department, but from his many contacts with Dean Rusk and his satellites, he knew that the message would probably never come to the attention of the President, or if it did, it would be presented in a sort of offhand, half-hearted manner.

This message was so urgent that Dr. Banerjee asked me if I would talk to the President about it at once. He would wait about twelve hours before officially sending the message through channels to the State Department. I said I would be very happy to do so, and that night I got the President on the telephone at the White House. I had not finished giving the entire message when he interrupted to say that this was a typical Russian trick, that messages like this had been coming through at a very rapid rate for a long time, that this was not a bona-fide effort, that there was a plan afoot to embarrass him, etc. He, therefore, did not want me to bother myself with the message. I reported this conversation to Banerjee, and, of course, nothing ever did happen.

Again, in February 1968, Banerjee came to see me saying he had an important message from Ho Chi Minh through the Indian foreign office. He thought it was of utmost urgency and that the President should know about it. Once again he felt that he could not trust the normal channels of the State Department to get it through, and he wanted me to try to communicate again with the President. I said I was doubtful I could accomplish much. I did, however, dictate a letter to Clark

Clifford, which was delivered to him by hand. Fortunately, he was having dinner with the President that night, and Clifford handed the note to LBJ himself.

The message dealt with the main questions raised by Americans who did not trust Hanoi. It was indeed responsive to the President's statement at San Antonio, September 29, 1967, when he said, "The United States is willing to stop all aerial and naval bombardment of North Vietnam when this will lead promptly to productive discussions. We, of course, assume that while discussions proceed, North Vietnam would not take advantage of the bombing cessation or limitation."

The message that I delivered to Clark Clifford from Ho Chi Minh was as follows:

Q. If the bombing ceases, when will talks start?
A. 7 to 15 days.
Q. What will be the subject matter of the discussion?
A. Anything within the frame of reference of the Geneva Conference.
Q. Who will be parties to the talks?
A. North Vietnam and the United States. Either can bring in another party.
Q. Will any advantage of the United States be taken in case of cessation of the bombing?
A. Hanoi accepts Clark Clifford's statement of January 25, 1968.

The position taken on that date by Clifford before the Senate Armed Services Committee was as follows:

SENATOR THURMOND: When you spoke of negotiating, in which case you would be willing to have a cessation of bombing, I presume you would contemplate that they would stop their military activities, too, in return for a cessation of bombing.

MR. CLIFFORD: No, that is not what I said. I do not expect them to stop their military activities. I would expect to follow the language of the President when he said that [he would stop the bombing] if they would agree to start negotiations promptly and not take advantage of the pause in the bombing.

SENATOR THURMOND: What do you mean by taking advantage if they continue their military activities?

MR. CLIFFORD: Their military activity will continue in South Vietnam, I assume, until there is a cease-fire agreed upon. I assume that they will continue to transport the normal amount of goods, munitions, and men, to South Vietnam. I assume that we will continue to maintain our forces and support our forces during that period. So what I am suggesting, in the language of the President, is that he would insist that they not take advantage of the suspension of the bombing.

In February 1968 Clark Clifford became Secretary of Defense and I was at the White House for the occasion of his swearing-in. Afterward, as I was going through the line, LBJ thanked me for the message from Hanoi and said, "I am going to do something about it." There was a great ring of sincerity in his voice, and I felt that he meant it. But there seldom was anything sincere about LBJ.

On March 31 he announced on television that he was willing to undertake peace talks with North Vietnam, and announced at the same time that he was not and would not be a candidate for re-election that fall. What all the implications were I did not know. LBJ doubtless saw in Hanoi's latest advance an opportunity to make political capital out of negotiating, and while the negotiations went on he might even use them to liquidate any other presidential candidate—Democrat or Republican, and if everything went all right, the decision not to run might be converted into the first presidential draft in American history.

One who takes the pains to dissect the public statements Lyndon Johnson made over the years about the Vietnam war and the terms for discussion which he would accept will find, when all those various statements are put together, that every subsequent statement qualified something which was in the previous statement. There never was any one statement that could be trusted as the complete, final, authentic, official, trustworthy statement of the President. He was constantly shifting and changing grounds and conditions, and in the meantime creating the greatest credibility gap in American politics— up to Nixon's second term. As things turned out, LBJ never had the slightest intention of following up the Indian message concerning Ho Chi Minh's proposal.

Other events, however, were soon to engulf LBJ, and what happened subsequently is to the credit of Clark Clifford, not the President.

•   •   •

When Clark Clifford became Secretary of Defense he felt that his main contribution would be to bring the war in Vietnam to a conclusion. It was costing the country $2.5 billion a month; wasting the lives of thousands of American boys; tearing the people to pieces; and in terms of the settlement of world problems, it was achieving precisely nothing. So one of the first things Clifford did was to arrange a luncheon meeting in his office at the Pentagon to which he invited no one except the Joint Chiefs of Staff. Clifford, who eats very sparingly, spent the entire hour telling of his plans to bring Hanoi and Washington together, to settle the war. He asked for the Chiefs' prayerful consideration of this and for their support. By the time lunch was over, no one else had said a word. The Joint Chiefs of Staff rose in unison, thanked him for the luncheon and walked out of the room, still silent.

Clifford realized he had a major problem on his hands. He knew that each member of the Joint Chiefs of Staff had a senator or two or a congressman who, at the signal, would sound the alarm and arouse public opinion behind some Pentagon proposal. Therefore Clifford knew that it was important to confer with the key senators and congressmen, briefing them and their assistants as to what the developments might possibly be vis-à-vis the Vietnam war. So Clifford spent the next two weeks on the Hill. He covered all the important bases. And then he had a second lunch with the Joint Chiefs of Staff. He went over his original proposal, broadened and embellished it a bit, and then pressed for approval. Clifford told me that he did not get resounding approval, but he did get a vote of three to two that the Joint Chiefs of Staff would go along. It was enough for the next step, which was to try to line up LBJ. He went at once to the White House and talked to LBJ, told him of his discussion with the Joint Chiefs of Staff, his proposals for a peace settlement, and the vote among the Joint Chiefs of Staff.

As Clifford related the story to me, the President was very displeased. In fact, LBJ was so unhappy at the news that not only would he not speak to Clifford, but for one week Clifford tried to get through to the President to talk with him or to see him, but to no avail. Clifford was certain that in a very short period he had exhausted his influence as Secretary of Defense and would shortly be returning to private life.

What happened in the inner workings of the President's mind no one knows. But this is the background of the speech he made on March 31, 1968, in which he said he would be happy to talk with Hanoi and that he would not be a candidate for re-election.

I think what actually happened was that following Clifford's reconnaissance of the situation, LBJ, too, sounded out opinion around the country and discovered that the public sentiment was overwhelmingly for the liquidation of the Vietnam situation. LBJ, who loved popularity more than anything else, was at as low an ebb as any man ever in the White House—prior to Nixon—as far as popularity went. Though this disapproval had been obvious to most people long before, it was not clear to LBJ, who was so insulated by his own stubbornness as well as by his firm conviction in the soundness of his political judgment.

The offer which LBJ had for an overall settlement of the Vietnam situation was outstanding. The 1954 Geneva Accords had contained the basic ingredients of a rule of law for settlement of the hostilities. Such a settlement could only be successful if it took into consideration the interests of all the Southeast Asian neighbors and if it marshaled world opinion behind the enforcement of any ultimate solution. The Geneva Accords were, in other words, the natural frame of reference for a discussion of the entire Vietnam situation.

LBJ chose a different method. He proposed direct talks between Hanoi and Washington; and in time Paris was agreed upon as the site. This method suited LBJ's political techniques because it was wholly freewheeling, and he could make the policy decisions as he went along. Unlike the Geneva Accords of 1954, Johnson's formula contained no basic principles. No other nations, except the United States and North Vietnam, were implicated, and there was no agreement to abide by any decisions. LBJ's way gave only a shadowy resemblance to a rule of law, though in theory it offered the possibility of a peaceful solution.

One day I was visiting with LBJ in the White House about a conservation matter. Since he knew I was opposed to his Vietnam policy, he waited patiently to see what side I was on concerning the matter at hand. When I had finished he crumpled the memo I had given him without reading it and put it in his pocket. I knew my cause was lost, as indeed it was. Then he asked me questions about Supreme Court vacancies and what replacement he should make of Tom Clark. He mentioned names and I commented on them. Regarding one, I said, "He will be very conservative on economic matters, and occasionally for liberty and justice on other matters."

"Liberty and justice," he said, "that's all you apparently think of. And when you pass over the last hill, I suppose you will be shouting 'Liberty and justice!' "

"You're goddamn right, Mr. President," I replied as I left by one door and he by another.

LBJ and I had been through many crises together. Yet mostly he was a fair-weather friend. He wouldn't even speak to me in public when I issued the stay in the Rosenberg case. Once at Johnson City, while standing in a small group, I told him I was headed for Siberia and asked if he had any objections.

Before he could answer, an aide spoke up and said, "Tomorrow's press will carry a story that Justice Douglas is off to Siberia after clearing the trip with the President."

I watched LBJ's face freeze. He did not answer my question but changed the subject. He was so alarmed by the implications that when the announcement came from the summer White House about the social events of that weekend, I—the guest of honor—was not even mentioned as being present.

He was forever on the move and full of endless energy. Once in Johnson City we went out on Johnson Lake in a speedboat going sixty miles an hour while Secret Service men nervously rubbed suntan lotion on his exposed skin. He would direct the boat around one buoy and head for another, all the while screaming for more speed. Finally we slowed down and I left the speedster for the patrol boat, giving my place to one of his favorite blondes. As I rejoined Lady Bird I asked, "What is Lyndon doing when he's not going sixty miles an hour in a speedboat?"

"Going six hundred miles an hour in an airplane" was her answer.

In 1967, when LBJ made a lightning-fast round-the-world trip, he gave me a personal account. The reason for the trip was a memorial service for Prime Minister Harold E. Holt in Australia. He spent 59 hours on the ground and 53 hours in the air. He recounted every landing and every conversation. On the plane he slept a few hours every night, had a masseur relax him, worked on stacks of mail, signed dozens of laws just passed by Congress, and talked almost every hour with the White House on the phone. It was a needless, reckless journey. Some of us who knew him well were talking about the insane or meaningless nature of the trip; and we agreed that it was symbolic of a deep-seated urge in LBJ for self-destruction. He had to hurry, hurry, hurry. He went at lightning speed to court disaster.

Was he carrying the United States on the same suicide course? Many of us wondered.

He certainly developed a formula for the destruction of this country. Putting down the Vietnam "revolution" was draining the nation's coffers. How much more would be spent should Guatemala, Peru or the Philippines ask to be "saved"?

Modern wars are too costly to be fought. They rob domestic programs of necessary support. We are in a period of mounting disemployment due to technological "advances" that "save labor." Employment in the public sector is our only hope. Yet with the vast military expenditure, money for other purposes is hard to get from a conservative Congress. Without employment, the racial problem worsens, for the first to feel the bite of a layoff is the black; and the hard core of unemployed and disemployed is the black. So as we spun faster and faster in the Vietnam orbit, we spun faster and faster toward riots and chaos at home.

Another characteristic that had a corrosive influence on the country was Johnson's refusal to believe in the basic integrity of men. Gifted though LBJ was, he felt, I think, that every man has his price—and of course every country, too. He exercised shrewdness in trying to determine what the price was and what the vulnerable spot in the particular individual was. The result was tragic, for his tactics in time became transparent. A degenerative process set in; specific issues of war and peace were affected; a downgrading of values took place both at home and abroad. In the end, few trusted him. His lieutenants were trapped between loyalty to him, a commanding, dynamic person, and loyalty to the nation. Confidence was undermined; we became a nation whose power turned on manipulation, slickness and outwitting an opponent.

An insight into the growth of the "credibility gap" is seen in the following episode. In May 1968, after the Senate had passed the restrictive legislation concerning the wiretapping decisions of the Court, it sent the legislation to the House and to a conference committee. The chairman of the House conference committee was Emanuel Celler, an old friend whom I saw at a dinner in New York City in late May of that year. He arrived at the dinner late, with apologies.

He whispered to me that he had been detained, that LBJ had called him on the phone and laid out the following strategy: Our Court had held in the Berger case, in June 1967, that wiretapping was a search within the meaning of the Fourth Amendment, and that warrants had to be obtained before taps could be placed. But LBJ wanted sweeping exceptions. So he implored Celler, in fact he *directed* Celler, to get through the House broad, sweeping exceptions in favor of wiretapping by having such provisions attached to an appropriations bill. LBJ explained to Congressman Celler that in that way he would not be able to veto the provision. It would go sailing through and he, LBJ, would have the public excuse that to veto wiretapping he would have to veto the entire appropriations bill.

Years before, he had taken on Communism as the all-weather, foolproof political touchstone. The idea grew and grew in his mind as good opposing evil. He was the apostle of good, so even Vietnam became a holy affair. Thus a gifted man, propelled by a messianic cause which in turn was intertwined with a desire for self-destruction, became a dangerous world figure.

LBJ leaned heavily on all sorts of advisers but seldom on his Cabinet. Walter Jenkins, later cruelly dropped from government, was LBJ's key man. Knowing LBJ, he realized that many of the things LBJ would order him to do would not be proper or judicious. But he never debated his boss. He solemnly promised to carry forward on that line. He also knew that in the onrush of events, LBJ would not remember his foolish requests. So Walter let many orders disappear in the limbo of forgetfulness. Thus he became a unique buffer for his boss—utterly loyal but with a discernment that LBJ needed great protection.

LBJ's invitations to people to come and help him ran into the hundreds each year. He was leery of some Kennedy men, particularly Bobby Kennedy, the Attorney General. When Bobby resigned in 1964 to run for the Senate, Nicholas deB. Katzenbach took his place and was confirmed as Attorney General in 1965. Katzenbach was a Kennedy man and LBJ feared him, too. He feared both of them because he thought they might dredge up some historic things against him. In 1966 he talked Katzenbach into joining the State Department, not because he thought he would be better there, but because he distrusted him near the helm of law enforcement. LBJ had long known and admired Tom Clark and had come to know and like Ramsey, Tom's son. That was how Ramsey became Attorney General, not because he would "cover up" for LBJ, but because he was a trusted friend.

Abe Fortas and Clark Clifford were constant advisers to LBJ—not for fees, not for a retainer, not for any rewards, but because LBJ knew them and respected them. An inside adviser who has no post or office may see things one way. As the case of Clark Clifford reveals, an insider moved into the post of Secretary of Defense, began to see the Vietnam "war" from the inside, and seeing it then, thought quite differently about it than when he was merely discussing policy questions with the President.

Lyndon Johnson wanted to be like Franklin Roosevelt. Yet it was not possible for him. Moreover, as I have said, he was obsessed with the desire to be loved. He never realized how strong he could be if, choosing principle rather than expediency, he had stood the line and let his enemies attempt to wax strong. He had to win them over, convincing them that he was right or stilling their voices out of fear or through bribery.

Still, when LBJ was not playing or thinking politics but was relaxing with friends, he was the most engaging, lovable person I ever knew and a storyteller *par excellence.*

David Ginsburg, my first law clerk, was Hubert H. Humphrey's right-hand man in the 1968 election. After LBJ announced that he would not run, Ginsburg urged Humphrey to resign as Vice President. He said, "Then you'll be free of LBJ and not tied to his policies."

But Humphrey refused. And commencing at least with the convention, Humphrey began to pay the price. When he started to maneuver to get out of LBJ's shadow on Vietnam, LBJ promptly pushed him back into it. Ginsburg's negotiations with LBJ over the Vietnam plank in the Democratic platform were drawn out and acrimonious. LBJ was dictating, not negotiating. Humphrey was to be his Charlie McCarthy.

LBJ knew Humphrey well. He knew that if Humphrey was independent of him, he would radically change the Vietnam policy. Hence LBJ kept HHH on a short leash.

While he was doing that, he was working under cover to get Nixon elected. (For example, Johnson entertained Nixon in his home in Texas, but never Humphrey.) Nixon was his man because he and Nixon saw eye to eye on Vietnam. It was on Vietnam that LBJ wanted his foreign policy judged. And Nixon was the one who would most likely perpetuate that program in a light favorable to LBJ. By the same token, LBJ's social program on the home front was one which Nixon would never outflank. Nixon, as President, would do LBJ and history two good turns! As Ginsburg told me after the election, "We had to beat both LBJ and Nixon. The combined opposition was too much for Hubert."

The last time I saw LBJ was at a White House reception on the eve of his permanent departure. Lady Bird was as friendly and vivacious as ever. Lyndon never spoke to me. At this time, his plans were afoot for the LBJ Library in Austin. I was invited to the dedication of the library but I did not attend. Hugo Black went, and well he might. He had a special relationship with LBJ, of which the following incident was a part:

In 1941 I was a guest of the Texas Bar Association in Fort Worth, and at the end of the ceremonies I drove West to California. My first night's stop was Big Spring, Texas, and as I was registering, the motel radio was on.

"The voice is familiar," I said.

"That's Lyndon Johnson campaigning for the Senate," the proprietor replied.

"Where's he speaking?"

"Down the street four blocks in the Courthouse Square."

So I hurried down to hear my friend, not waiting for dinner. There he was, on the top steps, haranguing an audience of three thousand people. He was taking out after Willkie, who had run against FDR, and LBJ lambasted Willkie without mercy. That night he introduced Willkie's theory of feeding the chickens: "Keep the horses well fed with oats, and the chickens can scratch for their oats." This theory was known as the Trickle-Down Theory and was heard on every Democratic platform in the thirties and forties.

As LBJ came to the close of his speech, he shouted, "I want all you good folks of Big Spring to line up and shake the hand of the next Senator from Texas, Lyndon B. Johnson."

The audience dutifully lined up, me included. I noticed that Lyndon gave each of them two pumps with the arm and one slap on the back before greeting the next comer. He did the same to me, only when he had given me the two pumps he said, "Where in hell did you come from? Step aside and wait for me—you're the man I want to see."

In time we walked to a restaurant to have a sandwich and he called his Big Spring staff to meet me. Then he started his diagnosis of the campaign. His opponent was Governor W. Lee ("Pappy") O'Daniel, who campaigned with a lively orchestra and a stove that handed out hot biscuits. "Pass the Biscuits, Pappy" was a song and a slogan; and Pappy talked of little else except the old-time religion represented by the Fundamentalist version of the Bible. That night in Big Spring, Lyndon had it all figured out how to beat Pappy. He'd get the Johnson precincts in early, swamping Pappy. He did get them in early; *and he lost.*

I saw him some weeks later in Washington and asked why that had happened. "I was a fool," he replied. "Because I got all *my* votes in early, Pappy knew exactly the votes he needed to win."

"How many?" I asked.

"Less than fourteen hundred."

"Where did he get them?"

"From the cemeteries, of course."

The next time, Lyndon ran against former Governor Coke Stevenson and he got his votes in late—so he knew how many he'd need. Johnson won by 87 votes.

A federal District Court in Texas issued a stay against the chairman and the secretary of the State Democratic Convention who had certified that LBJ had won the primary against Stevenson. The stay was temporary and the hearing on it was set for September 21, 1948, at Fort Worth. On September 22 the District Court announced that it would grant relief to Stevenson. On September 25 LBJ petitioned the Court of Appeals for mandamus. If LBJ was to get on the ballot, a decision had to be reached by September 30.

LBJ's lawyers—Alvin J. Wirtz, James V. Alfred, Thurman Arnold, Abe Fortas and Hugh Cox—applied to Hugo Black for a stay. Black held a hearing in his office, and on September 29 he stayed the District Court injunction, thereby putting Lyndon's name back on the ballot.

I never talked to Hugo about the case, but one attorney opined, "Justice Black was a wise, long-headed man. He knew there were cemetery votes cast for each candidate but that Lyndon had fewer cemetery votes than Stevenson." I think Hugo smelled the rat in Texas politics and that therefore he had only the choice of answering the question, "What kind of guy is this?" Johnson, at that time, was flying all the colors of a New Dealer. The Texas conservatives behind Coke Stevenson were trying to stop him, and the choice Hugo made was for Johnson.

Around the time of the inauguration of the library, CBS released a documentary on LBJ. Walter Cronkite was the interviewer, and Burton Benjamin the producer. It was filmed at Johnson City and technically was a beautiful thing to watch. But it was for me a sad dismemberment of a man I had loved. LBJ himself did the dismembering in trying to put all the blame on others and all credit on himself. Knowing the man, I realized the agony he was going through before my very eyes and those of eighty million other people. He was begging for trust, for approval, for confidence. And he could gain none of them because the partial record, the deceitful versions made him cruelly vulnerable.

I have been too harsh on LBJ. He was what Lady Bird always said—a "can-do" President. He pushed through laws at great speed, using the finesse he had developed as Majority Leader in the Senate. Earl Warren, writing in the *Texas Law Review* (51, 1973) after his retirement, told in detail of the great contribution to the cause of civil rights that LBJ made as President, with particular emphasis on the Civil Rights Act of 1964, the Voting Rights Act of 1965, and the Civil Rights Act of 1968. Those were the highlights of his broad vision in the field of racial problems. Johnson knew that, in Lincoln's words, a house divided against itself cannot stand. He named blacks to many posts in the federal government, among them Constance Motley and Spottswood Robinson to the federal District Court, and Thurgood Marshall, the first black man to sit on the Supreme Court. Overall, LBJ made the pluralistic society a living force as no President had done before him. That is an achievement that balances out many of the adverse memories I have of him.

Lyndon's great desire as I have said, was to walk in the steps of FDR and to be known as the man of the people who served the common good. I think that, in certain respects, he succeeded. For one thing, the legislative program that he finally got through was the most significant group of laws affecting the black race that has been produced in our history. Although Lyndon couldn't talk to the people as a group in the caring way FDR did, he could talk an individual into a corner and overwhelm him with his reasons. Some people called him garrulous, but his garrulity was associated with converting nonbelievers, and he was very, very successful.

Lyndon was never at ease with the intellectuals—the "eggheads," to use his expression. Part of his hostility to them was because, in his time, some of the most prominent were Kennedy men; and Lyndon had an abiding distrust of all Kennedy fans. The prize "egghead" he ridiculed was Adlai Stevenson, whom he deemed to be a competitor in 1960. Lyndon would mimic Adlai, walking with dainty steps and speaking prissy English. But when it came to appointments to the Court he named Abe Fortas, as his number one choice. Abe, too, was as elitist, and as intellectual and as brilliant as any of the "eggheads." Though Lyndon was not at home with the "intellectuals," over the years he became very dependent on Abe Fortas for all his decisions. Not that he always followed Abe's advice; he often did not. But he had such confidence in Abe that he was crippled without him. Lyndon was suspicious of "intellectuals" because they were so remote, so distrustful of him. But Lyndon knew no barriers where friends were involved. In spite of our disagreements he clung tightly to me, for he knew I would never make an unfriendly move against him.

Our friendship bloomed anew when I wrote my book *Farewell to Texas.* He did not like the title and he did not share my view that Texas —in matters of conservation—was going down the drain, but he threw himself with enthusiasm into getting pictures for the book. He came up with a great collection for me. The publisher chose line drawings instead, but at my insistence printed one of Lyndon's color photos taken on one of his ranches. It was rich in color and warm in sentiment—a picture of the bluebonnets that he and Lady Bird and I loved so much.

Richard M. Nixon

In my time it seemed as if the costs of public office were running so high that an officeholder had to be very rich or very poor to hold it. If he was rich, his predilections would usually run with his investments. If he was poor, he might be sorely tempted to become an adventurer. That is why I felt the salaries for public officials should be high, not miserly. But every effort to get a pay raise stirred up momentous opposition.

There probably has always been some corruption in Washington, D.C. When I was there, the lobbies were well financed and active. Big Business promised large sums to political parties and pretty much had their way—whether the Republicans or Democrats were in power. By the 1970s the industrial interests had 3,200 advisory committees in Washington, and they were the watchdogs over the federal agencies. They waxed particularly strong under Richard Nixon, who upped the secret levy on corporate givers, who in turn exacted their prices.

One of the most powerful of these behind-the-scenes corporate advisory committees sat with the Bureau of the Budget. It would, for example, slash funds that would serve the conservation cause by cleaning up the rivers because of the increase in the costs of the industrial polluters. The control of that committee was so great that for years we had no monitoring of industrial poisons entering our waterways.

Another device was the infiltration of industrial personnel into agency positions, one of the most notorious being the staffing of the Pesticide Division of the Department of Agriculture with chemical company employees.

Other, more subtle practices prevailed. Pentagon officials on retirement became officers of companies doing a big procurement business with the United States. How can a government official be vigilant to protect the public interest against these contractors if he knows that as a reward for friendly behavior he may one day become vice president of such a company and draw a huge salary in addition to his federal retirement pay? Forest Service employees on retirement frequently become officers of lumber companies. How can an agency employee adequately represent "We, the People" if his reward on retirement is to go with a company over which he is supposed to be a watchdog?

I debated this subject on television with General Omar Bradley after World War II. In the discussion I submitted that an officer who took such a post should give up his retirement pay. Bradley held the opposite view. Bradley, an honest person, saw absolutely nothing wrong with the practice. At the time he himself was retired and was a high officer in a company making large sales to the Pentagon. I thought it was as wrong for him to do that as it would be for a member of the Securities and Exchange Commission to resign to become president of the New York Stock Exchange, or for a commissioner on the Interstate Commerce Commission to leave his job to head a railroad, or a member of the Federal Aviation Agency or the Civil Aeronautics Board to depart government service to head an airline. Government service, to have integrity, can never be the stepping stone to professional advancement. It is an end in and of itself.

General Bradley was hurt to the quick by my jibes. I never thought he had personally done anything immoral when, on retirement, he signed up for a fat job with a Pentagon contractor. But the system that rewards men for serving two masters is inherently wrong.

In 1346 in England a law was passed that required judges to take an oath that they would not take a "gift nor reward by themselves, nor by other privily nor apertly, of any Man that hath to do before them by any Way, except Meat and Drink, and that of small Value." Canon 5 (C) (4) of the American Bar Association's Code of Professional Ethics reflects the same philosophy.

In the days of Queen Elizabeth, public officials were paid nominal salaries and were expected to make up the difference on their own. The end result was that officials levied taxes, so to speak, on those wealthy enough to have favors to ask. Consequently, the custom evolved of having in Parliament only members of the upper classes, endowed with riches. But a legislator with interests in commercial enterprises and financial institutions often has conflicting interests, for a bill regulating his empire might be good for the people but a setback to him and his investments.

The Nixon-Agnew regime reflected both crude and subtle corruption. The Agnew activities were those of a common crook—receiving kickbacks from contractors and not reporting the revenues as income. The Nixon activities, among others, ran to cutting income-tax corners to profit a President. Beyond that was the use of the Office of the President not "to execute the laws faithfully," as required by the Constitution, but to badger, beat and destroy anyone who asserted a First Amendment right to disagree with the Administration or register a protest against its policies or acts. This was the first time in history that both President and Vice President polluted and desecrated their high positions of trust and public confidence.

Roger Crampton, a law clerk for Justice Burton in 1956 and 1957, was a bright, conscientious, principled lawyer with a conservative cast of mind. He headed the Administrative Conferences for a few years and did a commendable job. He worked hard for the election of Nixon and especially for his re-election in 1972. He was rewarded by a position as Assistant Attorney General in the Department of Justice. After serving a few weeks, he was relieved of his job and in due course became Dean of the law school at Cornell. I asked him why he had been let go. He said that he was told that he was not sufficiently "malleable" to suit the Administration. Principled men are not "malleable" when it comes to questions of the proprieties of morality, and of honesty. Nixon could not fulfill his manifest destiny if those around him were not "malleable" enough to carry through his clandestine and unethical projects. The example of honest Roger Crampton is, in minuscule, the entire story of Nixon's life.

I first knew Nixon in the thirties when he was a law student at Duke University. I had gone there on invitation to give a lecture to the law school. I talked about predatory practices in finance, with special emphasis upon the disclosures that emerged after the many autopsies of companies and syndicates following the 1929 crash. Some years later

Nixon told me that I had been an inspiration to him, that my lecture had affected his life. I did not ask in what way, for the uneasy thought crossed my mind that predatory practices had inspired him.

At the beginning of World War II Nixon was an obscure lawyer in a vast pool of attorneys who worked for the Office of Price Administration. The person in charge was David Ginsburg, who has no recollection of the young lawyer shortly to start his climb up the political ladder. In 1946 the Republican candidate for Congress from the Twelfth District of California died and the committee called Nixon to see if he was interested—and he was. His opponent in the race was Congressman Jerry Voorhis, a staunch liberal.

The Bill of Rights and the Jeffersonian tradition were a part of his very being. He had served on the House Un-American Activities Committee (HUAC) and, as a member, had protested some of its most extreme and shocking tactics. In Congress from 1937, he had promoted Social Security, unemployment insurance, legislation protective of labor, First Amendment rights of witnesses called before investigative committees, and the right of those people to have and enjoy due process of law as respects the mode of the investigation, the right of counsel, and the like.

RMN took his political formula from Murray Chotiner, a Los Angeles lawyer. The Murray Chotiner method was, first, to discredit one's opponent in every possible way; second, to associate one's opponent with a subversive or treasonous program; third, always to attack, never defend; and fourth, if your opponent tries to defend himself against untrue charges, whimper and accuse him of using unfair political tactics when he calls you a liar.

The Chotiner formula made it easy to translate the principles of Jerry Voorhis into badges of Communism: for example, Social Security and unemployment insurance were telltale signs, for Russia had their counterparts. In those days such an accusation was equivalent to a conviction in the public mind. RMN, who knew the law, should have known better, but he also knew that the public mind had been saturated with fears of Communism, and that therefore anti-Communism was the best ticket through the treacherous path leading to the top. While Jerry explained what his ideas and beliefs were and what he had achieved, RMN set out to destroy him by innuendos, by direct false charges, by snide remarks.

At the time, the CIO had a Political Action Committee (PAC). One of RMN's slogans was that a vote for him was a vote against PAC and "its Communist principles."

Jerry Voorhis was also in favor of a reciprocal trade agreement, abolition of the poll tax, a school lunch program, abolition of some price subsidies, and for the Hobbs anti-racketeering bill, which included controls on labor leaders. He was against aid to countries not having a free press, against making HUAC a permanent committee, against giving federal oil in tidelands to the states and exempting insurance companies from the antitrust laws.

But RMN kept pounding away. His campaign literature said:

> Don't Be Fooled Again!
> Five times Jerry Voorhis has had the support of the radical groups because he was at one time a registered Socialist . . .
>
> Voorhis has the endorsement of the National PAC because he voted their viewpoint 43 times out of 46 opportunities during the past four years.
>
> While he has been carrying the Democratic colors in recent years for his political purposes, REMEMBER, Voorhis is a former registered Socialist and his voting record in Congress is more Socialistic and Communistic than Democratic.

The campaign was capped by an episode somewhat reflected in the Watergate episode some twenty years later. The Voorhis office was broken into one night, and much of the Voorhis literature taken. The next day, men hired through theatrical agencies rang doorbells in the Twelfth District. They were dressed in caps, tightly buttoned coats and high collars. They spoke a guttural English with a Russian accent. Handing a piece of Voorhis literature to a housewife, one would say, "We are Russians and we want you to vote for Mr. Voorhis."

This campaign started one week before the election, and Jerry could not catch up with it. RMN won by 65,586 votes against 49,994, in a district that Jerry had carried easily in 1942 and 1944.

In the House, Nixon became a member of HUAC. He was in hot pursuit of the Hollywood Ten (which I discussed in *Go East, Young Man*). He advocated vigorously that they be cited for contempt. Of the sixteen who voted against the motion, one was Helen Gahagan Douglas. That day it was intimated on the floor that those who sided with the Hollywood Ten were suspicious characters—Danny Kaye, it was said, was David Kaminsky; Eddie Cantor was Edward Isskowitz; Edward G.

Robinson was Emanuel Goldenberg; Melvyn Douglas (Helen's husband) was Melvyn Hesselberg—and so the snide anti-Semitic innuendo came into wide use, and Nixon was among the first to exploit it (93 *Cong. Record,* Pt. 9, p. 10778; Pt. 107, p. 92).

In 1950 Helen and Nixon both decided to run for the Senate. Helen, like Jerry Voorhis, was extremely sensitive to the civil rights of minorities as well as of majorities. She was opposed to many of the RMN tactics, including the great political capital he made out of the Alger Hiss case. I was at a dinner when Helen was debating with herself whether to try for the Senate. She asked me what I thought, and I counseled against it, saying she held a strategic post in the House and would be dreadfully smeared by RMN in any Senate race.

But Helen thought that it was time for liberals to stand up and be counted, and also time that another woman reach the Senate. So she announced, and soon RMN started to give her the "Communist" image. Helen, I think, thought that intelligent people would not fall for that line. But this was a time when the public was frightened. Senator Joseph McCarthy rode high and greatly conditioned American thought. Nixon bided his time, and a week before the election he did to Helen something similar to what he had done to Jerry. On the front page of the California papers were pictures of Helen embracing a well-known Communist, kissing a black, and shaking hands and beaming at another Communist. The pictures were composite—that is to say, doctored. The person Helen actually embraced had nothing to do with Communism. His picture was cut out and the picture of a Communist was substituted. But Helen was unprepared for the assault and did not have a chance to show how phony the manufactured photos really were. Nixon received 59 percent of the votes.

Nixon's 1950 campaign was said to be "one of the best-financed, well-publicized, and most underhanded campaigns in California's history." He charged that Helen's party had "caused the loss of China to Communism," which led to the Korean War. On domestic issues he relied on Communist subversion, Communist subversion, Communist subversion. His legislative record was said to be conservative, but, in fact, it was rather unprincipled in that it was so rubbery as to suggest largely an indifference to policy. He rode every little wave, played every little trick that pointed to popularity.

He was by no means the first person in American politics to stoop so low. In 1950 Frank Graham, a highly principled man, was running for the Senate from North Carolina. His opponents forged the name of Walter White, the famous leader of the NAACP, to thousands of letters imploring voters to cast their ballots for Graham. In the campaign, civil rights were the main issue and the prejudiced white electorate voted Frank Graham down.

In 1962 RMN ran for governor of California against Pat Brown. Nixon and his assistant, Bob Haldeman, formed a Committee of Concerned Democrats. They put up $70,000 and sent over 500,000 postcards to registered Democrats expressing doubts and fears about Brown and the forces below him, intimating there were subversives running the shop. There was no disclosure that Nixon and Haldeman were the promoters of the Committee of Concerned Democrats. The concern expressed in the postcards was that below Brown were people who

1. Wanted to admit China to the United Nations, and
2. Refused to bar Communists from joining the Democratic Party

One of my outstanding lawyers with SEC, Roger Kent, brought suit against Nixon. Judge Byron Arnold of the California Superior Court found that the scheme concocted by Nixon and Haldeman was fraudulent and enjoined them from pursuing it.

That was not all of Nixon's fraudulent actions in the 1962 election. But Pat Brown and his staff were wise to RMN's tactics that had defeated Jerry and Helen, so they prepared for the worst. Sure enough, a week before the election there appeared pictures of Pat Brown on the front pages of the California papers—embracing, shaking hands with and kissing the so-called subversives. The next day Pat's staff broke down the faked pictures into their separate parts and prepared a mat for the press that showed how the composite pictures had been created. Pat won the election by about 53 percent of the votes.

One who knew Nixon's previous political strategy could have predicted Watergate—as many of us did. Nixon had a long time before shown to the American people his mastery of the art of deceit. On September 23, 1952, when he was the vice-presidential candidate on the Eisenhower ticket, Nixon made a TV broadcast concerning his practice, while in the House and Senate, of taking $18,000 a year from a private group in California, not for his personal use but for helping to pay expenses of his office—such as making television speeches and traveling back to his district. Most men and women in public office receive outside funds—from their investments, from speeches they make, from book royalties, from law, medical or engineering firms with which they are professionally connected. Those clients often have interests wrapped up in legislative measures before Congress. When judges have remunerative ties to individuals, groups or corporations that have cases before the Court, the judges do not sit. That same ethical problem confronts legislators. They, too, should not vote on measures in which their patrons have financial stakes.

That was part of the problem confronting RMN in 1952. He never faced up to it in his famous TV address. He said he never personally pocketed the money, that it was not "income" for tax purposes. Nevertheless, the $18,000 served him well. He said in his speech, "I'm proud of the fact that not one of them [the contributors] ever asked me to vote on a bill other than my own conscience would dictate." But who were these interests? And in what bills did they have high stakes? And how did Nixon actually vote on those measures? He said at the start of his TV address that it was "morally wrong if any of the contributors got special favors for the contributions that they made." Nixon told who the administrator of the fund was, but the contributors remained faceless; the tax, tariff and subsidy measures they were interested in and how RMN voted on those precise measures were left undisclosed. The American people swallowed the explanation without realizing that it was no explanation at all of the real vice underlying the gifts. For we all know that "he who pays the piper calls the tune"—perhaps not invariably, but usually. The precise votes which Nixon made in the House favoring the group on tax laws, on housing, on maritime and air subsidies, and the like, were never revealed and no one could research the point on his own without knowing who the contributors were.

Adlai Stevenson had such a fund when he was governor of Illinois, and Nixon asked him to disclose "what favors, if any" the contributors received from Illinois during that time. But RMN, a clever manipulator of scenario, did not answer such questions concerning his own fund but rather turned the episode into an account of a penniless man from a poor family who was barely getting by, financially speaking.

Nixon's 1952 TV speech marked an ethical decline in the management of our public affairs. He was not the only one in public office to play fast and loose, but in a facile manner he showed the way it could be done—with public applause.

Those who knew him intimately, as Earl Warren did, were fully aware of his low ethical standards in the political arena. In 1948 Earl Warren was California's favorite son for the Republican nomination.

The convention was in Chicago. The delegation, which included Nixon, was pledged to cast its vote as a unit for Warren at least on the first ballot. Nixon no sooner reached Chicago than he contacted Tom Dewey, the contender from New York State, and had a session with him. California, said Nixon, wanted none of Warren; the delegates were for Dewey; Nixon would lead the defection. He did, and the result was that Warren—a man of far greater stature than Dewey—got second place; and the Dewey ticket went down to defeat. Warren never forgot that episode and never forgave Nixon.

In 1948 a storm brewed in the House Un-American Activities Committee concerning Dr. E. U. Condon, head of the National Bureau of Standards, charged by HUAC with being a subversive. The FBI had made a report to the Secretary of Commerce, under whom the Bureau operated, concerning Dr. Condon. The committee asked the Secretary of Commerce for the letter, and the Department of Justice recommended that a House resolution calling for its production not be passed. President Truman had indeed signed an executive order making all reports relative to the government-employee "loyalty security program" confidential and directing that all subpoenas issued for them "be respectfully declined." RMN, addressing himself to Truman's executive order and to the proposition that Congress has no right to question the judgment of the President, made a statement that reads ironically in the light of later events:

> I say that that proposition cannot stand from a constitutional standpoint or on the basis of the merits for this very good reason: That would mean that the President could have arbitrarily issued an Executive order in the Meyers case, the Teapot Dome case, or any other case denying the Congress of the United States information it needed to conduct an investigation of the executive department and the Congress would have no right to question his decision.

Referring to Truman's desire to protect government personnel against the discrimination of unfounded or disproved allegations, RMN went on to say,

> This point constitutes one of the strongest arguments for making the letter public rather than from keeping it secret.

Because as a result of the portions of the letter which have already been released, allegations have been made which reflect upon Dr. Condon. Some sources say that the letter in fact clears him of these charges. In the interest of a complete airing of all the facts and of dispelling these unfounded allegations, if they are that, it is essential that the entire content of the letter be released to the Congress.

RMN voted for the House resolution. Helen Gahagan Douglas was one of twenty-nine voting against it.

On January 26, 1950, speaking in the House about Alger Hiss, Nixon said,

Most important of all, we must develop and put into effect an extensive educational program which will teach the American people the truth about communism as well as the truth about democracy. The tragedy of this case is that men like Alger Hiss who come from good families, are graduates of our best schools, and are awarded the highest honors in Government service, find the Communist ideology more attractive than American democracy. The statement of Mr. John Foster Dulles when he commented upon the Hiss verdict last Saturday is particularly pertinent: The conviction of Alger Hiss is human tragedy. It is tragic that so great a promise should have come to so inglorious an end. But the greater tragedy is that seemingly our national ideals no longer inspire the loyal devotions needed for their defense.

Five years ago, at the time of the Dumbarton Oaks Conference in 1944, when Alger Hiss served as director of our secretariat, the number of people in this world in the Soviet orbit was 180,000,000, approximately the population of the Soviet Union. Arrayed on the anti-totalitarian side there were in the world at that time, in 1944, 1,625,000,000 people. Today there are 800,000,000 in the world under the domination of Soviet totalitarianism. On our side we have 540,000,000 people. There are 600,000,000 residents of United Nations countries which are classified as neutral such as India, Pakistan, and Sweden. In other words, in 1944, before Dumbarton Oaks, Teheran, Yalta, and Potsdam, the odds were 9 to 1 in our favor. Today, since those conferences, the odds are 5 to 3 against us.

The great lesson which should be learned from the Alger Hiss case is that we are not just dealing with espionage agents who get 30 pieces of silver to obtain the blueprint of a new weapon—the Communists do that, too—but this is a far more sinister type of activity, because it permits the enemy to guide and shape our policy; it disarms and dooms our diplomats to defeat in advance before they go to conferences; traitors in the high councils of our own Government make sure that the deck is stacked on the Soviet side of the diplomatic table.

America today stands almost alone between communism and the free nations of the world. We owe a solemn duty, not only to our own people but to free peoples everywhere on both sides of the iron curtain, to expose this sinister conspiracy for what it is, roll back the Red tide which to date has swept everything before it, and to prove to peoples everywhere that the hope of the world lies not in turning toward totalitarian dictatorship but in developing a strong, free, and intelligent democracy.

(96 *Cong. Record,* Pt. I, 81st Cong., 2nd Sess., p. 1007)

Nixon, to his credit, changed his tune in 1972 when he went to Peking and to Moscow to establish a détente with China and with Russia. Looking at the problem in a cool, objective way, he did more in 1972 to make the way of Russia and China easier than any "subversive" he had denounced. I do not condemn him for what he did in 1972. I mention the matter only to state that Nixon's hunt for the so-called subversive did more to perpetuate the Cold War than the activities of any other single person. The things he did in 1972 were sorely needed in the fifties. He and his ilk are mainly responsible for the glacial movement we as a nation have taken to developing a cooperative world regime—a rule of law, if you please.

Over twenty years of the "witch hunt" was good politics for a few headline hunters, but it corrupted the American mind and froze our actions to those who were suspicious, aggressive and blatantly offensive when viewed from the world scene. This un-American stance of intolerance gave us an overseas image that associated us not with ideas of freedom, but with bombs, subversion of other governments, and secretive corrupt plans to overthrow foreign regimes.

Ironically, in the end Alger Hiss, whom Nixon had used to step upward politically, "saved" Nixon's financial neck. Hiss had been convicted of perjury while a government employee and therefore came within the terms of a law (5 U.S.C., Sec. 8312 [c] [3]) enacted on September 6, 1966, which barred him from receiving his Social Security. In *Hiss* v. *Hampton* (338 F Supp. 1141), decided in 1972, the Court of Appeals held the act unconstitutional because it was an ex post facto law. Nixon's annuity or pension was also saved by that decision if any of the crimes for which he was pardoned had occurred prior to the date of the 1966 act. As to later crimes, the *Hiss* decision was warning to Congress that an ex post facto law was not the vehicle for cutting down Nixon's pension rights.

In 1968, when the Nixon-Agnew campaign was under way, an event occurred that could have changed the character of American politics for some years. Sheldon Cohen, a man of impeccable honesty, was Commissioner of Internal Revenue. I knew him well. He had for years been my attorney, preparing my federal income-tax returns. When he was named Commissioner, I had sworn him in.

I learned much later that a responsible man from Baltimore had come to Sheldon saying that he had uncontestable evidence that a contractor had been making kickbacks to Agnew. Sheldon was asked to check Agnew's tax returns for the years in question to see if these assessments were reported. The man who was making this request wanted to make public the expected news that Agnew had not reported that income and so blast the Nixon-Agnew ticket into oblivion.

Sheldon Cohen, respectful of the law governing the secrecy of a taxpayer's returns, declined the request to let this Baltimore man see Agnew's returns and said that even he, the Commissioner, would not examine them. For if he opened them up for an anti-Agnew man, where could he draw the line? Everyone in public office has enemies, and if the enemy of one can get his income-tax returns, why may not the enemy of another?

Grand juries, one of the bastions of strength of a free people, eventually caught up with Agnew. But they worked under a regime of law, not a regime of politics designed to destroy as many "opponents" as possible. For Congress had made explicit (26 U.S.C., sec. 6103) those persons entitled to see income-tax returns, and these provisions, even as enlarged by a Treasury regulation (Sec. 301.6103[a] [b], [c] and [d]) confine them to very small groups.

On April 30, 1973, Nixon said, in a TV broadcast,

> Political commentators have correctly observed that during my twenty-seven years in politics, I've always previously insisted on running my own campaigns for office.
>
> In both domestic and foreign policy, 1972 was a year of crucially important decisions, of intense negotiations, of vital new directions, particularly in working toward the goal which has been my overriding concern throughout my political career—the goal of bringing peace to America, peace to the world.
>
> And that is why I decided as the 1972 campaign approached that the Presidency should come first and politics second. To the maximum extent possible, therefore, I sought to delegate campaign operations, to remove the day-to-day campaign decisions from the President's office and from the White House.

In this much publicized TV speech on Watergate, RMN was offering, as an excuse for wrongdoing on the part of his White House staff, the fact that he, Nixon, had not been running the 1972 campaign. And he emphasized that the campaign was in that respect unlike his earlier campaigns, which he did run and supervise. Yet when he ran against Helen Douglas for the Senate, he made quite the contrary representations. The halls where he spoke were littered with handbills printed on pink paper denouncing Helen Douglas as being Communist-allied—a "pinko" in those days being the label attached to fellow travelers. When Nixon was leaving the halls, littered with these pink handbills, he was accosted and asked about them and often criticized by angry people who resented this devastating slur on Helen Douglas. Nixon's reply was that he had no idea who did it, that it was nothing for which he was responsible. So he lied then or he lied on April 30, 1973, when he spoke on television. His pronouncement on April 30, 1973, was also contradicted in his unsuccessful campaign against Pat Brown for governor, for Nixon was found by the court to have conceived of the formation of the Committee of Concerned Democrats and to be the mastermind behind its creation and operation.

Those who knew Nixon had predicted that he would personally be on his best behavior during his first term, performing as the real Nixon in the second. That is the psychological reason why he picked Agnew as his running mate, for he saw in Agnew the potential for evil that he, Nixon, could use in his first term as a front to do the things Nixon instinctively wanted to do. Agnew performed, attacking the "enemy" —mass media, newsmen, telecasters, unruly youngsters—in the best Nixon tradition. I. F. Stone, who was a Nixon authority, summed up the sorry spectacle: "Every nation has two souls, a good one and a bad one, and Nixon got to the top by making sure he appealed to the bad one."

We all knew that his first term would be quite "proper," and that his true image would not appear unless and until he was re-elected for a second term. It was a foregone conclusion that once he was safely ensconced he would run a predictable course—any means to destroy any competitor or to still any dissent or to put down unfavorable press comment. He had the federal agencies that license radio and television stations all set to render the "necessary" decisions. He had laid fright in the hearts of the mass media. Some networks—for example, CBS— stayed fairly firm. But others began to retreat; yet none capitulated.

The level at which RMN operated the White House was deplorable. Look at the "good" men he poisoned. Roger Crampton was not "malleable enough"—bless him. But many others were—good men tempted to play the role of the Mafia because of the Mafia leadership in the White House. Why did they do it? I do not know; I can only speculate. I saw men around FDR who wanted to know only his wish, and they would do it. Some of us had a higher regard for the presidency and would never become prostitutes—which, to be sure, he never asked us to become. But the White House has a strange attraction—it is where the power is; and power can catapult one into presidencies of multinational corporations, into seats of corporations, into lucrative law practices. Thus RMN spread out the honey that attracted customers for power.

We did not know Spiro Agnew before Nixon selected him as his running mate. But having known Nixon since 1937, we knew that he had to be of the same unethical cast as RMN. How RMN picked Agnew I do not know, but his instinct for "malleable" men was sound. And Agnew had Mafia-like tendencies to cut corners, violate the law and enrich himself. By RMN standards these were endearing ones.

We also predicted that Gerald Ford would be his choice for Vice President. It had to be Ford because of his mediocrity. RMN—like LBJ before him—could not stand to be overshadowed. So he picked a man who represented the doldrums of conservatism, though Ford, unlike Agnew, was an honest man.

Nixon was an amoral man. Deceit, simulations, telling lies marked the character of the man. He was bright, able and wholly unethical. The end, in his view, justified the means. No man is perfect, but deeply ingrained in our character has been the conviction that man has moral standards that are not subservient to expediency. Nixon had a compulsion to put expediency first. The appetite of his ego was devastating. Nothing could stand in his way.

During Nixon's political hiatus in the sixties, when he went into private practice, he proved to be an able lawyer and a good appellate advocate. He argued *Time, Inc.* v. *Hill* (385 U.S. 374) both on the original argument and on reargument. There came up for discussion a precedent in California in the case of *Melvin* v. *Reid* (112 Cal. App. 285, 193). Nixon on oral argument referred to it as resting on the common law. Warren—also a California lawyer—questioned if there was common law in California. Nixon hesitated and then corrected himself, saying it was under the Code. All of which only shows that even top-notch advocates sometimes nod. I should add that Nixon's native ability was obvious in his oral argument. The untrustworthy side of his character was not obvious. The only telltale sign was a degree of obsequiousness and eagerness to please and to be accepted.

Nixon lived not for his "friends," but for his "enemies." Everyone who crossed his path, everyone who was a competitor, had to be destroyed. That was the case of Jerry Voorhis and of Helen Douglas. It was true of Pat Brown in the governor's race in 1962. It was true of Ed Muskie in the 1972 campaign.

The "enemies" list was endless—a newsman, a cartoonist, a congressman or senator, anyone who crossed his path. Being on his "enemies" list that surfaced in 1973 during the Watergate hearings was, to most people I knew, an honor. I was disappointed that I was not on that list, especially because so many less deserving characters made it. The regime of the politics of destruction, which Nixon headed, thrived on "enemies." If he did not have one, he was forced to create one. He had to make every offbeat person a Communist to feed his insatiable appetite. Alger Hiss was only symbolic. Everyone who criticized, who took countermeasures, who filled the specifications which his mania dictated, had to be destroyed. Military overkill and political overkill marked his technique. His use of threats against the lower economic classes, as illustrated by his dispersion of neighborhood legal services and other features of the Office of Economic Opportunity illustrated the same technique. He had to shatter and suppress every latent force that sponsored opposition to him and his regime. This attitude toward "enemies," this use of "threats" marked the essence of Nixon's *Mein Kampf.*

He was actually envious of Soviet ruthlessness and helped design the American counterpart. He was interested not in the clash of ideas, but in the clash of power. Telling lies was so customary a technique, so much a proverb of his life, that he was unaware when he did lie. His compulsion was never to admit an error or a weakness. If he ever does make such an admission, it is solely for tactical reasons, as when in the Watergate affair he conceded that he should have been more watchful of the noxious culprits who surrounded him at the White House. Morality was no part of his technique but only a part of the appearance, as when he sprayed himself with the essence of godliness emanating from Billy Graham. Respect for ideological differences and for the sense of moral obligation that once made up our political ethic became obsolete as he fashioned the monoliths of sheer power. He sponsored a new value system in which truth played no part of what he called "operable realities." He became the embodiment of the blatant secularism which emerged through our business practices and our commercial advertising and which took the place of our old morality. He represented no culture or belief except the necessity to win by destroying people. That is why I personally thought his ascendancy to power marked the inquest on the Free Society which had been our boast since Jefferson and Madison.

That may seem to be a harsh conclusion. But from my ringside seat I saw only contempt for the American system—the Constitution, the Bill of Rights, Congress, the Courts and the restrictions of law—and not only contempt, but the atmosphere of secrecy. A cloak-and-dagger regime was launched, with wiretaps galore, *agents provocateurs,* the use of the CIA and the FBI (supposedly neutral investigating agencies) for the ends of party politics. Government became, as Henry Steele Commager has said, "a giant public relations enterprise" in which "policies are to be argued not on principle but on the merits of their packaging."* Great issues of war and peace were decided through the manipulation of public opinion polls, through falsification of the issues, through the spreading of lies by the President.

Before the 1960 election I was visiting with Sam Rayburn in his hideout den in the House, sipping bourbon and branch water. The topic of Nixon came up and Sam said, "Sometime I wish you would sit and watch the face of that man. Look at his profile from each side, look him in the eyes. You can see what kind of a person he is. I hate to say it, Bill, but that man is a crook." Memories of that analysis by the shrewd Sam Rayburn came back to me in 1973 when Nixon announced "I am not a crook."

When Jack Kennedy was installed in the White House, I went over to see him about a minor matter. But before leaving the Oval Office I said, "Jack, you will be praised and criticized on many issues during your presidency. But one distinction can never be taken from you. You drove Nixon into political oblivion and saved the nation from an awful curse." Jack replied, "The guy is plainly no good. One should never trust him even the distance he could throw his grandmother."

Never did I make a worse calculation. I had grossly underestimated the decline in American morality to the point that the White House could become a huge public relations forum, operating with Madison Avenue techniques. Nixon did not create that attitude; he merely exploited it. That is why the specter of the inquest seemed so ominous for a while.

Adlai Stevenson (who according to Nixon "got a Ph.D. from Dean Acheson's College of Cowardly Communist Containment") summed up Nixon in a fitting sentence:

"Nixonland—a land of slander and scare, of sly innuendo, of a poison pen, the anonymous phone call and hustling, pushing, and shoving—the land of smash and grab, anything to win."

One who contemplates the career of Richard M. Nixon should read Joachim C. Fest's biography of *Hitler*. Germany's elite either actively supported him or passively tolerated him. Words had become so "cheap" that even brutal language ceased to cause alarm. We might have followed the same path under Nixon but for three forces: (1) a free press that dared shake its fist at its incipient censor; (2) a public opinion that rated moral values high and that began to puke at chicanery in high

*Washington *Post* (May 27, 1973), pp. C1, C5.

places; and (3) a stoutly independent judiciary. Nixon did not invent the politics of destruction but he used them to the limit. His technique was to destroy those who crossed him, those who criticized him, the dissenters; and I, as one of his targets, can say that the power of the federal government leveled against the lone individual is ominous and forbidding, though I loomed very small in his plan of conquest.

It was a great credit to the people and to their institutions—the press, Congress, the Constitution and the courts—that Nixon finally was cornered, and to escape likely impeachment and disgrace, resigned.

Chapter XV

My
Impeachment

Every federal judge, I suppose, is on tenterhooks when his nomination is before the Senate. Even Holmes, named by Teddy Roosevelt, and confirmed by voice vote, felt uneasy before the vote was in. He wrote Sir Frederick Pollock on September 23, 1902:

> . . . now as to my judicial career they don't know much more than that I took the labor side in *Vegelahn* v. *Guntner* and as that frightened some money interests, and such interests count for a good deal as soon as one gets out of the cloister, it is easy to suggest that the Judge has partial views, is brilliant but not very sound, has talent but is not great, etc., etc.

But, worrisome though the nomination proceedings may be, an impeachment endeavor sears more deeply and drives a person away from the crowd, makes him less gregarious and leaves him mostly in the embrace of dear friends and his immediate family and the unimpeachable resolution of his conscience and conviction.

My particular seat on the Court traces back to John Blair, Virginian, named in 1789. The following men subsequently occupied that seat:

Samuel Chase, Maryland, 1796
Gabriel Duvall, Maryland, 1811

Philip P. Barbour, Virginia, 1836
Peter V. Daniel, Virginia, 1841
Samuel F. Miller, Iowa, 1862
Henry B. Brown, Michigan, 1890
William H. Moody, Massachusetts, 1906
Joseph R. Lamar, Georgia, 1910
Louis D. Brandeis, Massachusetts, 1916

Of these, Chase, Daniel, Miller and Brandeis were outstanding.

Prior to my time, impeachment proceedings as respects members of the Court had been started only against Chase—and these failed. Two attempts against me also failed. I do not attribute predestination to this line of Justices. But I do suggest that if my record is to be broken, the successor will have to be prepared to turn back three times the assaults on him. I would remind him that the cause is great—the independence of the judiciary that in many ways sets us apart.

When Nixon chose Agnew as his running mate in 1968, few people could understand why he did so. The reason soon became apparent: Agnew was the old Nixon who was on the payroll of real-estate and oil men while he was in Congress, doing favors that no congressman ethically could do; Agnew was the Nixon who was intolerant of ideas, who gave every liberal thought or leftist idea a sinister Communist tinge. Agnew soon began saying what the new, bland Nixon would not say. The old Nixon, speaking through Agnew, took up the cudgels against exercise of First Amendment rights.

Agnew denounced the mass media on November 13, 1969, for following Nixon's speech on Vietnam with some critical comments. The people, Agnew said, were entitled to make up their minds on Nixon's message without having his words and thoughts "characterized through the prejudices of hostile critics before they can even be digested." What Nixon needed, in other words, was a symphony of approval—or dead silence. A week later Agnew denounced the press for having anti-Nixon and anti-Agnew views. His main targets were the Washington *Post* and the New York *Times.*

Agnew's attacks on the First Amendment were of course under the disguise of defending it. His talk that the "rotten apples" of dissent should be "separated" from society was ugly and ominous.

Katharine Graham of the Washington *Post,* speaking on May 22, 1970, said that Agnew's campaign against dissent was reminiscent of the

McCarthy era, though the latter was "less potentially dangerous than the present." For McCarthy raised "a one-issue conflict—the problems of communist infiltration." The problems of the sixties and seventies were much more numerous, centering on the use of threats, surveillance, wiretapping, investigation, impeachment, and so on, to bring dissidents into line and make them conform.

The TV and radio station owners who need to get their licenses renewed were one target. A Nixon-Agnew commission sitting in judgment on an application could make a license-renewal hearing disastrous. Nothing in America has ever been more nervous than one billion dollars, and Agnew's assault on the mass media noticeably brought it into line.

Another target was the dissenter who joined with others (and therefore conspired) to cross state lines to make speeches, inciting people to riot. Thus the "conspiracy" concept and "interstate commerce" concept were used to level dissenters. All speech, as Holmes said, is incitement. To reduce speech to tranquilizers or to poems of praise is to rob the First Amendment of vitality.

Federal officials reachable by impeachment were another target. If judges could be intimidated and controlled, then the *status quo* could stay comfortably in the saddle, dealing with minorities and the discontented pretty much as it chose.

Chance played into Nixon's hands. A man by the name of Louis E. Wolfson had been a client of the Abe Fortas firm before Fortas came on the Court in 1965. The next year Wolfson was indicted for violations of the Securities and Exchange Act.

In charge of the Criminal Division of the Department of Justice was Will Wilson, the man who soon was forced to resign because of scandals in his Texas practice. In 1969, Wilson rummaged through the files on Wolfson and found papers which an evil mind would say implicated Abe Fortas. These papers were certainly no evidence of Abe's involvement in any criminal matter. Nevertheless, Wilson leaked this privileged information to the press as he was later to leak unsubstantiated material on me to Gerald Ford when Ford was working to have me impeached.

It appeared that Wolfson had created a foundation in 1966, and made Fortas a director and an adviser, at an annual salary of $20,000. Moreover, a contract had been signed by Fortas and Wolfson that would have paid Fortas $20,000 a year for life, and $20,000 a year for life for his wife,

Carolyn Agger, a member of the law firm which Fortas quit when he came to the Court. That contract, however, had been "canceled" by mutual agreement. The first and only $20,000 check had been received by Fortas prior to the indictment of Wolfson. The money was returned to Wolfson by Fortas during the same calendar year, but eleven months after its receipt and several months after the indictment.

The charge made was that Fortas, while a Justice, was rendering legal service to Wolfson. The story gained credence from the fact that even after Fortas became a member of the Court, he continued as an adviser to LBJ. That aspect of the matter had been exposed in 1968 when Fortas went before the Senate Judiciary Committee and failed to obtain confirmation as Chief Justice. But a year later the disclosure in *Life* of the fee paid by Wolfson, the long delay in returning it, and the fact that Wolfson was in deep trouble with the federal government all brought matters to a head and gave Nixon the opportunity to free another Court seat.

I was in Brazil at the time, giving lectures on habeas corpus at the Candido Mendes University, and by the time I returned, the hounds were in full pursuit of Fortas.

I sat up with him two nights, serving as a sounding board. I asked him if he had tried to get LBJ to do something to help Wolfson. His reply was an emphatic negative. I asked him if he had directly or indirectly contacted Manny Cohen, Chairman of the SEC, or any other SEC official to aid Wolfson. He said he had not. He apparently had held Wolfson's hand, so to speak, but had never undertaken to give legal advice or acted as counsel after coming on the Court.

I urged Abe not to resign, though parts of the press were demanding it. At first Abe agreed with me, but he quickly changed. I saw him the next night and he was then resolved to resign. My son Bill was with me and he too pleaded with Abe not to resign. "Blood will taste good to this gang. And having tasted it, they will want more," my son said. I told Abe that if he decided to resign, to do so on his own timetable, not on someone else's.

Abe Fortas' acceptance of a salary from the Wolfson Foundation had nothing to do with his performance of his judicial duties as a member of the Court. He meticulously refrained from sitting on or voting in any cases with Wolfson connections. Nevertheless, it was a juicy morsel that was seized upon in order to denounce the Justice for unethical conduct.

The problem was that Fortas had never wanted to be a Justice and had left his law practice most reluctantly. I think he had regretted it almost every day on the Court. So the urge to stay was not strong to begin with, and he quickly magnified the gravity of the charges against him.

The Fortas matter was discussed at Conference in Abe's presence. He explained that while he had done nothing improper, he thought that in view of the outcry in the press, it would be in the best interests of the Court for him to resign. He did so the next day, on May 14, 1969, with a public statement. He told me in private that he had done so because of the advice of Clark Clifford, who, apparently sensing the unhappiness of Fortas on the Court and feeling that the unpopularity of LBJ would most likely result in the opposition taking revenge on Fortas, recommended that he resign. Within a year Fortas sincerely regretted he had not faced the storm of criticism and stared his detractors down.

The first person to call him, offering condolences, was Richard Nixon, the man who had arranged it all. He sympathized with Abe because Nixon, too, had experienced the hostility of the press and knew how vicious and unreasonable it could be. The talk lasted almost an hour. I understand that Abe made a record of that conversation so that historians will have an accurate and complete account.

Having disposed of Fortas, Nixon turned loose on me, and there were indications that Brennan would be next. The impeachment effort against me was the direct result of the failure of the Senate to confirm Clement Haynsworth and Harrold Carswell, whom Nixon had named to take the place of Fortas. As I have discussed earlier, I knew little of Carswell at the time, but I did know Haynsworth slightly and I thought he would have been a good appointment to the Court. While Carswell's nomination was pending, House Minority Leader Gerald R. Ford said, "If the Senate does not confirm Carswell, we'll impeach Douglas." That threat cost Carswell five votes in the Senate—he lost by a vote of 51 to 45.

The ease with which Fortas had been dispatched quickened the assault on me, which crystallized after Haynsworth and Carswell failed to be confirmed. On April 11, 1970, Agnew said the Administration should "take a good look" at what I had been saying and thinking. "At the present time all I'm advocating is that Justice Douglas' record be thoroughly examined, including his writings and his verbal opinions, to see whether they are compatible with the position he holds."

Thus, the ground was being laid for my impeachment. Gerald Ford followed suit. Speaking in the House on April 15, he said:

> What, then, is an impeachable offense? The only honest answer is that an impeachable offense is whatever a majority of the House of Representatives considers to be at a given moment in history; conviction results from whatever offense or offenses two-thirds of the other body considers to be sufficiently serious to require removal of the accused from office. Again, the historical context and political climate are important; there are few fixed principles among the handful of precedents.
>
> I think it is fair to come to one conclusion, however, from our history of impeachments; a higher standard is expected of Federal judges than of any other "civil officers" of the United States. . . .
>
> Let us now objectively examine certain aspects of the behavior of Mr. Justice Douglas, and let us ask ourselves in the words of Mr. Justice Cardozo, whether they represent "not honesty alone, but the punctilio of an honor the most sensitive."
>
> Ralph Ginzburg is editor and publisher of a number of magazines not commonly found on the family coffee table. For sending what was held to be an obscene edition of one of them, *Eros,* through the U.S. mails, Mr. Ginzburg was convicted and sentenced to 5 years' imprisonment in 1963.
>
> His conviction was appealed and, in 1966, was affirmed by the U.S. Supreme Court in a close 5-to-4 decision. Mr. Justice Douglas dissented. His dissent favored Mr. Ginzburg and the publication, *Eros.*
>
> During the 1964 presidential campaign, another Ginzburg magazine, *Fact,* published an issue entitled "The Unconscious of a Conservative: A Special Issue on the Mind of Barry Goldwater."
>
> The thrust of the two main articles in Ginzburg's magazine was that Senator Goldwater, the Republican nominee for President of the United States, had a severely paranoid personality and was psychologically unfit to be President. This was supported by a fraction of replies to an alleged poll which the magazine had mailed to some 12,000 psychiatrists—hardly a scientific diagnosis, but a potent political hatchet job.
>
> Naturally, Senator Goldwater promptly sued Mr. Ginzburg

and *Fact* magazine for libel. A Federal court jury in New York granted the Senator a total of $75,000 in punitive damages from Ginzburg and *Fact* magazine. *Fact* shortly was to be incorporated into another Ginzburg publication, *Avant Garde.* The U.S. court of appeals sustained this libel award. It held that under the New York Times against Sullivan decision a public figure could be libelled if the publication was made with actual malice; that is, if the publisher knew it was false or acted with reckless disregard of whether it was false or not.

So once again Ralph Ginzburg appealed to the Supreme Court which, in due course, upheld the lower courts' judgment in favor of Senator Goldwater and declined to review the case.

However, Mr. Justice Douglas again dissented on the side of Mr. Ginzburg, along with Mr. Justice Black. Although the Court's majority did not elaborate on its ruling, the dissenting minority decision was based on the theory that the constitutional guarantees of free speech and free press are absolute.

This decision was handed down January 26, 1970.

Yet, while the Ginzburg-Goldwater suit was pending in the Federal courts, clearly headed for the highest court in the land, Mr. Justice Douglas appeared as the author of an article in *Avant Garde,* the successor to *Fact* in the Ginzburg stable of magazines, and reportedly accepted payment from Ginzburg for it.

(116 *Cong. Record* 11912 *et seq.*)

I understand why Gerald Ford might think I should not have sat in the *Ginzburg* v. *Goldwater* lawsuit. But I actually did not realize that *Avant Garde* was a Ginzburg publication. Indeed, up to that time it never occurred to me to inquire as to the ownership of any of the publishers that printed my articles.

Ford went on to denounce me for writing my book *Points of Rebellion,* published in 1970, and he bore down heavily on the fact that parts of that book had appeared in *Evergreen.* I had, however, had no part in placing the excerpts there. I had heard of *Evergreen* and knew it to be a low-grade publication. Without notice to me, an employee of my publisher, which held these magazine rights, contracted with *Evergreen.* I learned about it only when it was too late to stop the sale.

The rest of Ford's criticism of me related to my association with the Parvin Foundation, which, as I have mentioned, was engaged in an educational program involving people in underdeveloped nations but which was accused of having gambling and underworld connections. Ford also charged that my association with the Center for the Study of Democratic Institutions was a mark of culpable conduct.

Another charge arose out of the fact that I knew Juan Bosch, then the newly elected President of the Dominican Republic. He had come to Washington in 1963 and asked me if I could get the Parvin Foundation to launch a literacy program in his country. The board agreed and we worked with Leroy Collins, the head of the Broadcasters Association, to prepare a TV literacy program. By the time of the coup against Bosch there were about fifty of the eighty TV films ready for the start of the series. Juan Bosch also asked me to advise the members of his committee who were writing a new constitution. Ford conceived of that association with Bosch as a device for me to get a gambling casino license on the island—which was sheer fantasy.

On May 13, 1970, Nixon wrote the House Judiciary Committee when it was considering a resolution to impeach me:

> The power of impeachment is, of course, solely entrusted by the Constitution to the House of Representatives. However, the executive branch is clearly obligated both by precedent and by the necessity of the House of Representatives having all the facts before reaching its decision, to supply relevant information to the legislative branch, as it does in aid of other inquiries being conducted by committees of the Congress, to the extent compatible with the public interest.

As a result of Nixon's instructions to the FBI and the CIA, hundreds of documents concerning me were turned over to the House. The tempo quickened in the executive branch, so that some forty federal agents spent an amount of time investigating me equivalent to one man working fifteen years for eight hours a day.

The Nixon letter about me came back to plague him in 1974 when Congress was seeking documents from the White House concerning the impeachment of Nixon himself. Ford's statement that impeachment means anything the House says it means came home to roost, for in 1974 Ford, as Vice President, was taking Nixon's position that an impeachable offense includes only criminal acts.

Ford and his associates were planning a Roman Holiday in the summer of 1970, with my impeachment the main event. First on their program was obscenity. I, along with Black, had consistently taken the position that under the First Amendment, censorship is barred, even of things that we do not like, such as obscenity or pornography. So one of the things Ford had planned was a series of anti-smut hearings in which they would try to cast me in the role of a proponent of smut.

Second, they would use the Mafia. The propaganda which had been emanating linked me with the underground, the Mafia, all of which was totally fictitious. I never met, knew or had any dealings with a Mafia man. Ford had planned to bring underworld characters to the stand in conjunction with my hoped-for appearance, and thus create a public impression that organized crime was sitting on the Supreme Court.

Third, they planned to go into gambling. They spread the rumors that I was tied up with Bobby Baker in Las Vegas deals, and that my Dominican Republic project was merely a cloak to get a gambling casino there, all of which was sheer fabrication. But in that ring of the circus they would try to create the impression that the gambling syndicates were represented on the Court.

Fourth would be the ring of their circus to display the subversives. The John Birch Society in the state of Washington had long advertised that I was the only "known Communist" in Yakima County. My votes on the Court to give Communists procedural due process, and to extend to them the protection of the First Amendment, led to the easy charges from the right that I was a Communist. This indeed was the ring of the circus that Louis Wyman of New Hampshire easily exploited when he was Attorney General of that state and later its congressman. His great contribution, according to his propaganda, was that but for him and his vigilant investigation of Communism, New Hampshire would long before have been an enclave of Soviet Russia. His loss of the Sweezy case in our Court (354 U.S. 234), which he personally argued, was very much a part of his crusade.

Perhaps none of these programs would have been particularly relevant in a normal year, but even though they were all built on completely manufactured facts, the timing was perfect for a circus. Nineteen-seventy was an election year; and Nixon and Agnew had decided it should be a year of relentless exposure, reckless charges and the spread of malicious lies. They were masters in the art of the politics of destruction.

The upshot was that the matter of my impeachment was referred to the House Judiciary Committee, of which Emanuel Celler was chairman. Celler instructed the committee to form a subcommittee on the impeachment, and it was that group that conducted an investigation.

When the matter first broke into the open as a result of Gerald Ford's speech of April 15, 1970, my close friends in the legal business had a meeting in Clark Clifford's office. They included Si Rifkind and some of his staff, Sidney M. Davis and Dave Ginsburg, as well as Clark Clifford and some of his staff. Clifford indicated to me at once that he could not serve as my counsel because *Points of Rebellion* severely criticized President Johnson (not as severely as Clifford criticized him after he resigned as Secretary of Defense; nevertheless, Clark thought it would compromise him).

My own personal choice for counsel was Si Rifkind; he accepted at once and did a splendid job.

When the House Judiciary Committee announced it was taking action I wrote the chairman, saying I had appointed Judge Simon H. Rifkind of New York as my attorney, and had instructed him to make available to the committee any or all of my files the committee wanted to see, including bank accounts, income-tax returns, etc. Si Rifkind assembled a considerable staff in Washington—Ramsey Clark and Gerald Stern, and Dan Levitt of his office. Dave Ginsburg was brought in at my suggestion, and he assigned to the job one of his associates, Fred W. Drogula. I also asked Charles Miller, a former law clerk, of Covington & Burling, to work with the Rifkind firm on the matter, and Warren Christopher of O'Melveny & Myers in Los Angeles, another law clerk. Then there was Vern Countryman of Harvard Law School, who spent the summer of 1970 doing a lot of research. All told, they were eight in number.

Judge Rifkind worked out an arrangement with the committee whereby its members would indicate which documents they would like to see from my files; Rifkind's staff would dig them out, make Xerox copies and turn the copies over to the committee. The staff did a tremendous amount of work on the historical nature of impeachment proceedings—the procedures, precedents, and the like—and made their memos available to the special subcommittee. Since I had been on the Court for over thirty years, there were a goodly number of special complaints from disgruntled litigants, and these were all investigated, many of them in the field. Many old records of state courts were also gone through. So it was a busy summer in 1970.

It is easy to make a charge against a public official and put him to the test of defending himself. But when the accuser is the federal government itself with all its resources behind it, the person attacked is at a tremendous disadvantage. It costs money, and a lot of it, to transport eight lawyers across the country, put them up at hotels, pay telephone calls and all the incidentals necessary to do the work. Over and above all that, there is the question of compensating the lawyers.

This was a matter of some importance because the Rifkind firm, the Covington firm and the O'Melveny firm, not to mention Dave Ginsburg, heading a smaller firm, were all busy law firms having many, many cases in the federal courts, a lot of which reached the Supreme Court. Since these firms were representing me, I stepped out of all the cases in which they were counsel and on which the Supreme Court acted either on motions or on the merits. Moreover, the continuing nature of the investigation, and the fact that after the final report four congressmen—Robert Sikes of Florida, Joe Waggoner of Louisiana, William Scott of Virginia and Louis Wyman of New Hampshire—insisted that there be a further investigation, raised the prospect that this would be an ongoing matter for which I would need counsel for some months or even a year. Hence, as long as these men were my counsel I could not sit in any of their cases. Yet I did not want the fact that they once had been my lawyers to be a continuing disqualification after the ordeal was over. So I insisted they all be paid a fee and not serve *pro bono publico.* In other words, I wanted the case handled professionally. That raised a staggering problem as to how a salaried person can afford the luxury of these long-range investigations.

My connection with the Parvin Foundation had been well known for years. The directors included Robert M. Hutchins, the eminent educator, and Robert Goheen, president of Princeton. Harry Ashmore was a director, and so was Sidney M. Davis, New York lawyer of note and a close friend of mine who had once been Hugo Black's law clerk. As I mentioned earlier, the foundation financed a program whereby mature young men, between the ages of twenty-five and thirty-five, were brought from underdeveloped nations for a year at the Woodrow Wilson School at Princeton. We were indeed turning out future prime ministers trained in the values of the democratic society. By 1969 we had graduated sixty to eighty people. The foundation also sponsored a series of convocations around the world, dealing with the problems of the developing nations. The Conference on Latin American Problems held in Mexico City on September 9 and 10, 1969, had been organized by me—the one that ended with the publication in 1971 of the book *Holocaust or Hemispheric Co-op: Cross Currents in Latin America.*

Moreover, we had been trying to do with Latin American students at UCLA what we had done at Princeton with Asian and African students. The UCLA program had not worked out well. UCLA had been attracting Latinos, but they were all English-speaking. That meant they were in the upper crust—the elite of South America. I thought it important to comb the lower strata to find an occasional genius and give him some education in Jeffersonian and Madisonian ideas. But the search for that kind of person involved extraordinary efforts, for it meant finding him and equipping him with English and then starting his political education. That meant increasing burdens on the president of the foundation. Those considerations, plus the fact that between June 1968 and April 1969 I had had three major operations, made me think I should relinquish my presidency in favor of a younger man. A meeting was indeed scheduled for April 9, 1969, at which I planned to resign. But my third operation caused that meeting to be postponed, and my resignation was actually tendered on May 21, 1969, a few weeks after the story broke about Abe Fortas' association with Wolfson.

Some of the press took my resignation as a confession of "guilt"—guilt of what, I never knew. There was no conflict of interest with Court matters. My activities all related to overseas education in the democratic cause.

Some criticized me for taking a fee from the foundation. It did pay me $12,000 a year, on which I paid income tax. Out of the balance I paid all my expenses, never billing the foundation for any of them. There was net profit, though as one lawyer who reviewed the whole file of the foundation said, "You worked for twenty-five cents an hour."

But that was not all. The foundation had received an eighth interest in a trust fund from Albert Parvin, the *res* being a mortgage on a hotel in Las Vegas, as I have mentioned. The directors of the foundation finally got rid of the investment, though it took a couple of years. Parvin had given stock to the foundation, which so far as anyone knew was "pure." But after the stock was received, the company acquired interests in Las Vegas.

The Washington, D.C., *Evening Star* charged that I had been practicing law by giving legal advice to Parvin. They wanted an indictment and/or impeachment. In fact, however, the foundation had hired a lawyer—Carolyn Agger, eminent in the tax field—to advise it on tax matters.

Furthermore, the directors felt that Parvin, the donor, was playing too active a role in managing the portfolio, so they engaged a fiscal agent in New York City to handle the investments. But Parvin raised hell with that arrangement. Our lawyer kept sending me advice and messages and I routinely passed them on to the board, particularly to Parvin, the one who kept kicking over the traces. Calling that "practicing law" was evidence enough of the animus behind the drive to get me off the Court.

The sensationalism also was reflected in the stories linking Parvin with Wolfson, though so far as I know the only thing they had in common was that both were Jewish and financiers. Linking me with Abe Fortas was, of course, the motive; and the fact that his wife, Carolyn Agger, was the foundation's lawyer was enough to make a "common nest" out of the Fortas and Douglas cases.

One of the staff members of the Court summed it all up when he said, "When you put the devil in the White House, almost anything can happen."

While the storm over me was still raging, Warren E. Burger was nominated as Chief Justice by Nixon. Burger had been a director of the Mayo Foundation for some time, receiving a fee for his services, but that fact caused hardly a ripple when the hearings were held before the Senate Judiciary Committee and when the nomination reached the floor of the Senate.

The moral is: What is demanded of one judge is not necessarily demanded of another. The issue is basically an ideological one: How does the judge vote?

On June 10, 1969, the Judicial Conference adopted the following code to be obeyed by district judges and judges of the Courts of Appeal:

> A judge in regular active service shall not accept compensation of any kind, whether in the form of loans, gifts, gratuities, honoraria or otherwise, for services hereafter performed or to be performed by him except that provided by law for the performance of his judicial duties.
>
> Provided however, the Judicial Council of the Circuit (or in the case of courts not part of a circuit, the judges of the court in active service) may upon application of a judge approve the

acceptance of compensation for the performance of services other than his judicial duties upon a determination that the services are in the public interest or are justified by exceptional circumstances and that the services will not interfere with his judicial duties. Both the services to be performed and the compensation to be paid shall be made a matter of public record and reported to the Judicial Conference of the United States.

At the June 13 Conference, Warren urged that the Court adopt the foregoing resolution as its own. Earl Warren said he had made many speeches and written articles, but never for a stipend. Black spoke strongly against the resolution, saying that Congress should pass all the laws and that judges do not have the right to supervise other judges. Harlan said he had never voted in an election since coming to the Court and had accepted very few invitations, never for a fee. I remarked that Black's dissent in *Chandler* v. *Judicial Council* (382 U.S. 1003), expressed my view, and while I was in favor of publicity of income of all public officials, I was strongly against a licensing system for judges.

Stewart said he had accepted a few fees but that it was "wrong" and that he would never do it again.

White, who apparently had accepted some fees, did not say much.

Marshall, who said he had received as much as $10,000 for one lecture, said he would never do it again, as it was all "wrong."

Brennan, who had been very active—to his credit, I thought—in outside affairs, said he was canceling all engagements, resigning from the bar associations, engaging in no outside activities with or without fees.

Apparently the consensus was that it was not ethical for a Justice to take an honorarium. The talk had gone on for two hours when I gave my opinion. I said that I had written nearly thirty books and that it was not "wrong" for me to do so, that everything I had done I would do again, that giving lectures for travel expenses and for a fee was up to the individual Justice. I told the Conference what my principles were:

1. I would not speak to an industry group for expenses or for a fee, because they would be apt to have cases coming to the Court.

2. University groups or lecture forums were different—they were not litigants; the propriety of what a Justice did was dependent on what he said.

3. Some members of the Court—notably Warren, Stewart and Marshall—went overseas at the State Department's expense. I thought that was improper, as it implicated a Justice in the Executive's overseas policies. I traveled at my own expense.

All in all, I said that what a Justice did was up to him and his own conscience. I added that engaging in outside activities was good for the administration of justice, as it kept a judge from becoming a prisoner within the narrow confines of "the law."

The Court was divided and decided to defer action. I had prepared a dissent that read as follows:

> I have long favored full disclosure by all elected or appointed federal officials of the amount of their income and the source of it. I have never owned any stocks or bonds or other securities —apart from federal government bonds—since I have been on the Court. I indeed disposed of the small amount of government bonds I owned, as the Government is the largest litigator in the federal courts. The full disclosure requirements of the Judicial Conference therefore meet with my approval.
>
> I strongly oppose the permit system by which one group of judges determines whether it is in the "public interest" for a judge to write a book or article or give a lecture or make a speech.
>
> That system of surveillance is plainly unconstitutional for the reasons stated by Mr. Justice Black dissenting in *Chandler* v. *Judicial Council,* 382 U.S. 1003, 1004.
>
> I have no plan or project which would collide with the new permit system. But I protest with all my being the principle of surveillance, control, and censorship now saddled on judges. Apart from constitutional procedures for disciplining them, judges can no more be controlled respecting their thoughts and ideas than can preachers, editors, or authors. What judges do with their private lives is their own business.

While the Court did not adopt Warren's recommendation, the Judicial Conference (representing the circuit and district judges) did adopt it in substance. Each circuit and district judge was to disclose his income twice a year. From stocks and bonds? No. From trust funds? No. From real estate or other market transactions? No. The only disclosure required was of income from lectures or income from book royalties.

Hugo Black, true to principle, refused to file. I felt philosophically the same way, but I was under attack and the whole Nixon power was out to remove me. So I compromised—I did file; but with each filing I protested the discrimination being shown against some judges and the favor being shown the rich judges who fattened on dividends from stocks, on interest from bonds, on capital gains, and on real estate investments.

When, in June 1975, I received the John Muir Award from the Sierra Club I raised the question of whether acceptance of that award should disqualify me from sitting as a judge in any future Sierra Club case. I said:

> I have resolved that it should not, so long as I have had nothing whatsoever to do with any of these cases. At times in the past Mrs. Douglas and I have hiked or in other ways protested certain government projects. In such cases the protester should not sit as judge because he has at least a partial commitment on the merits. The question of conflict of interest is not always easy to resolve. The disclosure rules covering federal judge's income clouds the whole problem. A judge need not disclose income from stock investments, in trading in securities, or in interest in banks. He must, however, disclose all income from books, articles, reviews and the like. What rational difference can be made between the two is difficult to state. Income, whether in royalties or in dividends from a particular company would be relevant only if the judge contemplated sitting in the case.
>
> If we turn the clock back a hundred years and find the future of a federal judge in the slave trade, disclosure of that fact would have had an acute bearing on his fitness to sit in slave cases. I know a judge whose family owned practically the entire equity in a railroad, yet he sat in cases involving that railroad; and so far as is apparent he did a fair and impartial job. But the present disclosure rules do not require disclosure of the nature of the interest in business or industrial enterprises —only the amount of income from them regardless of their number or size.
>
> If the target is the prejudices of the judge, what he writes or puts into speeches is relevant, but producing a Zane Grey movie would hardly be revealing in that respect. If prejudice

of the judge were the target, then the category of his investments would be the most revealing.

I was once a director of the Sierra Club. I received no salary and I ceased being a member because the meetings were usually in San Francisco and I could not attend many meetings.

Being a director made me realize that my views as to policy in environmental matters do not always jibe with those of others, but my views are patterned after models. John Muir was a powerful influence in my early years. So were Gifford Pinchot, Clarence Darrow, Hiram Johnson, and William Borah. But I would not dream of stepping out of a case merely because Borah's name or Darrow's name was on the brief. A lawyer who is friendly with someone on the bench carries a heavy burden of proving he is right on the merits. For a friend on the bench bends over backwards to take that factor out of his decision.

The appearance of fairness is to me as important as fairness itself. For example, television and radio programs often pay small fees to those who appear on them. My practice has been not to accept them, no matter how small. The Court sits in judgment on FCC orders that are very important to the industry and it is important that no one with the power of final decisions have a financial interest with the applicant.

The New Testament was a powerful influence in my life; so was Thorstein Veblen. Such prejudices are the reason why confirmation by the Senate is important in the federal system. They are often components in the forces leading to a particular decision. Yet it would have been a gross erosion of judicial independence to have undertaken to drive Hugo Black out of a case involving First Amendment rights merely because he felt passionately that the First Amendment was the heart of our constitutional system.

On April 30, 1970, I had my physical checkup with Dr. Thomas Connally and went directly to Court. As we were sitting I wrote Black a note telling him: "My blood pressure is 140 over 70—which indicates that the Bastards have not got me down." Black responded: "Fine! Keep your smile! Mr. Ford and his crowd cannot get you. I am delighted to know of the results of your medical examination. After my appointment to the

Court when my opponents were after me most viciously, I told my wife we needed an inscription on our bed reading as follows, 'This too will pass away.' And it did. So will the flurry and the noise about you. Of course you know I am on your side. Keep up your smile and health and read the 13th chapter of 1st Corinthians now and then."

Out of the blue, in July 1970 came a letter from my old friend Irving Brant, who had, without any urging or solicitation, prepared a paper that he sent to Celler on the scope of the impeachment power; the theme of that paper was that unless the impeachment satisfies the standards of Article II, Sec. 4, of the Constitution—namely, "conviction of treason, bribery, or other high crimes and misdemeanors"—any removal from office would be a bill of attainder. I think the Brant report (published in book form in 1972 and entitled *Impeachment—Trials and Errors*) had a powerful impact in the House.

Ford's case against me was built up by analogy to Fortas. Yet the fact that I had a salary from the foundation seemed immaterial. As I have said, Burger was on the Mayo Foundation board while he was a member of the U.S. Court of Appeals. Blackmun, soon to reach the Court, likewise had long served on the board of the Mayo Foundation while he was a member of the U.S. Court of Appeals. Judges were often on law school faculties and received salaries for their services. Activities of that kind run afoul of ethical standards if they implicate the judicial function; they are unwise if they require the energy needed for court work. But when one has the time and energy, I always thought, outside civic endeavors were good for judges; and I seemed to meet the requirements, as the work of the Court never took more than four days a week for me.

In the late spring of 1970 Warren Burger told me that he had word from the President and that the President was very much opposed to this effort to impeach me. When I told that to Earl Warren he roared with laughter and said, "If that son of a bitch is opposed to your impeachment he could stop it in one minute."

That was my feeling—that Nixon, being an artist of dissimulation, would, if he planned to use a knife against a person, send him a message of cheer, friendship and good will.

While the investigation was under way in the House Judiciary Committee, Congressman Waggoner of Louisiana announced that he had hired Benton L. Becker, a lawyer of Kensington, Maryland, to help make a separate investigation of me. In the summer of 1970 Becker contacted Louis Wolfson through his attorney, William O. Bitman, and asked to interview Wolfson. In a letter of September 3, 1970, Becker referred to "my clients, Congressmen Ford, Wyman, Waggoner, and others." At that time Wolfson had finished a prison term, had been indicted again on another matter, and had been found guilty but not sentenced. His conviction was on appeal to the Second Circuit Court of Appeals. Becker, in his letter to Bitman, referred to Wolfson's "recent plight" and stated that he, Becker, "would be anxious to assist him in any way available to me." In a letter dated September 8, Bitman wrote to his client Wolfson saying that Becker had told him that if Wolfson "cooperated," "the Congressmen he referred to probably could be of some assistance" to Wolfson "in connection with the second case."

Becker was anxious to get Wolfson to testify against me. Wolfson, whom I remember having met only once, said he had no information adverse to me and declined to pursue the matter with Becker. Wolfson, however, sent copies of the correspondence to Si Rifkind, who in due course sent them on to Chairman Celler of the House Judicial Committee.

Becker's reference to "Ford, Wyman, Waggoner, and others" led us to think that he probably was in contact with the Department of Justice, which, after all, controls the course of criminal litigation, and with the President, who dispenses the pardoning power. The letters indicated that Nixon was seizing on every possible straw to make a case against me.

The hate mail to my office increased in tremendous volume; and it seemed for a while that the only segment of the press at all friendly were the cartoonists. Yet that was not a fair measure of public opinion. By chance my wife and I were at the dinner meeting of the Antitrust Section of the ABA in Washington, D.C. We received tremendous applause when introduced, which indicated the deep feeling of lawyers as to the implications of the Ford charges on the independence of the judiciary. Later, when Mrs. Douglas and I attended the ABA meeting in St. Louis in August 1970, I also received a tremendous ovation from the lawyers at the Assembly, which probably was not entirely spontaneous. We had been invited as guests of Bernard Segal, the president, who, I am sure, did much to spread the word as to what the nature of the battle was.

The truth is that by 1970 American society had become fairly submissive, dissent was becoming more and more difficult, and people marched more and more in conformity.

Those in public office are of course often "fair game" for politicians and muckrakers. As I related in the first volume of my autobiography, when Thomas Dewey, one of my classmates at law school, was running for the presidency in 1948, I was invited to Portland to address the Oregon Bar Association. The state bar put me up at the Benson Hotel. When I checked out after the speech, the hotel told me the bill had been paid by the bar association.

In October I was back in Washington, D.C. and the campaign was getting hotter and hotter. One day I received a telephone call from a friend, Lindsay C. Warren, the Comptroller General. He told me that the Oregon Bar Association, instead of paying my Benson Hotel bill itself, had routed it to a shipbuilding company that had a contract with the United States Navy, and that the contractor had in fact paid my hotel bill. The Comptroller knew about it because one of Dewey's men had been tipped off and had checked with him to make certain the facts were correct. Lindsay Warren looked into it and reported to Dewey that the facts were correct, and he promptly called me.

I called the Benson Hotel to get the amount of the bill and sent a check off in payment of it. I wrote a rather excoriating letter to the president of the Oregon Bar Association for doing this thing that linked a member of the Supreme Court with a highly unethical practice. The bill, as I recall, was not much over $50, but the story would have made headlines and been in all the papers. It would perhaps have hurt Truman, who had tried to get me to be his running mate. And how would any judge, who had been the guest of a bar association, like to be told later that his expenses had been paid by the Mafia?

Henry Hess, former U.S. Attorney in Portland, Oregon, had been a close personal friend over the years. We had been on many a fishing trip into the woods, and we had sat for hours around my fireplace in the big tamarack cabin I built in the early forties on the Lostine River in eastern Oregon. His greatest disappointment was that I had not given him the nod in 1944 to nominate me as FDR's running mate. He had his speech memorized, and when in a relaxed mood before an open fire, would give it over and again. He was a powerful speaker and a dear friend who died at an advanced age on March 15, 1974. I did not hear from him while the impeachment proceedings were on, nor did I hear from him after they were over. But some time later one thing he did brought tears to my eyes.

For years he had run the campaign for Edith Green, who served in the House from Oregon for twenty years. But in 1970 she made a speech about me, endorsing the Ford proposal to launch an impeachment investigation against me. Henry went directly to Edith Green and told her that in light of her statement against me, he and his brother Lee would no longer be associated with her campaign for Congress but would throw their financial support and weight behind her opponent. He did just that. Like the friendship of Abe Fortas, Si Rifkind, Sidney Davis and Joe Kennedy, his was a total commitment. One does not often find that quality in people anywhere.

What happened as a result of the impeachment proceedings of 1970 is a matter of history recorded in the Reports of June 20* and September 17, 1970,† of the Special Subcommittee of the House Judiciary Committee headed by Emanuel Celler. These Reports canvassed all the charges made by Ford, and each of them was found to be without any substance.

When the September 17, 1970, Report of the Committee was finally released to the public on December 16, 1970, the press was agitated and wanted interviews. Television crews were staked out at our home and at the exit of the Supreme Court garage. I arranged for a press conference at the Court, to which everyone was invited and at which I made the following statement:

> When the investigation of me was launched nine months or so ago, I instructed my counsel, the Honorable Simon H. Rifkind, to make available to the Select Committee all my files relevant to the inquiry, with no restraints as to privilege or immunity.
>
> The Select Committee has now performed its constitutional duties and I will try to continue to perform mine. I have always been proud to be a member of the Court, an institution which I think all will agree is distinguished at least in one respect— it always has been and always will be stoutly independent.
>
> We have a fine Chief Justice and it is a pleasure to work with

*Associate Justice William O. Douglas, Interim Report, Special Subcommittee on H. Res. 920, H. Jud. Committee, 91st Cong., 2d Sess.
†Associate Justice William O. Douglas, Final Report, Special Subcommittee on H. Res. 920, H. Jud. Committee, 91st Cong., 2d Sess.

him. Our newest member, Harry Blackmun, is what the mountain men I knew in the Far West would call a "stout fellow." There's no higher compliment.

I have not read the Report, even casually, up to now. The Report will speak for itself. And it would probably not be appropriate for me to comment on it in any event.

Perhaps I should add a few words. I have been to practically every country in the world.

This beautiful America cannot be equaled, I assure you.

The internal problems of America are the problems of humanity everywhere. Racial conflicts, religious intolerance, ideological wars rage on all the continents.

Unlike most countries, we have the political instruments to resolve them. I speak of the Bill of Rights.

Our main problem, apart from pollution, is to make our multiracial, multireligious, multi-ideological community a viable one.

To the young generation—in whom I have unbounded faith —I say, let that be your goal.

When you succeed—as you will—the world will witness the greatest Renaissance ever known. So I say to you—

Keep the Faith!

That was, however, not the end of the matter. In 1972 the Dayton, Ohio, press started rehashing the old record. The only thing "new" it came up with was that Meyer Lansky, the alleged Mafia figure in hiding in Israel, was linked to Parvin and therefore to me because Parvin gave him a finder's fee on a Las Vegas real estate deal. The trouble with that "new" evidence was that it happened (1) before the Parvin Foundation was formed and (2) before I ever met Parvin. Moreover, at no time did I ever know Lansky or have any relations of any kind with him.

In the spring of 1969 I had talked with Earl Warren, the then Chief Justice, just before his retirement in June. I told him I too wanted to retire because it was my thirtieth anniversary on the Court. So he made arrangements to reserve a suite of offices for himself and another suite for me as a retired Justice. But as early as May and June of 1969 the hound dogs, having got Justice Fortas to resign, had started baying at me. I felt that if I did retire under those circumstances, it would be an indication that somewhere, somehow, there had been some deep dark sin committed and that I was seeking to escape its exposure. So I changed my mind about retiring and decided to stay on indefinitely until the last hound dog had stopped snapping at my heels—and that promised to be a long time, as Nixon naturally wanted to have my seat on the Court.

After the impeachment proceedings were over and closed, in fact more than a year later, Hugo L. Black, Jr., who practices law in Florida, talked with me on a visit to Washington, D.C. He said that while the matter was pending before the House, several Southerners came to him asking if he would not sound out his father concerning their plans to remove me from the Court. Young Hugo took the matter up with his father, who said, "I have known Bill Douglas for thirty years. He's never knowingly done any improper, unethical or corrupt thing. Tell his detractors that in spite of my age, I think I have one trial left in me. Tell them that if they move against Bill Douglas, I'll resign from the Court and represent him. It will be the biggest, most important case I ever tried."

The message brought tears to my eyes, for by then Justice Black had died and I had never had the chance to thank him.

Chapter XVI

The End
of a Cycle

The basic jurisdiction of the Court was not changed much during my time, though by Article III of the Constitution, as we have seen, Congress can make our appellate jurisdiction as it likes. In one ten-year period I counted fifty-four bills that had been introduced in the House or Senate to take jurisdiction away from the Court as respects problems or areas where someone had been annoyed at our holdings. But none of these bills passed. In 1925 Congress, influenced by Chief Justice Taft, reduced our obligatory jurisdiction and increased our discretionary jurisdiction. With the passage of time the number of cases filed with us increased.

The First Congress provided by law that every litigant had the right to represent himself (Act of September 24, 1789, Sec. 35, 1 Stat. 92), but it soon became apparent that the expenses of litigation were too heavy for the poor to pay. It took a long time for a remedy to be provided.

The *in forma pauperis* practice at long last came into the federal system in 1892. The House Report stated:

> The question is narrowed therefore to this: Will the Government allow its courts to be practically closed to its own citizens, who are conceded to have valid and just rights, because they happen to be without the money to advance pay to the tribunals of justice? Even then they will not have an equal chance

with other men, for [*sic*] men able to prosecute gain cases that would be dismissed by the court had it the power. Many humane and enlightened States have such a law, and the United States Government ought to keep pace with this enlightened judgment.

The Government will not determine questions involving the liberty of the citizen without furnishing him his witnesses on his demand. Property is next in importance, and the less a man has the more important it is to him, and the more reprehensible to deprive [*sic*] of it unjustly.

(H. Rep. No. 1079, 52d Cong., 1st Sess., p. 2)

The overall statistics for *in forma pauperis* cases at the federal level since 1892 are not available. Even the Court's statistics are not complete. In 1930, the first year for which statistics are available, 22 *in forma pauperis* petitions were filed; the figures have steadily mounted until in the 1977 Term the number was 2,015. (In 1978 the number dropped to 1,939.)

Most of these cases come from prisons, and practically all of them have already been before two courts or more. So it is the rare case that needs a third or fourth review. Moreover, a very large percentage of the *in forma pauperis* cases before us present frivolous questions. For various reasons we seldom grant the petition and we hear oral argument in only a very small percentage of the cases. For example, of the 2,015 filed during the 1977 Term, only 14 were heard by the Court. Approximately 2 percent of these cases are subject to summary disposition—grant and affirm, or grant and reverse, or vacate and remand—all without oral argument. Nevertheless, the processing of these cases is an important function of the Court.

The tradition of giving them close scrutiny traces back to Chief Justice Hughes, who had a nose for injustices inflicted in police precincts and in the courts. An account of his energizing influence is summed up by one of his law clerks, Edwin McElwain in the *Harvard Law Review* (63, 5, 21–26 [1949]).

The growth of the laymen's interest in the law and demand for its protection were due to numerous circumstances. First is the growing complexity of the law. Social Security presented a maze for the unsophisticated when the statute, regulations and court decisions were pieced together. It usually took a law-trained mind to find the path and keep on it. A housing complaint might lead to any one of nineteen different agencies that only an expert can identify.

Second was the growth of federal and state laws dealing with the right of minorities. Since 1868 Congress has passed eleven civil rights acts, and five of these came in this century—the Civil Rights acts of 1957, 1960, 1964, 1968, and the Voting Rights Act of 1965. The upward surge in sentiment for the realization of the equality in political matters and economic opportunity implicit in the Bill of Rights created mounting claims.

Third was the increase in communication of ideas across the world. Buckminster Fuller properly said that the radio communized the world. News from far-off places stirred discontent in many places and led to dreams of a better life here. Courts did not sit to design blueprints for our society. But the dream of a better world had repercussions in hundreds of lawsuits each year filed in courts or germinated in administrative agencies.

Fourth was the growing discontent with and the unrest in the prisons. It was the Jacksonian theory which conditioned the start of the prison system in this country. The idea was that environment caused crime. Hence, if a prisoner were kept in solitary, having only his thoughts and his conscience for companions, he would reform. It took some years for that philosophy to become passé and some more years for ideas of rehabilitation to take hold. To say that rehabilitation became our pattern would be a distortion. Some prisons headed in that direction, but there was little progress; and increased discontent among prisoners, as measured by petitions and complaints filed, multiplied.

Until well into this century it was generally true that a prisoner was considered to be a "nonperson" in the constitutional sense. That has been changed by many decisions, perhaps the most dramatic being *Johnson* v. *Avery* (393 U.S. 483), where federal habeas corpus was used to relieve a prisoner from solitary confinement in a state prison, since solitary confinement was used to bar the prisoner from the exercise of a federal right—viz., access to federal habeas corpus.

In Russia, Khrushchev transformed the insane asylum to an institution for dissenters. We have never stooped quite so low. But the discontent over civil commitments—and the mounting demand for procedural due process—has fed an increasingly large number of cases into state and federal courts. Bruce Ennis' book *Prisoners of Psychiatry* shows how coercion is used to commit troublesome or eccentric people—

those usually being poor, old or black. After our school-segregation cases were decided in 1954, a young man from Georgia came into my office saying he had just escaped from an asylum there. It appeared his family had had him committed because he long maintained that school-children should not be segregated by races.

The use of the asylum to commit those who have been convicted of a crime has given rise to mounting litigation. And court decisions have emphasized that due process can no longer be a stranger to institutions whose names or operations identify them with "criminally insane" or "defective delinquents." (*Jackson* v. *Indiana,* 406 U.S. 715; *McNeil* v. *Patuxent Institution,* 407 U.S. 245.)

It would be a mistake to assume, however, that the bulk of prisoners' complaints relate to criminal matters. People in prison have a wide variety of problems—Social Security, domestic relations, veterans' rights, landlord-tenant problems involving their families, and the like. The central problem of a prisoner often relates to civil rights far removed from his criminal trial and conviction.

The fifth reason for the mounting need for lawyers are three decisions of the Court. In 1932, in the famous Scottsboro case, the Court held (in *Powell* v. *Alabama,* 287 U.S. 45) that in state trials involving capital offenses, an indigent defendant was entitled to a court-appointed lawyer.

In 1963 in *Gideon* v. *Wainwright* (372 U.S. 335) we held that in all felony cases an indigent is entitled to a court-appointed lawyer.

In 1972 we held in *Argersinger* v. *Hamlin* (407 U.S. 25) that in any case where a jail sentence is imposed, the sentence must be preceded by a trial in which an indigent is represented by a court-appointed lawyer.

The American Bar Association sounded one of the first calls to lawyers across the nation to respond to these mounting needs. (13 *La. Bar Journ.* 11 [1965]; 90 Rep. Amer. Bar Assoc. 391 (1965); 50 *Amer. Bar Assoc. J.* 1103 [1964].) Justice Powell, then president of the ABA, made clear in his reports that "the poor" embraced not only the indigents but the "20 per cent of our population in the lowest income bracket" (51 *Amer. Bar Assoc. J.* 3 [1965]).

By 1965 the Office of Economic Opportunity was providing legal aid. These services covered civil as well as criminal cases. Neighborhood Legal Services, an arm of OEO, spread across the land. Several hundred groups were formed; and soon the crunch was on, for landlords and finance companies no longer got easy default judgments. Rights of tenants and rights of borrowers were now also presented; and howls from the powers that be went up—most notably from Ronald Reagan and Richard Nixon.

Branches of the traditional Legal Aid Society also multiplied their efforts. Soon we had law schools working under the aegis of state supreme courts and making arrangements for students under supervision to render aid to indigents in civil cases (such as Social Security questions) and minor offenses on the criminal side. Maryland, I thought, experienced a minor rennaissance in that regard. The University of Virginia Law School was organized to use student help in processing state and federal habeas corpus petitions filed by indigents in the Commonwealth. In 1972 Virginia passed a law authorizing a state judge in charge of criminal offenses to appoint lawyers to represent indigents in matters of state prisons, regarding "any legal matter relating to their incarceration." The machinery was to be set in motion by the superintendent of the state penitentiary making a request of the county or city attorney, and the attorney would be paid from the state's criminal fund plus reasonable compensation (L. 1972 C. 773). The New York University Law School with its student participation was a powerful force in helping the Vera Institute and the Supreme Court of Manhattan launch their amazingly successful bond program. The law school at Moscow, Idaho, arranged for students to work on legal problems in Idaho's prisons. The examples ran into the dozens; there is no area of the country that has not been inspired by these unsung law school efforts.

The response to the demand for and the need of legal services was greatly accelerated by the various bar associations. The oncoming generation responded dramatically by flocking in large numbers to the law schools, practically swamping them. I am not sure what all the influences in that drive were. One reason at least was the existence of a deep concern on the part of youngsters that parts of our legal and economic system needed restructuring and that no one not skilled in the law could really be the architect.

Some legal communes were formed. Some public-interest law firms were created. More and more emerging young lawyers became identified with ad hoc committees, aimed at correcting one condition and serving one cause. Large law firms freely gave their young recruits time to spend, say, 10 percent or 15 percent of their working hours in public-interest projects.

Lawyers are not the sole participants in these ongoing projects. In 1972 the Public Interest Economics Center was established in Washington; it seeks to apply sociology and the discipline of economics to public-policy questions. Its interests are wide, ranging from housing, mass transit, energy, the environment and taxation. In these and other innumerable ways the energy and idealism of the new generation have become a yeast in the problems of society and in the workings of the law. Older heads began to realize that they were not necessarily wiser than the younger ones, so a new force started to shape our thinking and in part our lives.

It is, I think, a very healthy prospect for an America that is vital and aware. Our budgetary priority in the seventies was still armaments, but there were a few signs that our real priority was the quality of our lives.

Federally funded legal-aid services were reshaped. The opponents of the system, though not numerous, had powerful voices. Some thought that public aid should not be extended to legal aid for the poor if it involved political questions. Yet there is no question more political than the disenfranchisement of minorities. Some cases revealed local practices that use literacy tests to eliminate minorities from voting. In some sections in the North they were used against blacks and Americans of Puerto Rican birth. They have been used in the West to disenfranchise Chicanos who may be literate in Spanish but unable to pass English literacy tests. Removal of cases of that vast political impact from legal aid was a grave injustice.

Others placed a "political" cast on a case if it was a suit against state or federal officials. Yet one of the great characteristics of our system of government is that it places the people above government, making them indeed the real sovereigns. Our Constitution also makes clear that government should not ride the backs of people. So bringing suit against officials, whether under Civil Rights acts or under other heads of jurisdiction, was in the finest American tradition.

Some thought legal aid should leave the prisons alone, that prison problems were administrative problems over which the prison authorities had exclusive jurisdiction. Yet prison officials also represent government and at times they denied prisoners federal and/or state constitutional rights. Prisoners, as I have said, are not "nonpersons." The Bill of Rights extends to them as well as to others. We can never expect to have healthy prison regimes unless those behind the walls enjoy the same constitutional rights as those outside.

Some, like Ronald Reagan, inveighed against legal aid when it was used to bring class actions (which take place when one case is brought on behalf of separate individuals with the same complaint). But true class actions—as lawyers know—serve a high purpose in making unnecessary dozens of separate suits which the meager legal-aid resources could never finance.

We as a people cannot afford to deny the poor the same range of legal remedies which the affluent enjoy. We often act as if we are a government of the corporations, by the corporations, and for the corporations. As I have said, corporations were early held to be "persons" within the meaning of the Fourteenth Amendment, thus giving them the shield of the Constitution as well as the sword of financial power and political clout. Black and I took the opposed position that corporations are not "persons" within the meaning of the Fourteenth Amendment. What a vast difference in economic and business history that view would have made. The dominant view, which we opposed, pervaded American life from roughly 1882 to 1937. But starting with the Roosevelt Court, America was rediscovered—it is the individual that our Constitution and Bill of Rights exalt. Only through the individual is our real quality of life revealed.

That quality is improved by the tensions we remove, by the frictions we reduce, by the prospect of true equality of opportunity for every human in our midst. To some, the law may look like grubby business, but it is the instrument through which law and order are achieved. Equally important, it is the device through which justice is dispersed.

As Learned Hand once said: "If we are to keep our democracy, there must be one commandment: Thou shalt not ration Justice" (264 F 2d 35).

Under Hughes the Court sat five days a week two weeks a month, holding our Conferences on Saturday. Under Warren we sat four days a week two weeks a month, holding our Conferences on Friday. Under Burger we sat three days a week two weeks a month, holding our Conferences on Friday. Under Hughes, we had put some cases on the summary calendar, though most were on the regular calendar that gave each side one hour. By 1968, Warren's time, we had most of our argued cases on the summary calendar which gave each side thirty minutes.

Each argument day lasted four hours, so under Hughes, if all cases argued one week were on the regular calendar, we should hear 20 cases a week. Under Warren, if all cases were on the summary calendar, we'd hear only 16 cases a week. Under Burger's three-day week we heard 12 cases a week. Yet by the time Warren retired and Burger replaced him, the docket of the Court was running at about 4,000 cases a Term.

We sat hearing cases two weeks a month for seven months, very seldom hearing cases argued later than April. That seven months gave us fourteen weeks of argument. Under Hughes we would at that rate hear 280 cases, under Warren 224 cases, under Burger 168.

Yet a hue and cry went up to relieve the Court of its burden. Several proposals were made, one to create a mini-court which would pass on all petitions to the Court and indicate the ones we should hear. A variation was to design a system under which we would spin off to a mini-court cases that we thought needed additional review. A prestigious committee headed by Paul Freund of Harvard submitted a report to the Chief Justice recommending some such action.

The reason given was that we were overworked—which was insane. The full-fledged opinions written for the Court in recent Terms were:

1970	109	1975	138
1971	129	1976	126
1972	140	1977	129
1973	140	1978	130
1974	123		

When I went on the Court in the 1938 Term, there were 138 Court opinions; in 1939, 137; in 1940, 165; in 1941, 151.

The per curiams (unsigned opinions from the Court) in argued cases added to those Terms were:

1970	20	1975	16
1971	24	1976	22
1972	18	1977	8
1973	8	1978	8
1974	20		

In the 1938 Term there were 11 per curiams; in 1939, 6; in 1940, 4; in 1941, 11.

Our work, as measured by the opinions written for the Court, certainly did not increase during the Burger years. They had dropped low under Vinson. (In the 1953 Term we only wrote 83 Court opinions.) But under Hughes and Stone, opinion writing for the Court increased. Black and I wrote over 60 opinions for the Court a Term. Stone, Black and I wrote over 90 opinions a Term for the Court. Under Burger it was seldom that any Justice wrote as many as 18, the average being about 16.

How, then, could it be said that we were overworked and needed relief? The number of filings had increased to about 4,000 a Term, yet 2,500 of them came from prisons. We read them all carefully and out of them came nuggets of history: *Chambers* v. *Florida* (309 U.S. 227), *White* v. *Texas* (310 U.S. 530), *Hamilton* v. *Alabama* (358 U.S. 850), *Griffin* v. *Illinois* (351 U.S. 12), *Gideon* v. *Wainwright* (372 U.S. 335) and *Miranda* v. *Arizona* (384 U.S. 436). But the great bulk of the prison cases (about 99 percent) tendered frivolous issues. Moreover, the cases tendered us had already been through at least two courts and usually through three to ten courts, as many involved collateral attacks on their convictions.

Reading these cases takes time, and exposure to their problems is an adult-education program for the Justices. By sitting five days a week *à la* Hughes we could hear 20 cases a week and increase our output by nearly 100 cases a Term. Slackening off under Burger gave us more and more idle time. The impassioned plea for relief from overwork was ridiculed by Earl Warren, (59 *ABAJ* July 1973, p. 725) and Tom Clark —both retired; by Justice Brennan (*Ibid.,* August 1973, p. 835) and me on the Court; by Peter Weston, a former law clerk of mine on the law faculty at Michigan; by Eugene Gressman, former law clerk to Murphy (*Ibid.,* March 1973, p. 253) and many many others.

Yet the drive continued, even the American Bar Association joining the hue and cry. That hue and cry could not possibly entail any resemblance of proof of overwork. The real reason was political—and lay deeper. It had to do, to a large extent, with an attempt to enforce "law and order," not "constitutional" law and order, especially in regard to the Court's role in interpreting the Fourth and Fifth Amendments.

Our Fourth Amendment is demanding. It bars "unreasonable searches and seizures," and it requires warrants for the arrest of a person or for a search of his premises or effects to be based on a finding by a magistrate that "probable cause" exists for believing that a crime has been committed. These safeguards were products of our 1776 Revolution. British revenue officers used general warrants to search the colonists for smuggled goods. The general warrant was good for any time and place; it was official license to ransack a place. The American who made himself famous proclaiming against the general warrant was James Otis (to whom I have referred previously), who engaged in a famous debate about the general warrant in February 1761 in Boston. The feelings of the Americans ran so high over that debate that John Adams reported: "Then and there the child independence was born."

In 1914 the Court held that evidence seized in violation of the Fourth Amendment could not be used in federal courts against the person in a criminal prosecution (*Weeks* v. *United States,* 232 U.S. 383). That was the well-known exclusionary rule. Three possible sanctions could have been used: civil action against the violators, criminal prosecution of them, or exclusion of the illegally obtained evidence. Of these, only the last is a real sanction.

Our Court in 1966 by a five-to-four vote held in the famous Miranda case (384 U.S. 436) that when the police zero in on a suspect and hold him for a crime, there can be no in-custody interrogation unless he is warned of his right to remain silent, is advised of his right to counsel, and is furnished counsel if he is too poor to hire one.

That was the regular FBI procedure in apprehending suspects. The *Miranda* rule, however, was adopted not because of the FBI, but because of the right to counsel guaranteed by the Sixth Amendment and the right of an accused to remain silent guaranteed by the Fifth Amendment.

The cry went up that *Miranda* made the police helpless and ineffective. But the FBI had lived under those standards, and it was probably the most efficient police force in the world.

In 1928 the Court had ruled that a wiretap was not a "search" within the meaning of the Fourth Amendment (*Olmstead* v. *United States,* 277 U.S. 438), Taft writing for the majority, with Holmes, Brandeis and Butler dissenting. It was in that case that Holmes dubbed wiretapping "dirty business." In 1967 the Court in another six-to-three decision overruled *Olmstead* (*Berger* v. *New York,* 388 U.S. 41).

The outlawry of torture and coercion was one purpose of the provision in our Fifth Amendment that no person "shall be compelled in any criminal case to be a witness against himself." The concept of self-incrimination goes deeper than that. There were hated oaths that minorities were required to take. The Star Chamber exacted the oath *ex officio* that the Puritans hated (the phrase *ex officio* meant "by mere office of judge"). The examination of a suspect was made without any necessity of a charge being levied against him. It was a procedure taken over from the ecclesiastical courts. The accuser was seldom, if ever, known. The defendant, or even the witness, was forced under oath to tell the truth and answer any question that might be asked of him. The great rebellion against the oath arose because of the compulsion to answer unknown charges and the inability to know who the accusers were. Any refusal on the part of a person to answer constituted contempt, which was followed by imprisonment. Any partial or incomplete answers were followed by imprisonment. Those who believed in liberty of thought and speech violently opposed that oath.

In a famous trial held in 1637, John Lilburn refused the oath, stating: "But as for that Oath that was put upon me, I did refuse to take it as a sinful and unlawful oath, and by the strength of my God enabling me, I will never take it, though I be pulled in pieces by wild horses, as the ancient Christians were by the bloody tyrants in the Primitive Church."

In 1803 Levi Lincoln was Attorney General, and Jefferson was President. A contest arose over the midnight judicial appointments made by John Adams before he retired, litigation that ended in the Supreme Court with *Marbury* v. *Madison* (5 U.S. 137). The Attorney General was asked certain questions. Among the reasons Lincoln gave for not replying was his view that "He ought not to be compelled to answer anything which might tend to criminate himself" (*Id.* 144). The impasse was resolved and the objection was not pursued. But no stigma was attached to Lincoln for raising the objection. Later Madison offered Lincoln a seat on the Supreme Court, an offer Lincoln rejected because he was fast becoming blind.

Thirty years ago the plea of self-incrimination fell into popular disrepute. The phrase "Fifth Amendment Communist" was freely used to condemn recalcitrant witnesses. What people forgot was that the plea of self-incrimination preserved by the Fifth Amendment was made for the protection of the innocent as well as the guilty. Innocent people are often caught up in ambiguous circumstances that might lead to prosecution or even conviction. Moreover, under established decisions, a witness would be considered to waive the privilege if he testified to any episode that might be considered a link in the chain of evidence against him (*Rogers* v. *United States*, 340 U.S. 367, 373). He must object at the very threshold or find himself caught in a web from which he cannot escape.

Since our Fifth Amendment provides that no person "shall be compelled in any criminal case to be a witness against himself," it was early argued that the clause became applicable only in a criminal prosecution against the person claiming the privilege. But in 1892 it was held that while the clause was applicable in criminal prosecutions, it was also applicable in investigations that might lead to a criminal prosecution (*Counselman* v. *Hitchcock,* 142 U.S. 547, 562–563). And so American federal law proceeded for years on the basis that the prosecution may not make its case against an accused out of admissions or concessions forced from him by fear or coercion of any kind, whether those admissions are made before legislative committees; or to a policeman seeking to obtain a confession from a suspect or prisoner; or to a governmental agency seeking by a requirement of regulation the admission of the ingredients of a crime; or to mental coercion as well as to physical force; or to subtle pressures as well as coarse and vulgar ones.

There were some on the Court, including Black and me, who felt that the Self-Incrimination Clause gave a general right to silence. Talmudic law disallows the use of confessions because many are attributed to the Death Wish made manifest by completely fabricated confession or by exaggerations of the real facts. Our Self-Incrimination Clause has not, however, been construed as containing a general right of silence. Four Justices in 1896 felt that the protection against "compelled" testimony was the desire to give a witness complete immunity from prosecution for specific admissions made, for prosecution for collateral crimes whose clue was furnished by the "compelled" testimony, for the shame and infamy that might descend on him for any such "compelled" admissions (*Brown* v. *Walker,* 161 U.S. 591). And in 1956 two of us shared the same view (*Ullmann* v. *United States,* 350 U.S. 422). Yet that has never been the majority view. Moreover, in *Kastigar* v. *United States* (406 U.S. 441), decided in 1972, the Court cut down the Fifth Amendment from its original historic breadth. It had long been held that an immunity granted by government to a witness if he testified covered all of the transaction. In *Kastigar* a five-to-two decision held that an immunity was adequate provided it barred the use of the compelled testimony against the witness in a subsequent criminal prosecution. Such immunity, called "use immunity," would bar prosecution of a witness only for the exact crime about which he testified. For example, it would protect the witness against robbery to which he testified, but not against assault that accompanied the robbery. *Kastigar* watered down the protection of the Fifth Amendment to fit the Nixon idea of "law and order," not the constitutional standard that had existed for nearly two hundred years.

Up to the advent of the Burger Court, the Fourth and Fifth Amendments were rather liberally construed, apart from exceptions noted. Harlan, Stewart and White wrote many of our solid decisions. But Nixon wanted more and more expansion of the power of the police, less and less protection to the citizen. That is why he needed not four Court appointments, but nine.

Under Hughes, Stone and Warren, the Court had struck many "blows for liberty"—to use Jack Garner's old phrase. The civil rights of minorities had been vindicated over and over again, yet oppressive neighborhood and community racial problems festered. Bureaucracy got stronger, but the protests of employees grew louder. Power of government increased; and though the rights of the nonconformist were protected by the Court, the chances of the nonconformist in general diminished. The old game of doing in the Indian fell into different hands; for a while it had looked as if the Indians might win justice, but that was short-lived.

Prisoners were still subject to severe restrictions as to books they could read, letters they could receive, letters they could write, the extent to which their religious principles would be honored in prison discipline and management.

The death penalty had been held unconstitutional, but the voices of the Establishment for its reinstatement were strident.

School busing—long used in consolidated school districts to provide students with an excellent though distant school—was now used to break down segregated school systems. Busing of blacks fifty miles a day past white schools had long been the custom; busing blacks shorter distances to a better white school was now viewed with alarm.

American police—save for the FBI—had long been picked for their brawn, not their brain. American police were rough, ready to use vigilante methods to elicit "the truth." Holding the police to the requirements of the Constitution set up a powerful resistance, fanned by fear germinated by yellow journalists.

Mormon prayers in public schools or Moslem prayers in public schools would be anathema to Catholics or Baptists. Yet Catholics or Baptists in control of school boards saw no reason why their prayers should not be imposed on all public-school children.

Allowing a woman to have a lawful abortion in the first trimester of her pregnancy loosened a storm of protest in the country, though three of the four Nixon appointees to the Court approved.

What was happening, I think, was that Nixon and his followers wanted *law and order.* What the Hughes, Stone and Warren Court had been giving the country was *constitutional law and order.* The Establishment did not like it; few church groups liked it. Minority groups were pleased, yet their exultation created fear in the hearts of the majority.

The Richard Nixon–George Wallace philosophy of irritating those raw spots activated forces that prevented the healing of past conflicts. *Constitutional law and order* was shouted down. *Constitutional law and order* was discarded so that Watergate could flourish. The king (in the White House) and his council (the fourth branch of government) made up the laws as they worked their mischievous designs and plundered the nation.

Everyone was promised "a piece of the action," which meant plunder to Agnew, inside "cuts" off public projects to others, and brazen manipulation of government by others to serve the interests of clients.

The Supreme Court, an important symbol of the Constitution, was shoved more and more into the background. Cutting down its "workload," letting it sit one day a week (i.e., two a month) would keep it alive as a symbol but it would no longer be able to vindicate rights of the oppressed. It would keep the solemn, benign face of the Establishment, letting the country know that "law and order" was in control and that the Constitution—so far as human rights were concerned—was kept on ice.

That is the real reason why the Supreme Court was said to be overworked and should let others do its work. Big business, power politics, the regime under which the poor got poorer and the rich richer could not possibly have it otherwise.

There was always one comfort at day's end. When I shut the door to my home I seemed to shut out the world, for the house was set near the northern line of the lot and faced south looking into an acre and a half of lawn, garden and woods. I nourished a bevy of quail there. Raccoon and muskrats came to visit, and cardinals stayed all winter long. Across a rear fence was a city reservoir lined with grassy banks where turkey vultures forgathered on clear days to dry out their wings, one morning over a hundred appearing. On my side of the fence was a Himalayan rose bush germinated from seed which I brought back in 1951, and nearby was a cutting from a famous magnolia owned and admired by Andrew Jackson, who grew the tree in Nashville.

I like to sit in the woods at night and listen to the nocturnal sounds. There is the lovely call of the loon that takes me back in memory to the lakes of Minnesota and Canada. By March the spring peepers, swarming crickets and bullfrogs are in chorus. And on nights when gales blow and the people in nearby Washington, D. C. are asleep, the sky is filled with great travelers—mallard ducks, pintails, mergansers and some Canadian geese pass noisily overhead. Most impressive of all are the white whistling swans that often settle for a rest on the river below me and then take off in a tremendous armada.

Those travelers of the air seldom meet the travelers on the ground. Each passes in the dark as if wholly oblivious of the other. Each is on an important mission of life and reproduction. I have always felt more at home with those that travel overhead. They are "lesser" species than men—not craven, corrupt or deceitful, and bent on using the biosphere to sustain and perpetuate their lives, not to destroy it nor to exclude all others.

"Darest Thou . . ."

And darest thou, then,
To beard the lion in his den,
The Douglas in his hall?

These lines of Sir Walter Scott were
drummed into my ears from my earliest days. Mother would recite
them to us out of her reverence for Father and her conviction that
through his bloodstream we had acquired an indomitable will and capacity for achievement. Her purpose was to create a distinctive person,
one with courage and fortitude to take on the big battles of life that lay
ahead. She also had a little speech nominating me for President of the
United States, and always recited the Walter Scott lines at the start and
end of her speech.

Actually, Mother knew little about Douglas history. As I researched
it later I realized that the Douglas influence within England was largely
on the side of the Establishment, for the kings raised their tribal chiefs
pretty much as some shahs of Iran used tribal chiefs to strengthen their
hold on the people. Thus, as the tribal leaders became heads of military
or diplomatic missions, a Douglas might well be a judge or finance
minister in some faraway segment of the Empire. The Douglases did,
however, acquire a reputation for being strong.

Whatever their achievements, the picture Sir Walter Scott drew had
a great impact on this element of the Douglas clan in Yakima, and
greatly influenced my life—not as to what I did, but how I did it. Thus,
the night I left Yakima for Wenatchee to hop a freight train that would
take me East, to New York City and law school, Mother walked with

me to the alley where I picked up my shortcut to the freight yard. She held my head in both her hands and kissed me. Then she spoke the lines of Sir Walter Scott and added, "Go to it, son, you have the strength of ten because your heart is pure," by which I am sure she meant that I would always have that tenfold strength *if* my heart was pure.

Her words helped carry me through that long, tedious freight-car journey to New York City. As I described in the first volume of my autobiography, while I rode the rods by day, under the car, at night I was usually in a boxcar. By dusk it would fill up with people who were not only unkempt and smelly but suspicious-looking as well. By seven o'clock each car was pretty well organized with a committee in charge. Its function was to sort out the desirable from the undesirable. The committee members were liable to toss out the door any brother who seemed to have money, with the result that no well-heeled traveler could ride free. I'd wake at night hearing a scream or a yell and look up to see someone—on the count of three—fly across the car through the open door, followed by another scream and a third as the poor devil hit the ground on the side of the rail line.

Some of the boxcar occupants would try to buy the right not to be tossed into the darkness, and they would often ask me to use my influence to keep the price low. While I did save some frightened souls from being tossed into the pitch-darkness, I refused to be a broker or arbiter over the price to be paid. These men were all strangers to me, yet I learned from whispered conversations that they thought that I was the richest of all—apparently because I looked so clean. At times I was nervous when I went to sleep, wondering whether I would be the next one to be tossed out the side door.

By the time I reached New York I felt that nothing worse could possibly happen to me in the future. The "Darest Thou" philosophy had not made my freight-car journey safe, but it gave promise of greener pastures in the days ahead and helped me through the other barriers and obstacles I was to encounter in my life.

Appendix

The Constitution
of the United States of America

We the People *of the United States, in Order to form a more perfect Union, establish Justice, insure domestic Tranquility, provide for the common defence, promote the general Welfare, and secure the Blessings of Liberty to ourselves and our Posterity, do ordain and establish this Constitution for the United States of America.*

ARTICLE I.

SECTION 1. All legislative Powers herein granted shall be vested in a Congress of the United States, which shall consist of a Senate and House of Representatives.

SECTION 2. The House of Representatives shall be composed of Members chosen every second Year by the People of the several States, and the Electors in each State shall have the Qualifications requisite for Electors of the most numerous Branch of the State Legislature.

No Person shall be a Representative who shall not have attained to the Age of twenty-five Years, and been seven Years a Citizen of the United States, and who shall not, when elected, be an Inhabitant of that State in which he shall be chosen.

[Representatives and direct Taxes shall be apportioned among the several States which may be included within this Union, according to their respective Numbers, which shall be determined by adding to the whole Number of free Persons, including those bound to Service for a Term of Years, and excluding Indians not taxed, three fifths of all other Persons.][1] The actual Enumeration

---

[Note: The Constitution and all Amendments are presented in their original form. Items which have since been amended or superseded, as identified in the footnotes, are bracketed.]

1. Changed by Section 2 of the Fourteenth Amendment.

shall be made within three Years after the first Meeting of the Congress of the United States, and within every subsequent Term of ten Years, in such Manner as they shall by Law direct. The Number of Representatives shall not exceed one for every thirty Thousand,[2] but each State shall have at Least one Representative; and until such enumeration shall be made, the State of New Hampshire shall be entitled to chuse three, Massachusetts eight, Rhode-Island and Providence Plantations one, Connecticut five, New-York six, New Jersey four, Pennsylvania eight, Delaware one, Maryland six, Virginia ten, North Carolina five, South Carolina five, and Georgia three.

When vacancies happen in the Representation from any State, the Executive Authority thereof shall issue Writs of Election to fill such Vacancies.

The House of Representatives shall chuse their Speaker and other Officers; and shall have the sole Power of Impeachment.

SECTION 3. The Senate of the United States shall be composed of two Senators from each State, [chosen by the Legislature thereof,][3] for six Years; and each Senator shall have one Vote.

Immediately after they shall be assembled in Consequence of the first Election, they shall be divided as equally as may be into three Classes. The Seats of the Senators of the first Class shall be vacated at the Expiration of the second Year, of the second Class at the Expiration of the fourth Year, and of the third Class at the Expiration of the sixth Year, so that one-third may be chosen every second Year; [and if Vacancies happen by Resignation, or otherwise, during the Recess of the Legislature of any State, the Executive thereof may make temporary Appointments until the next Meeting of the Legislature, which shall then fill such Vacancies.][4]

No Person shall be a Senator who shall not have attained to the Age of thirty Years, and been nine Years a Citizen of the United States, and who shall not, when elected, be an Inhabitant of that State for which he shall be chosen.

The Vice President of the United States shall be President of the Senate, but shall have no Vote, unless they be equally divided.

The Senate shall chuse their other Officers, and also a President pro tempore, in the absence of the Vice President, or when he shall exercise the Office of President of the United States.

The Senate shall have the sole Power to try all Impeachments. When sitting for that Purpose, they shall be on Oath or Affirmation. When the President of the United States is tried, the Chief Justice shall preside: And no Person shall be convicted without the Concurrence of two thirds of the Members present.

Judgment in Cases of Impeachment shall not extend further than to removal from Office, and disqualification to hold and enjoy any Office of honor, Trust or Profit under the United States: but the Party convicted shall nevertheless be liable and subject to Indictment, Trial, Judgment and Punishment, according to Law.

SECTION 4. The Times, Places and Manner of holding Elections for Senators and Representatives, shall be prescribed in each State by the Legislature thereof; but the Congress may at any time by Law make or alter such Regulations, except as to the Place of Chusing Senators.

---

2. Ratio in 1965 was one to over 410,000.
3. Changed by Section 1 of the Seventeenth Amendment.
4. Changed by Clause 2 of the Seventeenth Amendment.

The Congress shall assemble at least once in every Year, and such Meeting shall [be on the first Monday in December,][5] unless they shall by Law appoint a different Day.

SECTION 5. Each House shall be the Judge of the Elections, Returns and Qualifications of its own Members, and a Majority of each shall constitute a Quorum to do Business; but a smaller number may adjourn from day to day, and may be authorized to compel the Attendance of absent Members, in such Manner, and under such Penalties as each House may provide.

Each House may determine the Rules of its Proceedings, punish its Members for disorderly Behavior, and, with the Concurrence of two thirds, expel a Member.

Each House shall keep a Journal of its Proceedings, and from time to time publish the same, excepting such Parts as may in their Judgment require Secrecy; and the Yeas and Nays of the Members of either House on any question shall, at the Desire of one fifth of those Present, be entered on the Journal.

Neither House, during the Session of Congress, shall, without the Consent of the other, adjourn for more than three days, nor to any other Place than that in which the two Houses shall be sitting.

SECTION 6. The Senators and Representatives shall receive a Compensation for their Services, to be ascertained by Law, and paid out of the Treasury of the United States. They shall in all Cases, except Treason, Felony and Breach of the Peace, be privileged from Arrest during their Attendance at the Session of their respective Houses, and in going to and returning from the same; and for any Speech or Debate in either House, they shall not be questioned in any other Place.

No Senator or Representative shall, during the Time for which he was elected, be appointed to any civil Office under the Authority of the United States, which shall have been created, or the Emoluments whereof shall have been encreased during such time; and no Person holding any Office under the United States, shall be a Member of either House during his Continuance in Office.

SECTION 7. All Bills for raising Revenue shall originate in the House of Representatives; but the Senate may propose or concur with Amendments as on other Bills.

Every Bill which shall have passed the House of Representatives and the Senate, shall, before it become a Law, be presented to the President of the United States; If he approve he shall sign it, but if not he shall return it, with his Objections to that House in which it shall have originated, who shall enter the Objections at large on their Journal, and proceed to reconsider it. If after such Reconsideration two thirds of that House shall agree to pass the Bill, it shall be sent, together with the Objections, to the other House, by which it shall likewise be reconsidered, and if approved by two thirds of that House, it shall become a Law. But in all such Cases the Votes of both Houses shall be determined by Yeas and Nays, and the Names of the Persons voting for and against the Bill shall be entered on the Journal of each House respectively. If any Bill shall not be returned by the President within ten Days (Sundays excepted) after it shall have been presented to him, the Same shall be a Law, in like Manner as if he had signed it, unless the Congress by their Adjournment prevent its Return, in which Case it shall not be a Law.

---

5. Changed by Section 2 of the Twentieth Amendment.

Every Order, Resolution, or Vote to which the Concurrence of the Senate and House of Representatives may be necessary (except on a question of Adjournment) shall be presented to the President of the United States; and before the Same shall.take Effect, shall be approved by him, or being disapproved by him, shall be repassed by two thirds of the Senate and House of Representatives, according to the Rules and Limitations prescribed in the Case of a Bill.

SECTION 8. The Congress shall have Power To lay and collect Taxes, Duties, Imposts and Excises, to pay the Debts and provide for the common Defence and general Welfare of the United States; but all Duties, Imposts and Excises shall be uniform throughout the United States;

To borrow money on the credit of the United States;

To regulate Commerce with foreign Nations, and among the several States, and with the Indian Tribes;

To establish an uniform Rule of Naturalization, and uniform Laws on the subject of Bankruptcies throughout the United States;

To coin Money, regulate the Value thereof, and of foreign Coin, and fix the Standard of Weights and Measures;

To provide for the Punishment of counterfeiting the Securities and current Coin of the United States;

To establish Post Offices and post Roads;

To promote the Progress of Science and useful Arts, by securing for limited Times to Authors and Inventors the exclusive Right to their respective Writings and Discoveries;

To constitute Tribunals inferior to the supreme Court;

To define and punish Piracies and Felonies committed on the high Seas, and Offenses against the Law of Nations;

To declare War, grant Letters of Marque and Reprisal, and make Rules concerning Captures on Land and Water;

To raise and support Armies, but no Appropriation of Money to that Use shall be for a longer Term than two Years;

To provide and maintain a Navy;

To make Rules for the Government and Regulation of the land and naval Forces;

To provide for calling forth the Militia to execute the Laws of the Union, suppress Insurrections and repel Invasions;

To provide for organizing, arming, and disciplining the Militia, and for governing such Part of them as may be employed in the Service of the United States, reserving to the States respectively, the Appointment of the Officers, and the Authority of training the Militia according to the discipline prescribed by Congress;

To exercise exclusive Legislation in all Cases whatsoever, over such District (not exceeding ten Miles square) as may, by Cession of particular States, and the acceptance of Congress, become the Seat of the Government of the United States, and to exercise like Authority over all Places purchased by the Consent of the Legislature of the State in which the Same shall be, for the Erection of Forts, Magazines, Arsenals, dock-Yards, and other needful Buildings;—And

To make all Laws which shall be necessary and proper for carrying into Execution the foregoing Powers, and all other Powers vested by this Constitution in the Government of the United States, or in any Department or Officer thereof.

SECTION 9. The Migration or Importation of such Persons as any or now existing shall think proper to admit, shall not be prohibited by the prior to the Year one thousand eight hundred and eight, but a tax or dut. be imposed on such Importation, not exceeding ten dollars for each Pers.

The privilege of the Writ of Habeas Corpus shall not be suspended, unle when in Cases of Rebellion or Invasion the public Safety may require it.

No Bill of Attainder or ex post facto Law shall be passed.

No capitation, or other direct, Tax shall be laid, unless in Proportion to the Census or Enumeration herein before directed to be taken.[6]

No Tax or Duty shall be laid on Articles exported from any State.

No Preference shall be given by any Regulation of Commerce or Revenue to the Ports of one State over those of another: nor shall Vessels bound to, or from, one State, be obliged to enter, clear, or pay Duties in another.

No Money shall be drawn from the Treasury, but in Consequence of Appropriations made by Law; and a regular Statement and Account of the Receipts and Expenditures of all public Money shall be published from time to time.

No Title of Nobility shall be granted by the United States: And no Person holding any Office of Profit or Trust under them, shall, without the Consent of the Congress, accept of any present, Emolument, Office, or Title, of any kind whatever, from any King, Prince, or foreign State.

SECTION 10. No State shall enter into any Treaty, Alliance, or Confederation; grant Letters of Marque and Reprisal; coin Money; emit Bills of Credit; make any Thing but gold and silver Coin a Tender in Payment of Debts; pass any Bill of Attainder, ex post facto Law, or Law impairing the Obligation of Contracts, or grant any Title of Nobility.

No State shall, without the Consent of the Congress, lay any Imposts or Duties on Imports or Exports, except what may be absolutely necessary for executing its inspection Laws: and the net Produce of all Duties and Imposts, laid by any State on Imports or Exports, shall be for the Use of the Treasury of the United States; and all such Laws shall be subject to the Revision and Controul of the Congress.

No State shall, without the Consent of Congress, lay any duty of Tonnage, keep Troops, or Ships of War in time of Peace, enter into any Agreement or Compact with another State, or with a foreign Power, or engage in War, unless actually invaded, or in such imminent Danger as will not admit of delay.

ARTICLE II.

SECTION 1. The executive Power shall be vested in a President of the United States of America. He shall hold his Office during the Term of four Years, and, together with the Vice-President, chosen for the same Term, be elected, as follows.

Each State shall appoint, in such Manner as the Legislature thereof may direct, a Number of Electors, equal to the whole Number of Senators and Representatives to which the State may be entitled in the Congress: but no Senator or Representative, or Person holding an Office of Trust or Profit under the United States, shall be appointed an Elector.

---

6. But see the Sixteenth Amendment.

[The Electors shall meet in their respective States, and vote by Ballot for two persons, of whom one at least shall not be an Inhabitant of the same State with themselves. And they shall make a List of all the Persons voted for, and of the Number of Votes for each; which List they shall sign and certify, and transmit sealed to the Seat of the Government of the United States, directed to the President of the Senate. The President of the Senate shall, in the Presence of the Senate and House of Representatives, open all the Certificates, and the Votes shall then be counted. The Person having the greatest Number of Votes shall be the President, if such Number be a Majority of the whole Number of Electors appointed; and if there be more than one who have such Majority, and have an equal Number of Votes, then the House of Representatives shall immediately chuse by Ballot one of them for President; and if no Person have a Majority, then from the five highest on the List the said House shall in like Manner chuse the President. But in chusing the President, the Votes shall be taken by States, the Representation from each State having one Vote; a quorum for this Purpose shall consist of a Member or Members from two thirds of the States, and a Majority of all the States shall be necessary to a Choice. In every Case, after the Choice of the President, the Person having the greatest Number of Votes of the Electors shall be the Vice President. But if there should remain two or more who have equal Votes, the Senate shall chuse from them by Ballot the Vice-President.][7]

The Congress may determine the Time of chusing the Electors, and the Day on which they shall give their Votes; which Day shall be the same throughout the United States.

No person except a natural born Citizen, or a Citizen of the United States, at the time of the Adoption of this Constitution, shall be eligible to the Office of President; neither shall any Person be eligible to that Office who shall not have attained to the Age of thirty-five Years, and been fourteen Years a Resident within the United States.

[8][In Case of the Removal of the President from Office, or of his Death, Resignation, or Inability to discharge the Powers and Duties of the said Office, the same shall devolve on the Vice President, and the Congress may by Law, provide for the Case of Removal, Death, Resignation or Inability, both of the President and Vice President, declaring what Officer shall then act as President, and such Officer shall act accordingly, until the Disability be removed, or a President shall be elected.]

The President shall, at stated Times, receive for his Services, a Compensation, which shall neither be encreased nor diminished during the Period for which he shall have been elected, and he shall not receive within that Period any other Emolument from the United States, or any of them.

Before he enter on the Execution of his Office, he shall take the following Oath or Affirmation:—"I do solemnly swear (or affirm) that I will faithfully execute the Office of President of the United States, and will to the best of my Ability, preserve, protect and defend the Constitution of the United States."

SECTION 2. The President shall be Commander in Chief of the Army and Navy of the United States, and of the Militia of the several States, when called

---

7. Superseded by the Twelfth Amendment.
8. This clause has been affected by the Twenty-fifth Amendment.

into the actual Service of the United States; he may require the Opinion in writing, of the principal Officer in each of the executive Departments, upon any subject relating to the Duties of their respective Offices, and he shall have Power to Grant Reprieves and Pardons for Offenses against the United States, except in Cases of Impeachment.

He shall have Power, by and with the Advice and Consent of the Senate, to make Treaties, provided two-thirds of the Senators present concur; and he shall nominate, and by and with the Advice and Consent of the Senate, shall appoint Ambassadors, other public Ministers and Consuls, Judges of the supreme Court, and all other Officers of the United States, whose Appointments are not herein otherwise provided for, and which shall be established by Law: but the Congress may by Law vest the Appointment of such inferior Officers, as they think proper, in the President alone, in the Courts of Law, or in the Heads of Departments.

The President shall have Power to fill up all Vacancies that may happen during the Recess of the Senate, by granting Commissions which shall expire at the End of their next Session.

SECTION 3. He shall from time to time give to the Congress Information of the State of the Union, and recommend to their Consideration such Measures as he shall judge necessary and expedient; he may, on extraordinary Occasions, convene both Houses, or either of them, and in Case of Disagreement between them, with Respect to the Time of Adjournment, he may adjourn them to such Time as he shall think proper; he shall receive Ambassadors and other public Ministers; he shall take Care that the Laws be faithfully executed, and shall Commission all the Officers of the United States.

SECTION 4. The President, Vice President and all civil Officers of the United States, shall be removed from Office on Impeachment for, and Conviction of, Treason, Bribery, or other high Crimes and Misdemeanors.

ARTICLE III.

SECTION 1. The judicial Power of the United States, shall be vested in one supreme Court, and in such inferior Courts as the Congress may from time to time ordain and establish. The Judges, both of the supreme and inferior Courts, shall hold their Offices during good Behaviour, and shall, at stated Times, receive for their Services, a Compensation, which shall not be diminished during their Continuance in Office.

SECTION 2. The judicial Power shall extend to all Cases, in Law and Equity, arising under this Constitution, the Laws of the United States, and Treaties made, or which shall be made, under their Authority;—to all Cases affecting Ambassadors, other public Ministers and Consuls;—to all Cases of admiralty and maritime Jurisdiction;—to Controversies to which the United States shall be a Party;—to Controversies between two or more States;—between a State and Citizens of another State;—between Citizens of different States;—between Citizens of the same State claiming Lands under Grants of different States, and between a State, or the Citizens thereof, and foreign States, Citizens or Subjects.

In all Cases affecting Ambassadors, other public Ministers and Consuls, and those in which a State shall be Party, the supreme Court shall have original Jurisdiction. In all the other Cases before mentioned, the supreme Court shall have appellate Jurisdiction, both as to Law and Fact, with such Exceptions, and under such Regulations as the Congress shall make.

The trial of all Crimes, except in Cases of Impeachment, shall be by Jury; and such Trial shall be held in the State where the said Crimes shall have been committed; but when not committed within any State, the Trial shall be at such Place or Places as the Congress may by Law have directed.

SECTION 3. Treason against the United States, shall consist only in levying War against them, or in adhering to their Enemies, giving them Aid and Comfort. No Person shall be convicted of Treason unless on the Testimony of two Witnesses to the same overt Act, or on Confession in open Court.

The Congress shall have Power to declare the Punishment of Treason, but no Attainder of Treason shall work Corruption of Blood, or Forfeiture except during the Life of the Person attainted.

ARTICLE IV.

SECTION 1. Full Faith and Credit shall be given in each State to the public Acts, Records, and judicial Proceedings of every other State. And the Congress may by general Laws prescribe the Manner in which such Acts, Records and Proceedings shall be proved, and the Effect thereof.

SECTION 2. The Citizens of each State shall be entitled to all Privileges and Immunities of Citizens in the several States.

A Person charged in any State with Treason, Felony, or other Crime, who shall flee from Justice, and be found in another State, shall on demand of the executive Authority of the State from which he fled, be delivered up, to be removed to the State having Jurisdiction of the Crime.

[No Person held to Service or Labour in one State, under the Laws thereof, escaping into another, shall, in Consequence of any Law or Regulation therein, be discharged from such Service or Labour, but shall be delivered up on Claim of the Party to whom such Service or Labour may be due.][9]

SECTION 3. New States may be admitted by the Congress into this Union; but no new State shall be formed or erected within the Jurisdiction of any other State; nor any State be formed by the Junction of two or more States, or parts of States, without the Consent of the Legislatures of the States concerned as well as of the Congress.

The Congress shall have Power to dispose of and make all needful Rules and Regulations respecting the Territory or other Property belonging to the United States; and nothing in this Constitution shall be so construed as to Prejudice any Claims of the United States, or of any particular State.

SECTION 4. The United States shall guarantee to every State in this Union a Republican Form of Government, and shall protect each of them against Invasion; and on Application of the Legislature, or of the Executive (when the Legislature cannot be convened) against domestic Violence.

ARTICLE V.

The Congress, whenever two-thirds of both Houses shall deem it necessary, shall propose Amendments to this Constitution, or, on the Application of the Legislatures of two-thirds of the several States, shall call a Convention for proposing Amendments, which, in either Case, shall be valid to all Intents and

---

9. Superseded by the Thirteenth Amendment.

Purposes, as part of this Constitution, when ratified by the Legislatures of three-fourths of the several States, or by Conventions in three-fourths thereof, as the one or the other Mode of Ratification may be proposed by the Congress: Provided that no Amendment which may be made prior to the Year One thousand eight hundred and eight shall in any Manner affect the first and fourth Clauses in the Ninth Section of the first Article; and that no State, without its Consent, shall be deprived of its equal Suffrage in the Senate.

ARTICLE VI.

All Debts contracted and Engagements entered into, before the Adoption of this Constitution, shall be as valid against the United States under this Constitution, as under the Confederation.

This Constitution, and the Laws of the United States which shall be made in Pursuance thereof; and all Treaties made, or which shall be made, under the Authority of the United States, shall be the supreme Law of the Land; and the Judges in every State shall be bound thereby, any Thing in the Constitution or Laws of any State to the Contrary notwithstanding.

The Senators and Representatives before mentioned, and the Members of the several State Legislatures, and all executive and judicial Officers, both of the United States and of the several States, shall be bound by Oath or Affirmation, to support this Constitution; but no religious Test shall ever be required as a Qualification to any Office or public Trust under the United States.

ARTICLE VII.

The Ratification of the Conventions of nine States shall be sufficient for the Establishment of this Constitution between the States so ratifying the Same.

DONE in Convention by the Unanimous Consent of the States present the Seventeenth Day of September in the Year of our Lord one thousand seven hundred and Eighty seven and of the Independence of the United States of America the Twelfth.

In Witness whereof We have hereunto subscribed our Names.

Go *WASHINGTON*
Presidt and deputy from Virginia

New Hampshire.

JOHN LANGDON
NICHOLAS GILMAN

Massachusetts.

NATHANIEL GORHAM
RUFUS KING

New Jersey.

WIL: LIVINGSTON
DAVID BREARLEY.

WM PATERSON.
JONA: DAYTON

Pennsylvania.

B FRANKLIN
ROBT. MORRIS
THOS. FITZSIMONS
JAMES WILSON
THOMAS MIFFLIN
GEO. CLYMER
JARED INGERSOLL
GOUV MORRIS

Delaware.

GEO: READ
JOHN DICKINSON
JACO: BROOM
GUNNING BEDFORD jun
RICHARD BASSETT

Connecticut.

WM SAML JOHNSON
ROGER SHERMAN

New York.

ALEXANDER HAMILTON

Maryland.

JAMES MCHENRY
DANL CARROL
DAN: of ST THOS JENIFER

Virginia.

JOHN BLAIR
JAMES MADISON Jr.

North Carolina.

WM BLOUNT
HU WILLIAMSON
RICHD DOBBS SPAIGHT.

South Carolina.

J. RUTLEDGE
CHARLES PINCKNEY
CHARLES COTESWORTH
  PINCKNEY
PIERCE BUTLER

Georgia.

WILLIAM FEW
ABR BALDWIN

Attest: WILLIAM JACKSON, *Secretary.*

ARTICLES IN ADDITION TO, AND AMENDMENT OF, THE CONSTITUTION OF THE UNITED STATES OF AMERICA, PROPOSED BY CONGRESS, AND RATIFIED BY THE LEGISLATURES OF THE SEVERAL STATES, PURSUANT TO THE FIFTH ARTICLE OF THE ORIGINAL CONSTITUTION.[10]

(The first 10 Amendments were ratified December 15, 1791, and form what is known as the "Bill of Rights")

AMENDMENT I

Congress shall make no law respecting an establishment of religion, or prohibiting the free exercise thereof; or abridging the freedom of speech, or of the press; or the right of the people peaceably to assemble, and to petition the Government for a redress of grievances.

AMENDMENT II

A well regulated Militia, being necessary to the security of a free State, the right of the people to keep and bear Arms, shall not be infringed.

10. Amendment XXI was not ratified by state legislatures, but by state conventions summoned by Congress.

AMENDMENT III

No Soldier shall, in time of peace be quartered in any house, without the consent of the Owner, nor in time of war, but in a manner to be prescribed by law.

AMENDMENT IV

The right of the people to be secure in their persons, houses, papers, and effects, against unreasonable searches and seizures, shall not be violated, and no Warrants shall issue, but upon probable cause, supported by Oath or affirmation, and particularly describing the place to be searched, and the persons or things to be seized.

AMENDMENT V

No person shall be held to answer for a capital, or otherwise infamous crime, unless on a presentment or indictment of a Grand Jury, except in cases arising in the land or naval forces, or in the Militia, when in actual service in time of War or public danger; nor shall any person be subject for the same offence to be twice put in jeopardy of life or limb; nor shall be compelled in any criminal case to be a witness against himself, nor be deprived of life, liberty, or property, without due process of law; nor shall private property be taken for public use, without just compensation.

AMENDMENT VI

In all criminal prosecutions, the accused shall enjoy the right to a speedy and public trial, by an impartial jury of the State and district wherein the crime shall have been committed, which district shall have been previously ascertained by law, and to be informed of the nature and cause of the accusation; to be confronted with the witnesses against him; to have compulsory process for obtaining witnesses in his favor, and to have the Assistance of Counsel for his defence.

AMENDMENT VII

In suits at common law, where the value in controversy shall exceed twenty dollars, the right of trial by jury shall be preserved, and no fact tried by a jury, shall be otherwise reexamined in any Court of the United States, than according to the rules of the common law.

AMENDMENT VIII

Excessive bail shall not be required, nor excessive fines imposed, nor cruel and unusual punishments inflicted.

AMENDMENT IX

The enumeration in the Constitution, of certain rights, shall not be construed to deny or disparage others retained by the people.

AMENDMENT X

The powers not delegated to the United States by the Constitution, nor prohibited by it to the States, are reserved to the States respectively, or to the people.

AMENDMENT XI

(Ratified February 7, 1795)

The Judicial power of the United States shall not be construed to extend to any suit in law or equity, commenced or prosecuted against one of the United States by Citizens of another State, or by Citizens or Subjects of any Foreign State.

AMENDMENT XII

(Ratified July 27, 1804)

The Electors shall meet in their respective states and vote by ballot for President and Vice-President, one of whom, at least, shall not be an inhabitant of the same state with themselves; they shall name in their ballots the person voted for as President, and in distinct ballots the person voted for as Vice-President, and they shall make distinct lists of all persons voted for as President, and of all persons voted for as Vice-President, and of the number of votes for each, which lists they shall sign and certify, and transmit sealed to the seat of the government of the United States, directed to the President of the Senate;—The President of the Senate shall, in presence of the Senate and House of Representatives, open all the certificates and the votes shall then be counted;—The person having the greatest number of votes for President, shall be the President, if such number be a majority of the whole number of Electors appointed; and if no person have such majority, then from the persons having the highest numbers not exceeding three on the list of those voted for as President, the House of Representatives shall choose immediately, by ballot, the President. But in choosing the President, the votes shall be taken by states, the representation from each state having one vote; a quorum for this purpose shall consist of a member or members from two-thirds of the states, and a majority of all the states shall be necessary to a choice. [And if the House of Representatives shall not choose a President whenever the right of choice shall devolve upon them, before the fourth day of March next following, then the Vice-President shall act as President, as in the case of the death or other constitutional disability of the President.—][11] The person having the greatest number of votes as Vice-President, shall be the Vice-President, if such number be a majority of the whole number of Electors appointed, and if no person have a majority, then from the two highest numbers on the list, the Senate shall choose the Vice-President; a quorum for the purpose shall consist of two-thirds of the whole number of Senators, and a majority of the whole number shall be necessary to a choice. But no person constitutionally ineligible to the office of President shall be eligible to that of Vice-President of the United States.

---

11. Superseded by Section 3 of the Twentieth Amendment.

AMENDMENT XIII

(Ratified December 6, 1865)

SECTION 1. Neither slavery nor involuntary servitude, except as a punishment for crime whereof the party shall have been duly convicted, shall exist within the United States, or any place subject to their jurisdiction.

SECTION 2. Congress shall have power to enforce this article by appropriate legislation.

AMENDMENT XIV

(Ratified July 9, 1868)

SECTION 1. All persons born or naturalized in the United States, and subject to the jurisdiction thereof, are citizens of the United States and of the State wherein they reside. No State shall make or enforce any law which shall abridge the privileges or immunities of citizens of the United States; nor shall any State deprive any person of life, liberty, or property, without due process of law; nor deny to any person within its jurisdiction the equal protection of the laws.

SECTION 2. Representatives shall be apportioned among the several States according to their respective numbers, counting the whole number of persons in each State, excluding Indians not taxed. But when the right to vote at any election for the choice of electors for President and Vice-President of the United States, Representatives in Congress, the Executive and Judicial officers of a State, or the members of the Legislature thereof, is denied to any of the male inhabitants of such State, being twenty-one years of age,[12] and citizens of the United States, or in any way abridged, except for participation in rebellion, or other crime, the basis of representation therein shall be reduced in the proportion which the number of such male citizens shall bear to the whole number of male citizens twenty-one years of age in such State.

SECTION 3. No person shall be a Senator or Representative in Congress, or elector of President and Vice-President, or hold any office, civil or military, under the United States, or under any State, who, having previously taken an oath, as a member of Congress, or as an officer of the United States, or as a member of any State legislature, or as an executive or judicial officer of any State, to support the Constitution of the United States, shall have engaged in insurrection or rebellion against the same, or given aid or comfort to the enemies thereof. But Congress may by a vote of two-thirds of each House, remove such disability.

SECTION 4. The validity of the public debt of the United States, authorized by law, including debts incurred for payment of pensions and bounties for services in suppressing insurrection or rebellion, shall not be questioned. But neither the United States nor any State shall assume or pay any debt or obligation incurred in aid of insurrection or rebellion against the United States, or any claim for the loss or emancipation of any slave; but all such debts, obligations and claims shall be held illegal and void.

---

12. Changed by Section 1 of the Twenty-sixth Amendment.

SECTION 5. The Congress shall have power to enforce, by appropriate legislation, the provisions of this article.

AMENDMENT XV

(Ratified February 3, 1870)

SECTION 1. The right of citizens of the United States to vote shall not be denied or abridged by the United States or by any State on account of race, color, or previous condition of servitude—

SECTION 2. The Congress shall have power to enforce this article by appropriate legislation.

AMENDMENT XVI

(Ratified February 3, 1913)

The Congress shall have power to lay and collect taxes on incomes, from whatever source derived, without apportionment among the several States, and without regard to any census or enumeration.

AMENDMENT XVII

(Ratified April 8, 1913)

The Senate of the United States shall be composed of two Senators from each State, elected by the people thereof, for six years; and each Senator shall have one vote. The electors in each State shall have the qualifications requisite for electors of the most numerous branch of the State legislatures.

When vacancies happen in the representation of any State in the Senate, the executive authority of such State shall issue writs of election to fill such vacancies: *Provided,* That the legislature of any State may empower the executive thereof to make temporary appointments until the people fill the vacancies by election as the legislature may direct.

This amendment shall not be so construed as to affect the election or term of any Senator chosen before it becomes valid as part of the Constitution.

AMENDMENT XVIII

(Ratified January 16, 1919)

[SECTION 1. After one year from the ratification of this article the manufacture, sale, or transportation of intoxicating liquors within, the importation thereof into, or the exportation thereof from the United States and all territory subject to the jurisdiction thereof for beverage purposes is hereby prohibited.

[SECTION 2. The Congress and the several States shall have concurrent power to enforce this article by appropriate legislation.

[SECTION 3. This article shall be inoperative unless it shall have been ratified as an amendment to the Constitution by the legislatures of the several States as provided in the Constitution, within seven years from the date of the submission hereof to the States by the Congress.][13]

---

13. Repealed by Section 1 of the Twenty-first Amendment.

AMENDMENT XIX

(Ratified August 18, 1920)

The right of citizens of the United States to vote shall not be denied or abridged by the United States or by any State on account of sex.

Congress shall have power to enforce this article by appropriate legislation.

AMENDMENT XX

(Ratified January 23, 1933)

SECTION 1. The terms of the President and Vice President shall end at noon on the 20th day of January, and the terms of Senators and Representatives at noon on the 3d day of January, of the years in which such terms would have ended if this article had not been ratified; and the terms of their successors shall then begin.

SECTION 2. The Congress shall assemble at least once in every year, and such meeting shall begin at noon on the 3d day of January, unless they shall by law appoint a different day.

SECTION 3. If, at the time fixed for the beginning of the term of the President, the President elect shall have died, the Vice President elect shall become President. If a President shall not have been chosen before the time fixed for the beginning of his term, or if the President elect shall have failed to qualify, then the Vice President elect shall act as President until a President shall have qualified; and the Congress may by law provide for the case wherein neither a President elect nor a Vice President elect shall have qualified, declaring who shall then act as President, or the manner in which one who is to act shall be selected, and such person shall act accordingly until a President or Vice President shall have qualified.

SECTION 4. The Congress may by law provide for the case of the death of any of the persons from whom the House of Representatives may choose a President whenever the right of choice shall have devolved upon them, and for the case of the death of any of the persons from whom the Senate may choose a Vice President whenever the right of choice shall have devolved upon them.

SECTION 5. Sections 1 and 2 shall take effect on the 15th day of October following the ratification of this article.

SECTION 6. This article shall be inoperative unless it shall have been ratified as an amendment to the Constitution by the legislatures of three-fourths of the several States within seven years from the date of its submission.

AMENDMENT XXI

(Ratified December 5, 1933)

SECTION 1. The eighteenth article of amendment to the Constitution of the United States is hereby repealed.

SECTION 2. The transportation or importation into any State, Territory, or possession of the United States for delivery or use therein of intoxicating liquors, in violation of the laws thereof, is hereby prohibited.

SECTION 3. This article shall be inoperative unless it shall have been ratified as an amendment to the Constitution by conventions in the several States, as provided in the Constitution, within seven years from the date of the submission hereof to the States by the Congress.

AMENDMENT XXII

(Ratified February 27, 1951)

SECTION 1. No person shall be elected to the office of the President more than twice, and no person who has held the office of President, or acted as President, for more than two years of a term to which some other person was elected President shall be elected to the office of the President more than once. But this Article shall not apply to any person holding the office of President when this Article was proposed by the Congress, and shall not prevent any person who may be holding the office of President, or acting as President, during the term within which this Article becomes operative from holding the office of President or acting as President during the remainder of such term.

SECTION 2. This article shall be inoperative unless it shall have been ratified as an amendment to the Constitution by the legislatures of three-fourths of the several States within seven years from the date of its submission to the States by the Congress.

AMENDMENT XXIII

(Ratified March 29, 1961)

SECTION 1. The District constituting the seat of Government of the United States shall appoint in such manner as the Congress may direct:

A number of electors of President and Vice President equal to the whole number of Senators and Representatives in Congress to which the District would be entitled if it were a State, but in no event more than the least populous State; they shall be in addition to those appointed by the States, but they shall be considered, for the purposes of the election of President and Vice President, to be electors appointed by a State; and they shall meet in the District and perform such duties as provided by the twelfth article of amendment.

SECTION 2. The Congress shall have power to enforce this article by appropriate legislation.

AMENDMENT XXIV

(Ratified January 23, 1964)

SECTION 1. The right of citizens of the United States to vote in any primary or other election for President or Vice President, for electors for President or Vice President, or for Senator or Representative in Congress, shall not be denied or abridged by the United States or any State by reason of failure to pay any poll tax or other tax.

SECTION 2. The Congress shall have power to enforce this article by appropriate legislation.

AMENDMENT XXV

(Ratified February 10, 1967)

SECTION 1. In case of the removal of the President from office or of his death or resignation, the Vice President shall become President.

SECTION 2. Whenever there is a vacancy in the office of the Vice President, the President shall nominate a Vice President who shall take office upon confirmation by a majority vote of both Houses of Congress.

SECTION 3. Whenever the President transmits to the President pro tempore of the Senate and the Speaker of the House of Representatives his written declaration that he is unable to discharge the powers and duties of his office, and until he transmits to them a written declaration to the contrary, such powers and duties shall be discharged by the Vice President as Acting President.

SECTION 4. Whenever the Vice President and a majority of either the principal officers of the executive departments or of such other body as Congress may by law provide, transmit to the President pro tempore of the Senate and the Speaker of the House of Representatives their written declaration that the President is unable to discharge the powers and duties of his office, the Vice President shall immediately assume the powers and duties of the office as Acting President.

Thereafter, when the President transmits to the President pro tempore of the Senate and the Speaker of the House of Representatives his written declaration that no inability exists, he shall resume the powers and duties of his office unless the Vice President and a majority of either the principal officers of the executive department or of such other body as Congress may by law provide, transmit within four days to the President pro tempore of the Senate and the Speaker of the House of Representatives their written declaration that the President is unable to discharge the powers and duties of his office. Thereupon Congress shall decide the issue, assembling within forty-eight hours for that purpose if not in session. If the Congress, within twenty-one days after receipt of the latter written declaration, or, if Congress is not in session, within twenty-one days after Congress is required to assemble, determines by two-thirds vote of both Houses that the President is unable to discharge the powers and duties of his office, the Vice President shall continue to discharge the same as Acting President; otherwise, the President shall resume the powers and duties of his office.

AMENDMENT XXVI

(Ratified July 1, 1971)

SECTION 1. The right of citizens of the United States, who are eighteen years of age or older, to vote shall not be denied or abridged by the United States or by any State on account of age.

SECTION 2. The Congress shall have power to enforce this article by appropriate legislation.

Law Clerks of
William O. Douglas

C. David Ginsburg (Harvard)	4-17-39 9-30-39	Charles E. Ares (U. of Arizona)	7-1-52 8-31-53
Stanley C. Soderland (U. of Wash.)	10-1-39 9-30-40	James F. Crafts, Jr. (Stanford)	9-1-53 8-31-54
Donald G. Simpson (U. of Wash.)	10-1-40 9-30-41	Harvey M. Grossman (UCLA)	9-1-54 8-6-55
Jed King (U. of Wash.)	10-1-41 4-15-42	William A. Norris (Stanford)	8-8-55 8-3-56
Walter B. Chaffe (U. of Calif.)	3-28-42 9-23-42	William Cohen (UCLA)	7-23-56 8-24-57
Vern Countryman (U. of Wash.)	9-24-42 7-31-43	Charles E. Rickershauser, Jr. (UCLA)	8-26-57 8-2-58
Eugene A. Beyer, Jr. (Yale)	8-3-43 10-1-44	Charles A. Miller (U. of Calif.)	8-4-58 8-8-59
Lucille Lomen (U. of Wash.)	10-22-44 9-30-45	Steven Duke (U. of Arizona)	8-10-59 8-14-60
Donald Colvin (U. of Wash.)	10-1-45 9-30-46	Bernard E. Jacob (U. of Calif.)	8-15-60 8-19-61
James Roger Wollenberg (U. of Calif.)	10-1-46 9-30-47	Thomas J. Klitgaard (U. of Calif.)	7-10-61 8-26-62
Stanley E. Sparrowe (U. of Calif.)	10-1-47 9-30-48	Jared G. Carter (Stanford)	7-16-62 8-19-63
Gary J. Torre (U. of Calif.)	10-1-48 9-30-49	Evan L. Schwab (U. of Wash.)	7-24-63 7-25-64
Warren M. Christopher (Stanford)	10-1-49 9-30-50	James S. Campbell (Stanford)	6-22-64 8-10-65
John Burnett (Yale)	10-2-50 9-29-51	Jerome B. Falk, Jr. (U. of Calif.)	6-28-65 8-13-66
Hans Linde (U. of Calif.)	10-2-50 9-29-51	Lewis B. Merrifield (USC)	7-5-66 7-26-67
Marshall L. Small (Stanford)	10-1-51 6-30-52	Carl J. Seneker II (U. of Calif.)	7-5-67 7-17-68

William A. Reppy, Jr. (Stanford)	10-12-67 8-19-68	Richard Benka (Harvard)	7-9-73 7-28-74
Peter Kay Westen (U. of Calif.)	7-8-68 7-31-69	Michael J. Clutter (USC)	7-1-73 7-26-74
Thomas C. Armitage (UCLA)	7-69 7-15-70	Ira M. Ellman (U. of Calif.)	7-9-73 7-26-74
Lucas A. Powe, Jr. (U. of Wash.)	7-1-70 8-15-71	Alan Austin (Stanford)	6-17-74 7-27-75
Dennis Brown (UCLA)	9-14-70 7-24-71	Donald Kelley (Stanford)	6-24-74 7-19-75
Kenneth R. Reed (U. of Arizona)	6-28-71 8-28-72	Jay Wright (Harvard)	7-15-74 7-19-75
Richard L. Jacobson (USC)	7-6-71 8-28-72	Robert Deitz (Harvard)	6-16-75 11-12-75
William H. Alsup (Harvard)	8-2-71 7-29-72	George Rutherglen (U. of Calif.)	6-30-75 11-12-75
Janet Meik (USC)	7-14-72 8-13-73	Alan Sternstein (U. of Arizona)	6-16-75 11-12-75
Carol S. Bruch (U. of Calif.)	8-3-72 7-20-73	Dennis Hutchinson (U. of Texas)	8-1-76 7-22-77
Peter Kreindler (Harvard)	11-14-72 6-9-73	Monty James Podva (U. of the Pacific)	8-15-77 6-30-80

Index of
U.S. Supreme Court Cases
in This Volume

Index